The Social Life of Emotions

This book showcases new research and theory about the way in which the social environment shapes, and is shaped by, emotion. The book has three sections, each of which addresses a different level of sociality: interpersonal, intragroup, and intergroup. The first section refers to the links between specific individuals, the second to categories that define multiple individuals as an entity, and the final to the boundaries between groups. Emotions are found in each of these levels, and the dynamics involved in these types of relationships are part of what it is to experience emotion. The chapters show how all three types of social relationships generate, and are generated by, emotions. In doing so, this book locates emotional experiences in the larger social context.

Larissa Z. Tiedens is Associate Professor of Organizational Behavior at the Stanford Graduate School of Business. She earned her B.A. in Psychology at Carleton College and her Ph.D. in Social Psychology at the University of Michigan. Her research has focused on emotions in social contexts, cognitive consequences of emotions, and processes involved in stratification.

Colin Wayne Leach is Associate Professor in the Social Psychology Program at the University of California, Santa Cruz. He received his academic training at Boston University, the University of Michigan, and the University of California, Berkeley. He is co-editor of *Immigrant Life in the U.S.: Multi-disciplinary Perspectives*.

Studies in Emotion and Social Interaction

Second Series

Series Editors

Keith Oatley
University of Toronto

Antony S. R. Manstead
University of Cambridge

This series is jointly published by Cambridge University Press and the Editions de la Maison des Sciences de l'Homme, as part of the joint publishing agreement established in 1977 between the Fondation de la Maison des Sciences de l'Homme and the Syndics of Cambridge University Press.

Catte publication est publiée en co-édition par Cambridge University Press et les Editions de la Maison des Sciences de l'Homme. Elle s'intègre dans le programme de co-édition établi en 1977 par la Fondation de la Maison des Sciences de l'Homme et les Syndicats de Cambridge University Press.

Titles published in the Second Series:

The Psychology of Facial Expression
James A. Russell and José Miguel Fernández-Dols

Emotion, the Social Bond, and Human Reality: Part/Whole Analysis
Thomas J. Scheff

Intersubjective Communication and Emotion in Early Ontogeny
Stein Bråten

The Social Context of Nonverbal Behavior
Pierre Philippot, Robert S. Feldman, and Erik J. Coats

Communicating Emotion: Social, Moral, and Cultural Processes
Sally Planalp

Emotions across Languages and Cultures: Diversity and Universals
Anna Wierzbicka

Gender and Emotion: Social Psychological Perspectives
Agneta H. Fischer

Metaphor and Emotion: Language, Culture, and Body in Human Feeling
Zoltán Kövecses

Feeling and Thinking: The Role of Affect in Social Cognition
Joseph P. Forgas

The Causes and Consequences of Feelings
Leonard Berkowitz

Emotions and Beliefs: How Feelings Influence Thoughts
Nico H. Frijda, Antony S. R. Manstead, and Sacha Bem

Identity and Emotion: Development Through Self-Organization
Harke A. Bosma and E. Saskia Kunnen

Speaking from the Heart: Gender and the Social Meaning of Emotion
Stephanie A. Shields

The Hidden Genius of Emotion: Lifespan Development of Personality
Carol Magai and Jeannette Haviland-Jones

The Mind and Its Stories: Narrative Universals and Human Emotion
Patrick Colm Hogan

Feelings and Emotions: The Amsterdam Symposium
Anatony S. R. Manstead, Nico H. Frijda, and Agneta H. Fischer

The Social Life of Emotions
Larissa Z. Tiedens and Colin Wayne Leach

The Social Life of Emotions

Edited by

LARISSA Z. TIEDENS
Stanford University

COLIN WAYNE LEACH
University of California, Santa Cruz

PUBLISHED BY THE PRESS SYNDICATE OF THE UNIVERSITY OF CAMBRIDGE
The Pitt Building, Trumpington Street, Cambridge, United Kingdom

CAMBRIDGE UNIVERSITY PRESS
The Edinburgh Building, Cambridge CB2 2RU, UK
40 West 20th Street, New York, NY 10011-4211, USA
477 Williamstown Road, Port Melbourne, VIC 3207, Australia
Ruiz de Alarcón 13, 28014 Madrid, Spain
Dock House, The Waterfront, Cape Town 8001, South Africa

http://www.cambridge.org

First published 2004

Printed in the United States of America

Typeface Palatino 10/12 pt. *System* LaTeX 2_ε [TB]

A catalog record for this book is available from the British Library.

Library of Congress Cataloging in Publication Data

The social life of emotions / edited by Larissa Z. Tiedens, Colin Wayne Leach.
p. cm. – (Studies in emotion and social interaction)
Includes bibliographical references and index.
ISBN 0-521-82811-2 (hb) – ISBN 0-521-53529-8 (pbk.)
1. Emotions – Social aspects – Textbooks. I. Tiedens, Larissa Z. II. Leach, Colin Wayne, 1967– III. Series.
BF531.S634 2004
152.4 – dc22 2003063546

ISBN 0 521 82811 2 hardback
ISBN 0 521 53529 8 paperback

For Mark, with love and gratitude.

L.Z.T.

For my first and best mentors: Mom and Phil

C.W.L.

Contents

Acknowledgments

This book began as a symposium at the 2001 American Psychological Association convention in San Francisco called, "Social Emotions: Feelings in Interpersonal and Intergroup Relations." We are grateful to Heather Smith for coorganizing the symposium and to Sharon Panulla for suggesting that the topic would make a good book. In addition, Russell Spears provided valuable encouragement and advice in the early stages.

More generally, "The Los Gatos Group" provided a wonderful environment for more discussion of ideas related to the social context of emotion and we thank Eileen Zurbriggen for her insights and her patience with us. Tony Manstead introduced us to Phil Laughlin at Cambridge, who made the process as easy as possible. We have also been greatly helped by Ena Inesi and Sandy Berg, and we very much appreciate the long hours they spent with the manuscript. In addition, Zachary Dorsey at TechBooks was extremely helpful and flexible in getting the final version put together. This book came into existence during a period in which both of our emotional lives were enriched by new contexts and relationships, and we are thankful for those.

Contributors

Cameron Anderson, New York University

Nyla R. Branscombe, University of Kansas

Margaret S. Clark, Carnegie Mellon University

Laura B. Citrin, University of Michigan

Mark H. Davis, Eckerd College

David S. Fearon, Jr., University of California, Santa Barbara

Eli J. Finkel, Northwestern University

Agneta H. Fischer, University of Amsterdam

Christina T. Fong, University of Washington

Barbara L. Fredrickson, University of Michigan

Elaine Hatfield, University of Hawai'i

Cheryl R. Kaiser, Michigan State University

Dacher Keltner, University of California, Berkeley

Thomas Kessler, University of Jena

Colin Wayne Leach, University of California, Santa Cruz

Diane M. Mackie, University of California, Santa Barbara

Brenda Major, University of California, Santa Barbara

Antony S. R. Manstead, Cardiff University

Rowland S. Miller, Sam Houston State University

Anca M. Miron, University of Kansas

Thomas F. Pettigrew, University of California, Santa Cruz

Richard L. Rapson, University of Hawai'i

Tomi-Ann Roberts, Colorado College

Patricia M. Rodriguez Mosquera, University of Amsterdam

Lisa A. Silver, University of California, Santa Barbara

Eliot R. Smith, Indiana University

Heather J. Smith, Sonoma State University

Richard H. Smith, University of Kentucky

Russell Spears, Cardiff University

Robert I. Sutton, Stanford University

Larissa Z. Tiedens, Stanford University

Linda R. Tropp, Boston College

The Social Life of Emotions

Introduction

A World of Emotion

Colin Wayne Leach and Larissa Z. Tiedens

> In every human attitude – for example in emotion ... – we shall find the whole of human reality, since emotion is the human reality which assumes itself and which, "aroused," "directs" itself toward the world. [...] There is, in effect, a world of emotion.
>
> Jean-Paul Sartre

In agreement with Sartre (1948), many theorists have argued that emotion is a way in which people imbue the world with meaning (see Abu-Lughod & Lutz, 1990; Harré, 1986; Osgood, 1971). Although this perspective emphasizes the individual as making the social world meaningful through emotion, it also suggests that individual emotion is necessarily about people's experience of the world. Thus, many contemporary thinkers argue that understanding emotion is essential to understanding social experience and behavior. For example, in the past fifteen years, the sociology of emotion has grown into a vibrant subfield (for reviews, see Kemper, 1990; Thoits, 1989) with examinations of emotion in the context of social relationships (e.g., Scheff, 1994), social status (e.g., Kemper, 2001), and social movements (e.g., Goodwin, Jasper, & Polletta, 2001). The anthropology of emotion has also grown in this same period and offers a challenge to individualistic and universalistic approaches to emotion (for reviews, see Lutz & Abu-Lughod, 1990; Lutz & White, 1986). Political scientists have also become fascinated with the way in which emotions influence political behaviors, including voting, policy support, and party support (e.g., Goodwin et al., 2001; Iyengar et al., 1984; Kinder & Sanders, 1996).

Unlike much of the work in other social sciences, psychologists have tended to study emotions as individual, internal, and private states. Thus, emotions are conceptualized as being caused by (and causing) *individual* processes, such as perception, inference, attribution, or bodily change. This approach locates emotion within the individual as though the human skin contains and restrains them – separating the emotions from the social world individuals inhabit. Fortunately, this tendency away from the social is neither ubiquitous nor necessary. In fact, concentration on the individual is not what most distinguishes the psychological approach from others. It is concern for the subjective meaning in emotion that best characterizes the psychological approach (for reviews, see Frijda, 1986; Lazarus, 1991; Ortony, Clore, & Collins, 1988; Scherer, Schorr, & Johnstone, 2001). Although the examination of subjective meaning can lean toward an individualistic approach, it can also demand attention to the social basis of the meaning in emotion (see Abu-Lughod & Lutz, 1990; Harré, 1992; Henriques et al., 1984; Leach, Snider, & Iyer, 2002; Voloshinov, 1986).

Those interested in human perception, judgment, and evaluation have long understood that individuals' meaning-making cannot occur in a vacuum. Indeed, the necessity of a social approach to understanding the process of subjective meaning is apparent in most of social psychology. Many pioneering social psychologists asserted that people are especially keen to give meaning to social events and other people (see Asch, 1952; Bruner, 1994; Cartwright, 1951; Erdelyi, 1974; Heider, 1958; Katz, 1960; Krech & Crutchfield, 1948). The classic social psychological approach also emphasized the importance of the social context – especially as it is represented in the shared reality constructed in groups – to peoples' evaluations of subjective meaning (e.g., Cartwright, 1959; Sherif, 1958; Sherif & Sherif, 1964; for discussions, see Bruner, 1994; Turner, 1991; Turner et al., 1987). In these ways, social psychology has already recognized that states that might initially appear to be individual and internal are rarely, if ever, separate from the social world. Instead, they cannot be disentangled from that social world. A social approach to emotion requires that we conceptualize emotion in the same way; that we stop seeing it as an individual response, and start considering it as a bridge between the individual and the world that blurs the boundaries between individuals and their contexts. From this perspective, emotions are one channel through which the individual knows the social world, and the social world is what allows people to know emotion. This volume seeks to conceptualize emotions and social relationships in this way.

THE SOCIAL LIFE OF EMOTION

There are numerous ways that emotions can be social. The term social, after all, has a number of definitions. Some of these have been quite prevalent in the psychological study of emotion. For example, psychologists have long conceptualized emotion as *responsive* to social events and entities. Emotions are typically considered as responses to important events in our lives, and social events are among the most important. Thus, social situations frequently generate emotional episodes.

Individual emotions have also been conceptualized as *regulated* by the social constraints and affordances provided by norms, morals, and values. In the most conventional version of this approach, individual emotion is constrained by society (e.g., Ekman, 1984; Ekman, Friesen, & Ellsworth, 1972). In this vision, people have internal, natural, and biological responses that are harnessed by societal practices and demands. In the more radical form of this approach, society defines the nature of emotion. That is, we are socialized into our ideas about specific emotion and into our understanding of how particular situations link up to emotional feelings (Harré, 1986). Emotional experiences then are dictated by our social surroundings in a way that is so thorough, we do not even notice the influence.

Finally, and perhaps most provocatively, there is the version of sociality with which Sartre was concerned. In this case, emotion is conceptualized as socially *constituted*. In this form of sociality, emotion is seen as being defined by and defining social relationships. This perspective suggests that we cannot know anything about our social relationships without the emotions that we use to navigate ourselves through these relationships. But, similarly, emotion is fully encompassed by those social relationships. This implies that emotion does not exist within the solitary individual because it depends on social configurations to not just trigger it, but also to actually form it. The chapters in this volume speak to all three of these kinds of sociality, including this latter – more novel and perhaps most fundamentally social – approach to emotion.

Emotion as Socially Responsive

There is wide agreement that social events and entities outside the individual play a role in the generation of emotion. Many of us are familiar with the infamous bear debated so hotly by William James and his critics. Exactly what occurs after the presence of the bear (and in what order) might not be agreed on, but there is a consensus that the external figure of the bear sets the emotion process in motion (see Ellsworth, 1994, p. 227). But not all external sources are equal. Although confronting a bear provides an especially dramatic example, most researchers have noted the particular force other humans have to generate emotions. Whether they are parents (Campos & Stenberg, 1981), friends (Clark & Brissette, 2001), or even strangers (Murphy & Zajonc, 1993), other humans seem to have a unique ability to generate affective responses in us.

This book speaks to this theme. Many of the chapters illustrate the way in which other people generate emotional responses in us. Sometimes this is because we feel the emotions of those around us (Anderson & Keltner;

Davis; Hatfield & Rapson). Sometimes this is because we have emotions about the things that other people do or the things that happen to other people (Clark & Finkel; Davis; R. H. Smith; Spears & Leach). Sometimes it is concern for our very relationship to others that generates emotion in us (Fearon; Miller; Rodriguez Mosquera, Fischer, & Manstead).

The groups to which we belong can also elicit emotions (Hatfield & Rapson; Mackie, Silver, & Smith). We can feel emotion about the success and failure of our own group (Branscombe & Miron; Tiedens, Sutton, & Fong) or of other groups (Mackie et al.; Smith & Kessler; Spears & Leach). In addition, groups may make salient cultural concerns (Rodriguez Mosquera et al.) or societal expectations (Citrin, Roberts, & Fredrickson) that shape our emotion.

Emotion as Socially Shared and Regulated

Early discussions of "display rules" (e.g., Ekman, 1984; Ekman & Friesen, 1971) emphasized that the social environment provides information about what emotion should and should not be expressed, by whom, and in what situations. Display rules vary across cultures, groups, and situations, such that individuals likely have very complex knowledge about what emotions are appropriate and when. Although Ekman and his colleagues were particularly concerned with differences in display rules across national cultures, some emotion rules are instantiated in a very local, relationship-specific way and pertain not just to expression, but also to feeling. For example, Hochschild's (1983) research on flight attendants illustrated the way that local environments provide quite explicit guidelines about the expression and experience of emotion. The training provided to flight attendants does not just teach them safety precautions and food preparation, but also how emotions can and should be used to provide the best possible experience for the customer. Flight attendants' success on the job is tied to their ability to regulate their emotions in the way dictated by the airlines.

The explicit regulation of emotion expression is one way in which emotion is social and several of the chapters discuss this kind of force. For example, Clark and Finkel suggest that people are well aware of the inappropriateness of expressing too much emotion to acquaintances, R. H. Smith discusses strong prohibitions on the acknowledgment of envy, and Spears and Leach discuss the moral proscriptions against the related feeling of *schadenfreude*. In addition, Tiedens et al. argue that groups occasionally dictate that some group members express one emotion and other group members another emotion. Citrin et al. discuss some of the dictates delivered to women about their emotions, such as the importance of smiling and suppressing expressions of anger.

Not all social knowledge of emotion expression is delivered in an explicit fashion, however. Research concerned with society and social relationships as regulators of emotion have pointed to the implicit and unconscious ways peoples' emotions become socialized. From this perspective, social forces direct our attention and concern toward some kinds of events and away from others. The chapter by Rodriguez Mosquera et al. does a particularly good job of explaining this way in which emotions are social. They describe how in honor cultures people are particularly concerned with family reputation and as such pay more attention to insults, sexual behavior, and the ability to provide protection for others than people from non–honor cultures. These things become particularly emotional. Importantly, people are unaware of the regulation that the cultural context is providing. For the individual, emotions are experienced as natural and automatic. Yet, this implicit form of influence is particularly powerful precisely because people do not experience it as influence (see Bourdieu, 1984).

Both implicit and explicit information about what people ought to feel are aspects of the moral code that defines and unites groups and societies. For example, Averill (1983) has shown that there is great agreement among European Americans that feelings of anger are most appropriate when one is wronged or insulted. As such, anger in the absence of injustice can make one appear immature or even pathological to those who share this cultural theory of justice-based anger. Several of the contributions to this volume also emphasize the ways in which peoples' notions of broad values, such as justice and morality, are involved in the production of emotion (Branscombe & Miron; Citrin et al.; Hatfield & Rapson; Kaiser & Major; Rodriguez Mosquera et al.; H. J. Smith & Kessler; R. H. Smith; Spears & Leach). For example, R. H. Smith provides many examples of the ways in which social actors can attempt to cloak their untoward envy in an effort to portray their hostility toward successful others as moral and just.

Sharing an emotion with others may also alter the experience itself (see Manstead & Fischer, 2001; Parkinson, 1995). For example, in their chapter, Clark and Finkel argue that the expression of emotions can either repel people from one another or promote a strong bond, all depending on the nature of the initial relationship. In addition, several contributors to this volume emphasize the ways in which sharing an emotion within a collective provides the feeling with a certain social reality. Indeed shared emotion within a group may indicate a shared understanding of the world. This sharedness can serve to coordinate (and regulate) social interaction within the group (e.g., Anderson & Keltner; Fearon; Hatfield & Rapson; Miller) or collective action against another group (e.g., Mackie et al.; Smith and Kessler). For example, in their contribution to this volume, Smith and Kessler review research suggesting that disadvantaged group members are more likely to engage in collective action designed to benefit their group as a whole if they appraise their group as enduring *collective* injustice. These group-level appraisals appear to promote feelings of anger and resentment about the group's shared mistreatment (see also Mackie, Devos, & Smith, 2000).

Viewing emotion as socially shared and regulated by social pre- or proscriptions begins to suggest that felt and expressed emotion also *provide* social meaning. That is, people are likely to make a number of social inferences based on the presence or absence of particular emotions in their social settings. Such effects are unlikely to be restricted to inferences about individuals. Indeed, emotions may be the basis of judgments regarding our relationships and the groups to which we belong. Suggestions of this link are provided in many chapters, including those by Tropp and Pettigrew; Mackie et al.; Fearon, Clark, and Finkel; Citrin et al.; and Anderson and Keltner. From this perspective, emotion becomes the bond associating or disassociating people and thus provides a basis for the maintenance and change of social relationships. This way of considering emotion as social moves toward locating emotions *between* people rather than *within* an individual person. This begins to suggest that emotion is not constrained by the skin of the human body, but instead provides a link between that which is inside and that which is outside.

Emotion as Socially Constituted

Sartre (1948) argued that "consciousness does not limit itself to projecting affective signification upon the world around it. It *lives* the new world which it has just established" (p. 75, italics in original). From his point of view, emotion *constitutes* the human world. This means that emotion is not simply a phenomenological or physiological response to the social world, but rather the form that human existence takes (in a world that does not exist free of our existence within it). Sartre's radical claim is that emotion is more than our attempt to make meaningful a preexisting world. In his view, by making meaning through emotion, we actually make the world itself. Thus, the world is constituted – comes into existence – through our emotion. This is how Sartre can claim that our emotion is not simply a reaction to the world, but rather that emotion "is a transformation of the world" (p. 58). According to Sartre, ours is a world of emotion because our emotion makes us and the world a unified whole. In this way, emotion is what is *between* us and the world. This suggests that emotion is always, at the same time, inside us and outside us.

Clearly, viewing emotion as socially constituted and constituting is a profoundly social approach. By conceptualizing emotion as existing between the person and the world (which includes other individuals, groups, and social mores), it causes the opposition between the psychological and the social to implode. Although this approach to human experience has been discussed in philosophy (e.g., Cassirer, 1944), social theory (e.g., Bourdieu, 1984; Hall, 1977), and psychology (Cartwright, 1951; Henriques et al., 1984; Voloshinov, 1986), it has been complicated for emotion researchers to instantiate.

We believe that the chapters in this volume begin to instantiate the perspective that emotion and the social world are mutually constitutive. For example, Anderson and Keltner discuss data that show emotional convergence among college roommates. In this study, it seems as though the emotion that the roommates come to share is at once an expression of the importance of the relationship and what that relationship itself is. Anderson and Keltner discuss this shared emotion as akin to a relational schema, where what it is to be in the relationship is to have the emotion. In general, what we see as most novel about this volume is that, when taken together, these chapters point to the quite radical notion Sartre suggested. Because chapter after chapter weaves together emotional experiences and expressions with social relationships, the emotional is seen as very social and the social as very emotional. In these chapters, emotions are not simply internal events that respond to the outside world. Instead emotions constitute the social context. As such, this volume examines emotion that shapes and is shaped by social life.

OVERVIEW OF CONTRIBUTIONS

One reason that the study of the social nature of emotions is difficult is because the social world is so varied. There are hundreds of types of relationships and as many emotions. This volume is organized to address three levels, of sociality: interpersonal, intragroup, and intergroup. The first form refers to the links between specific individuals, the second to categories that define multiple individuals as an entity, and the final to the relations between groups. Emotions are found in each of these levels, and the dynamics involved in these types of relationship are part of what it is to experience emotion. By examining emotion at all three levels, the volume as a whole shows how emotions are social and the social is emotional, regardless of the type of social relationship considered.

Interpersonal

Much of daily life is filled with interactions with other individuals, and often we encounter the same individuals over and over. These interactions and the relationships that grow out of them can come to be the most memorable and meaningful aspects of people's lives (e.g., Baumeister & Leary, 1995). Not surprisingly, they are a fertile context for the examination of the social life of emotions. Because social interaction and relationships are so important, emotions respond to them. Given the pull and importance of other people to us, their presence creates a regulating force. We also see in these chapters that many relationships are not understandable without the emotions that define them. An emotion captures and describes an interpersonal dynamic in a way that no other description can, and in that sense constitutes the relationship (see Heider, 1958).

The first section has some chapters focused on specific emotions – empathy, envy, embarrassment, and shame. In each case, the authors are concerned with the ways in which these emotions arise in particular kinds of social settings, the ways in which there are explicit and implicit rules about whether the emotion can and should be felt and expressed, and how the emotion itself forms a particular kind of dynamic between relationship partners. Davis argues that empathy is the transformation of another's experience into a response within the self that then shapes the interpersonal relationship. Here, we see that a blurred distinction between self and others generates an emotion that instantiates this perception of oneness. Davis argues that the emotional connection in empathy benefits interpersonal relationships and thus those in them.

The interrelation between self and other takes a more sinister form in the case of envy, as discussed by R. H. Smith. He argues that envy is based in a dual focus on a superior other and an inferior self. This dual focus suggests that the feeling of envy cannot exist without experiencing the self *relative* to another. This relational conceptualization of envy serves to integrate into a coherent whole (other-focused) feelings of hostility with (self-focused) feelings of self-loathing and shame.

The chapters by Fearon and Miller agree with the earlier ones by seeing interpersonal emotion as constituting a particular social relation. However, they emphasize the degree to which shame and embarrassment come out of a more generic human concern for social belonging that functions to maintain social relationships. In his chapter, Fearon conceptualizes shame as a reaction to a "social bond" under threat. As such, shame moves those who experience it to attempt to repair the damage done to their bond with others. Miller, on the other hand, emphasizes the functional nature of embarrassment by arguing that it is adaptive communication aimed at preventing others' devaluation or rejection.

In the final chapter of the first section, Clark and Finkel discuss the implications of expressing or suppressing emotion and argue that the effects depend on the type of relationship one has with the other to whom one might express the emotion. In this way, they discuss how people's emotions respond to the emotions of others and are regulated by others. Clark and Finkel also suggest that people's emotions appear to constitute social relationships. Using two different typologies of relationships (communal versus exchange and attachment style), Clark and Finkel show that emotion is part of what varies with and defines relational style. The amount and type of emotion expression both depend on and promote a style of interaction, suggesting that critical to understanding these forms of relating is understanding the emotions that constitute them.

Intragroup

A sense of "we" is a basic component of human sociality (Turner et al., 1987). The chapters in the second section, which focuses on emotions in intragroup contexts, are all concerned with the role of emotions in forming a "we" and the way in which collectives shape the emotions of those who are part of them.

The first two chapters in this section delve into the processes by which people, when associated with one another, come to share emotions. Hatfield and Rapson outline the unconscious and immediate responses individuals have to one another that frequently result in their coming to experience the same emotions. They argue that this phenomenon is not culturally and historically bound, but that instead the likelihood of transferring emotion from one person to the next may be human nature. Furthermore, they suggest that, when this emotional contagion occurs in relationships and groups, it can become the basis of group definition and collective action. They provide historical examples of instances in which groups of people came to share emotions with the result of extreme and spiraling mass emotions. These examples are suggestive of how emotions that emerge through social interaction affect large-scale social phenomena – impacting the people who are present, but also guiding relations within and between groups into the future.

Whereas Hatfield and Rapson illustrate some of the disastrous consequences of socially shared emotion, Anderson and Keltner, in the next chapter, take a functionalist approach. They show that emotional convergence strengthens relationships. Indeed, they imply that, without modulating emotions to converge with others, relationships might not form or at least would be less close and strong than those in which matching occurs. They also suggest that the degree to which people emotionally converge to others will depend on their power in the relationship, which illustrates how the need and desire for a relationship can affect emotional processes within relationships. These two chapters, when taken together, underscore the likelihood for emotional similarity within collectives, and show how these shared emotions play an important role in forming the collectives' social realities. Thus, collective emotions are generated through social interaction and, once they have appeared, they define the collective and direct their social behavior.

The role of emotions in defining social relationships does not only occur through social negotiations in which collectives end up with the same emotion. In their chapter, Tiedens, Sutton, and Fong argue that many groups are characterized by emotion variation and differentiation. They suggest instances in which groups characterized by differences in emotion can be conceptualized as just as groupy as those with the same emotion and argue that some tightly intertwined groups may in fact intentionally promote emotion variation. Like the previous two chapters, Tiedens et al. imply that the emotion composition of the group plays a primary role in determining what the group is and who counts as a group member, as well as whether the group will be successful at achieving its goals. In their approach, emotional variation (and convergence) is neither necessarily functional nor dysfunctional. Instead, the emotional composition of a group facilitates some positive outcomes but inhibits others. Thus, emotions impact and form the future of the group, but whether that is good or bad depends on the goals that are most important to the group.

Whereas the first three chapters in this section consider face-to-face groups, the final two in the intragroup section are concerned with social categories and societal groups. Rodriguez Mosquera et al. discuss emotion and culture, and Citrin et al. discuss emotion and gender. Both chapters go far beyond documenting differences between social groups in their emotional responses. The authors of these chapters are concerned with how membership in a particular social group directs members' attention, concerns, and interpretations toward and away from particular social cues.

What counts as emotional and what emotions are expected and experienced are shaped by forces that group members are unaware of, yet these emotions come to characterize the nature of the group. As such, particular emotions are accepted by group members (and outsiders) as natural biological correlates of group membership. Rodriguez Mosquera et al. and Citrin et al. are concerned with the often masked or unobserved social processes and practices involved in sealing these associations. In addition, these two chapters emphasize the reciprocal nature of social groups and emotions, in which each constitutes the other. These arguments are made in terms of how cultures can encourage or discourage concerns with honor, as well as how gender expectations encourage and discourage attention to appearance and the body. Though honor and the (gendered) body may not seem as though they necessarily implicate emotions, the authors demonstrate that emotions are tightly intertwined with both. In these chapters, we see that emotion emerges in response to subtle messages provided by the social environment. These messages are not explicitly about emotions per se, but about how to be a good group member and a good person. In this way, they form emotional responses, as well as meta-emotions about succeeding and failing to live up to cultural ideals. As such, the authors of both chapters also argue that emotions are centrally involved in socialization practices. Thus, emotion, culture, and gender become mutually constitutive – emotions are shaped by social context, and so, too, do they come to define the social meaning of the cultural context. These chapters corroborate previous ones by viewing emotions and social life as in a recursive relation in which emotions are both defined by and define social life.

Intergroup

The final section of the volume focuses on how emotions are involved in relationships between groups. The contributors discuss how emotions are involved in the conflict, competition, prejudice, and political maneuvering that characterizes so many intergroup relationships. Although early work on intergroup relations did not examine emotion very directly, much of it recognized the importance of affective evaluations. For example, the earliest research of reference groups and relative deprivation identified peoples' affective evaluations of their group's standing relative to other groups as central to social and political judgment and motivation (e.g., Hyman, 1942; Merton & Lazersfeld, 1950; Stouffer et al., 1949; see also Sherif & Sherif, 1964).

In the opening chapter for this section, Mackie et al. describe how emotions can be embedded in group memberships that gain their meaning through their relationships to relevant outgroups. In this way, they bring forward the classic work on reference groups and relative deprivation to marry it with more contemporary theories of social identity and emotion appraisal. Mackie et al. add sinew to their conceptualization of intergroup emotion by describing a number of studies showing people's group membership to be important to their emotional life. For example, they show that the importance people give to a particular group identity increases their fear and anger in reaction to threats that make their group membership salient.

The remaining chapters in the intergroup section are steeped in the perspective introduced by Mackie et al. Two chapters in the intergroup section focus on the emotions possible among members of groups that enjoy a status advantage over, or the power to harm, other groups. In their contribution, Tropp and Pettigrew review evidence showing that interventions that promote positive, equal-status, intergroup contact have robust effects on majority groups' affective ties to minority and other outgroups. Thus, changing the quality of a higher status group's relation to a group of lower status appears to reduce prejudice by promoting feelings like sympathy, warmth, and liking that signal a positive social tie to the outgroup. In the absence of such interventions, however, there are numerous ways in which advantaged groups can defend prejudice and inequality. For example, Branscombe and Miron examine the appraisal processes by which ingroup members can deemphasize and legitimate the harm their group has caused others. They argue that those most invested in maintaining a positive group identity engage in strategies to protect their group image from the moral stain of prejudice. By seeing their ingroup's mistreatment of others as morally legitimate or of minimal harm, invested ingroup members can protect themselves against the pain and distress associated with belonging to an immoral group. In this way, emotional and other investment in one's group undermines the kind of positive affective ties discussed by Tropp and Pettigrew.

Three chapters in the intergroup section focus on the emotions possible when one's group suffers a status disadvantage. Given the well-established tendency to see one's disadvantage as unfair, something discussed at the interpersonal level in R. H. Smith's chapter, all three contributions emphasize the importance of perceived (in)justice. In their contribution, Kaiser and Major focus on the emotional reactions that those facing group-based prejudice may experience. They argue that the degree to which members of devalued groups appraise their disadvantage as deserved, or not, should determine the quality of their emotional reaction to prejudice. Thus, those who see their group as deservedly devalued, perhaps because they believe that their group is inferior, should feel little group pride and may even feel a sense of collective shame. These critical feelings about the group appear likely to encourage individuals to distance themselves from the devalued group, in an attempt to escape "the mark of oppression."

In their chapter, H. J. Smith and Kessler also focus on what might determine the various emotional reactions to intergroup inequality. Although they share Kaiser and Major's concern for relative deprivation theory and the appraised legitimacy of intergroup inequality, they also integrate insights from theories of collective political action (i.e., social identity theory, resource mobilization theory). This theoretical emphasis leads them to view appraisals regarding the stability of intergroup inequality and the group's collective efficacy as central determinants of their emotional response to disadvantage. In this way, H. J. Smith and Kessler can begin to explain why some group members can feel a justice-based resentment that motivates direct political action while others feel anxiety, based in a recognition of injustice with little efficacy to challenge it.

In the final chapter in the intergroup section and the volume, Spears and Leach argue that *schadenfreude* is one way in which individuals can compensate for threats to a valued in-group's status. By taking pleasure in another group's misfortune, *schadenfreude* seems to offer succor for the pain of group inferiority. Echoing earlier contributions, Spears and Leach also emphasize the degree to which people's experience of *schadenfreude* is moderated by the moral legitimacy of the emotion given the circumstances of the outgroup's misfortune. As in other forms of moral regulation, *schadenfreude* is moderated under circumstances that make it morally illegitimate to take such malicious pleasure in another's misfortune. This again shows how emotions rooted in particular relationships must take account of the moral and social implications of the emotion for the relationship and for the actors' social life.

CODA

Across three levels of analysis, the contributions to this volume show how emotions can respond to, be regulated by, and constitute social relationships. In this way, the volume emphasizes the social basis of emotion, and it conceptualizes emotion as more deeply and fundamentally social than most prior work on the social nature of emotion. Rather than framing emotion as always reactive to social events and entities, the chapters in this volume offer specific examples of the ways in which emotion constitutes social relationships. Here, empathy, envy, hatred, pride, anger, and guilt are not simply a product of one's emotional reaction to a social relationship. Rather, these emotions are the way in which our relationships to others and to the social world are lived. In the chapters that follow, you will see "a world of emotion," because all that we are is in all that we feel.

References

Abu-Lughod, L., & Lutz, C. (1990). Introduction: Emotion, discourse, and the politics of everyday life. In C. Lutz & L. Abu-Lughod (Eds.), *Language and the politics of emotion* (pp. 1–23). Cambridge, UK: Cambridge University Press.

Anderson, C., & Keltner, D. (this volume). The emotional convergence hypothesis: Implications for individuals, relationships, and cultures.

Asch, S. E. (1952). *Social psychology*. New York: Prentice Hall.

Averill, J. R. (1983). Studies on anger and aggression: Implications for theories of emotion. *American Psychologist, 38*, 1145–1160.

Baumeister, R. F., & Leary, M. R. (1995). The need to belong: Desire for interpersonal attachments as a fundamental human motivation. *Psychology Bulletin, 117*, 497–529.

Bourdieu, P. (1984). *Distinction: Outline of a theory of taste*. Cambridge, MA: Harvard University Press.

Branscombe, N. R., & Miron, A. M. (this volume). Interpreting the ingroup's negative actions toward another group: Emotional reactions to appraised harm.

Bruner, J. (1994). *Acts of meaning*. Cambridge, MA: Harvard University Press.

Campos, J. J., & Stenberg, C. (1981). Perception, appraisal, and emotion: The onset of social referencing. In M. E. Lamb & L. R. Sherrod (Eds.), *Infant social cognition: Empirical and theoretical considerations* (pp. 217–314). Hillsdale, NJ: Erlbaum.

Cartwright, D. (Ed.). (1951). *Field theory in social science*. New York: Harper & Row.

Cartwright, D. (1959). Lewinian theory as a contemporary systematic framework. In S. Koch (Ed.), *Psychology: A study of science* (Vol. 2; pp. 7–91). New York: McGraw-Hill.

Cassirer, E. (1944). *An essay on man; an introduction to the philosophy of human culture*. New Haven, CT: Yale University Press.

Citrin, L. B., Roberts, T.-A., & Fredrickson, B. L. (this volume). Objectification theory and emotions: A feminist psychological perspective on gendered affect.

Clark, M. S., & Brissette, I. (2001). Relationship beliefs and emotion: Reciprocal effects. In N. Frijda, A. Manstead, & G. Simin (Eds.), *Beliefs and emotions* (pp. 212–240). New York: Cambridge University Press.

Clark, M. S., & Finkel, E. J. (this volume). Does expressing emotion promote well-being? It depends on relationship context.

Davis, M. H. (this volume). Empathy: Negotiating the border between self and other.

Ekman, P. (1984). Expression and the nature of emotion. In K. R. Scherer and P. Ekman (Eds.), *Approaches to emotion* (pp. 329–343). Hillsdale, NJ: Erlbaum.

Ekman, P., & Friesen, W. V. (1971). Constants across cultures in the face of emotion. *Journal of Personality & Social Psychology, 71*, 124–129.

Ekman, P., Friesen, W. V., & Ellsworth, P. (1972). *Emotion in the human face: Guidelines for research and an integration of findings*. Oxford: Pergamon Press.

Ellsworth, P. (1994). William James and emotion: Is a century of fame worth a century of misunderstanding? *Psychological Review, 101*, 222–229.

Erdelyi, M. H. (1974). A new look at the new look: Perceptual defense and vigilance. *Psychological Review, 81*, 1–25.

Fearon, D. S. (this volume). The bond threat sequence: Discourse evidence for the systematic interdependence of shame and social relationships.

Frijda, N. (1986). *The emotions*. New York: Cambridge University Press.

Goodwin, J., Jasper, J. M., & Polletta, F. (2001). *Passionate politics: Emotions and social movements*. Chicago: University of Chicago Press.

Hall, S. (1977). Rethinking the "base and superstructure" metaphor. In J. Bloomfield (Ed.), *Class, hegemony, & party* (pp. 43–72). London: Lawrence & Wishart.

Harré, R. (Ed.). (1986). *The social construction of emotions*. New York: Blackwell.

Harré, R. (1992). *Social being: A theory for social psychology* (2nd Edition). Oxford: Blackwell.

Hatfield, E., & Rapson, R. L. (this volume). Emotional contagion: Religious and ethnic hatreds and global terrorism.

Heider, F. (1958). *The psychology of interpersonal relations*. New York: J. Wiley & Sons.

Henriques, J., Holloway, W., Urwin, C., Venne, C., & Walkerdine, V. (Eds.). (1984). *Changing the subject: Psychology, social regulation and subjectivity*. London: Methuen.

Hochschild, A. (1983). *The managed heart: The commercialization of human feeling*. Berkeley: University of California Press.

Hyman, H. H. (1942). The psychology of status. *Archives of Psychology, 269*, 5–94.

Iyengar, S., Kinder, D., Peters, M., & Krosnick, J. (1984). The evening news and presidential evaluations. *Journal of Personality & Social Psychology, 46*, 778–787.

Kaiser, C. R., & Major, B. (this volume). Judgments of deserving and the emotional consequences of stigmatization.

Katz, D. (1960). The functional approach to the study of attitudes. *Public Opinion Quarterly, 24*, 163–204.

Kemper, T. (Ed.). (1990). *Research agendas in the sociology of emotions*. Albany, NY: State University of New York Press.

Kemper, T. (2001). A structural approach to social movement emotions. In J. Goodwin, J. M. Jasper, & F. Polletta (2001). *Passionate politics: Emotions and social movements* (pp. 58–73). Chicago, IL: University of Chicago Press.

Kinder, D. R., & Sanders, L. M. (1996). *Divided by color: Racial politics and democratic ideals*. Chicago, IL: University of Chicago Press.

Krech, D., & Crutchfield, R. S. (1948). *Theory and problems of social psychology* (1st Edition). New York: McGraw-Hill.

Lazarus, R. S. (1991). *Emotion and adaptation.* New York: Oxford University Press.

Leach, C. W., Snider, S., & Iyer, A. (2002). "Poisoning the consciences of the fortunate": The experience of relative advantage and support for social equality. In I. Walker & H. J. Smith (Eds.), *Relative deprivation: Specification, development, and integration* (pp. 136–163). New York: Cambridge University Press.

Lutz, C., & Abu-Lughod, L. (Eds.). (1990). *Language and the politics of emotion.* Cambridge, UK: Cambridge University Press.

Lutz, C., & White, G. (1986). The anthropology of emotions. *Annual Review of Anthropology, 15*, 405–436.

Mackie, D. M., DeVos, T., & Smith, E. R. (2000). Intergroup emotions: Explaining offensive action tendencies in an intergroup context. *Journal of Personality & Social Psychology, 79*, 602–616.

Mackie, D. M., Silver, L. A., & Smith, E. R. (this volume). Intergroup emotions: Emotion as an intergroup phenomenon.

Manstead, A. S. R., & Fischer, A. H. (2001). Social appraisal: The social world as object of and influence on appraisal processes. In K. R. Scherer, A. Schorr, & T. Johnstone (Eds.), *Appraisal processes in emotion: Theory, research, application* (pp. 221–232). New York: Oxford University Press.

Merton, R. K., & Lazersfeld, P. F. (Eds.). (1950). *Continuities in social research: Studies in the scope and method of "The American Soldier."* New York: US Free Press.

Miller, R. S. (this volume). Emotion as adaptive interpersonal communication: The case of embarrassment.

Murphy, S. T., & Zajonc, R. B. (1993). Affect, cognition, and awareness: Affective priming with optimal and suboptimal stimulus exposures. *Journal of Personality & Social Psychology, 64*, 723–739.

Ortony, A., Clore, G. L., & Collins, A. (1988). *The cognitive structure of emotions.* New York: Cambridge University Press.

Osgood, C. E. (1971). Exploration in semantic space: A personal diary. *Journal of Social Issues, 27*, 5–64.

Parkinson, B. (1995). *Ideas and realities of emotion.* New York: Routledge.

Rodriguez Mosquera, P. M., Fischer, A. H., & Manstead, A. S. R. (this volume). Inside the heart of emotion on culture and relational concerns.

Sartre, J. P. (1948). *The emotions: Outline of a theory* (trans. B. Frechtman). New York: Philosophical Library.

Scheff, T. J. (1994). *Bloody revenge: Emotions, nationalism, and war.* Boulder, CO: Westview Press.

Scherer, K. R., Schorr, A., & Johnstone, T. (Eds.). (2001). *Appraisal processes in emotion: Theory, methods, research.* New York: Oxford University Press.

Sherif, M. (1958). Group influences upon the formation of norms and attitudes. In E. E. Maccoby, T. M. Newcomb, & E. L. Hartley (Eds.), *Readings in social psychology* (3rd Edition). New York: Holt, Rinehart & Winston. (Original work published 1935.)

Sherif, M., & Sherif, C. W. (1964). *Reference groups: Exploration into conformity and deviation of adolescents.* New York: Harper and Row.

Smith, H. J., & Kessler, T. (this volume). Group-based emotions and intergroup behavior: The case of relative deprivation.

Smith, R. H. (this volume). Envy and its transmutations.

Spears, R., & Leach, C. W. (this volume). Intergroup schadenfreude: Conditions and consequences.
Stouffer, S. A., Suchman, E. A., DeVinney, L. C., Star, S. A., & Williams, R. M., Jr. (1949). *The american soldier, Volume 1: Adjustment during army life*. Princeton, NJ: Princeton University Press.
Thoits, P. A. (1989). The sociology of emotions. *Annual Review of Sociology, 15*, 317–342.
Tiedens, L. Z., Sutton, R. I., & Fong, C. T. (this volume). Emotional variation in work groups: Causes and performance consequences.
Tropp, L. R., & Pettigrew, T. F. (this volume). Intergroup contact and the central role of affect in intergroup prejudice.
Turner, J. C. (1991). *Social influence*. Pacific Grove, CA: Brooks/Cole.
Turner, J. C., Hogg, M. A., Oakes, P. J., Reicher, S. D., & Wetherell, M. S. (1987). *Rediscovering the social group: A self categorization theory*. New York: Basil Blackwell.
Voloshinov, V. N. (1986). *Marxism and the philosophy of language* (trans. L. Matejka and I. R. Titunik; originally published 1973). Cambridge, MA: Harvard University Press.

PART I

THE INTERPERSONAL CONTEXT

1

Empathy

Negotiating the Border Between Self and Other

Mark H. Davis

Self and other. Ego and alter. Ingroup and outgroup. Us and them. Home and visitors. Shirts and skins. Eagles and Rattlers. Klee and Kandinsky. Potter and Malfoy.

As the number and variety of these (and countless other) terms attest, it is absurdly easy to generate ways of thinking about the world that emphasize the separation between self and other. In fact, the point is so obvious as to almost appear self-evident. A quick glance at the morning paper will reveal a depressing number of instances of individuals and groups acting in ways that increase their own welfare at the expense of other individuals or groups. This sad reality is echoed, moreover, in more formal investigations of human nature. Psychology's view of humanity has long included a strong emphasis on hedonism (e.g., Cialdini, Darby, & Vincent, 1973; Dollard & Miller, 1950; Spencer, 1870). In short, the tendency for humans to see their interests as separate from others, and to act so as to maximize their interests at the expense of others, is widespread and robust.

However, the gap between self and other is not unbridgeable. People do not *always* act in ways that maximize their own self-interest. We are capable of inhibiting our immediate and frequently destructive responses to provocation, and substituting more constructive ones. We can forgive transgressions, even quite serious ones. We often act toward others in friendly ways, and sometimes offer help at great risk to ourselves. Although such behavior occurs more frequently toward individuals with whom we share some kind of positive affective bond, nonselfish thought and action also occurs between strangers with no such emotional connection.

This kind of admirable behavior can spring from many sources, but the psychological process most frequently invoked to explain phenomena such as these is probably empathy (e.g., Batson, 1991; Davis, 1994; Eisenberg & Fabes, 1990; Hoffman, 1982). Definitions of empathy have been nearly as numerous as those interested in defining it, but virtually all such efforts have agreed on at least one core feature: that empathy in some way involves the transformation of the observed experiences of another person into a response within the self. In a sense, then, empathy is the psychological process that at least temporarily *unites* the separate social entities of self and other. Viewed in this way, empathy can perhaps be considered the most "social" of phenomena, because it can only arise within some kind of interpersonal context.

The focus of this chapter will be on the ways in which empathy shapes and influences social interaction. Moreover, given the complex and multidimensional nature of empathy, this can occur through a variety of mechanisms. To aid in our understanding of what is to follow, then, it is necessary to consider briefly the nature of empathy.

WHAT IS EMPATHY?

Attempts to define empathy have a long and convoluted history. Various writers over the years have conceived of empathy as a cognitive *process* (e.g., Wispe, 1986), as an accurate *understanding* of another (e.g., Dymond, 1950), as a *sharing* of emotional states with a target (e.g., Hoffman, 1984), and as the specific emotional response of *sympathy* (e.g., Batson, 1991). Previously, I offered a model designed to organize all of these approaches into a comprehensive treatment of the empathy process; Figure 1.1 contains a somewhat revised and updated version of this model (Davis, 1994). In contrast to much previous work, the spirit of this model is deliberately inclusive, designed to emphasize the connections between these constructs. Thus, empathy is broadly defined here as a set of constructs having to do with the responses of one individual to the experiences of another. These constructs specifically include both the *processes* taking place within the observer and the affective and nonaffective *outcomes* that result from those processes. Based on this definition, the model conceives of the typical empathy "episode" as consisting of an observer being exposed in some fashion to a target, after which some response on the part of the observer – cognitive, affective, motivational, and/or behavioral – occurs. Four related constructs can be identified within this prototypical episode: *antecedents*, which refer to characteristics of the observer, target, or situation; *processes*, which refer to the particular mechanisms by which empathic outcomes are produced; *intrapersonal outcomes*, which refer to cognitive, affective, and motivational responses produced in the observer that are not necessarily manifested in overt behavior toward the target; and *interpersonal outcomes*, which refer to behavioral responses directed toward the target. One critical feature of this model is that it considers both cognitive and affective outcomes to be part of empathy. Given the focus in this volume on the connections between emotions and social life, I will in general highlight the affective components of this model, although it will be impossible (and undesirable) to ignore some of the more cognitive elements.

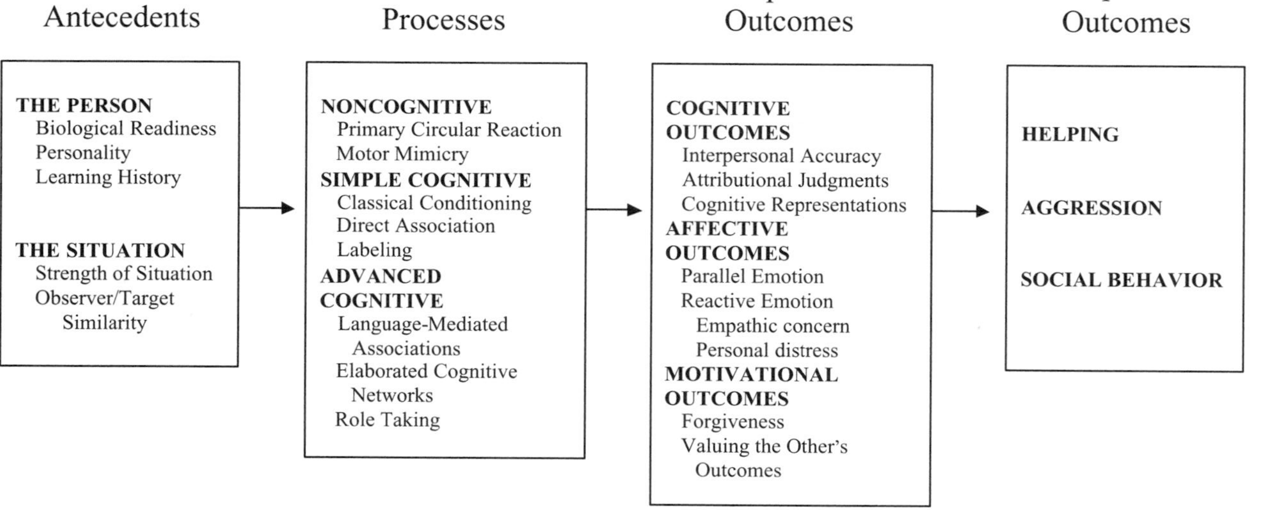

FIGURE 1.1. Comprehensive model depicting empathy-related processes and outcomes.

Antecedents

The Person

All observers bring to an episode certain characteristics that have the potential to influence both processes and outcomes. Of most importance for the purposes of this chapter are the *individual differences* that exist in the tendency to engage in empathy-related processes or to experience empathic outcomes. A variety of individual difference measures have been developed over the years for the purpose of assessing the dispositional tendency to engage in empathy-related processes, such as perspective-taking (e.g., Davis, 1980; Hogan, 1969), or to experience empathy-related affective responses (e.g., Davis, 1980; Mehrabian & Epstein, 1972). Of special note here are individual differences in the tendency to experience two particular affective states in response to the experience of other people. Specifically, the tendency to experience feelings of sympathy for a person in distress, and the tendency to experience personal unease in such cases, are especially important antecedent characteristics that have relevance for social interactions.

The Situation

All responses to another person, whether cognitive or affective, emerge from some specific situational context, and these contexts vary along certain dimensions. One such dimension is what we can call the *strength of the situation*, defined as its power to evoke an emotional response from observers. For example, a situation that includes a clear display of negative emotion by a weak or helpless target is particularly able to engender powerful observer emotions and would be classified as a "strong" situation. In contrast, situations lacking such evocative emotional cues would be characterized as relatively weak. A second situational feature is the *degree of similarity* between the observer and target. (Actually, of course, similarity is a joint function of both the target and the observer, but for the sake of convenience it is considered here.)

Processes

The second major construct within the model consists of the specific processes that generate empathic outcomes in the observer. Based on the work of Hoffman (1984) and Eisenberg (Eisenberg et al., 1991), the model identifies three broad classes of empathy-related processes, chiefly distinguished from one another by the degree of cognitive effort and sophistication required for their operation. In a sense, it is potentially misleading to characterize these processes as either "cognitive" or "affective." It is the *outcomes* of these processes that can be more clearly identified in this way, and each process is capable of producing both cognitive and affective outcomes. However, given the clear differences in the level of cognitive sophistication required for their operation, it seems reasonable to use this dimension to describe these three broad classes.

Noncognitive Processes

Some processes that lead to empathic outcomes require very little cognitive activity. The apparently innate tendency for newborns to cry in response to hearing others cry, which Hoffman (1984) refers to as the *primary circular reaction*, is one example. Another noncognitive process is *motor mimicry*, the tendency for observers automatically and unconsciously to imitate the target. Although early conceptions of mimicry viewed it as a somewhat deliberate strategy for "feeling into" the other, more recent approaches (e.g., Hoffman, 1984; Hatfield, Cacioppo, & Rapson, 1994) have treated it as a relatively automatic, largely noncognitive process.

Simple Cognitive Processes

In contrast to the noncognitive processes, other processes require at least a rudimentary cognitive ability on the part of the observer. *Classical conditioning* is an example; if an observer has previously perceived affective cues in others while experiencing that same affect (perhaps because both observer and target are simultaneously exposed to the same unpleasant stimulus), then the affective cues of targets may come to evoke that emotional state. Similar processes of comparably modest sophistication – *direct association* (Hoffman, 1984) and *labeling* (Eisenberg et al., 1991) – have also been proposed.

Advanced Cognitive Processes

Finally, some processes require rather advanced kinds of cognitive activity. One example is what Hoffman refers to as *language-mediated association*, in which the observer's reaction to the target's plight is produced by activating language-based cognitive networks that trigger associations with the observer's own feelings or experiences. For example, a target who says "My manuscript has been rejected" may exhibit no obvious facial or vocal cues indicating distress, but an observer may respond empathically because her relevant memories (perhaps of an especially undiplomatic review) are activated by the target's words. Eisenberg et al.'s (1991) *elaborated cognitive networks* refer to a very similar process. The most advanced process, however, and the one that has received the most empirical attention, is *role taking* or *perspective taking*: the attempts by one individual to understand another by imagining the other's perspective. It is typically an effortful process, involving both the suppression of one's own egocentric perspective on events and the active entertaining of someone else's.

Intrapersonal Outcomes

The model's third major construct consists of *intrapersonal outcomes* – the cognitive, affective, and motivational responses of the observer that result from exposure to the target. These outcomes are thought to result primarily from the various processes identified at the previous stage in the model.

Cognitive Outcomes

One cognitive outcome is *interpersonal accuracy*, the successful estimation of other people's thoughts, feelings, and characteristics; typically, such interpersonal judgments have been viewed as resulting to a considerable degree from cognitive role-taking processes (e.g., Dymond, 1950). Empathy-related processes have also been implicated in affecting the *attributional judgments* offered by observers for targets' behavior (e.g. Regan & Totten, 1975). More recently, perspective-taking has been linked to changes in the *cognitive representations* that perceivers form of targets – in particular, the degree to which these representations resemble the cognitive representations of the self (Davis et al., 1996; Galinsky & Moskowitz, 2000).

Affective Outcomes

This category consists of the emotional reactions experienced by an observer in response to the observed experiences of the target and is further subdivided into two forms: parallel and reactive outcomes. A *parallel emotion* may in a sense be considered the prototypical affective response: an actual reproduction in an observer of the target's feelings. This sort of emotional matching has clearly been the focus of several historical approaches (McDougall, 1908; Spencer, 1870). *Reactive emotions*, on the other hand, are defined as affective reactions to the experiences of others that differ from the observed affect. They are so named because they are empathic reactions *to* another's state rather than a simple reproduction of that state in the observer. One response clearly falling into this category is the feelings of compassion for others referred to variously as sympathy (Wispe, 1986), empathy (Batson, 1991), and *empathic concern* (Davis, 1983); another example would be *personal distress*, the tendency to feel discomfort and anxiety in response to needy targets.

Motivational Outcomes

A third category of intrapersonal outcomes, somewhat related to the second, are the motivational states produced in the observer by empathy-related processes. For example, *forgiveness* is often conceptualized as a transformation of motivation toward a transgressing partner in which desires for revenge are reduced and desires for reconciliation are increased

(McCullough, Worthington, & Rachal, 1997). More generally, empathic processes have also been linked to increased motivation to *value the other's outcomes* (Batson, Turk, Shaw, & Klein, 1995).

Interpersonal Outcomes

The final construct in the model consists of *interpersonal outcomes*, defined as behaviors directed toward a target that result from prior exposure to that target. The outcome that has attracted the most attention from empathy theorists and researchers is *helping behavior*; both cognitive and affective facets of empathy have long been thought to contribute to the likelihood of observers offering help to needy targets. *Aggressive behavior* has also been linked theoretically to empathy-related processes and dispositions, with the expectation that empathy will be negatively associated with aggressive actions. The effect of empathy on behaviors that occur within *social relationships* – a topic that has only recently begun to attract consistent research interest – also falls into this category. Conveniently enough, it is the focus of the remainder of this chapter.

HOW DOES EMPATHY INFLUENCE SOCIAL INTERACTION?

Given that the preceding model was explicitly formulated to account for the ways in which the experiences of one person come to evoke reactions in another, it is a short jump indeed to the proposition that empathy will play a significant role in shaping the nature of our social interactions. Using the model as a guide, it is possible to identify at least five ways in which empathy can be said to have such effects. Of course, this is not an exhaustive list, but it seems to capture several of the most likely avenues through which empathy can shape interactions. In each case, I will argue that empathy-related processes identified by the model produce intrapersonal outcomes that have beneficial effects on interpersonal relations. Some of these effects can be thought of as part of the day-to-day *maintenance* of relationships; others can best be thought of as operating to *repair* relationships when they are threatened by partner misbehavior. In the following pages, each of these five influences of empathy on social relationships will be considered separately. In brief, they are:

- The creation of an *emotional synchrony* between people that has generally positive effects on the perceived quality of the interaction and the relationship.
- The creation in the observer of *reactive emotions* (e.g., empathic concern; personal distress) that make certain kinds of pro-relationship social behavior more likely.

- The creation in the observer of *motivational states* that tend to elevate the interests of the target relative to those of the observer, thus making certain kinds of behavior (forgiveness, conciliation) more likely.
- A reduction in frequency or intensity of *aggressive* or *hostile reactions* following interpersonal provocation.
- An alteration of the observer's *cognitive representations of self and target* in a way that tends to produce outcomes that are beneficial for the relationship.

Emotional Synchrony

The notion that empathy creates an emotional sharing between observer and target is not new. McDougall (1908) and Spencer (1870) both argued that the essence of empathy (or sympathy, as it was then known) is to create in the observer the same emotional state as that experienced by the target. More recent approaches have broadened the range of observer emotions that can constitute empathy (e.g., Eisenberg & Strayer, 1987; Hoffman, 1984), but the concept of parallel emotional responses remains an important element in any comprehensive treatment of empathy.

Recent theory and research have tended to focus on a single mechanism by which these parallel emotions are created: the tendency of observers to mimic the target's facial expressions, vocal intonations, posture, and movements. Hatfield et al. (1992, 1994) have termed this general phenomenon *emotional contagion*, which they define as "the tendency to automatically mimic and synchronize facial expressions, vocalizations, postures, and movements with those of another person and, consequently, to converge emotionally" (Hatfield et al., 1992, pp. 153–154).

In order for emotional contagion to occur, two separate processes must unfold. First, it is necessary that observers mimic the behavior of targets, and second, it is necessary that this mimicry produces in the observers an emotional state that parallels that of the targets. Considerable evidence documents the operation of both of these processes. In this volume and elsewhere (Hatfield et al., 1992, 1994), Hatfield and Rapson have effectively summarized this evidence; and, given space constraints, I refer the interested reader to these sources for details. It is sufficient to note here that observers often seem to engage in a veritable symphony of unconscious mimicry during social interaction, imitating the facial expressions, bodily movements, posture, speech rate, and vocal intensity of their interaction partners. Moreover, evidence indicates that mimicry in each of these channels contributes to the creation of parallel emotional responding in the observer.

Given the considerable evidence that mimicry produces parallel emotional states in observers, what is the effect of the resulting emotional synchrony between observer and target? The most socially important outcome seems to be greater feelings of rapport between the target and observer – variously operationalized as feeling "in step," involved, or compatible with the other person. LaFrance (1979), for example, found that, when participants in an interaction had greater liking for one another, they also displayed greater posture similarity. Similarly, Bernieri (1988) reported that, following a ten-minute controlled interaction, members of a dyad expressed the greatest feelings of emotional rapport when their physical movements had been most synchronized. More recently, Chartrand and Bargh (1999) manipulated mimicry by having confederates mimic (or not) the physical actions of their partner during a fifteen-minute interaction; those in the mimicking condition reported greater liking for the confederate and a stronger perception that the interaction had gone smoothly. Thus, convincing evidence currently supports the view that the net effect of emotional synchrony is to increase feelings of closeness, connectedness, and rapport with others.

Reactive Emotions

In contrast to parallel emotions, reactive emotional responses do not match those of the target, but are in some sense a reaction *to* the target's situation. While this in theory could encompass a wide variety of emotions, practically speaking only two affective responses have received much sustained research attention. The first of these is *empathic concern* – the other-oriented emotional response of compassion for the target; the second is *personal distress* – the self-oriented response of discomfort and anxiety to another's misfortune (Davis, 1994). Theory and research support the view that both emotions play an important role in social interactions. To better organize this presentation, let us consider the impact that these two affective responses have on three specific kinds of social behavior: considerate social style, good communication, and generosity/helpfulness.

A *considerate social style*, in the sense intended here, includes such features as tolerance, cooperation, active support for others, and a general lack of egocentrism in thought and deed – characteristics that all reflect sensitivity to the other person's needs and desires. Evidence relevant to this topic comes in part from investigations that have measured individual differences in empathic concern and personal distress. For example, three studies using college populations have examined associations between dispositional empathy and measures of a considerate style. Davis and Oathout (1987, 1992) had college students report the frequency with which they engaged in a number of considerate behaviors toward their romantic partners, including "warmth" (acting in affectionate and supportive ways) and "positive outlook" (being friendly, positive, and dependable). In both studies, dispositional empathic concern was significantly and positively related to both kinds of behavior; although the pattern was not as consistent, dispositional personal distress was generally related to considerate behavior significantly but *negatively*. Davis (1983) had college students complete measures of dispositional empathy and a personality measure tapping other-oriented characteristics, such as awareness and understanding of others (the Femininity scale from the Extended Personal Attributes Questionnaire); although personal distress was not related to scores on the Femininity scale, empathic concern was very strongly and positively associated. Thus, the evidence suggests that empathic concern is positively and substantially related to a considerate style, and that personal distress is more weakly and generally negatively associated with such a style.

With regard to *good communication*, several studies indicate that empathic concern again has a constructive effect on social relationships. One set of studies (Davis & Franzoi, 1986; Davis, Franzoi, & Wellinger, 1985; Franzoi & Davis, 1985) examined the link between high school students' dispositional empathy and self-disclosure to peers; personal distress was not related, but empathic concern was significantly and positively related to disclosure *to females* (i.e., males' empathic concern scores were associated with disclosure to the opposite sex, and females' empathic concern scores were associated with same-sex disclosure). In two investigations mentioned previously, Davis and Oathout (1987, 1992) asked college students about the degree to which they "opened up" and "readily listened" to their romantic partner. For both men and women, empathic concern scores were significantly and positively associated with higher scores on this communication index; for women only, personal distress scores were negatively associated. Thus, for both men and women, dispositional empathic concern was rather consistently associated with better communication.

Finally, we come to the issue of *generosity/helpfulness*. Helping behavior, of course, has been studied by social psychologists for at least three decades (e.g., Latane & Darley, 1970), and for much of that time the role of empathy has been debated and examined. Evidence from a variety of sources suggests that both empathic concern and personal distress tend to be associated with offering help to a distressed other, although the theoretical explanations underlying each effect are somewhat different.

For example, considerable work has supported the view that people will help others to reduce the level of unpleasant arousal they are experiencing as a result of exposure to a distressed target. One influential approach in this vein has been the "arousal: cost-reward model" (Piliavin et al., 1981); another is the "negative state relief model" (Cialdini et al., 1973). Given the success of both approaches, it seems clear that, at least under some circumstances, the personal distress experienced in response to another's plight can serve to increase the helpfulness of an observer, if only to reduce his or her own discomfort.

There is also evidence that the other reactive emotion – empathic concern – can produce increased helping, but for a different reason. Batson (1987, 1991) has over the past two decades conducted a series of experiments designed to demonstrate the existence of "true altruism" – that is, helping motivated solely by a concern for the welfare of another. The proximal cause of such helping in this line of research is the state of empathic concern (simply termed empathy by Batson), and considerable evidence exists that this emotional response is associated with greater helping for another, even if there is some cost to the self. Such helping results, moreover, even if it is easy for the observer to escape the situation and thus avoid exposure to the victim's distress; in contrast, feelings of personal distress in this research tend to increase helping only when it is difficult for the observer to escape (see Batson, 1991, for a review).

Thus, both emotional states appear to generate more helpful behavior, although in the case of personal distress the motivation seems less "pure" and is much more dependent on situational factors, such as ease of escape. Coupled with the findings that personal distress was weakly or even negatively related to good communication and a considerate social style, reactive distress does not seem to be a very reliable source of constructive social behavior. In contrast, empathic concern appears to be consistently responsible for a variety of behaviors that are beneficial to social relationships.

Motivational States

A third mechanism by which empathy may affect social behavior is through its influence on the motivational states of the perceiver – that is, through its ability to trigger "the activation of internal desires, needs, and concerns" of the individual (Pittman, 1998, p. 549). In some ways, of course, this mechanism resembles the previous one – empathy's effect on reactive emotions – because of the link that often exists between emotional states and motivation. How are the two to be distinguished? One important difference between them, at least insofar as this chapter is concerned, is that motives and emotions frequently operate at somewhat different levels of specificity, with motivations typically being more general and emotions more specific. For example, the presence of a given motive (e.g., a general need for achievement) might give rise to a variety of specific emotional states (e.g., satisfaction following success; shame following failure).

One example of an empathy-mediated effect on motivation comes from the burgeoning literature on forgiveness. The past decade has seen an increasing amount of attention paid to this important interpersonal phenomenon (e.g., Enright, Gassin, & Wu, 1992; McCullough, Pargament, & Thoresen, 2000). Although a variety of definitions have been advanced, one influential approach is that of McCullough et al. (1997), who define forgiveness as a set of motivational changes characterized by lowered desires to retaliate against and maintain estrangement from an offending relationship partner, and a heightened desire for conciliation. Thus, forgiveness at its heart is a set of changes in the *motivations* of the offended party.

What is empathy's role in all this? McCullough et al. (1997) have proposed a model that identifies empathic concern for the transgressor (which they simply term "empathy") as the most important cause of forgiveness following a transgression. Only to the extent that the wronged party feels empathic concern (perhaps as a result of an apology by the transgressor) does s/he experience a motivational change such that "in place of the motivations for revenge and... estrangement, the increase in caring for the offending partner increases the offended partner's motivation to pursue conciliatory courses of action" (McCullough et al., 1997, p. 323).

Considerable recent evidence supports this model. In a pair of investigations, McCullough et al. (1997) found that feelings of empathy, as hypothesized, were associated with greater forgiveness for an individual who had previously transgressed against them; moreover, forgiveness was then associated with less avoidance and greater conciliation. McCullough et al., (1998, Study 4) reported similar findings in an investigation that examined two distinct behavioral responses to being wronged by another: avoidance and revenge. Feelings of empathy for the transgressor were associated with decreased motivation for both behaviors. In a sample of Italian married couples, Fincham, Paleari, and Regalia (2002) found the same pattern: more tolerant attributions for a partner's misbehavior led to feelings of empathy, which in turn led to increased forgiveness. Finally, in a pair of longitudinal studies, McCullough, Fincham, and Tsang (2003) repeatedly queried individuals for weeks after they suffered an interpersonal transgression. In both studies, empathy at the time of the transgression was significantly related to immediate forgiveness (termed "forbearance" by the authors), but was much less likely to predict additional forgiveness over time. Thus, it may be that empathic concern has its greatest effect on the motivation to forgive in the immediate aftermath of another's misbehavior.

There is an additional form of empathy-mediated motivational transformation that has attracted some attention in recent years. Batson, Turk et al. (1995) have argued that, because the emotional state of empathic concern reliably gives rise to an increased motivation to reduce the other's need, becoming aware of one's empathic feelings can also make one aware of the value that underlies such a motive: namely, a valuing of the other's welfare. Unlike emotions, which are quite transient, values are more stable; as a result, the effects of becoming aware of these values will be more long lasting. In a series of studies, Batson, Turk et al. (1995) found support for this hypothesis; most striking, perhaps, was the finding that although experimentally manipulated feelings of empathic concern dissipated once the target was no longer in need, the degree to which observers reported valuing the target's welfare did not.

In an interesting pair of studies, Batson, Klein, Highberger, and Shaw (1995) also found that, when empathic concern produces an increased valuing of a target's welfare, observers then act in ways that benefit the target, even when doing so contradicts usual principles of justice, such as equal treatment for all. These investigations suggest that a motivational "realignment" can result from empathic emotion – a realignment in which the welfare of another person becomes an increasingly important goal. In fact, a final set of studies by Batson et al. (1997) indicates that the increased valuing of the target can even generalize to other members of the group to which the target belongs (e.g., AIDS patients, homeless persons), and produce more positive evaluations of those groups.

Reducing Aggressive or Hostile Behavior

A fourth mechanism by which empathy can influence the course of social interactions is through its regulating effect on hostile and/or aggressive behaviors, and there are at least two major ways in which this might occur. The first possibility is that observers' emotional responses to the distress of others may lessen their likelihood of aggressing against those others. This might happen, for example, if observing the victim's distress cues leads to a sharing of the victim's distress. To escape this vicarious distress, the aggressor stops or reduces the aggression (e.g., Feshbach, 1964). Alternatively, victim distress cues can produce the reactive emotion of empathic concern in perpetrator-observers, and these feelings of sympathy may then lead the observer to stop or reduce the aggression (Miller & Eisenberg, 1988).

Evidence reviewed by Miller and Eisenberg (1988) suggests that, for adults, there is in fact a reliable association between measures of dispositional empathic emotionality (assessed via self-report) and aggressive behavior. Across the nine studies using adult samples included in that review, greater dispositional empathy was for the most part reliably associated with less aggressive behavior. Studies conducted since that review (Davis, 1994; Richardson et al., 1994) have found a similar pattern. In addition to these direct tests of the empathy–aggression link, a number of investigations have supported the related proposition that the simple presence of victim distress cues (because they trigger the empathic response) should serve to inhibit aggression (e.g., Buss, 1966; Geen, 1970). However, this effect is only reliable when the victim has not previously provoked the observer. When the victim *has* provoked the observer, victim distress cues sometimes reduce aggression, but sometimes do not (e.g., Baron, 1974, 1979). Thus, one important qualification on the "empathic emotions → aggression" link is the preexisting emotional stance that the observer has toward the target. In some cases, signs of victim distress may not have the effect of reducing aggression at all – in fact, they may even be reinforcing to the observer (Davis, 1994).

The second way in which empathy might reduce the occurrence of hostile and aggressive actions is through the process of perspective-taking. That is, adopting the point of view of a person who acts in a potentially provoking way may lead to a more tolerant and understanding perception of that person's actions; such tolerance can consequently reduce the likelihood that retaliation will occur. A number of studies have examined this possibility and found evidence consistent with it.

One set of investigations assessed dispositional perspective-taking, as well as some indicator of hostile/aggressive behavior and found higher perspective-taking to be associated with lower hostility. Davis and Kraus (1991) reported, in two samples of adolescent and preadolescent boys, a significant negative correlation between dispositional perspective-taking and their self-reported number of fights and arguments over the previous two years. Sessa (1996), in an investigation of thirty different nursing teams, found that teams with higher mean scores on measures of dispositional perspective-taking tended to perceive their group as having less "people-oriented" conflict (which is especially damaging) and more "task-oriented" conflict (which is less damaging). In a series of studies, Rusbult et al. (1991; Studies 3–5) presented undergraduate participants with a set of items that required them to estimate their likely response if faced with bad behavior by a romantic partner; both constructive (e.g., talk it over with the partner) and destructive (e.g., end the relationship) responses to the partner misbehavior were assessed. A general measure of dispositional perspective-taking was only sporadically related to lower levels of destructive responding; however, a measure of the specific tendency to adopt the *partner's* perspective was consistently related.

In two investigations (Richardson et al., 1994; Richardson, Green, & Lago, 1998), Richardson examined the link between dispositional perspective-taking and actual verbal aggression in a laboratory setting and found evidence that high perspective-takers were less likely to retaliate against opponents who had mildly provoked them; this held true even if the opponents increased the magnitude of their provocation across trials. Finally, in some interesting recent work, Giancola (2003) examined the effect of provocation, alcohol consumption, and dispositional empathy (both perspective-taking and empathic concern) on actual aggression (administering electric shocks). Using a sample of more than 200 "healthy social drinkers," he found that alcohol increased the level of aggressive responding, but that this was especially true for those who were lowest in dispositional empathy. Thus, not only does perspective-taking seem to make hostile responding less likely in general, it may also serve a buffering function by diminishing the harmful effects of other variables, such as alcohol consumption. It should also be noted here that some of the effects of perspective-taking on aggression may rely on emotional responses produced by taking the perspective of the provoker. Given the well-documented links between perspective-taking and emotional reactions (see Davis, 1994), it is likely that affective states, such as empathic concern and personal distress often accompany perspective-taking, and that they mediate – at least to some degree – the apparent influence of perspective-taking on hostility.

Cognitive Representation of Others

The final mechanism through which empathy may shape social interactions is a bit different from the others described thus far, and has to do with the way in which people construct and store mental representations of self and other. In short, the argument here is that empathy may play a significant role in affecting the nature of such representations and that this may have some significant implications for social behavior. This mechanism is undoubtedly the one in which cognitive processes and outcomes are paramount, and the role of empathy's affective components are the smallest. Nevertheless, it seems likely that even here the affective components of empathy still play a role, and this will be highlighted where appropriate.

Psychologists have been interested for some time in how social knowledge is mentally represented, and a variety of models have been proposed (Smith, 1998). Regardless of how such phenomena are conceptualized, however, considerable evidence supports the view that mental representations of self and other can influence social interaction in several ways: by affecting the way in which new social information is interpreted (e.g., Darley & Gross, 1983), the ease with which it can be recalled (e.g., Wyer & Srull, 1989), and the way in which other people are evaluated (e.g., Dunning & Hayes, 1996), to name only a few.

One topic in particular that has attracted attention in recent years has been the degree to which the cognitive representations of self and other can be said to overlap, or "merge," with one another. Importantly, for our purposes, empathy may play a significant role in this phenomenon. Just as empathy in general can be thought of as a process that bridges the gap between self and other, one effect of empathic processes may be to help create cognitive structures corresponding to self and other that are closer, more similar, or more intertwined.

At least two lines of research have focused on the "merging" of self and other. The first of these approaches was based originally on Aron and Aron's (1986) theory of "self-expansion." This theory argues that one consequence of falling in love is that the self-concept becomes enlarged; this happens at least in part because aspects of the romantic partner become included within the self. In support of this idea, Aron et al. (1991) found evidence that those in close relationships (e.g., best friends; spouses) appear to make fewer distinctions between the self and other in a variety of ways. In particular, spouses took longer to make "me/not me" decisions about traits that were different between self and spouse than for traits that were similar for both; such a pattern suggests a kind of "confusion" – at the level of cognitive representation – between self and other (Aron et al., 1991).

Another example of research addressing the possible "merging" of self and other representations is derived from cross-cultural psychology's notion of "interdependent self-construal" (Markus & Kitayama, 1991). This term refers to the fact that, in many collectivist cultures, the self is defined largely in terms of its connections to outside entities: family, significant others, and important groups. This stands in contrast to the kind of self-definition more common in individualist cultures; these definitions tend to emphasize internal attributes of the individual and view the self as essentially separate from other social entities. Thus, an interdependent self-construal appears to make fewer distinctions between "self" and "other." In fact, the very terms "self" and "other" may be less meaningful in this context; if self is defined in terms of its *connections* to others, then self and other may really occupy the same "cognitive space." Importantly, recent work has demonstrated that: (a) even among individuals from individualist cultures, there are differences in the degree to which people possess interdependent self-construals (Cross, Bacon, & Morris, 2000); and (b) it is possible to manipulate experimentally the degree to which interdependent self-construals are accessible (e.g., Haberstroh et al., 2002; Stapel & Koomen, 2001).

So, does empathy in fact make overlapping representations of self and other more likely? Evidence in support of this possibility has begun to accumulate. Davis et al. (1996) conducted two experiments in which perspective-taking or control instructions were given to participants prior to viewing another student on videotape. Those who received the perspective-taking set were more likely to use traits earlier identified as characteristic of the *self* (especially positive ones) to describe the other student; thus, the cognitive representations of self and other shared more common content. In three studies, Galinsky and Moskowitz (2000) extended this line of inquiry by examining the implications of perspective-taking for the use of stereotypes to characterize outgroups. College students who were instructed to take the perspective of an outgroup (the elderly) were less likely to later use stereotypes to characterize elderly people; moreover, and consistent with Davis et al. (1996), this effect was mediated by the fact that perspective-taking subjects again had a greater degree of overlap between self-traits and those seen as descriptive of the elderly. Taken together, these studies support the view that perspective-taking affects the cognitive representation of others in a particular way – by making them more similar to our own self-constructs. In a real sense, then, perspective-taking creates a merging of self and other.

More recent evidence also suggests that empathy may be related to the likelihood of possessing an interdependent self-construal. Cross et al. (2000) developed a measure of individual differences in the kind of interdependent self-concept that is most likely among those living in individualist cultures – one that is based on relationships with close or significant others, rather than ingroups. They term this construct "relational-interdependent self-construal," (RISC) and their measure of this construct is the RISC scale. In a sample huge by social psychological standards (*N* of over 2,500), Cross et al. found that both dispositional perspective-taking and empathic concern were positively related to scores on their measure. In the case of perspective-taking, this association was quite modest ($r = .13$), but for empathic concern it was more robust (.34). Thus, a dispositional tendency to experience the reactive emotions of sympathy and compassion is meaningfully associated with a tendency to define the self in terms of close social relationships. It should be noted here that it was the affective form of dispositional empathy that displayed by far the stronger association with scores on the RISC scale – an indication that affective constructs can play a significant role even for this most cognitive of mechanisms.

If it can provisionally be assumed, based on research to date, that empathy does tend to produce mental representations of self and other that overlap, what implications would this hold for social interaction? Several possibilities suggest themselves. For example, the Galinsky and Moskowitz (2000) investigation mentioned earlier demonstrates that one effect of self–other "merging" is a decreased use of stereotypes in characterizing other people. Because stereotypes have a well-documented effect on how new information about an individual is interpreted (e.g., Darley & Gross, 1983; Dunning & Sherman, 1997), anything that lessens the likelihood of their activation would have an influence on the resulting social judgments. In particular, such judgments should be less subject to the biases that stereotype activation typically brings (e.g., Mullen & Hu, 1989).

A second way that overlapping representations of self and other may affect social behavior has to do with such overlap's effect on perceptions of similarity to the other. Cross, Morris, and Gore (2002, Studies 5 and 6) examined the link between individual differences in interdependent self-construal (measured via the RISC scale) and measures of perceived similarity between the respondent and the respondent's "second-closest same-sex friend." Higher scores on the RISC scale were significantly associated with perceptions that the self and this friend were similar in abilities, values, and traits. In the same vein, Davis et al. (1996) found that greater self–other overlap was associated with perceptions of greater similarity to, and liking for, the target. Perceptions of similarity are important because considerable evidence from forty years of investigation documents the influence of similarity on liking (e.g., Newcomb, 1961; Sprecher & Duck, 1994). Importantly, such perceptions of similarity with the other can have beneficial effects for the relationship, regardless of their accuracy. Murray et al. (2002), for example, have demonstrated that even *false* assumptions of similarity between self and romantic partner nevertheless increase one's satisfaction with the relationship.

A third implication that self–other merging has for social interaction comes from Gardner, Gabriel, and Hochschild's (2002) investigation of the effect of interdependent self-construals on the social comparison process. Gardner et al. took as their starting point the well-documented effect – derived from self-evaluation maintenance SEM theory (Tesser, 1988) – that being outperformed by a close other in an important self-relevant domain frequently constitutes a threat to self-esteem. Gardner et al. argued that this effect makes sense if one's self-construal is independent of others, because in such cases others' success is seen as a threat to self. When self-construals are more interdependent, with significant others included *within* the self, such success by others would be less threatening. To test this idea, Gardner et al. manipulated the level of self-construal by priming either themes of individual achievement or group loyalty. As predicted, when an independent construal of self was primed, the usual SEM pattern was found; participants estimated that a close friend would outperform a stranger in a nonrelevant domain (performance on a trivia quiz), and that the stranger would prevail in a relevant domain (GRE questions). Following the priming of an interdependent self-construal, however, this pattern disappeared. Instead, the friend was predicted to outperform the stranger regardless of task. Thus, not only do overlapping cognitive representations of self and other produce less stereotypical thinking about others and increase one's perceived similarity to and liking for the other, they also appear to reduce the likelihood that good performance by a significant other will be perceived as a threat to the self, thus reducing at least one common and significant source of interpersonal friction.

A final means by which cognitive representations may influence social interaction is through the emotional responses we are likely to have when exposed to the experiences of someone with whom we feel some degree of cognitive "overlap." The genesis of this argument lies in a recent reinterpretation of evidence supporting the "empathy–altruism" link (Batson, 1991). Cialdini et al. (1997) argue that the apparent causal link between feelings of empathic concern (empathy) and helping may be mediated instead by a perception of "oneness" with the other that accompanies empathic feelings. In support of this position, Cialdini et al. (1997) offer evidence that such feelings of oneness are associated with both empathy and helping. Whether or not one is persuaded that such self–other overlap actually accounts for the empathy-helping relationship, it does seem that, in at least some circumstances, perceptions of oneness with another person are in fact accompanied by the emotional response of empathic concern. As a result, it seems plausible that yet another way in which overlapping cognitive representations may influence behavior is through their effect on affective states.

CONCLUSIONS

After considering the evidence reviewed in this chapter, it seems possible to reach at least three conclusions. First, it seems clear that empathic processes and outcomes have an overwhelmingly positive effect on the quality of social life. This is true for relatively primitive processes (such as motor mimicry), as well as for quite advanced ones (such as perspective-taking); both contribute to making social life less contentious and more enjoyable. A variety of intrapersonal outcomes – cognitive, affective, and motivational – all foster behaviors that enhance the quality of our relations with other people. With almost no exceptions, the effect of empathy on social life is beneficial.

Second, although both cognitive and affective facets of empathy are involved in influencing the course of social interactions, it seems clear that many of the most important effects involve emotional aspects. For example, the first two mechanisms described in this chapter – emotional synchrony and reactive emotions – by definition depend on the existence of particular affective states in the observer. Although cognitive processes may be involved in their creation, it is the presence of these specific emotional states that is crucial. The third mechanism – motivational states – also owes much to empathically created emotional responses; evidence suggests that both forgiveness and increased valuing of the other's welfare result from feelings of sympathy for another. The two remaining influences of empathy on social behavior – aggression reduction and cognitive representations of self and other – have a more cognitive flavor, but even here it is apparent that empathic emotional responses play a role. It is important, of course, to keep in mind that empathy is a multidimensional phenomenon in which cognitive and affective facets are usually intertwined. Nevertheless, and in keeping with the spirit of this volume, it is also fair to say that emotional responses to – and about – other people seem especially critical in shaping social life.

Finally, the constructive effects of empathy on social life can be characterized as operating in two broad ways. One is through their salubrious effects on the mundane details of everyday life. Unconscious and nearly constant mimicking of interaction partners produces an emotional synchrony that makes us feel closer and more attuned to those with whom we spend time. Dispositional empathic concern leads us to communicate more openly and to act in more considerate ways. The creation of overlapping cognitive structures corresponding to self and other produces greater feelings of similarity and liking, and reduces the degree to which we view the success of close others as a threat to our self-esteem. Thus, in a host of small and nearly invisible ways, empathy smoothes the rough edges of social intercourse and makes for more satisfying relationships.

But there is another way in which empathy makes its positive contribution to social life. It also operates during less routine, more dramatic moments – times of provocation, bad behavior, and betrayal by others. Perspective-taking reduces the tendency to respond immediately and destructively to bad behavior by relationship partners, and thus helps avoid the escalatory cycles that often result from provocation. Perhaps even more important, feeling empathic concern for transgressors contributes strongly to a willingness to forgive, and with this, a readiness to forgo retaliation and embrace reconciliation. Empathy may therefore be said to have at least two important functions in social life – a *maintenance* function that operates all the time to keep relationships running smoothly, and *reparative* function that is apparent during times of relationship strain. Which of the two is more important is probably impossible to determine; a case might be made for either. What does seem clear is this: because both are undeniably important to the long-term viability of social relationships, empathy's importance for the ongoing vitality of social relationships is substantial.

References

Aron, A., & Aron, E. N. (1986). *Love as the expansion of self: Understanding attraction and satisfaction*. New York: Hemisphere.

Aron, A., Aron, E. N., Tudor, M., & Nelson, G. (1991). Close relationships as including other in the self. *Journal of Personality and Social Psychology, 60*, 241–253.

Baron, R. A. (1974). Aggression as a function of victim's pain cues, level of prior anger arousal, and exposure to an aggressive model. *Journal of Personality and Social Psychology, 29*, 117–124.

Baron, R. A. (1979). Effects of victim's pain cues, victim's race, and level of prior instigation upon physical aggression. *Journal of Applied Social Psychology, 9*, 103–114.

Batson, C. D. (1987). Prosocial motivation: Is it ever truly altruistic? In L. Berkowitz (Ed.), *Advances in experimental social psychology* (Vol. 20; pp. 65–122). New York: Academic Press.

Batson, C. D. (1991). *The altruism question: Toward a social-psychological answer*. Hillsdale, NJ: Lawrence Erlbaum Associates.

Batson, C. D., Klein, T. R., Highberger, L., & Shaw, L. L. (1995). Immorality from empathy-induced altruism: when compassion and justice conflict. *Journal of Personality and Social Psychology, 68*, 1042–1054.

Batson, C. D., Turk, C. L., Shaw, L. L., & Klein, T. R. (1995). Information function of empathic emotion: learning that we value the other's welfare. *Journal of Personality and Social Psychology, 68*, 300–313.

Bernieri, F. J. (1988). Coordinated movement and rapport in teacher-student interactions. *Journal of Nonverbal Behavior, 12*, 120–138.

Buss, A. H. (1966). Instrumentality of aggression, feedback, and frustration as determinants of physical aggression. *Journal of Personality and Social Psychology, 3*, 153–162.

Chartrand, T. L., & Bargh, J. A. (1999). The chameleon effect: The perception-behavior link and social interaction. *Journal of Personality and Social Psychology, 76*, 893–910.

Cialdini, R. B., Brown, S. L., Lewis, B. P., Luce, C., & Neuberg, S. L. (1997). Reinterpreting the empathy-altruism relationship: When one into one equals oneness. *Journal of Personality and Social Psychology, 73*, 481–494.

Cialdini, R. B., Darby, B. L., & Vincent, J. E. (1973). Transgression and altruism: A case for hedonism. *Journal of Experimental Social Psychology, 9*, 502–516.

Cross, S. E., Bacon, P. L., & Morris, M. L. (2000). The relational-interdependent self-construal and relationships. *Journal of Personality and Social Psychology, 78*, 791–808.

Cross, S. E., Morris, M. L., & Gore, J. S. (2002). Thinking about oneself and others: The relational-interdependent self-construal and social cognition. *Journal of Personality and Social Psychology, 82*, 399–418.

Darley, J. M., & Gross, P. H. (1983). A hypothesis-confirming bias in labeling effects. *Journal of Personality and Social Psychology, 44*, 20–33.

Davis, M. H. (1980). A multidimensional approach to individual differences in empathy. *JSAS Catalog of Selected Documents in Psychology, 10*, 85.

Davis, M. H. (1983). Measuring individual differences in empathy: Evidence for a multidimensional approach. *Journal of Personality and Social Psychology, 44*, 113–126.

Davis, M. H. (1994). *Empathy: A social psychological approach*. Boulder, CO: Westview Press.

Davis, M. H., Conklin, L., Smith, A., & Luce, C. (1996). Effect of perspective taking on the cognitive representation of persons: A merging of self and other. *Journal of Personality and Social Psychology, 70*, 713–726.

Davis, M. H., & Franzoi, S. L. (1986). Adolescent loneliness, self-disclosure, and private self-consciousness: A longitudinal investigation. *Journal of Personality and Social Psychology, 51*, 595–608.

Davis, M. H., Franzoi, S. L., & Wellinger, P. (1985). *Personality, social behavior, and loneliness*. Presented at the 93rd annual convention of the American Psychological Association, Los Angeles.

Davis, M. H., & Kraus, L. A. (1991). Dispositional empathy and social relationships. In W. H. Jones & D. Perlman (Eds.), *Advances in personal relationships* (Vol. 3; pp. 75–115). London: Jessica Kingsley Publishers.

Davis, M. H., & Oathout, H. A. (1987). Maintenance of satisfaction in romantic relationships: Empathy and relational competence. *Journal of Personality and Social Psychology, 53*, 397–410.

Davis, M. H., & Oathout, H. A. (1992). The effect of dispositional empathy on romantic relationship behaviors: Heterosocial anxiety as a moderating influence. *Personality and Social Psychology Bulletin, 18*, 76–83.

Dollard, J., & Miller, N. E. (1950). *Personality and psychotherapy*. New York: McGraw-Hill.

Dunning, D., & Hayes, A. F. (1996). Evidence for egocentric comparison in social judgment. *Journal of Personality and Social Psychology, 71*, 213–229.

Dunning, D., & Sherman, D. A. (1997). Stereotypes and tacit inference. *Journal of Personality and Social Psychology, 73*, 459–471.

Dymond, R. F. (1950). Personality and empathy. *Journal of Consulting Psychology, 14*, 343–350.

Eisenberg, N., & Fabes, R. A. (1990). Empathy: Conceptualization, measurement, and relation to prosocial behavior. *Motivation and Emotion, 14*, 131–149.

Eisenberg, N., Shea, C. L., Carlo, G., & Knight, G. P. (1991). Empathy-related responding and cognition: A "chicken and the egg" dilemma. In W. Kurtines & J. Gewirtz (Eds.), *Handbook of moral behavior and development. Volume 2: Research* (pp. 63–88). Hillsdale, NJ: Lawrence Erlbaum Associates.

Eisenberg, N., & Strayer, J. (1987). Critical issues in the study of empathy. In N. Eisenberg & J. Strayer (Eds.), *Empathy and its development* (pp. 3–13). Cambridge: Cambridge University Press.

Enright, R. D., Gassin, E. A., & Wu, C. (1992). Forgiveness: A developmental view. *Journal of Moral Development, 21*, 99–114.

Feshbach, S. (1964). The function of aggression and the regulation of aggressive drive. *Psychological Review, 71*, 257–272.

Fincham, F. D., Paleari, G., & Regalia, C. (2002). Forgiveness in marriage: The role of relationship quality, attributions and empathy. *Personal Relationships, 9*, 27–37.

Franzoi, S. L., & Davis, M. H. (1985). Adolescent self-disclosure and loneliness: Private self-consciousness and parental influences. *Journal of Personality and Social Psychology, 48*, 768–780.

Galinsky, A. D., & Moskowitz, G. B. (2000). Perspective-taking: Decreasing stereotype expression, stereotype accessibility, and in-group favoritism. *Journal of Personality and Social Psychology, 78*, 708–724.

Gardner, W. L., Gabriel, S., & Hochschild, L. (2002). When you and I are "we," you are not threatening: The role of self-expansion in social comparison. *Journal of Personality and Social Psychology, 82*, 239–251.

Geen, R. G. (1970). Perceived suffering of the victim as an inhibitor of attack-induced aggression. *The Journal of Social Psychology, 81*, 209–215.

Giancola, P. R. (2003). The moderating effects of dispositional empathy on alcohol-related aggression in men and women. *Journal of Abnormal Psychology, 112*, 275–281.

Haberstroh, S., Oyserman, D., Schwarz, N., Kuhnen, U., & Ji, L. (2002). Is the interdependent self more sensitive to question context than the independent self? Self-construal and the observation of conversational norms. *Journal of Experimental Social Psychology, 38*, 323–329.

Hatfield, E., Cacioppo, J. T., & Rapson, R. L. (1992). Emotional contagion. In M. S. Clark (Ed.), *Review of personality and social psychology: Volume 14. Emotion and social behavior* (pp. 151–177). Newbury Park, CA: Sage.

Hatfield, E., Cacioppo, J. T., & Rapson, R. L. (1994). *Emotional contagion*. Cambridge: Cambridge University Press.

Hoffman, M. L. (1982). Development of prosocial motivation: Empathy and guilt. In N. Eisenberg (Ed.), *The development of prosocial behavior* (pp. 281–313). New York: Academic Press.

Hoffman, M. L. (1984). Interaction of affect and cognition in empathy. In C. E. Izard, J. Kagan, & R. B. Zajonc (Eds.), *Emotions, cognition, and behavior* (pp. 103–131). Cambridge: Cambridge University Press.

Hogan, R. (1969). Development of an empathy scale. *Journal of Consulting and Clinical Psychology, 33,* 307–316.

LaFrance, M. (1979). Nonverbal synchrony and rapport: Analysis by the cross-lag panel technique. *Social Psychology Quarterly, 42,* 66–70.

Latane, B., & Darley, J. M. (1970). *The unresponsive bystander: Why doesn't he help?* New York: Appleton-Century-Crofts.

Markus, H., & Kitayama, S. (1991). Culture and the self: Implications for cognition, emotion, and motivation. *Psychological Review, 98,* 224–252.

McCullough, M. E., Fincham, F. D., & Tsang, J. (2003). Forgiveness, forbearance, and time: The temporal unfolding of transgression-related interpersonal motivations. *Journal of Personality and Social Psychology, 84,* 540–557.

McCullough, M. E., Pargament, K. I., & Thoresen, C. E. (2000). The psychology of forgiveness: History, conceptual issues, and overview. In M. E. McCullough, K. I. Pargament, and C. E. Thoresen (Eds.), *Forgiveness: Theory, research, and practice* (pp. 1–14). New York: Guilford.

McCullough, M. E., Rachal, K. C., Sandage, S. J., Worthington, E. L., Jr., Brown, S. W., & Hight, T. L. (1998). Interpersonal forgiving in close relationships. II. Theoretical elaboration and measurement. *Journal of Personality and Social Psychology, 75,* 1586–1603.

McCullough, M. E., Worthington, L. L., Jr., & Rachal, K. C. (1997). Interpersonal forgiving in close relationships. *Journal of Personality and Social Psychology, 73,* 321–336.

McDougall, W. (1908). *An introduction to social psychology.* London: Methuen.

Mehrabian, A., & Epstein, N. (1972). A measure of emotional empathy. *Journal of Personality, 40,* 525–543.

Miller, P. A., & Eisenberg, N. (1988). The relation of empathy to aggressive and externalizing/antisocial behavior. *Psychological Bulletin, 103,* 324–344.

Mullen, B., & Hu, L. (1989). Perceptions of ingroup and outgroup variability: A meta-analytic integration. *Basic and Applied Social Psychology, 10,* 233–252.

Murray, S. L., Holmes, J. G., Bellavia, G., Griffin, D. W., & Dolderman, D. (2002). Kindred spirits? The benefits of egocentrism in close relationships. *Journal of Personality and Social Psychology, 82,* 563–581.

Newcomb, T. M. (1961). *The acquaintance process.* New York: Holt, Rinehart, and Winston.

Piliavin, J. A., Dovidio, J. F., Gaertner, S. L., & Clark, R. D. (1981). *Emergency intervention.* New York: Academic Press.

Pittman, T. S. (1998). Motivation. In D. T. Gilbert, S. T. Fiske, & G. Lindzey (Eds.), *The handbook of social psychology* (Vol. I, 4th Edition; pp. 549–590). New York: McGraw-Hill.

Regan, D. T., & Totten, J. (1975). Empathy and attribution: Turning observers into actors. *Journal of Personality and Social Psychology, 32,* 850–856.

Richardson, D. R., Green, L. R., & Lago, T. (1998). The relationship between perspective-taking and nonaggressive responding in the face of an attack. *Journal of Personality, 66,* 235–256.

Richardson, D. R., Hammock, G. S., Smith, S. M., Gardner, W., & Signo, M. (1994). Empathy as a cognitive inhibitor of interpersonal aggression. *Aggressive Behavior, 20*, 275–289.

Rusbult, C. E., Verette, J., Whitney, G. A., Slovik, L. F., & Lipkus, I. (1991). Accommodation processes in close relationships: Theory and preliminary empirical evidence. *Journal of Personality and Social Psychology, 60*, 53–78.

Sessa, V. I. (1996). Using perspective taking to manage conflict and affect in teams. *Journal of Applied Behavioral Science, 32*, 101–115.

Smith, E. R. (1998). Mental representation and memory. In D. T. Gilbert, S. T. Fiske, & G. Lindzey (Eds.), *The handbook of social psychology* (Vol. I, 4th Edition; pp. 391–445). New York: McGraw-Hill.

Spencer, H. (1870). *The principles of psychology*. London: Williams and Norgate.

Sprecher, S., & Duck, S. (1994). Sweet talk: The importance of perceived communication for romantic and friendship attraction experienced during a get-acquainted date. *Personality and Social Psychology Bulletin, 20*, 391–400.

Stapel, D. A., & Koomen, W. (2001). I, we, and the effects of others on me: How self-construal level moderates social comparison effects. *Journal of Personality and Social Psychology, 80*, 766–781.

Tesser, A. (1988). Toward a self-evaluation maintenance model of social behavior. In L. Berkowitz (Ed.), *Advances in experimental social psychology* (Vol. 21; pp. 181–222). San Diego, CA: Academic Press.

Wispe, L. (1986). The distinction between sympathy and empathy: To call forth a concept, a word is needed. *Journal of Personality and Social Psychology, 50*, 314–321.

Wyer, R. S., & Srull, T. K. (1989). *Memory and cognition in its social context*. Hillsdale, NJ: Lawrence Erlbaum.

2

Envy and Its Transmutations

Richard H. Smith

A routine fact of life is that we often meet people who are superior to us in some way. When their superiority matters to us, we can feel envy. Here is Shakespeare's Cassius, a literary prototype of the envying person, as he protests the honors being heaped on Caesar:

> Why, man, he doth bestride the narrow world
> Like a Colossus, and we petty men
> Walk under his huge legs and peep about
> To find ourselves dishonorable graves. (Shakespeare, 1599/1934, p. 41)

These words show an important quality of envy. The envying person notices another's advantage or superiority and feels *inferior*. Caesar was an exceptional man who had achieved military and political greatness, and Cassius felt undersized and trivial next to his grand presence. Envy begins with an unflattering social comparison resulting in a quick, painful perception of inferiority (e.g., Foster, 1972; Parrott, 1991; Salovey & Rodin, 1984; Silver & Sabini, 1978; Smith, 1991; Smith et al., 1999).

It is worth dwelling on why an unflattering social comparison might catch our attention and then create a painful emotion such as envy. From an evolutionary point of view, it is highly adaptive for people to have an inclination to scan their environment for threats of all kinds. In terms of potential threats from others, this also means that people should have the capacity and the inclination to assess their rank (e.g., Beach & Tesser, 2000; Buunk & Ybema, 1997; Frank, 1999; Gilbert, 1992; Smith, 2000). This would be especially true in situations where group members must compete for limited resources tied to sustenance and mating, as may have been typical when current human tendencies evolved (e.g., Gilbert, 1992). Low ranking signals that one should act submissively; high ranking enables dominance. There are potentially severe consequences for misjudging rank. Individuals who believe they can dominate a group, when in fact they cannot, will find that group members possessing actual superiority will assert themselves, perhaps with hostility and aggression. Those who exaggerate their rank on characteristics that matter in mate selection may find themselves rejected, unappeased, and made fools. Not surprisingly, empirical evidence indicates that assessments of rank are made quickly, at the earliest stages of social interactions, and, perhaps without much explicit cognitive processing (Kalma, 1991).

Social comparisons serve decisive inferential functions in ability assessments. As Festinger (1954) argued in his now classic analysis of social comparison processes, human beings are motivated for adaptive reasons to assess their abilities and opinions. Because objective, nonsocial standards are actually lacking for most such assessments, people typically look to others as a standard instead. Not only do social comparisons inform us about whether we have performed well or poorly, but they also localize the cause of our performance (e.g., Kelley, 1967). The more our performance is discrepant from how others have done, the more something about ourselves becomes the "cause" of our performance. An unflattering social comparison creates a direct route to a negative inference about the self, and so it is only natural for such a comparison to create an emotional reaction like envy.

It is difficult to overemphasize the broad and potent role of social comparisons in social life. Considerable research confirms Festinger's insights into the nature of self-evaluative judgments (see Buunk & Gibbons, 1997; Suls & Wheeler, 2000, for reviews). We need at least some sense of where we stand on important attributes because our effectiveness in group settings partly depends on it. It matters, and often matters profoundly, how we compare with others. The outcomes we receive across important domains of life, from work to romance, frequently result in no small way from where we fall on local distributions of valued traits and abilities (Frank, 1999). The accumulating pattern of these outcomes is a central contributor to our sense of self-worth and to the emotions we feel as we interact with others (Smith, 2000).

Paradoxically, the importance of social comparisons in self-evaluation may help to explain why research also shows that people use social comparisons not only for accurate self-assessment, but also for self-enhancement (e.g., Brickman & Bulman, 1977; Wills, 1981). Especially when the implications of social comparisons threaten our self-esteem, we tend to select or construe comparison information in a biased, ego-enhancing manner – serving our vanity as much as our need for accurate self-knowledge (see Suls & Wheeler, 2000, for recent reviews). The self-esteem implications of social comparisons can be so menacing that concerns over accurate self-assessment take a back seat. There is a basic antinomy between using social comparisons to assess our abilities and using them to maintain an ego-enhancing sense of superiority. As will be outlined later, that accuracy can be trumped by self-enhancement may help to explain how the invidious pain of an unflattering comparison can transmute itself into an emotion more bearable to the envying person's self-image.

WHAT ARE THE MAIN CONDITIONS NECESSARY FOR ENVY?

Similarity

We envy people who are similar to ourselves (e.g., Aristotle, 322 B.C./1941; Heider, 1958; Parrott, 1991; Tesser, 1991). Social comparisons, in general, work this way. We seek social comparisons and are affected by social comparisons with people who are like us (Festinger, 1954). Otherwise, we are unlikely to find social comparisons with them useful or consequential (e.g., Goethals & Darley, 1977). Envy involves "potter against potter," to use Aristotle's words. Cassius shares with Caesar commonalities of military background and patrician class, and so he is primed by such similarities to find Caesar's superiority invidious.

Self-Relevance

Envy also requires that the domain in question be self-relevant. We must link part of our core self-worth with doing well in this domain. This makes sense as it would be improbable for a social comparison to create an emotion of any kind unless it is linked to something important to the self. Without self-relevance, the disadvantaged person will feel little erosion in his or her sense of self. Cassius has military and political ambitions of his own that are typical for the social class that Caesar and he share, and so the enveloping shadow cast by Caesar's successes creates a personally charged contrast. Research by Tesser (1991) and by Salovey and Rodin (1984) confirms the important role of self-relevance. In fact, Tesser's research shows that low self-relevance, together with similarity or closeness, actually produces the opposite of envy – a kind of "pride in other" (Tesser, 1991).

A study by Salovey and Rodin (1984) offers especially good evidence for the importance of both similarity and self-relevance in envy. College student participants received feedback on a career aptitude test suggesting that their career prospects in their chosen field were promising or poor. Then, they were given the career aptitude information of another student (i.e., a comparison person of similar background), who had done well or poorly on either the same or different career domain. Envy arose only when the participants, having received negative feedback, compared themselves with the student who had done better on a self-relevant career domain.

The combining of similarity and self-relevance probably helps to account for why the other person's advantage matters when we envy. The advantaged person, most of whose attributes we see in ourselves, nonetheless has something that we want but do not possess. Part of envy involves a painful, inferiority-tinged longing for something dearly wished for but enjoyed by another who is otherwise much like ourselves (Parrott & Smith, 1993).

Low Control

People feeling envy must also believe that the desired attribute is beyond their power to obtain (Smith, 1991). This feature may seem contradictory. On the one hand, people are more likely to envy those who are similar to themselves – which implies that the envying person should be able to imagine the possibility of possessing the desired attribute. As Elster (1998) notes, envy "presupposes that I can tell myself a plausible story in which I ended up with the envied possession," which is why "princes may envy kings and starlets envy stars, but most people envy neither, or, only weakly" (p. 169). On the other hand, this sense of possibility is more characterized by it "*could* have been me" rather than it "*will* be me." The envying person believes that obtaining the desired attribute is unlikely even as he or she can imagine what it would be like to have it. It is near in one's imagination, but unreachable as a sober prediction. When we envy, we feel inferior because another person possesses something that we long for – and to make matters worse, it is a frustrated longing. Control over altering one's inferiority is an important though little studied aspect of envy. However, it does appear that emotional responses to unflattering comparisons will tend to be free of inferiority and frustration if the advantage seems changeable (Lockwood & Kunda, 1997; Testa & Major, 1990).

Fairness of the Advantage

A final antecedent condition of envy concerns perceptions of fairness. Envy seems to have a resentful quality to it. When we envy, we often feel that the envied person does not quite deserve his or her advantage (e.g., Heider, 1958; Scheler, 1915/1961; Smith, 1991), or, at least that our disadvantage is undeserved (Ben-Ze'ev, 2000). But envy is not resentment proper (Rawls, 1971). Generally, if the advantage is unfair, especially in terms of *objectively* derived and agreed upon standards, the full-blown emotions of resentment and indignation rather than envy will result (e.g., Walker & Smith, 2002). Envy occurs when the advantage is painful but fair by such objective standards. Envy seems linked with a sense of injustice, but this sense of injustice is qualitatively different from that which produces indignation and resentment in their unalloyed forms. It is *subjectively* derived and nurtured. This notion of subjective injustice will be discussed further, but the key point here is that envy seems flavored by resentment, but of a kind qualitatively distinct from the feelings aroused by objectively unfair advantage. When we envy, we feel inferior because another person, otherwise like ourselves, possesses something that we long for but cannot have. Also, in a subjective sense, we usually feel that this advantage is not quite deserved.

THE HOSTILE COMPONENT OF ENVY

Definitions of envy and scores of scholarly treatments also point to the hostile side of the emotion. Cassius' envy is characterized by feelings of inferiority, painful longing, frustration, and subjective injustice, but he also feels hostile.

> ... What trash is Rome,
> What rubbish and what offal, when it serves
> for the base matter to illuminate
> So vile a thing as Caesar! (Shakespeare, 1599/1934, p. 52)

Hostility is a defining component of the envy. Without it, the emotion might better take another label, such as "admiration." Those who have studied envy usually acknowledge nonhostile forms (e.g., Parrott, 1991; Rawls, 1971; Silver & Sabini, 1978), but also argue that these benign varieties are less prototypic and are more straightforward to grapple with as an object of study (e.g., Foster, 1972). It is the hostile component of envy that moves the envious Cassius to bring Caesar down, that explains why envy is one of the seven deadly sins (e.g., Schimmel, 1993; Silver & Sabini, 1978), that accounts for why envious people will sacrifice their own outcomes to diminish the envied person's advantage (e.g., Zizzo, 2000), that suggests the reasons why envy is such a strong predictor of malicious joy when the envied person suffers (Brigham et al., 1997; Smith et al., 1996), that explains why people often worry when they are the targets of envy (e.g., Foster, 1972; Schoeck, 1969), and that, in general, shows why envy may produce a multitude of antisocial behaviors (e.g., Beck, 1999; Duffy & Shaw, 2000; Schoeck, 1969).

Why is envy a hostile emotion? If we feel inferior because of an unflattering comparison, why not simply surrender to this reality? Why not feel happy for the advantaged person and find ourselves inspired?

Defensive Reaction to Self-Esteem Threat

One approach to understanding the hostile component of envy is to see it as a natural defensive response (e.g., Beck, 1999; Schimmel, 1993). Many perspectives on human motivation claim that people have a strong desire to maintain a positive self-evaluation (e.g., Beach & Tesser, 2000). Invidious comparisons oppose this goal. The unflattering comparison either creates self-diminution or keeps in view a previously conceded sense of inferiority.

The resulting emotional pain may command a defensive reaction. It seems only natural to want to rid oneself of this pain, and an immediate, gut response may be to lash out at the spur cause of this pain, the envied person.

Perhaps the most simple way to channel such defensive ill-will and, at the same time, to repair the damage done to one's self-estimation is to find ways to derogate the envied person (Salovey & Rodin, 1984; Silver & Sabini, 1978; Tesser, 1991). What may often happen is that an envy-producing comparison on an ability dimension produces derogation on a moral dimension (D. Montaldi, unpublished data). It may be difficult to deny an ability difference, to convince oneself that a self-relevant domain is unimportant, or to do much to close this difference. But it may be quick and easy to construe the envied person as morally flawed. These perceived moral flaws can become an effective point of convergence for one's angry feelings. In social comparison terms, the experience of envy may begin with an upward comparison on a *non*moral dimension, which then inspires an immediate downward comparison on a moral dimension (Wills, 1981). The sting of the envied person's advantage yields to one's own quick-developing superiority on more "important" moral domains.

The study by Salovey and Rodin (1984) already cited provides good evidence for this downward comparison process. Participants who felt envy because they compared themselves with a fellow student who had outperformed them on their own career domain tended to derogate this person. The derogation emerged both on rating scales and in open-ended written comments. Salovey and Rodin (1984) cite one particularly telling comment:

> no matter how much I tried to get on with the task, my mind kept returning to that below-average profile. Soon, I was feeling a bit worried and very sensitive about my abilities. Then, when I tried to read the other guy's story, I couldn't help but think, 'If he's such a hot-shot premed and does so well in his classes, I bet he's really just a nerd: I bet he's one of those unfriendly, antisocial weenies that hang out in the library 20 hours a day; he probably couldn't have an interesting conversation with anyone.' (p. 790)

Violation of an "Ought" Force

Unfair advantages, judged by objective standards, create indignation and resentment proper rather than envy. But, as noted earlier, envy also appears to have a sense of injustice allied with it – a sense qualitatively different from that found in indignation and resentment proper. The envious individual does not quite believe that the envied person's advantage is fair. Heider (1958) argued that this is because envy will typically occur between people who are similar in terms of background, class, and the like, the first antecedent condition for envy mentioned previously. Psychological balance forces require that similar people should have similar outcomes, a principle that Heider called an "ought" force. The envious person feels a sense of injustice because the envied person's advantage violates what "ought" to be. Naturally, a person who feels unfairly treated will feel angry (Brown, 1986). Note again that this sense of unfairness captured by Heider is distinct from "objective unfairness" described earlier. Objective unfairness follows from clearly unjust procedures and is backed by the consensual power of local standards and norms. Such backing should whip up especially open and vigorous hostility. Violations of an "ought" force of the type that Heider describes are more private, much less consensual, and lead to bottled and constrained hostility, but hostility nonetheless.

If we go by how Cassius reacts to Caesar, we can see the process that Heider describes at work. Although Caesar's great achievements and talents make Cassius feel inferior, at the same time he also feels similar to Caesar in terms of background and experience. He tries to bring Brutus into his circle of conspirators by bringing Caesar down to a position of similar background and worth to Brutus.

> I was born free as Caesar: so were you:
> We both have fed as well, and we can both
> Endure the winter's cold as well as he.... (Shakespeare, 1599/1934, p. 40)

Cassius goes further to suggest that he is *more than* Caesar's equal in certain respects. He describes how "once, upon a raw and gusty day" Caesar dared Cassius to swim with him across the Tiber. They both plunged in, but before they reached the other side, Caesar cried for help. Cassius carried the "tired Caesar" from the waves to the shore. It frustrates and infuriates Cassius that a man of such a weak constitution should "get the start of the majestic world, and bear the palm alone" (p. 41).

> And this man
> Is now become a god, and Cassius is
> A wretched creature, and must bend his body
> If Caesar carelessly but nod on him. (Shakespeare, 1599/1934, p. 40)

Across the board, the envy-inspired conspiracy that fells Caesar is cobbled together by men who think of themselves in his general league. The ways in which they believe they are similar to Caesar contribute to the envy-rooted indignance they feel over his rise to an almost god-like status.

Subjective Injustice

As noted earlier, envy is more likely in situations in which the envying person has little power to change things. In many cases, the domain of comparison is also one in which the envying person feels little to blame for his or her inferiority either. People often envy another person's greater inborn talents, for example. Caesar is superior to Cassius in certain natural qualities, many of which may partially explain Caesar's ability to soar in popularity and power. Cassius is blameless for his natural inferiority (Ben-Ze'ev, 2000). Furthermore, Caesar should hardly be praised in a moral sense for his natural gifts. The consequences of natural superiority amplify over time if both the advantaged and the disadvantaged persons pursue their goals with equal intensity – just as a person with a longer stride makes quicker progress than a person with a shorter stride (Rousseau, 1754/1984). Although the envying person has no legitimate cause for making a public claim against the envied person's advantage, as most societal norms include natural ability as a legitimate basis for determining merit, the resulting sense of injustice can remain in the form of secret protest even so. Like violations of the "ought force," this subjective sense of injustice is also distinct from resentment proper. Resentment proper arises from obvious cases of unfairness in which societal norms support the outward display of indignation. But regardless of its societal legitimacy, because subjective injustice is still a justice-based phenomenon, hostile feelings can flavor the envying person's reactions. The focus of these hostile feelings is on the envied person who has the "unfair" advantage (Smith, 1991).

There is an existential complaint at the bottom of this subjective sense of injustice. In Parrott's (1991, p. 14) words, "One's place in the world, one's lot in life, is not quite what one wants, and it all seems the luck of the draw." Another person enjoys an advantage longed-for by oneself, and one feels impotent to attain this advantage. Furthermore, there seems no clear reason why this person is more deserving of this advantage than oneself. Any number of unspoken phrases can repeat themselves in an internal dialogue often infused with anger and ill-will, phrases such as: "Why does he deserve all the talent? It's not fair that she has such good looks!" We rarely voice these sentiments, especially if they contain explicit ill-will. If we do, observers will find them ignoble and illegitimate and will attribute them to envy (Silver & Sabini, 1978).

Some evidence for the role of subjective injustice in the hostile aspect of envy, as well as feelings of inferiority-caused discontent, emerged in a study by Smith et al. (1994). Participants wrote detailed, narrative accounts of experiences in which they felt strong envy. They then completed a set of items asking them to assess whether the envied person's advantage was "objectively" unfair (e.g., "Anyone would agree that the envied person's advantage was unfairly obtained."), "subjectively" unfair (e.g., "It seemed unfair that the person I envied started out in life with certain advantages over me."), and whether this advantage created a sense of inferiority (e.g., "The discrepancy between the person I envied and me was due to my own inferior qualities."). Additional items assessed the degree to which participants felt hostile toward the envied person and discontented because of this person's advantage. Beliefs about personal inferiority strongly predicted discontent but not hostile feelings, suggesting that feeling inferior alone is insufficient for the full experience of envy. Beliefs about objective injustice predicted hostility but not discontent, suggesting that obvious unfairness should create hostility, but should have little connection with seeing oneself as inferior and feeling depressed as a result. Beliefs about subjective injustice predicted both discontent and hostility, suggesting that subjective injustice is linked to both of these defining aspects of the experience of envy.

Envy and Shame

Yet another explanation for the hostility associated with envy stems from the affinity between envy and shame and the frequent co-occurrence of these emotions. Shame can be defined as "painful feeling of having lost the respect of others because of the improper behavior, incompetence, etc., of oneself" (*Webster's New World Dictionary*, 1982, p. 1308). Whether the emotion arises from moral or nonmoral failings, a large part of the shame involves a sense that the self has been rendered defective, and at least implicitly, inferior. Like envy, shame involves some form of negative self-evaluation (see Gilbert, 1998, and Tangney & Dearing, 2002, for reviews), although this negative self-evaluation need not have relativistic origins. Envy, of course, requires an unflattering social comparison. Even so, Kaufman (1989) has dubbed shame the "affect of inferiority," and work by Gilbert and his colleagues shows shame to be highly correlated with measure of unfavorable social comparisons (Gilbert, 1998). It may be that any sense of being defective tends to imply a relativistic judgment.

Shame is different from envy in that it involves a more constant self-focus (Smith, 2000). Whereas envy seems to produce a dual focus, on both the self and the envied person, shame emerges from situations in which the defective self dominates one's attention, without a necessary regard to the conspicuous presence of a particular unflattering social comparison. Another distinctive aspect of shame is that it is often the public exposure of moral or nonmoral failing that encourages this sharp focus on a negative self-appraisal (but see Tangney & Dearing, 2002); in fact, it may be that such public exposure can prick the emotion in the first place (Smith et al., 2002). Hence, the close connection exists between shame and shaming. Although public exposure directs concerns toward what others think of the self (in this sense the focus is external rather than internal), the spotlight is still directed at the self – and a negative aspect of the self.

Research evidence suggests a strong link between shame and anger (Tangney & Salovey, 1999), especially among people who are dispositionally shame-prone (e.g., Tangney, 1995). This link is surprising, at least in one sense. A consistent focus on one's own defects and failings should produce nonhostile, depressive responses (Gilbert, 1992) rather than anger.

However, the fact that shame is strongly associated with anger suggests that a person who is suffering a devalued self will tend to lash out at others. With shame, the focus of hostility, if it is not turned inward, may be on the person who seems to trigger or aggravate the feeling, perhaps the person who brings the moral or nonmoral failing out into the open, through shaming (Smith et al., 2002).

How might shame help to explain the hostile aspect of envy? First of all, if it is true that shame is one frequent result of a devalued self, then any instance of envy, which by definition creates a sense of inferiority, has the potential to create shame as well, along with the potential for hostility often associated with shame. Strictly speaking then, part of invidious hostility can be shame-based, rather than envy-based alone. However, when an unflattering social comparison is the dominating impetus for the overall affective state, the label of envy may be the best summary term to define the experience.

Shame enters into an explanation for the hostility associated with envy in another way. Envy violates a powerful social norm requiring that we be happy, rather than displeased and hostile, when others succeed (Heider, 1958). This is one reason why people feeling envy report thinking that others will disapprove of their feelings (Parrott & Smith, 1993). Thus, when we feel envy, we tend to be ashamed of it. The further combining of shame and envy may then lead to an even more painful self-diminishment, and perhaps an even more vigorous hostility directed outward as a result.

D. Montaldi (unpublished data) argues that some cases of envy involve shame exactly because the envying person feels both inferior and also to blame for his or her inferiority. That is, the envied person's superiority is something that might have been obtained if one had only done the necessary things to make it happen. One's sense of inferiority is compounded by the knowledge that one could have and should have done certain things but, in fact, did not. Montaldi labels this "merit" envy because there is a clear recognition that the envied person's superiority is deserved. However, positive feelings of admiration often fail to result because the superiority is such a threatening affront to the self. Envy arises instead, along with shame, originating from at least three sources: the shame of feeling envy and its concomitant sense of inferiority and hostility, the shame of realizing that one is to blame for one's inferiority, and the shame of feeling shame.

ENVY AS AN EMOTION EPISODE AND ITS TRANSMUTATIONS

Explanations for the hostile component of envy highlight the challenge of understanding the emotion generally. It is tempting to examine any emotion at the narrow point in which it is first evoked; in the case of envy, this point is at the first recognition of one's inferiority and the painful longing, frustration, subjective injustice, and ill-will that quickly follow. Perhaps for many emotions, this approach is adequate. But, as Parrott (1991) argues, envy is perhaps best understood as an evolving episode, "unfolding in time" (p. 12). It begins with unflattering comparison, and it can then proceed in various directions as the envying person grapples with the fact of his or her inferiority, the presence of hostile feelings, and the arousal of other, overlapping emotions, such as resentment proper and shame. The end point of this process can be a felt emotion very different from the incipient experience, attracting a label different from envy – from the envying person's point of view if not from an observer's perspective.

One reason why envy has the capacity to proceed in different directions comes back to the initial and repeated point made about envy, namely that it starts with the recognition of inferiority on a self-relevant domain – and that, again, the envying person will be motivated to resist this conclusion. As noted previously, inferiority is too painful a condition for most people to bear, for both internal and self-presentational reasons. When made to feel inferior because of an unflattering social comparison, people appear capable of numerous defensive maneuvers to turn the tables on this conclusion (e.g., Elster, 1998; Tesser, 1991).

An additional reason comes back to the second key point made about envy, its hostile nature. People are taught that it is wrong to feel hostile toward another person, even if they believe that on some subjective level, the envied person's advantage is not quite fair. As with inferiority, they will resist owning these feelings in their private mind, as well as in their public selves. It is certainly improper, in most cultures, to openly express envious hostility. It is shameful. Thus, people find ways to reframe or relabel these hostile feelings as well.

The repugnant nature of envy is an important point to highlight. As Silver and Sabini (1978, p. 106) note, "calling someone envious, like calling him greedy, arrogant, lazy, or gluttonous, is far from complimenting him.... Envy is one of seven deadly sins." It has a "vicious character" (Elster, 1998, p. 165), and "few things are more destructive to our self-image" (Foster, 1972, p. 165).

The self-threatening, abhorrent nature of envy works against its emerging in anything but an altered form. It is "normally suppressed, preempted, or transmuted to some other emotion" (Elster, 1998, p. 165). As Farber (1966, p. 36) puts it, envy has "protean character" and a "talent for disguise" and is "often simply impossible to recognize." This often seems true from the observer's point of view and "also for the envious one himself, whose rational powers may lend almost unholy assistance to the need for self-deception" (Farber, 1966, p. 36). Once again, an episode of envy will take different turns that depend on how the envious person reacts to the painful self-implications of the emotion and its socially repugnant nature.

People feeling envy will suppress the emotion to various degrees. At the one extreme are people who recognize their envy for what it is and who manage to avoid its suppression. They recognize their inferiority, acknowledge that it hurts, and own up to the ill-will that comes with it (Elster, 1998). Even if they feel a private sense of injustice, this sense is quickly discounted as an appropriate avenue for coping with the feeling. Any shame that arises works to diminish hostile feelings rather than aggravate them. At the other extreme are people who are so well-prepared with creative defenses that envy is suppressed before it can break through into consciousness. These people will feel hostile toward the envied person, but see no connection between this hostility and envy, and will feel no shame over feeling this ill-will. Awareness of the underlying cause of their ill-will is bypassed, and they see the envied person's advantage as unambiguously unfair and the advantaged person as worthy of hate. In between these extremes are perhaps the more typical cases in which the emotion is at least half-acknowledged for what it is. But, over time, it is either reframed to lessen the hurt (Parrott, 1991; Silver & Sabini, 1978; Tesser, 1991) or transmuted into another emotion, such as resentment proper, selected because it has more socially acceptable attributes (Elster, 1998).

None of the conspirators who assassinate Caesar construes their motives as envious. The sentiments expressed by Cassius (inferiority, painful longing, frustration, subjective injustice, and hostility) are all hallmarks of envy, but he sidesteps using the label of envy to characterize his motives, in his private soliloquies or in his public exhortations as he recruits Brutus into the conspiracy against Caesar. Rather, he focuses where he can on attributes of Caesar that he sees as inferior, such as noting Caesar's feeble inability to best him in swimming. He highlights the similarities between his own background and Caesar's, and evokes memories of experiences in which he in fact seemed superior to Caesar. Finally, he paints Caesar as arrogant and ambitious. All these construals provide ways for Cassius to lessen any sense that he is actually inferior to Caesar. Thus, he can come to believe that he is feeling outraged rather than merely envious.

The envying person may be able to transmute the feeling and thus succeed in self-deception, but often fails to convince observers (Silver & Sabini, 1978). There is something in envy that creates emotional leaks, despite efforts to hide its presence. Antony sees the telltale signs of envy in Cassius. In the classic speech following Caesar's assassination and in his retrospective remarks at the end of the play, Antony undermines the envy-inspired assumption on the part of the conspirators that Caesar was ambitious. He suggests that "private grievances" are the clearer motive for the conspiracy, rather than legitimate complaints. At the very end of the play, he sums up the motives of the conspirators, except for Brutus, as doing "that they did in envy of great Caesar" (p. 134). Caesar, himself, also saw Cassius as envious by disposition and sensed the danger in it:

> Yond Cassius has a lean and hungry look...
> Such men as he be never at heart's ease
> Whiles they behold a greater than themselves
> And therefore are they very dangerous. (Shakespeare, 1599/1934, p. 43)

One of the illuminating aspects of *Julius Caesar* is how envy invades so much of the play, even when it goes unstated. Cassius, seemingly in his every word and action, is vigorously pursuing the envy-triggered goal of ridding Rome of Caesar. Yet, he never uses the label of envy to identify his motives, even in his private moments. He seems to realize that the attribution of envy would undermine his conspiratorial goal, and this is especially evident in his method of recruiting Brutus into the fold. He knows that acting out of envy would seem vicious, small-minded, and unjustified – a shameful motive. His recruiting of Brutus is crafted to appeal to Brutus' high-minded sense of himself, the "noble" Brutus. He warns against the flatterer even as he flatters Brutus, reminding Brutus of the high regard people have for him and his ancestors. He makes it seem as though it would be impossible for Brutus to take an action that was sullied by base motives. Then, after arguing that Caesar has no natural superiority over Brutus in terms of character and worth, he makes the case that Caesar has overshot himself and that his ambition is dangerous to Rome – while those around Caesar decline in power and suffer a "falling-sickness." The lure works, and Brutus, now "whetted against Caesar," joins the conspiracy.

Was Brutus envious? If so, it was very well defended. To the end, he fashions an impervious wall of honorable motives to deflect both the public and private attribution of envy. Yet, it seems that one of the interesting aspects of envy is that it can come in such buried forms. When it does, it may be most dangerous. Brutus, convinced of his pure motives, now throws himself into the collective task of murder, damning Caesar for crimes that may be committed rather than ones already committed – all the while repeating phrases, such as "I have no personal cause to spurn at him."

> And therefore think him as a serpent's egg
> Which hatched, would as his kind grow mischievous,
> And kill him in the shell. (Shakespeare, 1599/1934, p. 56)

Interestingly, although Brutus is loath to conclude that he has a hint of envy toward Caesar, he is nonetheless very aware of how best to act so as to fend off its apparent presence. Brutus is acutely aware of appearances. As the conspirators plan the assassination of Caesar, the question arises whether others, such as Antony, should die with Caesar. But Brutus worries that their "course will seem too bloody" and that, afterwards, it will seem motivated by "wrath in death and envy" (p. 61). He worries further that they should kill Caesar "boldly" rather than "wrathfully."

> Let's carve him as dish fit for gods,
> Not hew him as a carcass fit for hounds.
> ... This shall make
> Our purpose necessary, and not envious....
> We shall be called purgers, not murderers. (Shakespeare, 1599/1934, p. 62)

There seems to be a special danger in the full suppression of envy, because its latent presence may motivate all the more hostile actions precisely because the underlying, baser motive never surfaces. In terms of awareness, Brutus gets nowhere close to admitting his envy. It is Cassius, perhaps sensing latent envy in Brutus, who provides the building blocks for moral outrage, giving the noble Brutus the noble motive of serving his ancestors and serving Rome. He urges Brutus to take action, emboldened and validated by a consensus born of conspiracy.

This analysis of the envy felt by Cassius and Brutus is largely speculative, as there is no direct empirical evidence for various turns that envy can take. Nonetheless, it suggests the noxious role of envy in social interactions. The more people can avoid the label of envy to describe their feelings, the more they might end up acting inappropriately because they are convinced of the righteousness of their cause. It takes a truly base nature to *know* that one is envious, and then to say "I will act on this envy." As Elster notes, "I do not know of any society in which an individual would consciously confess to envy ... that is, hostility towards the nonundeserved fortune of another, and justify aggressive or destructive behavior in terms of the motivation" (1998, p. 169). The person who correctly sees his or her destructive behavior as envy-based, embraces this motivation, and acts destructively in this spirit, seems a truly evil person, a dispositional attribution the self usually shuns with the greatest of passions. We can also look to Shakespeare for an example here. Iago, another immortal literary prototype of the envious person, envies Othello and confesses this motivation to himself and to those who join him in luring Othello into the abyss of morbid sexual jealousy. He seems to feel no shame over the nature of his motivation and, at the end of the play, among the human wreckage that he has caused, shows no remorse. Othello looks down at Iago's feet to check for the cloven hooves of the devil.

THE ENVY EPISODE

To summarize, any episode of envy begins with noticing a desired advantage enjoyed by another person. The advantage produces envy when the envied person is similar in background characteristics, when the advantage resides in a self-relevant domain, when prospects of obtaining the advantage seem unchangeable or blocked, and when the envying person is unable to claim that the advantage is objectively unfair. We want what the other person has, believe (subjectively but not objectively) that our similarities in background suggest that we should have it, but conclude that is beyond our grasp. All of these features appear necessary for envy to occur. Low similarity will tend to make the comparison inconsequential (Testa & Major, 1990). A comparison domain of low-self relevance creates admiration and basking in reflected glory (Tesser, 1991). The belief that the advantage is changeable creates inspiration and emulation (Lockwood & Kunda, 1997). Construing the advantage as objectively unfair brings about full-blown indignation and resentment proper (Walker & Smith, 2002).

Once the basic conditions are met, envy should result. Then, as the episode of envy evolves, as various other emotions come on board, and as the awareness of feeling envy waxes or wanes, it will take one of a number of forms. For example, if the focus is on one's own blameworthy inferiority, then, to use Montaldi's suggestion, "merit" envy results. The typical path for such envy to take may be a downward comparison on moral domains. This deflects a focus on one's inferiority, providing a justification for any lashing out at the envied person in a hostile manner. Such a course may be expanded further if envy arises in conjunction with shame, as this may create the potential for further defensive ill-will. However, to the extent the envying person can remain conscious of the unjustified nature of his or her hostile feelings, perhaps more constructive responses will occur – such as working hard to overcome the disadvantage, despite the odds, or, downplaying the importance of doing well on the domain (e.g., Tesser, 1991). Guilt, an emotion that seems less likely to induce self-degradation and defensive ill-will compared with shame (Tangney & Salovey, 1999), may help guide the emotion episode in this less hostile direction. Alternatively, a constant dwelling on one's own inferiority might lead to depression (Smith et al. 1994).

Another form of envy results when subjective unfairness of the advantage dominates the emotion. Privately, people feeling such envy will have a strong sense of being unfairly treated and may develop a simmering, frustrated resentment over their lot in life (Scheler, 1915/1961). They will avoid giving their feelings the label of envy, however, because this reduces the legitimacy of their hostility. They will sense that these feelings violate social norms and may realize that other people will quickly detect their hostility and attribute this hostility to envy. Thus, they avoid acting on their hostile envy, but are primed for feeling *schadenfreude* if misfortune befalls the envied person (e.g., Smith et al., 1996). Perhaps they will engage in backbiting, gossip, or indirect sabotage. Over time, if they keep a focus on the "unfair" advantage rather than their own contribution to the situation, they might be able to convince themselves as well as others that they have a legitimate cause for feeling hostile. If so, the attribution of envy will fade into a distant public and private background. Once hostile feelings are legitimized, any residual envy becomes fully transmuted into righteous indignation and resentment proper, giving free license for direct and open actions designed to undermine the advantaged person's position. An observer might still try to attribute the envying person's behavior to envy, but this claim will be rejected as preposterous by the envying person – so far removed is the indignation from its invidious origins.

EVIDENCE FOR THE TRANSMUTATION OF ENVY AND IMPLICATIONS

As noted earlier, the tracing of how episodes of envy might evolve remains largely speculative. Research by Smith and his colleagues suggests the role of subjective injustice concerns in hostile envy. Salovey and Rodin's (1984) work indicates that, under the conditions right for envy, people will express hostility. The research linking envy with *schadenfreude* (Smith et al., 1996) suggests how powerfully envious feelings are conducive to ill-will, even when the misfortune befalling the envied person is undeserved (Brigham et al., 1997). Studies by Tesser (1991) show how self-evaluation maintenance processes create disliking for the advantaged person or devaluing of the comparison domain. But no studies have examined precisely how envy might evolve over time and transmute itself.

One potentially fruitful approach to examining transmutational phenomena while also suggesting the value of understanding this process is suggested by a recent model of prejudiced responses (Fiske et al., 2002; Glick, 2002). In this model, prejudice directed at traditionally disadvantaged groups (Hispanics, African Americans) is distinguished from prejudice directed at advantaged groups (Asians, Jews). Both types of prejudice can have negative consequences, but Glick (2002) argues that envious prejudice can be uniquely virulent. Economically successful groups, if they are considered outgroups, tend to be viewed as both lacking in warmth and in competition with one's ingroup. The combination of coldness and competition suggests that the outgroup *intends* to use its success at one's own group's expense. A key feature of the model is that it is the *emotion* directed at the outgroup that will largely characterize the nature of prejudicial response. In the case of envious prejudice, there are a number of important implications.

Envious prejudice will be especially hostile if the envious person can find reasons to construe the envied outgroup as unfairly achieving its success. As would be expected, given the way that envy evolves, any hint of unfairness will be grasped quickly and held onto stubbornly. For example, envious prejudice will be especially strong if the majority group senses that its "social status has shifted downward" (Glick, 2002, p. 130) relative to the envied group, as if something rightfully its own has been taken away. Hostility will be enhanced still further if the envied group appears to have traits, such as shrewdness and cunning, that seem to explain its increasing advantage, at least in part. These traits provide the convenient downward comparison on moral dimensions that deflects invidious comparison on nonmoral dimensions and provide justification for hostile feelings and actions.

A historical example of envious prejudice is the treatment of Jews by the Nazis (Glick, 2002). Prior to Hitler's rise, many Germans held negative attitudes toward Jews. Glick argues that these attitudes were in part based on envy directed at the perceived economic power and cultural influence of Jews in Germany. Hitler capitalized on this prior envious prejudice to make Jews "a socially plausible cause of Germany's problems" (Glick, 2002, p. 133). Hitler emphasized stereotypes of Jews suggesting both superiority (e.g., shrewdness, cunning, power grabbing), as well as moral inferiority (e.g., lazy and unclean) to fuel both fear and contempt. Remarkably, Jews were "simultaneously portrayed as possessing a superhuman potency and will to dominate, yet also as servile, parasitical, and inferior" (Glick, 2002, p. 134). Jews were cast as threats to Germany and inherently deserving hostile treatment. The threat that Jews seemed to represent, together with their perceived vileness, all manufactured to suit social-psychological needs, masked the envy actually underlying the hostility. Hitler and many Germans hated the Jews, but were incapable of admitting or even realizing any role of envy in their hatred. The unconscious, yet all the more virulent, envy seems to explain the willingness and desire to exterminate the Jews, even at the expense of managing the war against the Allies. As the tide turned and Germany's military fortunes crumbled, Hitler took valuable resources away from the fighting to hasten the killing of as many Jews as possible. Of course, understanding the behavior of the Nazis resists single explanations, but envy provides a partial glimpse into the possible motivations capable of producing both genocide and self-destructive behavior.

CONCLUSIONS

So many of the examples in this chapter come from Shakespeare's *Julius Caesar* that it is worth noting that Shakespeare, himself, was the target of envy. We can thank envy for providing us with the spur that then produced the first recorded reference to Shakespeare by another Elizabethan playwright, Robert Greene.

> There is an upstart crow beautiful with our feathers that, with his 'tiger's heart wrapped in a player's hide,' supposes is as well able to bombast out a blank verse as the best of you; being an absolute Johannes Factotum, in his conceit the only shake-scene in a country. (Schoenbaum, 1975, p. 115)

Robert Greene was older than Shakespeare and yet less successful. He must have been envious of this "upstart crow" who, despite lacking the university education of most of his peers, was not only writing spectacularly successful plays of three major types (histories, tragedies, *and* comedies), but was also strutting his "feathers" on the stage as an actor as well.

And so envy is a natural, common response to another's advantage, and Shakespeare knew it well. He realized that it could be a painful and repugnant emotion that has the capacity to transmute itself into other feelings better suited to our private and public selves. He also realized that in this transmuted form it could provoke extreme behavior, such as murder in the case of Caesar's assassination and pure evil in the case of Iago's bringing down of Othello. Once transmuted, hostile feelings and actions could take malicious flight, untethered by the social constraints that quell aggression linked merely to envy that is out in the open.

But envy is not the inevitable response to another's advantage, and we can see this in Shakespeare's life as well. It is impossible to be sure about the feelings Shakespeare aroused in those around him. But we do know that two friends collected his plays for him, some years after his death. One of these friends, Ben Jonson, a fellow actor and playwright who may also have envied Shakespeare while the bard was still alive, wrote a fond eulogy for this "swan of Avon" once called an "upstart crow." Evidently, Shakespeare could even win over the heart of a competitor, and, in the more than 400 years since, the rest has been adoration.

ACKNOWLEDGMENTS

I wish to acknowledge the very helpful comments on the initial draft of this chapter from the Editors of this volume, Colin Wayne Leach and Larissa Tiedens, and from Sung Hee Kim and Walter Foreman.

References

Aristotle. (1941). Rhetoric. In R. McKeaon (Ed.), *The basic works of Aristotle*. New York: Random House.

Beach, S. R. H., & Tesser, A. (2000). Self-evaluation maintenance and evolution: Some speculative notes. In J. Suls & L. Wheeler (Eds.), *Handbook of social comparison: Theory and research* (pp. 123–140). New York: Kluwer Academic/Plenum.

Beck, A. (1999). *Prisoners of hate: The cognitive basis of anger, hostility, and violence*. New York: HarperCollins.

Ben-Ze'ev, A. (2000). *The subtlety of emotions*. Cambridge, MA: The MIT Press.

Brickman, P., & Bulman, R. J. (1977). Pleasure and pain in social comparison. In J. M. Suls & R. L. Miller (Eds.), *Social comparison processes: Theoretical and empirical perspectives* (pp. 149–186). Washington, DC: Hemisphere.

Brigham, N. L., Kelso, K. A., Jackson, M. A., & Smith, R. H. (1997). The roles of invidious comparisons and deservingness in sympathy and *schadenfreude*. *Basic and Applied Social Psychology, 19*, 363–380.

Brown, R. (1986). *Social psychology (2nd Edition)*. New York: The Free Press.

Buunk, B., & Gibbons, F. X. (Eds.). (1997). *Health, coping, and well-being: Perspectives from social comparison theory*. Mahwah, NJ: Lawrence Erlbaum.

Buunk, B. P., & Ybema, J. F. (1997). Social comparison and occupational stress: The identification-contrast model. In B. P. Buunk & F. X. Gibbons (Eds.), *Health, coping, and well-being: Perspectives from social comparison theory* (pp. 359–388). Mahwah, NJ: Lawrence Erlbaum.

Duffy, M. K., & Shaw, J. D. (2000). The Salieri syndrome: Consequences of envy in groups, *Small Group Research, 31*, 3–23.

Elster, J. (1998). *Alchemies of the mind: Rationality and the emotions* (pp. 165, 169). Cambridge: Cambridge University Press.

Farber, L. (1966). *Ways of the will* (p. 36). New York: Basic Books.

Festinger, L. A. (1954). A theory of social comparison processes. *Human Relations, 7*, 117–140.

Fiske, S. T., Cuddy, A. J. C., Glick, P., & Xu, J. (2002). A model of (often mixed) stereotype content: Competence and warmth respectively follow from perceived status and competition. *Journal of Personality and Social Psychology, 82*, 878–902.

Foster, G. (1972). The anatomy of envy. *Current Anthropology, 13*, 165–202.

Frank, R. H. (1999). *Luxury fever*. New York: The Free Press.

Gilbert, P. (1992). *Depression: The evolution of powerlessness*. New York: The Guilford Press.

Gilbert, P. (1998). What is shame? Some core issues and controversies. In P. Gilbert & B. Andrews (Eds.), *Shame: Interpersonal behavior, psychopathology, and culture* (pp. 3–38). Oxford: Oxford University Press.

Glick, P. (2002). Sacrificial lambs dressed in wolves clothing: Envious prejudice, ideology, and the scapegoating of Jews. In L. S. Newman & R. Erber (Eds.), *What social psychology can tell us about the Holocaust* (pp. 130–134). Oxford: Oxford University Press.

Goethals, G. R., & Darley, J. M. (1977). Social comparison theory: An attributional approach. In J. M. Suls & R. L. Miller (Eds.), *Social comparison processes* (pp. 259–278). Washington, DC: Hemisphere.

Heider, F. (1958). *The psychology of interpersonal relations*. New York: John Wiley.

Kalma, A. (1991). Hierarchisation and dominance at first glance. *European Journal of Social Psychology, 21*, 165–181.

Kaufman, G. (1989). *The psychology of shame: Theory and treatment of shame-based syndromes*. New York: Springer.

Kelley, H. H. (1967). Attribution theory in social psychology. In D. Levine (Ed.), *Nebraska symposium on motivation*. Lincoln, NE: University of Nebraska Press.

Lockwood, P., & Kunda, Z. (1997). Superstars and me: Predicting the impact of role models on the self. *Journal of Personality and Social Psychology, 73*, 91–103.

Parrott, W. G. (1991). The emotional experiences of envy and jealousy. In P. Salovey (Ed.), *The psychology of jealousy and envy* (pp. 3–30). New York: Guilford.

Parrott, W. G., & Smith, R. H. (1993). Distinguishing the experiences of envy and jealousy. *Journal of Personality and Social Psychology, 64*, 906–920.

Rawls, J. (1971). *A theory of justice*. Cambridge, MA: Harvard University Press.

Rousseau, J. (1754/1984). *A discourse on inequality* (M. Cranston, Trans.). New York: Viking Penguin Inc.

Salovey, P., & Rodin, J. (1984). Some antecedents and consequences of social-comparison jealousy. *Journal of Personality and Social Psychology, 47*, 780–792.

Scheler, M. (1961). *Ressentiment* (L. A. Coser, Ed., W. W. Holdhein, Trans.). Glencoe, IL: Free Press. (Original work published 1915.)

Schimmel, S. (1993). *Seven deadly sins*. New York: Bantam Doubleday.

Schoeck, H. (1969). *Envy: A theory of social behavior*. New York: Harcourt, Brace, and World.

Schoenbaum, S. (1975). *William Shakespeare: A documentary life* (p. 115). New York: Oxford University Press.

Shakespeare, W. (1934). *The tragedy of Julius Caesar* (pp. 40, 41, 52–62, 134). New York: Henry Holt. (Original work published 1599.)

Silver, M., & Sabini, J. (1978). The perception of envy. *Social Psychology Quarterly, 41*, 105–117.

Smith, R. H. (1991). Envy and the sense of injustice. In P. Salovey (Ed.), *Psychological perspectives on jealousy and envy*. New York: Guilford.

Smith, R. H. (2000). Assimilative and contrastive emotional reactions to upward and downward comparisons. In J. Suls & L. Wheeler (Eds.), *Handbook of social comparison: Theory and research* (pp. 173–200). New York: Kluwer Academic/Plenum.

Smith, R. H., Parrott, W. G., Diener, E., Hoyle, R. H., & Kim, S. H. (1999). Dispositional envy. *Personality and Social Psychology Bulletin, 25*, 1007–1020.

Smith, R. H., Parrott, W. G., Ozer, D., & Moniz, A. (1994). Subjective injustice and inferiority as predictors of hostile and depressive feelings in envy. *Personality and Social Psychology Bulletin, 20*, 705–711.

Smith, R. H., Turner, T., Leach, C. W., Garonzik, R., Urch-Druskat, V., & Weston, C. M. (1996). Envy and *schadenfreude*. *Personality and Social Psychology Bulletin, 22*, 158–168.

Smith, R. H., Webster, J. M., Parrott, W. G., & Eyer, H. (2002). The role of public exposure in the experience of moral and nonmoral shame and guilt. *The Journal of Personality and Social Psychology, 83*, 138–159.

Suls, J. M., & Wheeler, L. (Eds.). (2000). *Handbook of social comparison: Theory and research*. New York: Plenum.

Tangney, J. P. (1995). Shame and guilt in interpersonal relationships. In J. P. Tangney & K. W. Fischer (Eds.), *Self-conscious emotions: Shame, guilt, embarrassment, and pride* (pp. 114–139). New York: Guilford Press.

Tangney, J. P., & Dearing, R. L. (2002). *Shame and guilt*. New York, NY: Guilford Press.

Tangney, J. P., & Salovey, P. (1999). Problematic social emotions: Shame, guilt, jealousy, and envy. In R. M. Kowalski & M. R. Leary (Eds.), *The social psychology of emotional and behavioral problems: Interfaces of social and clinical psychology* (pp. 167–195). Washington, DC: American Psychological Association.

Tesser, A. (1991). Emotion in social comparison and reflection processes. In J. Suls & T. A. Wills (Eds.), *Social comparison: Contemporary theory and research* (pp. 115–145). Hillsdale, NJ: Erlbaum.

Testa, M., & Major, B. (1990). The impact of social comparison after failure: The moderating effects of perceived control. *Basic and Applied Social Psychology, 11*, 205–218.

Walker, I., & Smith, H. J. (2002). *Relative deprivation: Specification, development, and integration*. Cambridge: Cambridge University Press.
Webster's New World Dictionary of the American Language. (1982). (p. 1308). New York: Simon & Schuster.
Wills, T. A. (1981). Downward comparison principles in social psychology. *Psychological Bulletin, 90*, 245–271.
Zizzo, D. (2000). *Relativity-sensitive behavior in economics*. Unpublished doctoral dissertation, Oxford University, UK.

3

The Bond Threat Sequence

Discourse Evidence for the Systematic Interdependence of Shame and Social Relationships

David S. Fearon, Jr.

During the last decade there has been increasing attention to "social affect" as a category of emotion strongly associated with the assessment, formulation, and management of social relationships. There is a constant need during social interactions for individuals to evaluate the quality of the interpersonal association. A system of emotions devoted to the quality of "being social" may therefore be most visible when individuals encounter problems involving social relationships. Methods for examining the dynamics of social affect should also capture in detail their integration with the discourse in which they arise. Such methods, however, constitute an almost invisible fraction of the widening literature on social affect. By examining emotions and relationships as they occur, direct analysis of discourse allows exploration of social affect outside the confines of predetermined variables, scenarios, and participants' self-reports on scales.

This chapter presents evidence of a systematic link between social affect and the quality of social relationships. Specifically, it tests and expands Retzinger and Scheff's theory that shame represents a category of social emotion dedicated to maintaining social relationships and sociality among individuals and groups. Methods for analyzing the integration of conversation with affect and relationships are presented and illustrated in detail, and applied to an interview setting in which participants explain their answers to a standard self-evaluation scale. Analysis of discourse found that participants often display in speech and gesture varieties of shame. This negative social affect is triggered when participants describe problems with social relationships and, often simultaneously, when presenting a negative impression of themselves to the interviewer. Participants manage shame by immediately reformulating their references to the relationship such that it appears less problematic. I refer to the regular association between relationship threat, shame affect, and its management as a *bond threat sequence*. The bond threat sequence is illustrated in detailed analysis of interview excerpts. Also presented is a test of the sequential relationship by context-sensitive content analysis and Markov chain modeling of transitional probabilities.

SHAME AND SOCIAL RELATIONSHIPS

The category of "negative social emotions" is potentially quite wide, judging from the proliferation of terms both clinical (such as "social anxiety") and vernacular (such as guilt, embarrassment, remorse, or "awkwardness"). Retzinger and Scheff (Retzinger, 1991a, 1995; Scheff, 1990, 2000; Scheff & Retzinger, 1991) suggest that most if not all of these common terms for social affect are variations of a single category of emotion, which they refer to as shame or the "shame family." The terms may be grouped by a mutual function. Scheff and Retzinger propose that shame and its complementary positive emotion, pride, serve to regulate social interaction in the interest of maintaining secure social relationships. Although guilt and embarrassment may be distinguished by common situations that evoke them and intensity of feelings (Tangney & Dearing, 2002), these classifications share relationship trouble as a common denominator. The claim that shame adequately designates a single system of affect is debatable; however, it serves as a starting point for exploring a systematic link between social affect and relationships.

Empirical studies conducted originally by H. B. Lewis (1971) – and developed by Retzinger (1987, 1991a, 1991b, 1995) and Scheff (1990, 1997) – suggest that emotion systems underlying the "shame family" of affect are constantly engaged in assessing, in some form, the quality of one's immediate or imagined relationships. Pride arises when one's social relationships are secure; however, affect may go unnoticed if relationships are unproblematic. Troubles involving social association generally become a focus of one's attention, particularly when accompanied by overt feelings, such as embarrassment, guilt, or remorse.

Several early researchers of social psychology noted, often only in passing, the association of shame and pride with an individual's ubiquitous monitoring of self in relation to others (Darwin, 1887/1965; Lynd, 1958; MacDougall, 1908). Cooley (1902, p. 184), in his concept of "looking-glass self," suggested that shame and pride arise from seeing oneself from the viewpoint of others. Goffman (1959, 1967) made explicit the behavioral links between the "shame family" of affect and social relationships. Impression management, or maintaining "face," depends upon sensitivity to deference, including subtle signs from the other of social status and mutual evaluation, such as the duration of eye contact or pauses in speech. Indications of disrespect evoke feelings of embarrassment, a form of shame, and may mobilize negative attributions about the other. Goffman also demonstrated people's efforts to hide signs of embarrassment and the wider social stigma associated with displaying to others the painful effects of negative social evaluation.

This constant concern for the quality of relationships is a central premise of attachment theory (Ainsworth, 1978; Bowlby, 1988; Main et al., 1985), which considers a minimal degree of sociability and security in relationships to be as essential for adults as are the primary attachments of infants to their caretakers. In the last two decades, numerous studies have shown the integral role of social attachment and related emotions in many aspects of life (Bradley & Cafferty, 2001; Lewis et al., 2000). Similarly, many approaches in psychotherapy stress the importance of the "differentiation" of self from others (especially one's family members) for emotional well-being (cf., Bowen, 1978).

THE SOCIAL BOND

Retzinger and Scheff use the term "social bond" to refer to the complex social-emotional systems surrounding the expression and experience of social relationships. They propose that the regulation of social distance is an active component of face-to-face social interaction, during which participants implicitly assess the quality of their mutual understanding, attributions of each other's feelings, intentions, and signs of deference and status. Such assessments can also occur during private thought.

This emphasis on social association and evaluation as expressed during a course of action distinguishes the term social bond from "social relationship" or "social role," which can apply to broader categories of association that persist across time and situations. For example, a person can describe to a therapist in general terms the relationship with his or her mother. The relevance of the social bond is evoked by *the act of describing the relationship to the therapist*. I refer to individuals "orienting to the social bond" to capture two forms of social association in this example. A social relationship as an object of reference serves as a direction for cognitive and emotional resources, evaluation, and a potential trigger for emotional response. Second, during interaction, one orients all topical references to other listeners. This ongoing relevance of managing the social bond with co-present others, that Goffman (1959) calls "presentation of self," can occur simultaneously with the frequent references to self and other during everyday conversation. The empirical distinctions between both aspects of bond orientation are discussed herein.

Orienting to either the social bond with the other or a bond as object of reference can be a source of trouble. Maintaining bond security requires balancing closeness and separateness among people. Movement toward either extreme evokes strong affect and threatens the existence of that relationship. Individuals may perceive a threat to their social bonds when valued or desired relationships with other individuals or groups are too distant, or isolated. An individual, for example, may be rejected by a social group. More commonly, one encounters judgments, insults, disrespectful remarks, and other more subtle negative evaluations and attributions that may heighten one's immediate sense of "separateness" from others. Alternately, one may purposely distance oneself from others, for example, by blaming individuals or groups and becoming angry. Bonds that are too close may also be insecure. These "engulfed" bonds appear outwardly as intense attachment. People in engulfed relationships tend to conform to the "engulfing other" rather than emphasize their own needs, because their sense of self is dependent upon acceptance by the other. Those prone to engulfing others demand conformity as a sign of acceptance and maintain a sense of emotional security by controlling others.

Close analysis of interaction in the study herein and elsewhere (Fearon, 2001; Lewis, 1971; Retzinger, 1991a, 1995; Scheff, 1997) finds that individuals tend to mobilize attention and action to even minor signs of bond trouble as though in anticipation of potentially greater threat. Threats generally evoke emotional response. Social bond threat predominantly triggers affect from the shame family, although other emotions (such as anger, fear, and grief) may also be associated with bond trouble. Shame can potentially be experienced as intensely negative or "painful." More often, feelings of embarrassment or guilt are mild and transitory, yet may still be consequential to one's perceptions and course of action.

Affect from the shame family involves both direct feelings and visible displays that communicate this family of emotions to others during social interaction. Many of the common terms included in the family of shame (such as embarrassment, guilt, and disgrace) vary in intensity and context, but share common nonverbal indicators. From her analysis of psychotherapy sessions, Lewis (1971) identified two ways patients expressed shame: *overt* and *bypassed*. Overt displays of shame include blushing, laughter – particularly giggling or "nervous" laughter, touching or covering the face, lowering the eyes, and quiet or rapid speech. Retzinger (1987, 1991a, 1995) describes these as "hiding" behaviors, by which one, in effect, withdraws from the other's direct scrutiny, and by implication, deflects attention from the threatening aspect of what is being said or done. Conversely, people may bypass shame by activities such as "tense" laughter, biting the lip, and rapid or stammered speech that distract from internal negative feelings by controlling overt signs of affect. Controlling outward displays of embarrassment or guilt also assists impression management.

Another feature of a threat is the mobilization of efforts to alleviate the threatening conditions, in this case, the problematic aspects of the current social bond. The findings reported herein suggest that individuals manage threats to the bond by shifting the way they refer to self and others, changing attributions about their isolation from, or closeness to, others. For example, one may acknowledge a mistake but then blame that error on others, or mitigate a negative self-evaluation with a more positive statement about oneself. This process of mitigating, repairing, or otherwise altering the conditions that produced bond threat I term *reorienting the social bond*.

Resolving the bond threat shifts conditions that evoke shame and may assuage negative feelings. This suggests that shame functions both in signaling social bond trouble and motivating its repair. Participants monitor, often unwittingly, each other's emotional displays and gestures, as well as the content and implications of the discourse. When noticing signs of shame, embarrassment, or other discomfort in another, a participant may reorient the bond trouble by showing a perceived insult to be unintentional, mitigating a prior evaluation, or changing the topic. Thus, repairing bond trouble can be mutually beneficial. Ignoring the other's display of shame may lead to conflicts or other interpersonal trouble and may evoke other emotions, such as anger (Retzinger, 1991a, 1991b; Scheff & Retzinger, 1991).

The remainder of this chapter presents a study in which social bond trouble and shame were found to occur in a characteristic pattern I refer to as the *bond threat sequence*, consisting of three components typically occurring in the following order: (1) a participant orients action or attention to a threatened social bond, (2) shame occurs with or immediately following this orientation, and (3) the participant attempts to reorient the bond and conditions of threat. Social bonds and shame are related systematically because problems in social bonds trigger shame, which participants manage by adjusting the bond.

The study was conducted in two phases: qualitative and quantitative. Each phase will be presented separately, the first describing in detail the methods for analyzing social bonds and shame, and applying the analysis to interview excerpts illustrating the bond threat sequence. The second section presents methods and the results of content analysis testing the sequential relationship of bond threat, shame, and reorientation.

PHASE 1: TESTING THE BOND THREAT SEQUENCE IN INTERVIEW SETTINGS – SOCIAL BOND ANALYSIS

Methods

Data and Procedures

The data discussed herein were originally collected in an exploratory case study examining the relationship of emotions and self-evaluation in discourse (Fearon, 1994). Two first-year university students were interviewed and videotaped, a male given the pseudonym "Darryl" and a female, "Jessie." Each participant completed the Texas Social Behavior Inventory (TSBI) scale (Helmreich & Stapp, 1974) in which participants rate the degree to which responses to a variety of social situations are "characteristic" of them. In a structured interview based on seven of the TSBI questions, subjects were first asked to explain their choice for the written response to a scale question. They were then asked in prepared questions to recall and describe specific instances of problems with social situations like those in the inventory item.

The use of spontaneous assessments and life-history examples provide frameworks for participants' self-evaluation and for describing potentially problematic social bonds. Although these two cases are not necessarily representative of a larger population, the observed phenomena are unlikely to be unique. The findings are consistent with Lewis' (1971) studies of more than 100 psychoanalysis sessions, which share with the current study aspects of self-presentation and self-evaluation in an interview setting.

Conversation Analysis and Social Bond Analysis

The interviews were examined using two methods for analyzing recorded discourse in the moment-to-moment details of its production. Conversation analysis (Heritage, 1984, pp. 233–292) was combined with methods for examining the integration of affect with interaction and participants' ongoing management of interpersonal relationships that I call social bond analysis. This approach is based upon methods developed by Harrington (1990), Retzinger (1991a, 1995), and Scheff (1990, 1997). Both methods examine the details of recorded interaction to describe how participants bring forth organized courses of action and context oriented to each other. Conversation analysis focuses on procedures for making one's relevant interests recognizable to others, projecting next actions, assessing quality of shared orientation, and adjusting to troubles. Of particular interest are sequentially ordered actions, such as questions and answers, in which a first action provides a context of relevance and accountability for next actions.

Social bond analysis proposes that, in addition to building utterances and a course of interaction with others, individuals continually identify, manage, and share orientation to relationships by direct and indirect references to self, others present, specific nonpresent others, and "generalized others" (e.g., groups and institutions, such as "the government"). Managing social bonds is concurrent with, and often accomplished through, other conversational procedures, such as asking questions. Because individuals must convey their orientation to others through their talk, prosody, and gestures, much of the process is available to empirical description. Individuals may also show orientation and adjustment to aspects of the bond of which they are unaware or do not anticipate.

Illustration of Social Bond Analysis

Methods for locating social bond dimensions of the interview discourse are illustrated in Table 3.1, in which the interviewer reads one of the items of the self-evaluation scale and the participant's written response, and the participant answers by reframing the item as a personal trait. Transcript

TABLE 3.1. *Excerpt 1. Jessie: "Master Situations"*

1	**Interviewer:**	Okay. Let's go to number eight. U::m (1.0) I would descri:be myself as one who attempts to ma:ster situa:tions. (0.5) A:h
2		You put number >two not ver:y.<
		shakes head EL smile EC
3	**Jessie:**	N::o I don't (0.2) >°attempt° to< {ma:(h)ster si(hh)tuations}
		Eup, brows up-dwn EC, smile
4		°I mean° (1.5) I> (1.0) don't thi:nk,

conventions of conversation analysis (Jefferson, 1984) are listed in the Appendix. The participant's gestures are listed above the text where they occur.

Analysis begins by locating the social bonds to which participants orient within the given utterance. This is not a process of simply labeling "social roles," such as "interviewer" and "subject." Of interest, rather, is how participants both orient to and embody certain social associations through their actions, their contextual relation to surrounding talk, and especially any emotional responses these references apparently evoke.

Jessie, in her response, shows an orientation to two social bonds. First, she expresses a particular association with the interviewer through the act of responding. In the prior turn, the interviewer read one of the TSBI items and Jessie's written response. The interviewer relies in part on Jessie's recognition of how to be an interview participant when he uses the otherwise obscure reference "you put number two, not very." By rephrasing the item as a statement about herself, Jessie is in effect "being" a participant in the interview by confirming the interviewer's expectations. In the course of responding, Jessie orients to another social bond by making a self-evaluative statement from the abstract standpoint of "generalized others" who master situations.

A second task in analyzing social bonds is to locate indicators of the quality of association the participants express. An individual may make overt assessments of relationships in an utterance. More often, the quality of the bond is indirect and implicit as actors orient to potentially assessable aspects of utterances and actions. The orientation of a given bond in an utterance can often be assigned a "direction" along a spectrum of negative or positive, threatened or secure, isolated or engulfed. There is no objective scale for assessing the quality bond orientation, and the researcher's assignments are occasionally impressionistic. Evidence to support claims can, and should, be found in participants' words, context, and gestures that indicate how participants overtly intend a reference to be understood by the interviewer, and any unintentional responses to bond orientation.

Jessie confirms the interviewer's report of her written response, which maintains a positive face-to-face bond as interview participant. In agreeing, however, Jessie transforms "not very" into a characteristic of herself, stating overtly that she does not attempt to master situations. There are several indications that Jessie treats this self-evaluation as negative. From the contextual relevance, Jessie could likely guess that she has not given the preferred response to the TSBI question. The initial stretched "N::o" is a typical method of prefacing acknowledgment or admission of a fault. Jessie's behaviors and prosody suggest a negative emotional response, specifically embarrassment, which is a form of shame, as detailed herein.

Identifying Shame

In addition to assessing relationship dynamics, social bond analysis focuses explicitly upon the relation of emotions and indicators of affect, and shame in particular, to talk and social bonds. Retzinger (1991a, 1995) compiled from her own and others' research (Edelman et al., 1989; Ekman & Friesen, 1972, 1982; Gottschalk et al., 1969; Izard, 1977; Labov & Fanshel, 1977; Lewis, 1971) a list of the verbal, paralinguistic, and gesture indicators of shame, presented in Table 3.2. Retzinger, following Lewis (1971), classifies most of the characteristic shame behaviors by function as either hiding, which is associated with overt expressions of shame, or self-control indicating bypassed shame. Verbal indicators include phrases and statements that imply underlying shame. Paralanguage includes such aspects of nonverbal manner as tone of voice, rhythm and regularity of speech. Gestures include facial expressions, gaze, and body posture.

This list of shame indicators is neither definitive nor necessarily complete. Some of the indicators may occur with other affect, or could occur for reasons other than underlying shame. Stammered and fragmented speech, for example, can occur when one searches for a word. Although claims of a participant's experience of emotions are necessarily speculative, admissible operative descriptions of emotions can be built from recorded, publicly observable indicators, provided the researcher can show their relevance to surrounding talk.

In line 3 of the interview excerpt, indicators of shame surround Jessie's reference to not mastering situations. There is a slight hesitation before "I don't attempt," lowered eyes, more rapid and quiet delivery of "attempt to," and a slight laugh with the words "master situations." These "hiding behaviors" are likely an overt expression of mild shame or embarrassment. It is not fully distinguishable whether Jessie responds to evaluating herself as not mastering situations or to making a negative impression with the interviewer for saying so. Both factors can contribute to the affect; however, the laughter in particular may be oriented to the interviewer by presenting an affiliative acknowledgment that her statement can have a negative interpretation.

TABLE 3.2. *Verbal, Paralanguage, and Gesture Indicators of Shame*

A) **Gestural Indicators of Shame** (Ekman & Friesen, 1972; Izard, 1977; Retzinger, 1991a)
   1) **Blushing**
   2) **Hiding behavior:** covering all or part of face with hand (Edelman et al., 1989), averting gaze, lowering eyes or head
   3) **Self-control:** biting or licking lips, pressing lips together, wrinkling forehead, fidgeting hands, feet, or whole body, masking behaviors such as false smiling (Ekman & Friesen, 1982)

B) **Paralinguistic Indicators of Shame** (Labov & Fanshel, 1977; Retzinger, 1991a; Scheff, 1990)
   1) Hiding behavior (with transcript markings)
      a) **Quiet voice:** (°word°) volume drops to almost inaudible level, articulation becomes lax or breathy
      b) **Hesitation:** delay or drawn-out prefacing of sensitive or delicate topic
      c) **Self-interruption:** (word>) abrupt halt of an utterance preceding a change or censoring of a topic
      d) **Pause:** (1.5) Silences of more than a second are generally marked when preceding a threat-relevant or sensitive topic
      e) **Rapid speech:** (>words<) making all or part of an utterance less intelligible by rushing or running together words
      f) **Laughed words:** ({words}) spontaneous laughter or giggling surrounding words may indicate embarrassment, and tense laughter may mask shame or anger
   2) Control and disorganization of thought
      a) **Filled pauses:** frequent filling of pauses and lapses in speech with sounds such as "uh"
      b) **Irregular rhythm:** frequent halt and pauses giving a choppy quality to speech cadence
      c) **Stammer:** repeated words, syllables, consonants, and quick hesitations surrounding threat-relevant topics, sometimes making utterance incomprehensible
      d) **Incoherent speech:** rapid topic changes, incomplete topics, or other fragmentations of a topic, description, or narrative

C) **Verbal Hiding Behavior** (Harrington, 1992; Lewis, 1981; Retzinger, 1991a; Scheff, 1990)
   1) **Projection:** substituting reference to self with generic reference to person "you" or group, such as "people," disclaiming the experience as one's own by shifting it to the generalized "other" (e.g., "It just makes you feel kind of low.") (Harrington, 1992)
   2) **Abstraction:** suppressing or mitigating direct reference, to specific people and events by substituting generic references, such as "they" or "it," especially where use of pronouns is not conversationally relevant (i.e., when the recipient could not recognize the pronoun's referent)

3) **Verbal withdrawal:** Shifting speech from full sentences and narrative description to short clauses, single words, minimal responses, and long pauses
4) **Fillers:** frequently interjecting utterances with phrases such as "you know" or "kinda like," especially when use occurs with or increases during discussion of threat-oriented or sensitive topics
5) **Code words:** references to feeling inadequate, awkward, ridiculed, socially isolated or vulnerable, "dazed," empty, or indifferent, cf., Gottschalk et al.'s (1969) Shame-Anxiety scale

---

Identifying Reorientation of Social Bonds

In line 4 of the excerpt, Jessie follows the reference "master situations" immediately with "I mean," which prefaces a qualification of her prior statement. This is followed by a long pause of 1.5 seconds, after which "I don't think" qualifies and mitigates the impression that she was presenting a definitive assertion that she does not attempt to master situations. Thus, Jessie's words specifically address the problematic conditions in the social bond as she may perceive it, namely, presenting a negative self-evaluation to the interviewer.

Jessie's mitigation efforts are examples of reorienting the social bond. Actions that may qualify as reorientation are those that specify in a markedly different way a social bond indicated earlier, generally within immediately prior clauses, sentences, or turns of conversation. Although one's orientation can shift from positive to negative or neutral, this study focuses on shifts from negative to more positive or neutral orientations. Reorienting actions include:

1. *Mitigation*: words or phrases that qualify or downgrade an event or bond orientation to appear less severe or important.
2. *Redirecting the bond*: shifting responsibility for bond trouble from oneself to others, or from one "offending" party to another, through behaviors such as blaming, and justifications accounting for trouble. Accounts may include circumstances not involving social relationships.
3. *Denials or defensiveness*: denying relevance of a bond trouble or feelings, or showing indifference (e.g., "It didn't really matter.").

Social bond analysis was applied to video recordings and transcripts to identify instances in which participants oriented to social bond threat, indicated by: (1) orienting to a social bond with signs of negative evaluation or problems in impression management, (2) indicators of shame, and (3) efforts to reorient the threat by shifting the reference to the bond, or presenting to the interviewer a more positive impression.

Findings: Two Examples of Bond Threat Sequences

Analysis of two bond threat sequences further illustrates both the phenomena and the methods of conversation analysis and social bond analysis that describe the phenomena. In interview excerpts with "Darryl" and "Jessie," each participant encounters a bond threat and manages shame by reorienting the bond. Their bond threat sequences differ, however, in the source of threat and the methods by which they manage shame. Darryl orients toward an isolated bond by describing being negatively evaluated by friends, and shows efforts to bypass feelings of shame. Jessie expresses shame overtly when orienting toward an engulfed relationship with a male friend.

Darryl: Isolation Bond Threat, Bypassed Shame

In a probe question for an item on the TSBI scale, Darryl is asked to describe a specific instance of making a decision with a group of friends. He responds with a narrative in which he is repeatedly left to decide for his friends where to eat. Table 3.3 provides the discourse, beginning about forty seconds into his response, after Darryl has explained that, "after awhile everyone's kinda like 'What do you want to do Darryl?' Like – like I was always just imposing my opinion on them when they wouldn't make the decision."

ORIENTING TO ISOLATION BOND THREAT. In lines 1 and 2, Darryl orients to an isolated social bond as he describes how his friends blame him for making a decision. He refers to the bond twice, with "I – telling – them" and [I] – "getting my way" – [with them]. Emphases on the words "telling" and "getting" connote the impression that he is making an improper imposition, presented as an attribution of the friends' perspectives. The words "always" and "pretty-much" also extend the friend's attributed blame from the specific to general case, as though these were common judgments. Again, the empirical focus is not on the past relationship, but the present act of description that Darryl constructs for the interviewer and likely intends to be interpreted by the interviewer as negative. This incident of social rejection is fairly mild, and Darryl may have chosen it assuming it was the sort of story the interviewer was looking for. Darryl's subsequent emotional response to telling the story, and his effort to reorient the bond, distinguishes his presentation of the incident as a bond threat.

REORIENTATION. In lines 3 and 4, Darryl reorients the bond in two steps. First, he verbally denies that his friends' attributed evaluation of the situation was true, which he emphasizes and extends by the words "at all." Notice his use of indirect references "it" and "that," which mitigate another direct indication of his offending action. Darryl then blames the situation on his friends being unable to "make their own decisions." The blame statement is itself somewhat mitigated; he does not directly state what his friends "didn't have enough" of. Darryl reorients the implication of social rejection by shifting focus from Darryl's attributed faults to those of his friends.

SHAME. Darryl's act of orienting to bond trouble evokes an emotional response. Indicators of shame occur throughout the excerpt; however, the expression of affect shifts with Darryl's bond orientation. Overt indicators of shame occur as he describes his friends' negative judgments, in line 1, as he lowers his head and says rapidly, 'because of that.' He makes eye contact then lowers his head again in line 2 as he indicates his own actions, "telling them." He smiles slightly, which might be considered a "false smile" (Ekman & Friesen, 1982) performed with the mouth alone and operating to mask and control negative feelings. As he completes the references to the negative judgment, he stammers and pauses slightly, indicators of verbal disruption and a shift toward efforts to control and bypass feelings.

Darryl also shows efforts to control and bypass expression of shame during his reorientation of the blame. As Darryl begins to formulate the blame statement in line 3, he looks away, then hesitates, stammers, speaks rapidly, and draws a breath before arriving at "make their own decision." He seems to spit out the blame statement, anticipating its emotional tenor before he has cognitively formulated its linguistic content. He also hides direct reference to what his friends do not "have enough" of, in effect mitigating a more emotionally charged blame statement. Rapid speech and thought distract from feelings arising with the orientation to being rejected, or with the formulation of blame.

Darryl's shifts in gaze correspond to both shame affect and efforts to reorient the feelings. He maintains eye contact, in a sidelong glance, during his defense in line 3, "it wasn't like that at all." The eye contact may help solicit the interviewer's nod and verbal acknowledgment, "huh." Darryl lowers his eyes after "at all" keeping them lowered while he blames his friends. Lowering eyes is an overt shame indicator, hiding oneself from face-to-face attention; however, the gaze shift is followed immediately by the verbal disruption, indicating efforts to control feelings. He returns eye contact during the following reorientation, in which the interviewer's ratification is again relevant. Controlling shame is effective for both impression management and alleviating affect triggered by describing the situation. A display of shame, such as blushing or turning the head, would hamper his ability to present a legitimate case to the interviewer for laying blame on his friends. Also, overt feelings of shame could lead to guilt about blaming his friends.

The bond threat sequence in Table 3.3 shows Darryl's strategy for managing the isolation threat posed by orienting to a negative judgment by friends, and evoked by presenting its description to the interviewer. In the next excerpt, Jessie shows trouble when orienting to an engulfed social

TABLE 3.3. *Excerpt 2. Darryl: Interviewer's Question: Describe a Time When You Made a Decision for a Group of Friends*

		lowers head, rapid voice EC
1	**Bond threat**	and so: () >because of that< they thought I was like al:ways (1.1) pretty-
		lowers head, false smile verbal disruption
2		much telling them "let's do this" and an (0.3) >getting my< wa:y.
		EC, (interviewer nods, "huh" ↓) averts eyes, verbal disruption
3	**Reorients w/bypassed shame**	bu:t () it wasn't like that at all () >*Theyjs wr<() >th:ey we:ren't< () eno:ugh>*
		rapid voice inbreath EC
4		>*they didn't have enough to<() (•hhh)* make their ow:n dec:isio:ns

bond, and reorients the bond while expressing more overt indicators of shame.

Jessie: Engulfed Bond Threat, Overt Shame

As a follow-up to the question Jessie answered in the previous excerpt, the interviewer had asked Jessie to describe a situation that she has not mastered. She describes a troubled relationship with "this guy." She explained prior to this excerpt that, "from all outsiders' point of view . . . most people would think we were like boyfriend and girlfriend? But and totally like we're not at all? Like we don't feel that way at all." She continued: "It's kinda like real borderline. Like, we are in a way like, the way we act around each other? But then there's like no commitment or what> whatsoever." Numerous shame indicators, primarily overt, marked Jessie's description thus far, including pauses, lowered eyes, laughed words, and "filler" terms "like" and "you know." The excerpt displayed in Table 3.4 begins directly after this reference to their lack of commitment.

TABLE 3.4. *Excerpt 3a. Jessie: Interviewer's Question: Describe a Situation You Have Not Mastered*

		eyes averted EC
1	**Bond threat**	*An () and I guess* if I (1.2) wanted to master the situa:tion I could bring it
		soft voice
2		up and say wohl what's going o:n here yaknow wh:y *(1.3)* °*yaknow n*° *(0.6)*
		rapid voice eyes averted
3		should we be: (0.6) >*comm:itted to each other<* *or whatever*

ORIENTING TO ENGULFMENT BOND THREAT. Jessie's complaint about a lack of commitment seems on the surface to be another orientation to an isolated social bond evoking embarrassment about feeling rejected. The way she reorients the bond, however, suggests that she is threatened by commitment as a source of engulfment. Again, engulfed bonds are "too close for comfort" in one's feelings of dependence, conformity, or differentiation of self from others in which rejection is treated as the only alternative to commitment. Jessie describes a hypothetical situation in which if she "wanted to master the situation" she would confront the issue of their commitment. To "bring it up" with the friend and question the status of their relationship would create an opportunity to move the relationship toward either greater closeness, commitment, or to "whatever." "Whatever" could cover a reference to the alternative, "uncommitted," implying dissolution of the relationship, or it may refer to "whatever" nebulous state they are in now. Because confronting their relationship is a hypothetical case only if she wanted to "master the situation," she implies a preference for keeping their relationship *status quo*. Movement in the relationship risks either becoming more engulfed in the bond or possibly being rejected. This interpretive analysis of the possible state of the relationship Jessie describes is not fully verifiable. Her actions, however, show evidence that the act of describing the situation for the interviewer triggers a threat sequence. Her solution is to move away from engulfment, as she indicates in her next utterance, displayed in Table 3.5.

REORIENTATION. Jessie reorients the bond as presented to the interviewer by declaring, rather tentatively, that she doesn't want "that." She never directly specifies what "that" is. She may not want more commitment, or she may not want to confront the state of their relationship and risk rejection. If she desires to avoid greater commitment to her friend, then she reorients an engulfed relationship by asserting her needs as a conscious choice – "I don't . . . want," "I haven't really wanted to. . . ." Her reorientation, however, implies that another solution to engulfment is to not confront the bond, not to risk any movement in closeness or distance, but rather to maintain a *status quo*. If she avoids questioning their

TABLE 3.5. *Excerpt 3b. Jessie: Continued*

		eyes averted quieter EC laughed words
4	**Reorients w/overt shame**	but () °*I don't really*° *(1.9)* °*An I() don't*° *()* I'm not *{sure that} I wdn't>*
		tense smile, laugh EL, bites lip
5		I don't think I *{want}* that *{any}ways* so *(2.5)*
		tense smile, laugh
6		°*I guess* I haven't really wanted *{to mm (hh)mm}*°

bond, however, Jessie indirectly maintains a state of engulfment. In an engulfed bond, particularly within families, independent movement toward more separation risks attributions of abandonment by the other and dissolution of the bond (Bowen, 1978). People in engulfed relationships may resist negotiating the terms of a relationship because it evokes strong emotions. The more attachment, the greater the risk of dissolution of the bond and negative emotional consequences. Maintaining the *status quo* is a solution to the emotional risks of confronting an engulfed relationship. Thus, Jessie reorients expression of what she might identify as the bond threat, a lack of commitment, by asserting that she does not want more commitment.

SHAME. Shame may be evoked, however, by orienting to an underlying threat posed by confronting an engulfed bond. A cluster of shame indicators, italicized in the transcript, follows Jessie's talk about confronting their commitment. Laughed words, verbal mitigation, and hesitation surround her description of what she wants in the relationship. Softer speech hides the initial formulation of the reorientation, which is disrupted by pauses, hesitation, and verbal disorganization. She prefaces each statement of what she wants with verbal mitigation, "I don't really," "not sure that," "I don't think . . . anyways," "I guess," and "I haven't really." Following these qualifiers, she then laughs the words that make the self-assertions, "I'm not {sure that}," "I don't think I {want} that {any} ways," and "I haven't really wanted {to mm(h)mm}." Verbal mitigation and laughter cover a direct statement of what she wants, such as "I don't want commitment" or "I don't want to ask him."

The verbal mitigation and disruption, laughter, gestures, and paralinguistic hiding behaviors are primarily indicators of overt shame. The affect is more visible and less controlled than bypassed shame, as though her feelings "leaked" out. Jessie shows efforts to control the display at the (2.5) pause, pressing her lips together and perhaps biting them, and then speaking more quietly. The overt display suggests that Jessie has more direct experience of feelings than Darryl, whose rapidly produced reorientations could "crowd out" his attention to feelings.

As discussed, the interview participants can orient concurrently to social bonds described and the face-to-face bond with the interviewer. Both activities of description and impression management can trigger overt shame, and the analysis does not clearly distinguish which, if either, is a primary source of affect. Both Darryl and Jessie's efforts to control shame, however, appear directed primarily toward impression management, especially while reorienting the bond. For Darryl, bypassing expression of shame helps mitigate a display to the interviewer of any guilt about blaming his friends, which would undermine his reorientation. Jessie displays feelings more directly; however, the laughed words and verbal mitigation act as "hiding" behaviors, manage her impression by marking the commitment problem as not serious, and conveying conviction to the interviewer that she does not wish to confront an unusual relationship. The subtle details of their emotion management and reorientation methods are likely not a result of conscious deliberation. The efforts to manage both presentation of self and the personal experience of social bonds suggest a systematic functional integration of social affect with the pragmatics of talk; in this case, creating descriptive narratives in response to interview questions.

PHASE 2: QUANTITATIVE CONTENT ANALYSIS OF THE BOND THREAT SEQUENCE AND SHAME

Direct analysis of the interview discourse suggested that the bond threat sequence was predominant throughout the interviews, and that when indicators of shame occurred they were most often associated sequentially or concurrent with orientation to negative bonds and efforts to reorient the bond. These quantitative observations are not systematically addressed by conversation analysis and social bond analysis. These methods, however, allow precise coding of content, which in turn can address the following questions: (1) are there individual differences in sources of bond threats, whether isolated or engulfed, and in the type of shame participants display – overt or bypassed? (2) Do shame, orientation to bond trouble, and reorientation occur together more often than by chance and in what order? Addressing the second question tests the hypothesis that shame and social bond orientation are sequentially related, and that shame has a direct role in the detection, display, and management of social bond trouble. The results presented here are exploratory for this small participant pool, but suggest directions for larger studies.

Methods

Demarcating Interview Data into Units of Analysis

In preparation for content analysis, both interviews were transcribed using conventions of conversation analysis. Because each component of the bond threat sequence is either a contextual part of an utterance or, for gestures and paralanguage, is systematically related to that context, coding the interviews required full and detailed application of conversation analysis and social bond analysis described previously to support each coding decision. For content analysis, coding of shame indicators in relation to verbal actions of bond orientation requires a nonarbitrary unit of analysis that properly distinguishes one action from another. Transcripts, therefore, were demarcated by "turn construction units" (TCUs) (Sacks et al., 1974). Extensive research in conversation analysis finds that speakers and recipients naturally construct and monitor utterances with attention to where the next speaker might begin his/her next turn at talk, even when s/he does not actually begin a new turn. TCUs are also distinguishable in the multiturn narratives of the interview participants. For example, the following utterance, "No I don't attempt to master situations | I mean (1.5) I > (1.0) don't think" contains two TCUs separated between "situations" and "I mean." Ford and Thompson (1996) have concluded that TCUs are closely aligned with "intonation units," in which stretches of speech are distinguishable by rising and falling contours of intonation. Linguistics research has suggested that intonation units, and hence TCUs, may represent the "rhythm" and sequential building blocks of symbolic thought and semantic content. The TCU therefore provides a means of demarcating interview transcripts that reflect the participants' own orientation to the discourse. As a working hypothesis, I treat emotions as also organized within TCUs, because affect indicators usually can be found to correspond to their immediate verbal context.

Coding Criteria and Measures

For content analysis, each TCU was coded for the discourse and affect events occurring with it. Indicators of overt shame and bypassed shame were coded using the verbal, gesture, and paralanguage indicators listed in Table 3.2. Also distinguished were shame indicators with and without a clear relevance to the context. Using social bond analysis, each TCU was coded for the participant's orientation to a social bond, if any, and whether the bond orientation was positive, negative, or neutral. Also coded, when possible, was orientation to isolated or engulfed bonds. Bond reorientation was marked for TCUs containing mitigation, redirection, denials, defensiveness, or other shifts from negative to positive orientation.

A Filemaker database was constructed to assist in coding and statistical analysis. Coding allowed calculation of individual differences and overall ratio of shame and bond threat sequences to interview responses. Calculation of transitional probabilities, and Markov chain sequential modeling (cf., Bakeman & Gottman, 1986), was used to test the probability that an association between orientation to a negative bond, indicators of shame, and reorientation occur together more often than by chance, and in that particular order.

Findings: Content Analysis of Interview

Individual Differences in Shame and Bond Threat Sequences

Participants' bond threat sequences ranged from one to seven TCUs in duration. During interview responses, TCUs occurred as part of bond threat sequences in 64% of the male's TCUs and in 84% of the female's TCUs (Table 3.6). Shame indicators occurred in 33% of the 571 TCUs for Darryl and 45% of Jessie's 444 TCUs. These results indicate the effectiveness of the interview method for eliciting shame and bond threat orientation.

TABLE 3.6. *Proportions of TCUs with Bond Threat Sequences and Shame*

TCUs	Darryl (571 TCUs)	Jessie (444 TCUs)
Within bond threat sequence	64%	84%
With shame indicators	33%	45%

Note: TCU, turn construction unit.

In the excerpts presented previously, Darryl and Jessie differed in the sources of bond threat and types of shame they displayed. Content analysis suggested a pattern of difference throughout the interviews. Lewis (1971), in her analysis of psychotherapy sessions, found that an individual tends toward either overt or bypassed expression of shame in a variety of social situations, suggesting a possible personality trait. Jessie and Darryl displayed both overt shame and efforts to bypass shame, often intermingled within an utterance. Jessie, however, in addition to displaying more shame overall, expressed overt in 85% of the TCUs with shame indicators (Table 3.7). Darryl showed slightly more bypassed (54%) than overt (46%) shame indicators.

Darryl and Jessie also differed in the type of bond orientation that typically provoked shame during their interviews. Darryl tended to orient his discussion and life-history examples toward problems with isolated social bonds that involved social separation, negative judgments or blame from others, or perceptions of lack of control. Of Darryl's TCUs with bond orientation, 61% involved isolated bonds and 7% engulfed bonds (Table 3.7). Jessie, however, expressed shame most often when orienting discussion toward engulfed bonds, such as conforming to her peer group and parents or shyness in group situations. Of Jessie's TCUs with bond orientation, 45% were toward engulfed bonds and 30% toward isolated bond trouble. Participants' bond orientation expressed during the interview may reflect general tendencies in the type of bonds and situations they find problematic. Because participants choose their particular examples and control the length of their responses, overall proportions of bond orientations are arbitrary to a degree and not fully comparable. The individual differences in bond orientation and shame display in these two cases, however,

TABLE 3.7. *Comparing Types of Shame Expression and Direction of Bond Orientation*

	Shame		Bond Orientation		
Of TCUs with:	Overt	Bypassed	Engulfed	Isolated	Secure
Darryl (male)	46%	54%	7%	61%	32%
Jessie (female)	85%	15%	45%	30%	41%

Note: TCU, turn construction unit.

correspond to individual and gender differences found by Lewis (1971, 1976) and other shame research (Scheff, 1997; Tangney, 1990; Tangney & Dearing, 2002).

Transitional Probabilities

Sequential analysis of transitional probabilities among indicators of bond orientation and shame within and between TCUs provided preliminary support for the hypothesis that bond threats, shame, and reorientation are related sequentially. Markov analysis is more valid with a larger number of observations (TCUs) than were available for the two participants. Also, an Anderson–Goodman test of homogeneity (Gottman & Roy, 1990, pp. 67–76) found that the data for both participants could not be reliably pooled. Results for this exploratory analysis cannot be considered fully reliable; however, they are suggestive of what a larger study may show.

A series of individual tests for each participant were run to find significant probabilities of transition of bond states and shame within a single TCU, between adjacent TCUs, and across one or more TCUs. The number of TCU data points was not sufficient for a direct test of the sequential probability of negative bond orientation, shame, and reorientation occurring together. Although numerical results of each test could not be combined, significant results confirmed the three components of the hypothesis: (1) negative bond orientation occurs with or transitions to shame more often than by chance; (2) shame transitions to, or co-occurs with, reorientation/mitigation; and (3) negative bond orientation transitions to reorientation. These associations among the two-step transitions confirm qualitative observations that these three components usually occur in the sequential order.

DISCUSSION

The central, although preliminary, finding of this exploratory study is the significant sequential relationship between negative bond orientation, shame, and reorientation. The bond threat sequence suggests a central role of shame in the detection of troubles in one's current and imagined social associations, the signaling of trouble to self and others, and motivation for adjustment to the social bond. Unlike other emotions, those of the shame family appear almost exclusively social in their domain of operation, and are intimately tied to language, social self, and human group life. Social affect for human beings may have co-developed with language and specialized in their evolution from similar affect in other species, to alert oneself and others to changes in the quality of social relationships.

The operation of a bond threat sequence also suggests new methods for analyzing shame in both controlled and natural settings. If social bond trouble reliably indicates shame, the characteristic gestures and paralinguistic markers that occur with an utterance are evidence of underlying feelings. The integration of close analysis of conversation and of participants' orientation to social association accomplished through talk gives a more reliable context for both identifying shame and its operation in ways that self-reports, affect inventories, and self-evaluation cannot capture.

This exploratory study could be replicated with a larger sample, with the TSBI or other standard measures of self-esteem, social behaviors, or social affect, such as the Test of Self-conscious Affect (TOSCA) (Tangney & Dearing, 2002). In addition to providing a more valid basis for quantitative analysis, a wider sample would allow comparison of individual differences, including gender, age, culture, ethnicity, and language.

Research on the phenomena of the bond threat sequence could also be extended to studies of discourse in everyday situations, or specialized settings such as organizations. The sequence of bond orientation, shame, and reorientation is likely to be more complex and varied during face-to-face interaction. Either member in a conversation might trigger a threat, and reorienting the bond is often a process of negotiation, rather than "self-repair" alone as in the interview settings. Interesting patterns, however, become apparent when analyzing recorded interaction from everyday settings, including the involvement of other emotions. Retzinger (1987, 1991a, 1991b) documents in detail the patterns in marital quarrels in which conflicts escalate through "shame-rage spirals," and Scheff (1997) has explored interaction of shame and anger at a macro scale, specifically its contribution to the start of World War I. Scheff (1997) also found that abusive parents may have particular difficulty handling shame. In an exploratory study (Fearon, 2001), I found that a caretaker's unacknowledged shame precedes anger and physical punishment. Shame and social bond dynamics are also readily apparent in group interaction in settings such as business meetings, and are a largely unexplored dimension in understanding group dynamics.

APPENDIX: TRANSCRIPTION CONVENTIONS

><	Hurried speech within brackets.
>	"Cut off" of the prior word or sound.
oo	Words bracketed by degree signs are softer than surrounding talk.
–	Underscoring indicates some form of stress.
::	Colons indicate prolongation of the immediately prior sound.
: (underscored)	Underscoring of a colon and following letter indicates a rising intonation, "e.g., Does he work ha:rd?" and underscoring of letters prior to a colon indicate falling intonation, e.g., "I don't work ha:rd."

., ?	Punctuation markers indicate intonation rather than grammatical symbols.
(1:3)	Indicates measured time in one second, and a tenth of a second.
()	Indicates tiny gap, generally less than one second.
{word}	Laughed words.
(hh)	Parenthesized h's indicate explosiveness, associated with laughter, sighs, and outbreaths.
italics	Shame markers.
EC, EL, EA, Eup	Eye contact, eyes lowered, eyes averted, eyes up.

After Jefferson (1984) and Retzinger (1995).

References

Ainsworth, M. D. S. (1978). *Patterns of attachment: A psychological study of the strange situation*. Hillsdale, NJ: Lawrence Erlbaum Associates.

Bakeman, R., & Gottman, J. M. (1986). *Observing interaction: An introduction to sequential analysis*. Cambridge: Cambridge University Press.

Bowen, M. (1978). *Family therapy in clinical practice*. New York: J. Aronson.

Bowlby, J. (1988). *A secure base: Parent child attachment and healthy human-development*. New York: Basic Books.

Bradley, J. M., & Cafferty, T. P. (2001). Attachment among older adults: Current issues and directions for future research. *Attachment & Human Development, 3*(2), 200–221.

Cooley, C. H. (1902). *Human nature and the social order* (p. 184). New York: Scribner.

Darwin, C. (1887/1965). *The expression of emotion in men and animals*. London: John Murray.

Edelman, R. J., Asendorpf, J., Contarello, A., Georgas, J., Villanueva, C., & Zammuner, V. (1989). Self-reported expression of embarrassment in five European cultures. *Journal of Cross-Cultural Psychology, 20*, 357–371.

Ekman, P., & Friesen, W. (1972). *Emotion in the human face*. New York: Pergamon.

Ekman, P., & Friesen, W. (1982). Felt, false and miserable smiles. *Journal of Non-Verbal Behavior, 6*, 238–252.

Fearon, D. S. (1994). *The bond threat sequence: Discourse evidence for the systematic interdependence of shame and social relationships*. Unpublished Masters thesis, University of California, Santa Barbara.

Fearon, D. S. (2001). *Social bond threat, shame, and low perceived power in abusive caretaker relationships*: Paper presented at the 2001 Conference on Language, Interaction, and Culture, University of California, Santa Barbara.

Ford, C. E., & Thompson, S. A. (1996). Interactional units in conversation: Syntactic, intonational, and pragmatic resources for the management of turns. In E. Ochs & E. A. Schegloff & S. A. Thompson (Eds.), *Interaction and grammar* (pp. xii, 468). Cambridge: Cambridge University Press.

Goffman, E. (1959). *The presentation of self in everyday life*. Garden City, NJ: Doubleday.

Goffman, E. (1967). *Interaction ritual*. New York: Anchor.

Gottman, J. M., & Roy, A. K. (1990). *Sequential analysis: A guide for behavioral researchers* (pp. 671–76). Cambridge: Cambridge University Press.
Gottschalk, L. A., Winget, C. N., & Gleser, G. C. (1969). *Manual of instructions for using the Gottschalk-Gleser content analysis scales: Anxiety, hostility, and social alienation-personal disorganization.* Berkeley: University of California Press.
Harrington, C. L. (1990). *Emotion talk: The sequential organization of shame talk,* PhD thesis, University of California, Santa Barbara.
Harrington, C. L. (1992). Talk about embarrassment: Exploring the taboo-repression-denial hypothesis. *Symbolic Interaction, 15*(2), 203–225.
Helmreich, R., & Stapp, J. (1974). Short forms of the Texas social behavior inventory (TSBI), an objective measure of self-esteem. *Bulletin of the Psychonomic Society, 4*(5A), 473–475.
Heritage, J. (1984). *Garfinkel and ethnomethodology* (pp. 233–292). New York: Polity Press.
Izard, C. E. (1977). *Human emotions.* New York: Plenum.
Jefferson, G. (1984). Caricature versus detail: On capturing the particulars of pronunciation in transcripts of conversational data. *Tilberg papers on language and literature no. 31* (Vol. 31). Netherlands: University of Tilburg.
Labov, W., & Fanshel, D. (1977). *Therapeutic discourse: Psychotherapy as conversation.* New York: Academic Press.
Lewis, H. B. (1971). *Shame and guilt in neurosis.* New York: International Universities Press.
Lewis, H. B. (1976). *Psychic war in men and women.* New York: New York University Press.
Lewis, H. B. (1981). Shame and guilt in human nature. In S. Tuttman, C. Kaye, & M. Zimmerman (Eds.), *Object and self: A developmental approach.* New York: International University Press.
Lewis, T., Amini, F., & Lannon, R. (2000). *A general theory of love.* New York: Random House.
Lynd, H. M. (1958). *On shame and the search for identity.* New York: Harcourt Brace.
MacDougall, W. (1908). *An introduction to social psychology.* London: Methuen.
Main, M., Kaplan, K., & Cassidy, J. (1985). Security in infancy, childhood and adulthood: A move to the level of representation. In I. Bretherton & E. Waters (Eds.), *Growing points of attachment: Theory and research* (pp. 66–104). Chicago: University of Chicago Press for the Society for Research in Child Development.
Retzinger, S. M. (1987). Resentment and laughter: Video studies of the shame-rage spiral. In H. B. Lewis (Ed.), *The role of shame in symptom formation* (pp. 115–181). Hillsdale, NJ: Erlbalm.
Retzinger, S. M. (1991a). *Violent emotions: Shame and rage in marital quarrels.* Newbury Park, CA: Sage.
Retzinger, S. M. (1991b). Shame, anger, and conflict: case-study of emotional violence. *Journal of Family Violence, 6*(1), 37–59.
Retzinger, S. M. (1995). Identifying shame and anger in discourse. *American Behavioral Scientist, 38*(8), 1104–1113.
Sacks, H., Schegloff, E. A., & Jefferson, G. (1974). A simplest systematics for the organization of turn-taking for conversation. *Language, 50,* 696–735.
Scheff, T. J. (1990). *Microsociology: Discourse, emotion, and social structure.* Chicago: University of Chicago Press.

Scheff, T. J. (1997). *Emotions, the social bond, and human reality: Part/whole analysis*. Cambridge, UK: Cambridge University Press.

Scheff, T. J. (2000). Shame and the social bond: A sociological theory. *Sociological Theory, 18*, 84–99.

Scheff, T. J., & Retzinger, S. M. (1991). *Emotions and violence: Shame and rage in destructive conflicts*. Lexington, MA: D. C. Heath and Company.

Tangney, J. P. (1990). Assessing individual differences in proneness to shame and guilt: Development of the self-conscious affect and attribution inventory. *Journal of Personality and Social Psychology, 59*(1), 102–112.

Tangney, J. P., & Dearing, R. L. (2002). *Shame and guilt*. New York: Guilford Press.

4

Emotion as Adaptive Interpersonal Communication

The Case of Embarrassment

Rowland S. Miller

The last time I was embarrassed, events unfolded in a familiar pattern. I was in the presence of others when I discovered that I had committed a small gaffe of which they were aware; coincident with my realization of my mistake came aversive arousal and a warm face, a sheepish grin, and an averted gaze. I was mildly mortified and, genuinely regretful, I apologized. In response, my audience offered some mild teasing that seemed playful instead of malicious, and I was evidently forgiven: Our interaction then continued as if my blunder had not occurred, and my miscue was not mentioned again.

This was just a single, potentially idiosyncratic episode of embarrassment, but my guess is that you recognize that pattern of events. It's prototypical. All of its elements – the public misbehavior; the unbidden, involuntary wash of chagrin and abashment; the particular sequence of nonverbal behavior; the resulting helpful, conciliatory actions; and the tolerant, lenient responses from others – characterize embarrassment among adults all over the world (Miller, 1996).

Further, just as in my example – and given that one has transgressed in some manner – most embarrassments have a happy ending. Embarrassed emotion is certainly unpleasant; it is a blend of fretful mortification and chagrin that is discomforting and sometimes humiliating. Nevertheless, among adults, embarrassment usually elicits kinder reactions from others than those that would have been forthcoming had one's embarrassment not occurred (Miller, 1996).

This central fact about embarrassment – that it usually improves rather than harms difficult interactions – is the focus of this chapter. In what follows, I take a functional account of emotion: Coherent cross-cultural patterns of physiological, affective, and behavioral responses to certain situations are presumed to exist because they are (or were once) adaptive, promoting well-being and reproductive fitness (Cosmides & Tooby, 2000). As we will see, embarrassment appears to be a basic emotion that exemplifies the communicative and interactive roles of social emotions that evolved to manage our diverse dealings with other people. What does embarrassment do for us? Why does it exist? It is to those arguments that I now turn.

A FUNCTIONAL ACCOUNT OF EMBARRASSMENT

The notion that "emotions exist because they maximize reproductive fitness of individuals" dates back to Darwin's analyses of the origins of species (Turner, 1997, p. 212). Emotion theorists usually agree that, because nature is parsimonious and favors simple systems over those that are unnecessarily complex, emotions must be useful in some way or they would never have developed (Keltner & Gross, 1999). Thus, "the reason the primary, prototypic emotions developed in the first place, were shaped and reshaped over the millennia, and continued to survive, was because they were adaptive" (Hatfield & Rapson, 1990, p. 129). Being "adaptive" means that emotions helped solve specific problems of survival and adjustment; it does not mean that the emotions themselves were pleasant or desirable experiences.

Some emotions are *social* emotions because they emerge wholly from interpersonal concerns and occur "only as a result of real, anticipated, remembered, or imagined encounters with other people" (Leary, 2000, p. 333). Some types of social emotions (such as love, hatred, and envy) involve our feelings about others; Leary (2000) terms these the "social-evaluative" emotions. Other social emotions result from our perceptions of others' judgments of us; these "social-relational" reactions include embarrassment, jealousy, hurt feelings, and pride (Leary, 2000).

Many emotions that can result from the action of others may also be elicited by private, nonsocial events that do not involve interaction with others and so are not social emotions. For example, sadness, which is not a social emotion, may occur either for interpersonal reasons (such as a beloved's death) or for nonsocial reasons (such as losing a beloved belonging). Nonsocial emotions may occasionally stem from interpersonal events, but social emotions differ from them by their connections to our social (as opposed to physical) well-being. Social emotions are not triggered by impersonal events; they result solely from our feelings about others or others' feelings about us (Leary, 2000).

Social emotions presumably evolved to facilitate attachments among individuals and to manage group life. Such emotions would have been adaptive in serving the human *need to belong*, a fundamental, universal human motivation to establish and maintain close relationships with (at least a few) other people (Baumeister & Leary, 1995). A need to belong plausibly became prevalent in early hominids as those who eagerly sought the close company of others reproduced more successfully than did those who were more independent or disaffiliative. Early humans are presumed to have lived as hunter-gatherers in small tribal groups; those who lived happily in such settings may have surmounted the challenges of physical survival and reproduction more readily than did those who were less social and more solitary (Keltner & Haidt, 2001; Turner, 1996).

In particular, social-relational emotions elicited by threats to belongingness – that is, emotions that resulted from the prospect of rejection or exclusion by others – would have had several valuable effects (Leary, 2000). First, they would have alerted our forebears to their interpersonal problems, interrupting their objectionable behavior and promoting attention to their precarious predicaments. They also would have encouraged cognitive appraisals that delineated one's difficulty and subsequently motivated remedial responses designed to reduce one's jeopardy. Such emotions would thus have been interpersonal wake-up calls that got our ancestors to take action before it was too late.

Moreover, springing from public, interactive events, social-relational emotions may have served as *signals* of one's state to others (Hess & Kirouac, 2000). To the extent that such emotions engendered particular, patterned physiological or behavioral responses, they may have been visible, recognizable reactions that communicated one's feelings to others (Keltner & Ekman, 2000; Preuschoft & van Hooff, 1997). Not all emotions, whether social or nonsocial, are accompanied by distinctive nonverbal displays, but a select group of "basic" emotions do trigger such responses (Ekman, 1999). Basic emotions are members of a core group of discrete emotions of special importance and consequence; they are distinguished not only by their distinctive expressive displays, but also by their unique physiological responses and their connection to universal antecedent events that differ little from culture to culture (Ekman, 1992, 1999). Furthermore, because we do not choose what emotions to experience – because emotion is unbidden and involuntary and washes over us quickly when triggering events are encountered (Ekman, 1992) – any basic social-relational emotions may have been reliable and trustworthy signals of a person's inclinations that were hard or impossible to fake. Even if people regained conscious control over their actions after only a moment or two, the onset of such emotion might have been an unmistakable event to any attentive observer.

Now, in modern times, embarrassment appears to be such an event. It is certainly a social phenomenon: Almost all of the embarrassments we experience occur in the presence of others (Tangney et al., 1996), and if embarrassment does occur when we are alone, it invariably involves the real or imagined possibility that misbehavior will be discovered by others (such as the embarrassment felt by a woman who, finding herself mistakenly standing in an empty *men's* restroom, is mortified by the chance that someone could walk in at any moment; see Miller, 1992).

In addition, as we will see shortly, several other aspects of embarrassment fit the notion that it is a basic emotion that is an adaptive communication that serves the need to belong. In our distant past, abandonment by one's tribe may have endangered one's survival. Embarrassment conceivably evolved both to provide an emergency means of alerting one to transgressions that could engender banishment by others and to forestall such rejection by reassuring others of one's goodwill (Gilbert & Trower, 2001; Keltner & Haidt, 1999). In particular, embarrassment may have been designed to maintain and preserve status hierarchies that were essential for effective living in groups (Keltner & Haidt, 2001); in signaling one's chagrin and submission to the group after counter-normative behavior, embarrassment may have reduced the likelihood of retaliation or punishment from one's fellows. Thus, through natural selection, embarrassment may have become a "social counterpart to physical pain; just as it would be hard to survive if we had no pain to warn us of threats to our physical well-being, we would not last long if we had no social anxiety or embarrassment to warn us of possible rebuke and rejection" (Miller & Leary, 1992, p. 216). Let us consider how embarrassment fulfills these useful functions.

DEFINING CHARACTERISTICS OF EMBARRASSMENT

Antecedents

With few exceptions, embarrassment follows surprising, startling events that threaten to convey an unwanted image of oneself to others. Typically, these are mishaps in which someone personally "violates a norm of deportment, civility, self-control, or grace" (Miller, 2001, p. 283) through clumsy, maladroit behavior or mental errors or by losing control of possessions, such as clothes, cars, and pets. In such instances, "people may trip and fall, spill their drinks, rip their pants, stall their cars, fart inadvertently, and forget others' names" (Miller, 2001, p. 283), and most embarrassments – about two-thirds of the embarrassments we encounter – involve individual misbehavior of this sort (Miller, 1992).

In other cases that account for one-sixth of embarrassing episodes (Miller, 1996), embarrassment results from negative publicity that does not involve any personal impropriety, but that stems instead from the actions of others. Innocent people are occasionally put on the spot by practical jokers who are trying to embarrass them; the pranksters' intentions are usually more playful than malicious, but real humiliation can result (Sharkey, 1997). People can also be embarrassed merely by being linked in others' judgments with someone else who is misbehaving; in "team embarrassments" of this sort, a partner's actions make one look bad by association, even when one has personally done nothing wrong.

Most embarrassments, then, involve a sensible dread of social disapproval that stems from events that transmit undesired information about oneself, directly or indirectly, to others. This is not true of all embarrassments, however, because people are also occasionally embarrassed by excessive public scrutiny even when they have no salient reason to fear inspection by others (Sabini et al., 2000). For instance, simply picking a person at random from a sizable audience and asking the rest of the group to gaze silently at him or her reliably discomfits and embarrasses the target of such perusal (Lewis, 2000). Even singling someone out for public praise often causes the recipient of such compliments to become embarrassed (Miller, 1992). Conspicuousness can evidently cause embarrassment even when there's no hint of social disapproval in the air.

At first blush (so to speak), the embarrassing potential of such events suggests that embarrassment may spring from sources that do not always arouse a threat to belongingness. On the other hand, embarrassed reactions to excessive public scrutiny (unlike the inborn capacity for embarrassment that results from potential disapproval per se) may be learned generalizations that result from our many past experiences with such scrutiny that *did* result in rough treatment from others (see Buss, 2001). Most of us may learn to dread close inspection from others in elementary school. When Cathy Stonehouse and I asked fifth-graders to keep diary records of their embarrassments for a month, we found that any events that made young adolescents conspicuous typically resulted in teasing and derision from their peers (Stonehouse & Miller, 1994). Too often when we are young, public scrutiny results in "ridicule, scorn, criticism, or rejection" (Buss, 1980, p. 243), even when we have done nothing to deserve such disregard. No wonder, then, that simple conspicuousness can be embarrassing, even to adults; the trepidation one feels when singled out for public inspection can reasonably be considered to be the generalized result of many youthful lessons in which close observation by others was punishing.

In general, then, prototypical embarrassment occurs when surprising, unanticipated events increase the threat of unwanted social evaluations from real or imagined audiences, and these are events that threaten the need to belong. The specific events that elicit embarrassment range from mere conspicuousness to debasing pratfalls, but in every case the embarrassed person has reason to be concerned about what others may be thinking of him or her.

Moreover, although socialization and experience undoubtedly shape our susceptibilities to embarrassment (as my analysis of the embarrassing potential of conspicuousness would suggest), there is notable similarity in the events that elicit embarrassment across different cultures (Miller, 1996). Iranian children agree closely with Japanese children about the embarrassing potential of publicly falling off one's bicycle or walking in on someone in a toilet (Hashimoto & Shimizu, 1988), and college students in Illinois and in western Japan experience similar types of embarrassing predicaments with similar frequencies (Cupach & Imahori, 1993). Adolescents in Sweden, Hungary, India, and Yemen agree about the amount of embarrassment various predicaments cause (Stattin, Magnusson, Olah, Kassin, & Reddy, 1991), and embarrassment has been observed among Africans, Samoans, and the Balinese (Eibl-Eibesfeldt, 1989). Around the world, regardless of their religion, climate, or socioeconomic status, people suffer embarrassment when unwanted events transmit undesired information about them to others.

Embarrassment is thus a social-relational emotion elicited by specific antecedents that raise the specter of interpersonal devaluation or rejection, and its commonality and regularity across cultures are consistent with the possibility that it evolved to meet recurring human needs.

Phenomenology

Embarrassed people report a variety of different feelings, but their predominant sensations are surprise, a sense of exposure, fluster, and sheepishness (Miller & Tangney, 1994; Parrott & Smith, 1991). They feel self-conscious and ungainly, and awkward and abashed. These feelings strike without warning when one realizes that one's conduct has gone awry, so that prototypical embarrassment involves startled, clumsy chagrin. Embarrassment is thus a multifaceted sensation but, importantly, its feelings can be distinguished from those that characterize related states such as shyness (Izard & Youngstrom, 1996; Mosher & White, 1981) and shame (Miller & Tangney, 1994; Sabini, Garvey, & Hall, 2001). Embarrassed emotion gets one's attention, and people easily identify their embarrassments when they occur.

Physiology

Whether there is a particular pattern of sympathetic and/or parasympathetic activation that distinguishes embarrassment from other emotions remains undecided (cf. Harris, 2001; Lewis & Ramsay, 2002), but there is at least one physiological signature that makes embarrassment unique: the blush (Edelmann, 2001). The visible coloring of the cheeks and neck that often accompanies embarrassment is due to vasodilation of facial veins that brings blood closer to the surface of the skin. What's striking about that reaction is that elsewhere in the body, peripheral vessels are constricting in response to emotion, sending blood away from the skin and toward the muscles, readying the person to fight or flee (Drummond, 1989). The veins in our cheeks, ears, and neck behave differently because they are wired differently, being equipped with β-adrenergic receptors that are uncommon in venous tissue (Drummond, 1997; Mellander et al., 1982). People cannot consciously control their blushing – although the realization that one is visibly blushing may intensify one's embarrassment and exacerbate one's blush (Drummond, 2001) – and blushing can be reliably distinguished from the flushing that may follow exercise, sexual arousal, or intoxication (Leary et al., 1992). It is a genuinely specific behavior that almost always indicates that someone is presently embarrassed.

It is not only noteworthy that such a singular reaction exists at all, but also that it is limited to the face and neck, the region of the body that is most often visible to our conspecifics. Blushing does not appear to serve any self-regulatory function – people may be unaware that they are blushing until others inform them of that fact (Leary et al., 1992) – so the location of the blush may suggest its true purpose: Like other facial expressions that accompany basic emotions, blushing may exist, at least in part, to signal one's feelings to others.

Nonverbal Behavior

Even if blushing is hard to detect (as it can be in dark-skinned people; Drummond & Lim, 2000) or does not occur, a person's embarrassment is usually readily recognizable. This is because there is a specific, distinctive *sequence* of nonverbal actions that occurs when embarrassment strikes (Keltner, 1995; Keltner & Anderson, 2000). First, embarrassed people avert their gazes, looking away from others (usually to the left and then down). Then, they try to suppress emerging smiles with actions called *smile controls*, biting their lips or pressing them together or pulling down the corners of their mouths. These efforts usually fail, and most people break into a nervous, goofy, sheepish grin that reaches its apex $1\frac{1}{2}$ seconds after their gaze aversion begins (a pattern that clearly distinguishes an embarrassed smile from one of genuine amusement or delight; Asendorpf, 1990). Next, people typically lower their heads and turn them away, and, finally, hide their eyes or smile behind a hand. The entire tableau takes about five seconds from start to finish.

Idiosyncrasy exists, and not all embarrassed people will engage in all of these actions every time. Nevertheless, most of them are present most of the time, and Keltner (1995) demonstrated that if gaze aversion, smile controls, a sheepish grin, head movements, and face touches all occur, one's embarrassment is plain (and readily distinguishable from related states, such as amusement or shame; Keltner & Buswell, 1996).

Embarrassed people also exhibit more nervous body motion, shifting their postures and gesturing more frequently than they do when they are poised and calm (Edelmann & Hampson, 1981), and they make more speech errors by stuttering, stammering, and generally misspeaking, too (Edelmann & Hampson, 1979). Add up all these reactions, and embarrassment is usually obvious. Combine them with a blush, and embarrassment is positively unmistakable.

These coherent displays allow the possibility that others may be able to recognize when we are embarrassed. The situation plays a part – one's audience may influence the intensity with which some of these actions occur (Costa et al., 2001) – but the various behavioral reactions that accompany embarrassment usually provide a *reliable signal* that embarrassment has occurred, nonetheless. Are these signals normally noticed? Do embarrassed behaviors routinely communicate one's chagrin to others? Indeed, they do.

Others' Perceptions

My colleague, David Marcus, and I have explored the recognizability of embarrassment in two studies that focused on observers of others' embarrassments. In a first investigation (Marcus, Wilson, & Miller, 1996), we invited female collegians to attend laboratory sessions in groups of five, and then asked each of them, in turn, to perform either an embarrassing or innocuous task as the other women watched from an adjacent room. (For sixty seconds, the women either danced by themselves to recorded music – the embarrassing task – or simply sat and listened to the tune.) Our procedure was thus a round-robin design in which all of a group's members watched all of the others perform the task and were watched by them as well. As a result, the data were amenable to variance partitioning using Kenny's (1994) Social Relations Model, which allowed us to determine the extent to which perceptions of embarrassment were in the "eye of the beholder," varying substantially from perceiver to perceiver, or on the face of the beheld, being similar no matter who was watching.

We found that strong embarrassment was, in fact, perfectly plain to observers. There was little variability among different watchers when the women performed the embarrassing task; some actors were more embarrassed than others, of course, but the extent of a woman's embarrassment was usually evident to observers who agreed among themselves about what an actor was feeling. There was more idiosyncrasy in perceptions of the mild reactions that followed the innocuous task – observers who were more susceptible to embarrassment tended to perceive stronger chagrin than less easily embarrassed observers did – so that people differed in their recognition of mild embarrassment. Nevertheless, intense embarrassment was typically obvious to any attentive observer.

In a second study (Marcus & Miller, 1999), we took advantage of naturally occurring public performances to examine perceptions of authentic embarrassment in field settings. Students in 19 different classes at two different universities reported how embarrassed they felt during presentations to their classes and also judged the embarrassment felt by their classmates during the colleagues' presentations. The procedure offered the advantages of presenting observers with a variety of individual instances of "live" emotion that were encountered in a naturalistic manner, but the results replicated those we obtained in the lab. There was notable consensus in observers' judgments of who was and who was not embarrassed, and, importantly, those perceptions were reasonably accurate. The observers' judgments were reliably correlated with the speakers' self-reports of how embarrassed they had been during their talks. Any embarrassment that the students felt during their presentations tended to be mild, but it was plainly recognizable to their audiences when it occurred.

Overall, then, studies of embarrassed behavior suggest that embarrassment engenders more coherent responses than we may realize. We feel discombobulated and rattled when we are embarrassed, but our flustered actions may feel more chaotic than they really are. Not only *can* others tell when we are embarrassed, as the nonverbal signals of embarrassment would allow, they *do* discern our embarrassment with some precision. Individuals differ somewhat in their perception of mild embarrassment, with those who are more sensitive to the state usually believing it to be stronger in others, but even mild embarrassment is unlikely to go entirely unnoticed. When we are embarrassed, others are likely to know it.

Interactive Responses to Embarrassment

How do people behave toward others when they are embarrassed? This is not a simple question, because people may respond to embarrassment in several different ways (Miller, 1996), and they may not always choose the most efficacious response. Presumably, one of embarrassment's benefits is that it interrupts undesirable behavior and alerts the social miscreant that things have gone wrong. However, when they are in the throes of a negative affective state such as embarrassment, people may impulsively pursue short-term strategies that have long-term costs (Gray, 1999), and they do not always make advantageous decisions. Indeed, when I and my colleagues asked 257 young adults what they had done in response to a recent embarrassment, we found that in one of every eleven embarrassments, people simply fled their predicaments by running away (Miller et al., 1996). Such behavior obviously ends the misbehavior that triggered the embarrassment, but an abrupt departure usually makes a bad impression on any onlookers (Levin & Arluke, 1982), so it is not an optimal strategy.

Happily, however, people more often respond to embarrassment with more effective reactions. About one-third of the time, people apologize, expressing regret for their misbehavior and pledging to do better in the future, or they attempt to redress or repair any damage or inconvenience they have caused. If the situation permits – that is, if they have not done anyone any damage and just look silly – people may resort to humor, wryly acknowledging their misbehavior with a witticism or self-deprecatory remark. Humor occurs one-sixth of the time. Thus, people respond to about half of their embarrassments with behavior that is either explicitly ingratiating or remedial (Miller et al., 1996), and both are likely to elicit approval from audiences.

On other occasions, about one-third of the time, people offer accounts that reduce their apparent responsibility for their misbehavior, or they simply ignore the embarrassing event and continue on as if nothing has happened (Miller et al., 1996). As long as the accounts are reasonable or the transgressions trivial, either can be an effective strategy that allows an interaction to continue with only minimal disruption (Gonzales, 1992). Belaboring a minor infraction with an elaborate apology actually creates a larger nuisance than it resolves, so simply looking momentarily embarrassed and then returning to the flow of the interaction is often a reasonable, efficacious response (Cupach & Metts, 1994).

Despite their aversive arousal, people rarely respond to embarrassment with anger or aggression. We found that embarrassed people behaved in a surly fashion only 5% of the time, and then only when someone else had intentionally caused their embarrassment (Miller et al., 1996). Aggression never occurred when embarrassment was self-imposed, so embarrassment does not routinely foster hostility toward others.

To the contrary, although less desirable reactions may occur, it is clear that most responses to embarrassment involve amiable, conciliatory behavior that seeks to restore and maintain existing interactions. In addition, embarrassment appears to create a generalized desire for social approval and inclusion, so that embarrassed people are more generous and helpful than they would otherwise be. In a classic investigation, Robert Apsler (1975) embarrassed young adults by having them dance to recorded music and sing the "Star Spangled Banner" in front of an observer, and then, shortly thereafter, either the observer or a third person who was ostensibly unaware of the person's embarrassment asked for help with a class project. (Both the observer and the third person were part of the research team.) Embarrassed participants generously volunteered more help than did other, unembarrassed participants who had performed innocuous tasks, and they did so no matter who asked. Despite its unpleasant phenomenology, embarrassment engenders agreeable, acquiescent conduct. The flustered disorganization that can accompany embarrassment may be so complete that we occasionally behave stupidly, but "most of the time when we're embarrassed, we are contrite, humble, and eager to please" (Miller, 1996, p. 175).

Others' Reactions

We have seen that embarrassed emotion interrupts undesirable interactions with distinctive feelings of chagrin when events threaten to communicate unwanted information about us to others. In response, we may exhibit a singular physiological response that is a reliable signal of mortification and abashment, and we are likely to engage in a relatively automatic sequence of nonverbal behavior that further makes our embarrassment plain. Then, to the extent we choose a deliberate strategy of response, we are more likely than not to behave in a conciliatory, amicable, and accommodating manner. Others are likely to recognize that we are embarrassed.

How, then, are others likely to react to us? Perhaps the most remarkable aspect of embarrassment is that, despite its aversive nature, it has prosocial effects. Among adults, obvious embarrassment following a public predicament does not rouse rejection and make matters worse; instead, it ordinarily elicits empathy and support from one's witnesses. Surveys of onlookers' reactions to others' embarrassments have determined that, most of the time, audiences try to be helpful to embarrassed actors in their midst (Metts & Cupach, 1989). Their most common responses are reassurance and support in which they communicate their continued regard for, and acceptance of, the abashed actors despite the embarrassing event (saying things such as, "It's okay; don't worry about it"). They also often express empathy for the actors, suggesting that they are familiar with such predicaments and implying that they are not portentous events ("I know how you feel; it happens to me all the time").

Smiling and laughter may also occur, and these sometimes make the embarrassed actors feel even worse (Metts & Cupach, 1989). Often, however, an audience's obvious good humor reduces the actors' concerns by demonstrating that a predicament *is* a laughing matter rather than an ominous crisis. At a minimum, a lighthearted audience is unlikely to be spiteful or angry.

So, the interactive situations we encounter as adults are quite different than those we may have faced in elementary school. Fifth-graders often react to others' embarrassment with derision, but adults rarely do. The witnesses of our embarrassments are likely to be tolerant and kind, exhibiting supportive rather than rejecting behavior.

What, then, are they thinking? Are kindly audiences merely pretending to be forbearing while they privately denigrate and disparage embarrassed actors? Not at all. Remarkably, if people do transgress, others will judge them more favorably if they seem embarrassed by their misbehavior than if they remain collected and unperturbed. Gün Semin and Tony Manstead (1982) provided one of the first illustrations of this pattern when they showed young adults videotapes of a man accidentally dislodging a large stack of toilet paper rolls in a grocery store. Four different versions of events followed. In two cases, the shopper displayed evident embarrassment, whereas in the other two he did not, and (crosscutting that manipulation) he either repaired the damage by rebuilding the stack or he simply walked away. The observers respected the actors who cleaned up their messes, but they *liked* those who displayed chagrin at their awkward predicaments. The target who became embarrassed and repaired the damage was liked best, but even the fellow who just walked away in evident mortification was liked somewhat better than the one who picked up his mess with unruffled aplomb. Obvious chagrin clearly mollified the observers, who formed more favorable impressions of actors who became embarrassed than of those who remained calm.

Independently, blushing has similar ameliorative effects. Peter de Jong (1999) asked young adults to read scenarios depicting a shopper who was said either to blush or to remain cool and collected after a store mishap. Blushing mitigated the observers' disapproval, leaving audiences with the impression that the blushing actor was more trustworthy and conscientious than a target who did not blush. Importantly, the blushing actor was also believed to have more respect for the rules of common courtesy than did the unruffled actor.

Other investigations have obtained similar results. If their children seemed embarrassed after public misbehavior, for instance, parents levied less punishment than they would have inflicted if the children did not express chagrin (Semin & Papadopoulou, 1990). People who do poorly on laboratory tasks are liked better by observers when they express embarrassment about their poor performances than when they do not (Edelmann, 1982).

In fact, embarrassment seems to be such a desirable response to public predicaments that people who find themselves in embarrassing circumstances should *try* to make their embarrassment known to others – and they do. Mark Leary and his colleagues embarrassed college students by asking them to sing the soaring ballad, "Feelings," with an experimenter in the room; then, some of the students were allowed to express their embarrassment to the experimenter on an explicit questionnaire, whereas others were not. Later in the procedure, those who had informed the experimenter of their prior chagrin were no longer embarrassed, whereas those who had never communicated their abashment to their audience said they were still flustered. Once the researchers offered the participants the opportunity to make their prior embarrassment plain, the abashed singers gladly took it (Leary, Landel, & Patton, 1996).

In a second study, Leary et al. (1996) asked participants to sing "Feelings" into a tape recorder privately, but then embarrassed some of them by playing the tape. During the agonizing playback, the experimenter told some participants that they seemed to be blushing, but did not mention a blush to others. Thereafter, the participants were asked for various self-ratings, and, in an apparent effort to gain social approval, those who believed that a blush had not been noticed described themselves more positively to the experimenter than did those who believed their blushing had been evident. Without any blushing at work, the nonblushers seemed to turn to other means to avoid disapproval from their audience. In contrast, those who believed that they had visibly blushed described themselves less positively and no differently than those who had never been embarrassed in the first place; they behaved as if they understood that with a blush in place, their predicaments had been resolved.

Overall, then, the various data converge on intriguing conclusions: When we find ourselves in an embarrassing situation, "*others will like us and treat us better if we do become embarrassed* than they will if we remain unruffled, cool, and calm" (Miller, 1996, p. 152), and people behave as if they know, at some level, that it is helpful to communicate embarrassment to others after a predicament occurs. Embarrassment may be unpleasant, but it typically elicits favorable, rather than unfavorable reactions from others, quite possibly because they are reassured of an actor's good intentions when he or she is embarrassed by some misbehavior.

EMBARRASSMENT AS A GESTURE OF APPEASEMENT

Correlation does not prove causation, and although embarrassment deflects disapproval that would otherwise follow public predicaments, no one can prove that embarrassment evolved to fulfill that function. Nevertheless, nearly everything we know about the emotion is consistent with that possibility.

People are typically cowed by the threat of undesired evaluations from others when they become embarrassed. Their emotional wash of chagrin is also a guarantee that they care about others' opinions of them. In addition, the signs of embarrassment, especially blushing, are involuntary responses that cannot be feigned, so they can be taken as a reliable indication of a person's abashment and authentic regret. Indeed, theorists Cristiano Castelfranchi and Isabella Poggi (1990) have suggested that:

> Those who are blushing are somehow saying that they know, care about, and fear others' evaluations and that they share those values deeply; they also communicate their sorrow over any possible faults or inadequacies on their part, thus performing an acknowledgment, a confession, and an apology aimed at inhibiting others' aggression or avoiding social ostracism. (p. 240)

Thus, blushing and the other signals of embarrassment may plausibly operate as a trustworthy *nonverbal apology* that communicates one's genuine contrition to observers, and that is why audiences react more kindly to embarrassed actors than to cool customers after some predicament has occurred (e.g., de Jong, 1999).

Why does this pattern exist? Conceivably, as an exemplar of embarrassment, blushing came to be an interpersonal signal of chagrin, conciliation, and contrition after the facial veins developed their curious repertoire for some other reason. However, it seems more parsimonious to accept that embarrassment's unique characteristics developed because they fulfilled useful ends, as a functional account suggests. Considering embarrassment to be a *gesture of appeasement* that arose to help manage troubled social relations fits the facts nicely (Crozier, 2001; Keltner, Young, & Buswell, 1997). Indeed, human displays of embarrassment even resemble the appeasement displays of other species: The gaze aversion, sheepish grin, and lowered head of a chimpanzee that is trying to deflect the wrath of a dominant companion has much in common with embarrassment's nonverbal routine (Keltner & Buswell, 1997; Miller & Leary, 1992).

Embarrassment that follows a public predicament appears to reliably communicate a person's compliant desire to avoid rejection. Still, any gesture can be misinterpreted, and to communicate its intended meaning, embarrassed behavior may need to fit the situation in which it occurs. Exaggerated embarrassment that seems disproportionate to its circumstances may have the undesirable effect of portraying its author as inept or anxious. One such deleterious effect was illustrated by a study in which a young woman asked for help with a research project in several college classes (Levin & Arluke, 1982). In one case, she was poised as she described her project, and she distributed her sign-up sheets without incident. In contrast, in another case, she dropped her pile of sheets and gathered them up with evident embarrassment before proceeding with her appeal. Finally, in a third situation, she dropped the sheets, became flustered, and exclaimed "Oh, my god! I can't continue," before scurrying out of the room; the class's instructor then distributed the sign-up sheets for her. Interestingly, and in keeping with embarrassment's conciliatory appeal, the students offered her more help when she flubbed and then recovered than they did when a predicament did not occur. However, the students were quite unhelpful when her embarrassment caused her to flee after a relatively innocuous mistake.

So, appropriate embarrassment makes desirable impressions on onlookers, but exaggerated, overstated embarrassment may not. Embarrassed behavior communicates one's distress and regret to others, but whether that message is reassuring or exasperating probably depends on the events it follows.

CONCLUSIONS

Embarrassment is a self-conscious, social-relational emotion that springs from our concerns about what others are thinking of us (Miller, 1996). It is an unpleasant experience, but it serves useful functions, and we would be worse off without it. In particular, embarrassment is a prototypical example of the manner in which emotion can have both intrapsychic and interpersonal effects. Indeed, one can plausibly argue that, as a social mechanism in a very social species, embarrassment exists primarily to aid and abet our interactions with others.

References

Apsler, R. (1975). Effects of embarrassment on behavior toward others. *Journal of Personality and Social Psychology, 32*, 145–153.

Asendorpf, J. (1990). The expression of shyness and embarrassment. In W. R. Crozier (Ed.), *Shyness and embarrassment: Perspectives from social psychology* (pp. 87–118). Cambridge, UK: Cambridge University Press.

Baumeister, R. F., & Leary, M. R. (1995). The need to belong: Desire for interpersonal attachments as a fundamental human motivation. *Psychological Bulletin, 117*, 497–529.

Buss, A. H. (1980). *Self-consciousness and social anxiety*. San Francisco: W. H. Freeman.

Buss, A. H. (2001). *Psychological dimensions of the self*. Thousand Oaks, CA: Sage.

Castelfranchi, C., & Poggi, I. (1990). Blushing as a discourse: Was Darwin wrong? In W. R. Crozier (Ed.), *Shyness and embarrassment: Perspectives from social psychology* (pp. 230–251). Cambridge: UK: Cambridge University Press.

Cosmides, L., & Tooby, J. (2000). Evolutionary psychology and the emotions. In M. Lewis & J. M. Haviland-Jones (Eds.), *Handbook of emotions* (2nd Edition; pp. 91–115). New York: Guilford Press.

Costa, M., Dinsbach, W., Manstead, A. S. R., & Ricci-Bitti, P. E. (2001). Social presence, embarrassment, and nonverbal behavior. *Journal of Nonverbal Behavior, 25*, 225–240.

Crozier, W. R. (2001). *Understanding shyness: Psychological perspectives*. New York: Palgrave.

Cupach, W. R., & Imahori, T. T. (1993). Managing social predicaments created by others: A comparison of Japanese and American facework. *Western Journal of Communication, 57*, 431–444.

Cupach, W. R., & Metts, S. (1994). *Facework*. Thousand Oaks, CA: Sage.

de Jong, P. J. (1999). Communicative and remedial effects of social blushing. *Journal of Nonverbal Behavior, 23*, 197–217.

Drummond, P. D. (1989). Mechanism of social blushing. In N. W. Bond & D. A. T. Siddle (Eds.), *Psychobiology: Issues and applications* (pp. 363–370). Amsterdam: Elsevier Science.

Drummond, P. D. (1997). The effect of adrenergic blockade on blushing and facial flushing. *Psychophysiology, 34*, 163–168.

Drummond, P. D. (2001). The effect of true and false feedback on blushing in women. *Personality and Individual Differences, 30*, 1329–1343.

Drummond, P. D., & Lim, H. K. (2000). The significance of blushing for fair- and dark-skinned people. *Personality and Individual Differences, 29*, 1123–1132.

Edelmann, R. J. (1982). The effect of embarrassed reactions upon others. *Australian Journal of Psychology, 34*, 359–367.

Edelmann, R. J. (2001). Blushing. In W. R. Crozier & L. E. Alden (Eds.), *International handbook of social anxiety: Concepts, research and interventions relating to the self and shyness* (pp. 301–323). Chichester, UK: Wiley.

Edelmann, R. J., & Hampson, R. J. (1979). Changes in non-verbal behaviour during embarrassment. *British Journal of Social and Clinical Psychology, 18*, 385–390.

Edelmann, R. J., & Hampson, R. J. (1981). The recognition of embarrassment. *Personality and Social Psychology Bulletin, 7*, 109–116.

Eibl-Eibesfeldt, I. (1989). *Human ethology*. New York: Aldine de Gruyter.

Ekman, P. (1992). An argument for basic emotions. *Cognition and Emotion, 6*, 169–200.

Ekman, P. (1999). Basic emotions. In T. Dalgleish & M. J. Power (Eds.), *Handbook of cognition and emotion* (pp. 45–60). Chichester, UK: Wiley.

Gilbert, P., & Trower, P. (2001). Evolution and process in social anxiety. In W. R. Crozier & L. E. Alden (Eds.), *International handbook of social anxiety: Concepts, research and interventions relating to the self and shyness* (pp. 259–279). Chichester, UK: Wiley.

Gonzales, M. H. (1992). A thousand pardons: The effectiveness of verbal remedial tactics during account episodes. *Journal of Language and Social Psychology, 11*, 133–151.

Gray, J. R. (1999). A bias toward short-term thinking in threat-related negative emotional states. *Personality and Social Psychology Bulletin, 25*, 65–75.

Harris, C. R. (2001). Cardiovascular responses of embarrassment and effects of emotional suppression in a social setting. *Journal of Personality and Social Psychology, 81*, 886–897.

Hashimoto, E., & Shimizu, T. (1988). A cross-cultural study of the emotion of shame/embarrassment: Iranian and Japanese children. *Psychologia, 31*, 1–6.

Hatfield, E., & Rapson, R. L. (1990). Passionate love in intimate relationships. In B. Moore & A. Isen (Eds.), *Affect and social behavior* (pp. 126–151). Cambridge, UK: Cambridge University Press.

Hess, U., & Kirouac, G. (2000). Emotion expression in groups. In M. Lewis & J. M. Haviland-Jones (Eds.), *Handbook of emotions* (2nd Edition; pp. 368–381). New York: Guilford Press.

Izard, C. E., & Youngstrom, E. A. (1996). The activation and regulation of fear and anxiety. In D. A. Hope (Ed.), *Perspectives on anxiety, panic, and fear* (pp. 1–59). Lincoln, NE: University of Nebraska Press.

Keltner, D. (1995). Signs of appeasement: Evidence for the distinct displays of embarrassment, amusement, and shame. *Journal of Personality and Social Psychology, 68*, 441–454.

Keltner, D., & Anderson, C. (2000). Saving face for Darwin: The functions and uses of embarrassment. *Current Directions in Psychological Science, 9*, 187–192.

Keltner, D., & Buswell, B. N. (1996). Evidence for the distinctness of embarrassment, shame, and guilt: A study of recalled antecedents and facial expressions of emotion. *Cognition and Emotion, 10*, 155–171.

Keltner, D., & Buswell, B. N. (1997). Embarrassment: Its distinct form and appeasement functions. *Psychological Bulletin, 122*, 250–270.

Keltner, D., & Ekman, P. (2000). Facial expression of emotion. In M. Lewis & J. M. Haviland-Jones (Eds.), *Handbook of emotions* (2nd Edition; pp. 236–249). New York: Guilford Press.

Keltner, D., & Gross, J. J. (1999). Functional accounts of emotion. *Cognition and Emotion, 13*, 467–480.

Keltner, D., & Haidt, J. (1999). Social functions of emotion at four levels of analysis. *Cognition and Emotion, 13*, 505–521.

Keltner, D., & Haidt, J. (2001). Social functions of emotions. In T. J. Mayne & G. A. Bonanno (Eds.), *Emotions: Current issues and future directions* (pp. 192–213). New York: Guilford Press.

Keltner, D., Young, R. C., & Buswell, B. N. (1997). Appeasement in human emotion, social practice, and personality. *Aggressive Behavior, 23*, 359–374.

Kenny, D. A. (1994). *Interpersonal perception: A social relations analysis*. New York: Guilford Press.

Leary, M. R. (2000). Affect, cognition, and the social emotions. In J. P. Forgas (Ed.), *Feeling and thinking: The role of affect in social cognition* (pp. 331–356). Cambridge, UK: Cambridge University Press.

Leary, M. R., Britt, T. W., Cutlip, W. D., II, & Templeton, J. L. (1992). Social blushing. *Psychological Bulletin, 112*, 446–460.

Leary, M. R., Landel, J. L., & Patton, K. M. (1996). The motivated expression of embarrassment following a self-presentational predicament. *Journal of Personality, 64*, 619–636.

Levin, J., & Arluke, A. (1982). Embarrassment and helping behavior. *Psychological Reports, 51*, 999–1002.

Lewis, M. (2000). Self-conscious emotions: Embarrassment, pride, shame, and guilt. In M. Lewis & J. M. Haviland-Jones (Eds.), *Handbook of emotions* (2nd Edition; pp. 623–636). New York: Guilford Press.

Lewis, M., & Ramsay, D. (2002). Cortisol response to embarrassment and shame. *Child Development, 73*, 1034–1045.

Marcus, D. K., & Miller, R. S. (1999). The perception of "live" embarrassment: A social relations analysis of class presentations. *Cognition and Emotion, 13*, 105–117.

Marcus, D. K., Wilson, J. R., & Miller, R. S. (1996). Are perceptions of emotion in the eye of the beholder? A social relations analysis of embarrassment. *Personality and Social Psychology Bulletin, 22*, 1220–1228.

Mellander, S., Andersson, P., Afzelius, L., & Hellstrand, P. (1982). Neural beta-adrenergic dilatation of the facial vein in man: Possible mechanism in emotional blushing. *Acta Physiologica Scandinavia, 114*, 393–399.

Metts, S., & Cupach, W. R. (1989). Situational influence on the use of remedial strategies in embarrassing predicaments. *Communication Monographs, 56*, 151–162.

Miller, R. S. (1992). The nature and severity of self-reported embarrassing circumstances. *Personality and Social Psychology Bulletin, 18*, 190–198.

Miller, R. S. (1996). *Embarrassment: Poise and peril in everyday life* (pp. 152, 175). New York: Guilford Press.

Miller, R. S. (2001). Shyness and embarrassment compared: Siblings in the service of social evaluation. In W. R. Crozier & L. E. Alden (Eds.), *International handbook of social anxiety: Concepts, research and interventions relating to the self and shyness* (pp. 281–300). Chichester, UK: Wiley.

Miller, R. S., Bowersox, K. A., Cook, R. E., & Kahikina, C. S. (1996, April). *Responses to embarrassment*. Paper presented at the meeting of the Southwestern Psychological Association, Houston.

Miller, R. S., & Leary, M. R. (1992). Social sources and interactive functions of emotion: The case of embarrassment. In M. S. Clark (Ed.), *Review of personality and social psychology* (Vol. 14, pp. 202–221). Newbury Park, CA: Sage.

Miller, R. S., & Tangney, J. P. (1994). Differentiating embarrassment and shame. *Journal of Social and Clinical Psychology, 13*, 273–287.

Mosher, D. L., & White, B. B. (1981). On differentiating shame and shyness. *Motivation and Emotion, 5*, 61–74.

Parrott, W. G., & Smith, S. F. (1991). Embarrassment: Actual vs. typical cases, classical vs. prototypical representations. *Cognition and Emotion, 5*, 467–488.

Preuschoft, S., & van Hooff, J. A. R. A. M. (1997). The social function of "smile" and "laughter": Variations across primate species and societies. In U. Segerstrále & P. Molnár (Eds.), *Nonverbal communication: Where nature meets culture* (pp. 171–189). Mahwah, NJ: Erlbaum.

Sabini, J., Garvey, B., & Hall, A. L. (2001). Shame and embarrassment revisited. *Personality and Social Psychology Bulletin, 27*, 104–117.

Sabini, J., Siepmann, M., Stein, J., & Meyerowitz, M. (2000). Who is embarrassed by what? *Cognition and Emotion, 14*, 213–240.

Semin, G. R., & Manstead, A. S. R. (1982). The social implications of embarrassment displays and restitution behavior. *European Journal of Social Psychology, 12*, 367–377.

Semin, G. R., & Papadopoulou, K. (1990). The acquisition of reflexive social emotions: The transmission and reproduction of social control through joint action. In G. Duveen & B. Lloyd (Eds.), *Social representations and the development of knowledge* (pp. 107–125). Cambridge, UK: Cambridge University Press.

Sharkey, W. F. (1997). Why would anyone want to intentionally embarrass me? In R. M. Kowalski (Ed.), *Aversive interpersonal behaviors* (pp. 57–90). New York: Plenum.

Stattin, H., Magnusson, D., Olah, A., Kassin, H., & Reddy, N. Y. (1991). Perception of threatening consequences of anxiety-provoking situations. *Anxiety Research, 4*, 141–166.

Stonehouse, C. M., & Miller, R. S. (1994, July). *Embarrassing circumstances, week by week.* Paper presented at the meeting of the American Psychological Society, Washington, DC.

Tangney, J. P., Miller, R. S., Flicker, L., & Barlow, D. H. (1996). Are shame, guilt, and embarrassment distinct emotions? *Journal of Personality and Social Psychology, 70*, 1256–1264.

Turner, J. H. (1996). The evolution of emotions in humans: A Darwinian-Durkheimian analysis. *Journal for the Theory of Social Behavior, 26*, 1–33.

Turner, J. H. (1997). The evolution of emotions: The nonverbal basis of human social organization. In U. Segerstrále & P. Molnár (Eds.), *Nonverbal communication: Where nature meets culture* (pp. 211–223). Mahwah, NJ: Erlbaum.

5

Does Expressing Emotion Promote Well-Being? It Depends on Relationship Context

Margaret S. Clark and Eli J. Finkel

Questions concerning whether it is best to express or suppress felt emotions have long been of interest to psychologists. Is expressing pride in one's accomplishments a good thing? It does allow others to celebrate one's accomplishments, but it can lead to one being judged as arrogant. Are fears best confided to others or should they be suppressed? Expressing fears may elicit help and comfort or derision and exploitation. What will happen if one expresses sadness? Will companions express compassion and reassurance or pity and avoidance? Most generally, is expressing one's emotions good or bad for your personal well-being?

Our answer to all of these questions is, "It depends." To the extent that emotions carry information about one's needs, we argue, the wisdom of expressing them to others depends importantly, even crucially, on the relationship context within which one finds oneself. Our position is simple: Expressing emotion is likely to be beneficial in the company of others who care about one's welfare. The more companions care, the wiser expression of emotion is likely to be. Such expressions are more likely to be accepted, elicit care, and maintain or strengthen the caring relationship. In sharp contrast, if one finds oneself with companions who do not care about one's welfare, it is generally unwise to express emotions indicative of one's needs. At best, the expressions will be ignored; at worst, one may be avoided, derided, or exploited.

In this chapter, we review evidence supporting these claims. First, we make a theoretical case that expressing emotions – such as fear, sadness, happiness, and pride – is less risky and more beneficial in communal relationships (in which partners assume responsibility for one's welfare and provide benefits noncontingently) than in other relationships. Second, we review empirical evidence that, indeed, emotions are more often expressed when people perceive their partner to have a communal relationship with them than when they do not hold this perception. Third, we make a theoretical and empirical case that expressing emotion in communal contexts will produce a host of social, cognitive, and physiological benefits that are unlikely to accrue when emotion is expressed in noncommunal contexts.

A THEORETICAL CASE THAT PEOPLE SELECTIVELY EXPRESS EMOTION IN COMMUNAL RELATIONSHIPS

Our argument that it is wiser to express emotion in communal relationships than in other relationships is based on two assumptions. First, expressing most emotions conveys information about one's current need state (or lack thereof) to the target of the expression. Second, any given person's relationships with other people vary in terms of the extent to which the relationship partner assumes responsibility for that person's needs.

Expressed Emotion Conveys Information About Our Needs

Emotion researchers have long recognized that emotion, as experienced internally, communicates information to oneself. Negative emotions generally indicate that one has a need. They cause a person to pause and attend to that need (Frijda, 1993; Simon, 1967). The novice skier who takes a wrong turn and finds herself staring down an extremely steep and icy slope, for instance, is likely to feel fear. The fear is a signal that she has a need for safety and that she ought not ski down the slope. Positive emotions indicate that one's needs have been met and that an activity ought to be continued. For instance, the warm contentment a child feels as his mother reads him a picture book signals the child that being with his mom and reading books are good. Positive emotions can also encourage a person to try new things and to explore his or her environment (Frederickson, 1998).

However, emotions are not entirely private affairs. They can be perceived on one's face (Keltner et al., 2003), in one's tone of voice (Scherer, Johnstone, & Klasmeyer, 2003), and in one's posture (Riskind, 1984). In addition, of course, people often verbalize their emotions (Reilly & Seibert, 2003). Some have noted that such outward expression of emotion is adaptive because it conveys to others that they may share the same need (or opportunity to have a need be met) as the emotional other (Levenson, 1994). For instance, a skier's fearful facial expression may alert other skiers to the steep slope ahead, and a toddler's giggles may alert siblings that whatever is going on is enjoyable and prompt them to join the fun.

We would agree. However, we suggest that an additional and perhaps more important function of emotion expression is to communicate information about a person's welfare *to others*, thereby enabling and encouraging those others to attend and respond to the person's need states. For instance, the fearful skier's facial expression can summon reassurance from a companion, a toddler's giggles encourage his mom to keep reading to him, and, of course, an infant's cries of distress cause parents to come running.

Relationships Vary in Communal Strength

We refer to the degree to which one person assumes responsibility for another's welfare and will benefit that other noncontingently as the *communal strength* of a relationship (Clark & Mills, 1993; Mills & Clark, 1982; Mills et al. in press). That people perceive certain relationship partners to be more concerned with their welfare than other relationship partners is obvious. Most people, for instance, perceive their mothers to be more concerned about their welfare than, say, an acquaintance at work.

There are two determinants of perceiving that any particular relationship partner will or will not assume communal responsibility for our needs. One is obvious: Some partners really are more responsive to our needs than are others. It is wise to express emotion to these people. The other determinant lies in our own personality rather than in the reality of a partner's caring. Even when partners do care, many studies have shown that certain people may not perceive that care. Such people have been variously labeled as insecure (Ainsworth et al., 1978), rejection sensitive (Downey & Feldman, 1996), or low in self-esteem (Murray et al., 1998). These people are undoubtedly overrepresented among those who are chronically low in communal orientation (Clark, Ouellette, Powell, & Milberg, 1987) or low in perceived social support (Cutrona & Russell, 1987). These people tend not to express emotion even when partners do care (i.e., even when it would be wise to express emotion).

People Should Selectively Express Emotions Indicative of Their Needs to Those Who Care About Those Needs

Putting the assertion that expressions of emotions convey information about our needs to relationship partners, together with the assertion that a person's relationship partners vary in the extent to which they care about the person's needs, leads to the conclusion that people should selectively express emotions to communal partners. The stronger the relationship, the more emotion it makes sense to express. It is within communal relationships that partners are most likely to react positively to such expressions (Clark & Taraban, 1991), attend to the needs that are conveyed (Clark, Mills, & Powell, 1986; Clark, Mills, & Corcoran, 1989), provide support in response to the needs (Clark et al., 1987), and feel good about helping (Williamson & Clark, 1989, 1992). It is also within communal relationships that people expect partners to respond to their needs (Clark, Dubash, & Mills, 1998).

Relationship Type:
Does the Partner Actually *Behave* Communally Toward the Individual?

Personality: Does the Individual *Perceive* that Others Care About His or Her Needs?	Yes	No
Yes	High	Low
No	Low	Low

FIGURE 5.1. Emotion expression as a function of relationship type and personality.

In contrast, it ordinarily makes little sense to express emotions revealing one's needs outside the context of communal relationships. At best, the other will ignore one's needs. At worst, the other will exploit one by taking advantage of the vulnerabilities revealed. Consider, for example, a child who has been teased by peers and is distressed. Should he display this distress? Our analysis suggests that the answer is "yes," if the other cares about his welfare and "no" otherwise. The child would be wise to express the distress to a caring parent who is likely to react with comfort, reassurance, and advice, but unwise to reveal the distress to the taunting peers who may redouble their taunting as a result of knowing that they can get a reaction from him.

When Will People Express Emotion?

We have just argued that expression of emotion should be highest in normatively strong communal relationships. But will it be? Not necessarily. It is the *perception* of such responsiveness that will guide a person's emotion expression. It is important to keep in mind that some people are chronically low in perceiving that partners care (even when partners *do* care).

Given this, we suspect that a partner's actual communal orientation will combine with a person's chronic tendency to believe that close partners care to determine expression of emotion. In Figure 5.1, the type of relationship a partner actually has with a person (communal or not) is crossed with that person's chronic beliefs that "close" others care or do not care, thus creating four cells. We predict that expressions of emotion indicative of one's needs

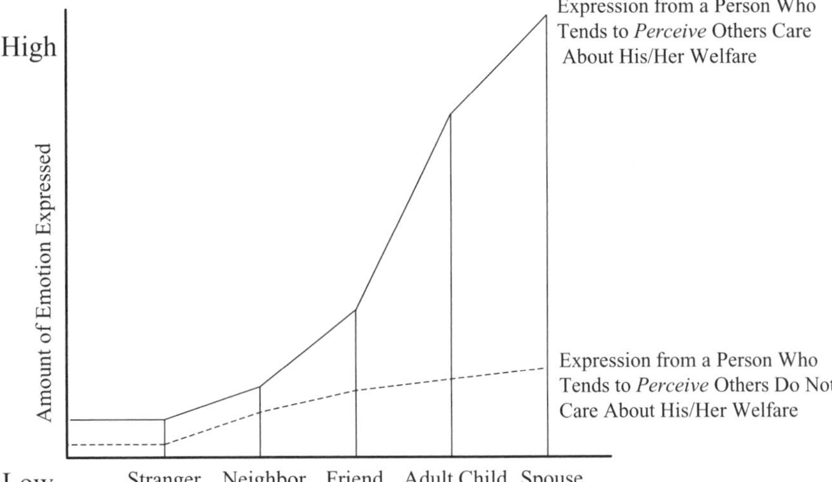

FIGURE 5.2. Two hypothetical people's level of emotion expression as a function of the degree to which various members of their social network care about their welfare. [For this figure, we assume that the amount that others actually care about their welfare increases from left (stranger) to right (spouse).]

are likely to be high (and to seem adaptive to the expresser) in just one cell – that in which people who have a chronic tendency to perceive that intimate partners do care are paired with partners who actually do care for them (e.g., friends, romantic partners, family members) (M. S. Clark & E. J. Finkel, in press). In all other cells, emotion expression should be low.

Having presented Figure 5.1, we hasten to add that it is too simple. Any given relationship is not simply "communal" or "not communal" in nature. Rather, communal relationships vary in strength. To some (small) extent, individuals expect communal behavior even from strangers. For instance, most people expect that even complete strangers would tell them the time without expecting compensation. Thus, to a very limited extent, we argue, it is perfectly appropriate to express emotion to strangers; it is appropriate as long as the expressed emotion does not call for them to be more than very mildly responsive to our needs. For instance, it seems fine to express mild annoyance regarding the weather to a stranger at a bus stop (because a sympathetic nod or comment is all that is expected). Other communal relationships are much stronger (e.g., ones with friends), and still others are very strong (e.g., ones with parents and spouses). The stronger the communal relationship, the more appropriate and common will be emotion expression conveying greater needs.

Given continuous variation in people's general tendencies to perceive that partners care, as well as in the actual strength of communal relationships, these two variables probably combine to influence emotion expression in something like the way depicted in Figure 5.2. In this figure, perceptions that others care are depicted along the y-axis running from low to high. A hypothetical hierarchy of communal relationships (from weak to strong) is depicted along the x-axis. The solid line running through the figure depicts the extent to which a person high in the chronic tendency to believe others care does believe that particular members of his or her network care. The area under that solid curve represents the situations in which that person is likely to express emotion indicative of his own needs. The dashed line running through the figure depicts the extent to which a person low in the chronic tendency to believe others care does believe that particular members of his or her network care. The much smaller area under that dashed curve represents the situations in which that person is likely to express emotion indicative of his own needs.

Strategic Emotion Expression

To this point, we have discussed when people are and are not likely to express the emotions they feel. It is worth noting that our analysis suggests that people can use emotion expression strategically. As one example, within relationships a person perceives to be communal, that person may exaggerate his needs in the hope of unfairly garnering greater support or getting out of some undesired task (Mills & Clark, 1986). For example, people may strategically express more sadness or distress than they are experiencing when in the presence of a communal partner in the hopes of receiving support, getting out of an undesired task, or being reassured that their relationship really is communal. They do so precisely because the other is likely to care. Others have noted the existence of such strategies as well, suggesting that "acting like one is in a bad mood can cause one to obtain desirable attention from others, as well as sympathy, aid and exemption from normal duties" (Parrott, 1993, p. 294; see also Hill, Weary, & Williams, 1986). Even quite young children seem to know they can gain assistance by strategically expressing sadness (Zeman & Shipman, 1996).

A second type of strategic emotion expression may be used when one does not presently have a communal relationship with a given person, but desires to have one and suspects that the other shares that desire. In such a case, expressing emotion may be risky but fruitful. Imagine, for instance, a new college student who knows no one on campus and is lonely. She expresses sadness to another student who is also new at the university and also interested in forming relationships. Her expression communicates her willingness to trust in the other student, suggests a desire for a new friendship, and sets the stage for the other to respond with sympathy and support. The other may avoid her; but, in this case, it is reasonable to suspect the other may respond in kind, and a new communal relationship may be formed. Indeed, we believe willingness to express appropriate amounts of emotions in such situations is a social skill that will enable people to form new communal relationships and to strengthen existing ones. Indeed, in a recent study, Clark, Graham, & Helgeson (2003) revealed that greater willingness to express emotions (as measured in students prior to their arrival as freshmen at a residential college) predicted the formation of more friendships and romantic relationships over college students' first semester at a residential university, and greater intimacy in the closest of those relationships, corroborated by their roommates' independent reports of providing those students with support.

EMPIRICAL EVIDENCE SUGGESTING THAT INDIVIDUALS SELECTIVELY EXPRESS EMOTION TO COMMUNAL OTHERS

Having made a case that more emotion ought to be expressed the more communal a relationship is, we turn to the considerable evidence supporting our contention. For instance, Pennebaker, Zech, and Rimé (2001) report having used several techniques (e.g., retrospective reports, diaries, emotion inductions, and observations of social sharing) to tap the extent to which people talk about their emotions (e.g., joy, anger, and fear) to various relationship partners. They found that sharing of emotion-eliciting experiences occurred frequently, but was directed selectively to "parents or close family members, best friends, and/or spouse or companion" – relationships we judge to be normatively communal in nature. Emotion was rarely disclosed to people who did not belong to these circles (see also Fitness, 2000; Rimé et al., 1998; Rimé et al., 1991).

Additional support for the idea that people selectively express emotions to communal partners comes from a study by I. Brissette and M. S. Clark (unpublished data). These researchers examined whether the extent to which people expressed emotion to others varied according to the extent to which those people felt these relationships were communal in nature. Participants rated the communal strength of a variety of their relationships (e.g., relationships with their mother, their father, a specific casual friend, a sibling, their boss, their professor, their cousin, their roommate), with communal strength defined as the extent to which the other person is willing to respond noncontingently to the participant's need. Next, on separate scales, participants rated their willingness to express happiness, contentment, hurt, sadness, anger, disgust, guilt, and fear to each of these partners (both when the emotion was caused by the particular other and when it was caused by someone or something else). As predicted, the within-subject correlations between each person's ratings of how communal their relationships were and their willingness to express each of the sixteen emotions within the relationship were all positive (ranging from +.23 to

+.57). Moreover, all were significant, with the exception of correlations between how communal one's relationship was and willingness to express anger and disgust when those emotions were caused by the partner. (Those two correlations may not have reached significance, because communal relationships are often mutual and expressing anger or disgust caused by a communal partner not only expresses one's own needs, but also may simultaneously interfere with the other person's needs.)

In the individual differences literature, there is also evidence for people expressing more emotion indicative of their own needs within relationships they perceive to be communal. J. A. Feeney (1995), for example, examined links between attachment styles and expression of emotion within dating relationships. She had members of dating couples complete an attachment measure, as well as a measure of emotional control. (The latter was completed with regard to emotions experienced in relation to their dating partner.) The scale tapped willingness to express/suppress anger, sadness, and anxiety. For our purposes, the interesting finding is that secure people were less likely to suppress expressions of emotion than were avoidant people. That is, the more securely attached members of couples were, male or female, the less likely they were to report suppressing anxiety and sadness. In addition, the more securely attached females (but not males) were, the less they suppressed anger. Importantly, these associations remained significant after controlling for the reported frequency of the emotion in question being experienced.

Similar results were obtained in a subsequent study reported by J. A. Feeney (1999), this time with married couples. In this study, attachment styles were used to predict expressions of anger, sadness, anxiety, happiness, love, and pride to the partner – both when these emotions were caused by the partner and when they were caused by something not involving the partner. More secure spouses reported less of a tendency to control/suppress each of these emotions, regardless of the cause (with the exception of wives' willingness to express partner-related pride). Again, all correlations remained significant after controlling for the frequency and intensity of these emotions (with the exception of wives' willingness to express partner-related love). In no case were the correlations reversed from what we would expect, given our theoretical position.

Other work supporting the idea that perceiving one's partner cares will be associated with greater expressions of emotions has been reported by R. L. Collins and DiPaula (R. L. Collins, 1994; R. L. Collins & DiPaula, 1997). These researchers had HIV-positive men fill out a perceived social support questionnaire with regard to five members of their close social network and also a "ways of coping index," which tapped their tendency to suppress the expression of distress when in the presence of others. Consistent with our analysis, after controlling for physical health, these authors observed a significant negative correlation between the average level of support the men perceived they had and their reported tendency to suppress distress.

Finally, a recent study by Clark and Finkel (in press) provides some evidence supporting all three of our postulates, namely that: (a) being in the context of a normatively communal relationship promotes expression of emotion, (b) being high in the tendency to trust others promotes expression of emotion, and, importantly, (c) that relationship context and personality variables related to trusting may *interact* to produce the highest levels of expressing emotions indicating that one has a need (as suggested by Figures 5.1 and 5.2). In this study participants filled out a measure of communal orientation and also provided reports on the extent to which they would express fear, anxiety, anger, happiness, and joy within a business relationship and within a close relationship. People were significantly more likely to say they would express all five emotions within a close relationship other than to someone with whom they did business. In addition, people high in communal orientation (an indicator of trust in partners' caring) were more likely to say they would express all five emotions than were those low in communal orientation. Importantly, for fear and anxiety (the two emotions of these five that indicate the most personal need and vulnerability), relationship context and communal orientation interacted in just the manner suggested in our figures. That is, within a business relationship (in which expressing emotion is normatively inappropriate) stated willingness to express fear and anxiety was not only very low, communal orientation did not make a difference. However, when participants were asked about willingness to express emotion within a close relationship in which such expressions are normatively appropriate, communal orientation made a difference. People high in communal orientation (who presumably are high in trust that others care) reported being significantly more willing to express these emotions than did people low in communal orientation (who presumably have lower trust that others care).

EXPRESSING EMOTION WITHIN COMMUNAL RELATIONSHIPS PRODUCES A HOST OF SOCIAL, COGNITIVE, AND PHYSIOLOGICAL BENEFITS

Thus far, we have argued that emotions carrying information about our welfare will most often be expressed to partners whom we perceive as being responsive to our needs. We now make a case that people who do express emotion in these contexts will reap many social, cognitive, and physiological benefits, whereas those who express emotion outside the context of communal relationships will suffer costs (Finkel & Clark, 2003). We make a theoretical case for these views and present empirical evidence as it is available. We note at the outset that there is not good empirical evidence for all the theoretical points we will make.

Does Expressing Emotion Produce Social Benefits? Yes, But Primarily Within Communal Relationships

The most straightforward benefit of expressing need-indicative emotions to those with whom one has a communal relationship is that the other person is likely to respond with social support. In line with this notion are studies such as one reported by Shimanoff (1988) involving married couples. Shimanoff found that, when spouses examined messages from their mates, messages including expressions of negative emotions, disclosures of vulnerabilities, and hostilities toward persons other than the spouse promoted more supportive responses than did messages that lacked these emotional contents. In addition, developmentalists have long noted that infants' and children's cries of distress elicit care from most mothers (Ainsworth et al., 1978).

Notably, this work involved people in normatively strong communal relationships (spouses, mothers and their children). Is there evidence that these benefits are limited to expressing emotions to others who care for us? There is some. For instance, women's weeping at work apparently elicits embarrassment for the women and confusion and even anger from their co-workers (Hoover-Dempsey, Plas, & Strudler-Wallston, 1986). Moreover, individuals' expression of negative emotions causes people who do not know them and/or do not wish to form close relationships with them to dislike them and to judge them to be unsociable and unpopular (Sommers, 1984).

Of course, the best evidence for the proposition that expressed emotion will be met with support within communal (but not within noncommunal) relationships would come from a study in which equivalent emotion is expressed both to a person who desires a communal relationship with the expresser and one who does not, and in which resulting support (or lack thereof) is observed. Such evidence emerges from an experimental study reported by Clark et al. (1987). In this study, participants were led to desire a communal or a noncommunal relationship with a confederate. In addition, participants were led to believe that the confederate was feeling sad (or not). Finally, all participants were given an opportunity to help the confederate. Not surprisingly, participants helped the other significantly more in the communal than in the noncommunal conditions. Most pertinent to the present point, however, is how the confederate's sadness influenced the amount of help that the confederate received. In the communal condition, the confederate's sadness significantly increased the amount of help participants provided. In fact, it doubled this help. In the noncommunal condition, in sharp contrast, the confederate's sadness had no effect on the participant's helping. (In this study, there was a "floor effect" on helping. Almost no helping was given in the neutral mood condition, and helping actually went down a little bit in the sad condition but did not have room to drop significantly. In actual social situations, we suspect that a noncommunal other's sadness might actually lead to avoidance of that person.)

If one assumes that securely attached individuals possess more caring, attentive communal attitudes toward their partners (meaning that they are more likely to assume communal responsibility for the partner's welfare) than are avoidant individuals – an assumption for which there is considerable evidence (N. L. Collins & Read, 1990; Crowell & Feldman, 1988; Kunce & Shaver, 1994) – then two additional studies support the point that expressing emotion leads to support in communal, but not in other, relationships. In one study reported by Simpson, Rholes, and Nelligan (1992), women expected that they (but not their spouses) would soon be experiencing a stressful laboratory experience. Among women with securely attached, caring, spouses, those who expressed greater anxiety received greater reassurance, emotional support, and helpful comments from that secure, caring, spouse. In sharp contrast, among women with avoidant, less caring husbands, those who expressed greater anxiety actually received fewer supportive comments. Analogous results also have been obtained by B. C. Feeney & N. L. Collins (2001), who found that, when secure individuals received a note from their partner indicating greater distress, they responded with more supportive comments. Avoidant individuals, in contrast, reacted to greater expressions of distress with fewer supportive comments.

These studies, taken together, suggest that expressing emotion (at least sadness and anxiety and distress) is wise, in that it will elicit social support, at least in existing communal relationships or to partners who desire communal relationships. However, it is less wise to express emotion to noncommunal partners because they do not wish to have a communally oriented relationship with one or because their personality is such that they are not communally oriented even when the situation calls for it. Expressing emotion to such partners actually may result in obtaining *less* support.

Although receipt of help is the most straightforward social benefit of expressing emotion to communal others, we suggest that the interpersonal benefits of expressing emotion to communal partners are unlikely to stop there. Expression of emotion is likely to strengthen communal relationships through a cascade of intra- and interpersonal processes. For example, through self-perception processes (Bem, 1972), the person expressing emotion is likely to conclude that he or she trusts the other and is willing to be dependent on the other. In addition, simply by being the target of expressed emotion, the partner is likely to feel trusted and to see him or herself as a person on whom the other depends. Both feelings and senses are, in our view, crucial to strengthening communal relationships and may be why expression of positive emotion and disclosure of negative emotion are linked with greater perceived intimacy in daily interactions (Lippert & Prager, 2001).

In addition, both social and developmental psychologists have suggested that expressing emotion in a social context often results in partners "catching" the emotion (Hatfield, Cacioppo, & Rapson, 1991; Hoffman, 1984) – a process that may lead to or heighten feelings of empathy, which, in turn, should result in the person feeling the empathy perceiving that he or she really does care about the emotional person (cf. Batson, Turk, Shaw, & Klein, 1995; Mills, Jellison, & Kennedy, 1976). Moreover, assuming the empathy is openly expressed, perceiving expressions of empathy should cue the person who had initially expressed emotion to feel cared for as well. Of course, empathy itself promotes helping (Batson, 1991; Eisenberg & Fabes, 1990) and any boost in helping due to felt empathy ought also to strengthen the communal relationship (Batson et al., 1995).

In sum, emotion expression to a person who is communally oriented toward one is likely to promote a cascade of empathy, care, perceptions of being trusted and caring (in the target of the expressed emotion), perceptions of trusting the other, being willing to be dependent on the other, and being cared for by the other (in the person who has expressed the emotion). In contrast, expression of emotion to a noncommunally oriented person is not likely to have these salubrious consequences. Instead, it may lead to a withdrawal of support and avoidance or, worse, rejection and dislike (in the target of the expressed emotion), and hurt feelings and regret (in the person who has expressed the emotion).

Does Expressing Emotion Produce Cognitive Benefits? Yes, and Perhaps Primarily Within the Context of Communal Relationships

We have noted that expressing emotion to a communal partner produces social benefits – benefits that are not apparent when emotion is expressed within other relationships. In this section, we briefly review evidence that, once emotions are experienced, expressing (and not suppressing) these emotions will also produce cognitive benefits. Given evidence that felt emotion is most commonly expressed (and least often suppressed) within communal relationships, it follows logically that these benefits are most likely to accrue within communal relationships.

What evidence exists for cognitive benefits of expressing rather than suppressing emotion? First, consider evidence that being asked to suppress emotion (relative to feeling free to express it) can impair memory. In one recent study, participants were either instructed to inhibit any emotion expression while watching an upsetting film or they received no emotion-regulation instructions (Richards & Gross, 2000, Study 1). Participants who suppressed their feelings later exhibited poorer memory for the film's auditory and visual details than did participants who simply watched the film. A follow-up study in the same article provides evidence that emotion suppression leads to cognitive self-monitoring strategies (e.g., subvocalizations). Presumably, this ensures that the emotion is suppressed. These strategies, in turn, however, may interfere with encoding new information.

These studies involved comparisons of the memory performances of those who have suppressed their emotions with those who have expressed their emotions. Studies have also compared memory performance among those who have been induced to *express* their emotions to those who have not received such instructions. In one study, researchers compared a group of participants who wrote on three consecutive days either about their emotions associated with coming to college or about a trivial topic (Klein & Boals, 2001). Working memory was assessed three times over the ensuing seven to eight weeks. Relative to participants who wrote about trivial topics, those who wrote about their emotions exhibited greater improvements in working memory seven to eight weeks later.

Why did this happen? Klein (2002) believes expressing emotion promotes the formation of coherent memory structures about the emotional events, particularly when causal words (such as "because" and "cause," and insight words such as "realize" and "understand") are used (Klein & Boals, 2001). Because emotional memories are often stored as fragmented and poorly organized cognitive structures (Foa & Kozak, 1986), they can remain very accessible and difficult to suppress. Such memories are likely to continue to intrude into consciousness until they are integrated into a schematic representation (Horowitz, 1975). These emotional memories either intrude into awareness or must be suppressed, the latter of which consumes limited cognitive resources (cf. Wegner, 1994). Such intrusive thoughts and efforts to suppress them then results in inefficient allocation of working memory resources and, ultimately, impaired reasoning and problem solving. Emotion expression may facilitate narrative development, allowing the emotion-eliciting event to be "summarized, stored and forgotten more efficiently" (Pennebaker & Seagal, 1999, p. 1248).

Indeed, there is evidence that forming a narrative of emotional events is an adaptive coping strategy (Frankl, 1955/1984; Horowitz, 1979; Janoff-Bulman, 1992; Silver & Wortman, 1980). Moreover, research investigating how people cope with emotional life events supports the idea that expressing emotion fosters insight and cognitive closure, thereby reducing demands on the cognitive system (e.g., Pennebaker, 1993; Pennebaker, Mayne, & Francis, 1997). Results from one study found that incest survivors who had at least one confidant were more likely to have made sense of their victimization than were those who had no confidants (Silver, Boon, & Stones, 1983). In fact, those participants who had *never* disclosed their incest experience were incapable of forming a coherent narrative thereof.

We have already noted that precisely because emotion appears to be selectively expressed within the context of communal relationships, the intrapersonal memory benefits of doing so ought to accrue in such relationships. Beyond this, we strongly suspect that expressing emotion to a communally oriented other will set in motion some interpersonal processes that will result in even bigger cognitive benefits than would have occurred if, say, the person merely expressed emotion in journal writing.

Here are the reasons why. First, when one talks to another person, that partner will send signals as to whether or not he or she comprehends what is being said. These signals will prompt the expresser to use coherent language and logical reasoning so that the partner can then understand. Moreover, and very importantly, an involved, communally minded listener is likely to help the individual construct a narrative by asking constructive questions ("Why do you think you feel that way?"), providing insights ("I think he does that because he's insecure – it probably has nothing to do with you."), or providing reasons why it might make sense to put the issue in the past and move on ("Why worry about it? You'll never see him again.") (cf. L. F. Clark, 1993). Thus, the cognitive benefits of expressing emotion should be more likely to accrue within communal than within noncommunal relationships not only because emotion expression occurs most often in such relationships, but also because it is primarily within such relationships that partners are likely to assist the individual in forming a coherent narrative. By forming such a narrative, rumination and the continued need to suppress the emotion are reduced.

What about the cognitive benefits (or lack thereof) of expressing emotion in noncommunal relationships? We have suggested that because emotion is less commonly expressed and more commonly suppressed in noncommunal relationships, such benefits will be uncommon in noncommunal relationships. But what happens when people *do* express emotion in such relationships? We believe that others almost certainly will not assist the person in analyzing the emotional experience, coming to an understanding of it, or putting it in the past. Instead, we think expressions of emotion indicative of one's own needs to noncommunal others will often create awkward social situations, which may well exacerbate cognitive problems with memory, intrusive thoughts, and rumination. Such expression may make such problems worse because it will add social problems (in addition to emotional reactions to those problems and the need to suppress those emotional reactions) to whatever needs the person expressing the emotion already had. For example, imagine a person who is interviewing for a job. He is nervous and fearful. Expressing that nervousness and fear to a friend ahead of time may be quite useful for all the reasons we have already discussed, but what if he expresses the nervousness and fear to the interviewer? The interviewer is not responsible for those needs. She may look surprised. She may end the interview abruptly. A likely consequence is that the person's fear and nervousness will be increased, leading to even less attention being available to encode information from the environment.

Intrusive thoughts may actually increase ("I can't believe I told her I was nervous!"), and more rumination is likely to take place.

Does Emotion Expression Produce Physiological Benefits? Yes, and Perhaps Primarily Within Communal Relationships

Beyond the social and cognitive benefits of expressing emotion to others, we also believe there are physiological benefits to expressing emotion. Moreover, we suspect that such physiological benefits occur primarily when emotion is expressed to communal partners. As with demonstrations of cognitive benefits to expressing emotion, those who have done research on the physiological benefits of expressing emotion have tended not to take relationship type into account. Thus, we first review some of the evidence that expressing emotion produces physiological benefits. Then, we will comment on why we suggest that these benefits ought to be most likely in communal relationships.

Generally speaking, evidence that expressing emotion produces physiological benefits falls within one of two categories. First, there is evidence that suppressing emotion, once it is felt, may result in immune system suppression. Second, there is evidence that suppressing emotion, once it is felt, may result in sustained physiological responding that exceeds metabolic demands.

Consider first the effects of emotion expression versus suppression on immune functioning. Petrie et al. (1995) have found that people who are asked to write (in private) about the most traumatic and upsetting experiences in their lives exhibited increased antibody levels over time relative to people who wrote about trivial topics. Work from the same laboratory revealed that participants assigned to write about traumas also exhibited lower CD4, CD8, and total lymphocyte numbers relative to control participants, although several other blood cell markers did not differ across experimental condition (Booth, Petrie, & Pennebaker, 1997). Researchers from an independent laboratory have examined the effects of both individual differences in tendencies to express emotion and experimentally induced expressive tendencies on participants' control of latent Epstein-Barr virus (EBV). One study revealed that people high in dispositional tendency to be emotionally expressive not only wrote especially emotional essays in a laboratory context, but they also exhibited lower antibody titer to EBV (signifying effective immune control of this latent viral infection) relative to people who were not as emotionally expressive. Another study used an experimental design in which participants were randomly assigned to write or to talk about emotion-eliciting events or to write about trivial topics. Those who talked about emotion-eliciting events exhibited the lowest EBV titer afterward, followed by those who wrote about emotional events, followed by those who wrote about trivial events (Esterling et al., 1994).

Other research suggests that suppressing emotion may result in sustained physiological responding that exceeds metabolic demands (e.g., Pennebaker, 1989). One marker of physiological activation that has been linked with expression of emotion is skin conductance levels (SCLs). Skin conductance provides an index of sympathetic activity (Dawson, Schell, & Filion, 2000). Suppression of emotion has been linked with higher SCLs, suggesting that when one suppresses emotion (relative to expressing it), general sympathetic arousal is higher (Gross & Levenson, 1993, 1997; Pennebaker, Hughes, & O'Heeron, 1987; Petrie et al., 1995). Gross and Levenson (1993), for example, either instructed participants to suppress emotional reactions to a disgust-eliciting film or gave participants no instructions in this regard. Ratings of participants' body movement revealed that the suppression subjects were able to mask their behavioral emotion expressions relative to control subjects. However, it appeared that they paid a price: They exhibited higher SCLs than those who were permitted to express their disgust.

Finally, we note some evidence that expressing high-intensity emotion, given that the emotion is felt, is linked with lower blood pressure than is suppressing emotion. For example, in one study among people who experienced their work environment as hostile and tense, those who held their emotions in experienced higher blood pressure than did those who did not (Julkunen, 1996). Another study revealed that high levels of both job stress and anger suppression interacted to predict hypertension (Cottington et al., 1986). More generally, a meta-analytic review of research in this area revealed that the combination of experiencing high levels of emotion and suppressing it results in higher levels of blood pressure (Jorgensen et al., 1996).

As noted, researchers who have linked emotion suppression versus expression to immune functioning, skin conductance, and blood pressure have not simultaneously focused on relationship context. However, because most people suppress expression of emotion outside the context of communal relationships and express emotion within the context of communal relationships, physiological benefits of expressing emotion ought to accrue most often when people are with partners who care about them. Beyond this, we also note that if emotion expression indicative of one's needs were to take place with a person who does not assume a commensurate degree of responsibility for one's welfare, we suspect the same physiological benefits would not accrue. Our reasoning parallels our analysis of why cognitive benefits would be similarly unlikely in such a circumstance. Whereas expressing emotion to another who cares about one's welfare should be both nonthreatening (as the other will not hurt one) and soothing (as one transfers some of one's concerns and needs to the other, allowing that other to assume some of the worry and receiving comfort and support in return), expressing emotion to a noncommunal is unlikely to be soothing. The other is unlikely to assume some of one's concern and help. Instead, the other may think less of one or even take advantage of one's emotions. Regretting one's expression of emotions, believing that others think less of one, and/or being exploited may, in turn, elicit increased rather than decreased physiological activation.

Imagine the difference between the child who is teased on the playground expressing distress to her parent versus expressing distress to a peer acquaintance in the classroom. The caring parent is likely to soothe the child, hug her, assure her of her own worth (and the other child's shortcomings), and even assume some of the worry of monitoring the situation. The child's physiological activation should drop. In contrast, after revealing her distress to noncaring peer acquaintance, the peer may simply shrug her shoulders and do nothing to comfort or reassure the child. Worse yet, the peer may join in the teasing. Either or both consequences may cause the child to regret revealing her distress and may ultimately heighten rather than diminish physiological activation.

CONCLUSIONS

At the start of this chapter, we asked whether it is better to express emotions or to suppress them. In the past, most researchers have addressed this question without taking the social context into account. We think this has been a mistake, for emotion expression is fundamentally social (Clark, 2002). It conveys to others both our needs and our vulnerabilities, and it is important to take this context into account when deciding whether to express one's emotions or not.

It is often wise, we have argued, to express emotion to others who assume communal responsibility for one's needs. These others are likely to focus on what the emotion indicates about one's needs and to respond to those needs. Expressing (rather than suppressing) emotions in such a context likely produces a cascade of positive social, cognitive, and physiological consequences. We have reviewed evidence that people do selectively express emotion in communal contexts and that doing so does benefit them. Sadly, we have noted, there are some people who are unlikely to take advantage of the benefits of expressing emotion to communal partners. These are people who are not confident that even the seemingly closest partners care about their welfare (e.g., people who are high in rejection sensitivity or people characterized by avoidant attachment).

It is typically unwise, we have further argued, to express emotion indicative of one's needs in noncommunal relationships. Instead, it may be best to suppress these emotions. We believe this is true despite the fact that suppressing emotion has been shown to produce some cognitive and physiological costs. The reason why is that noncommunal others are unlikely to respond helpfully to our needs and may even exploit our vulnerabilities. As a result, expressing emotion in a noncommunal context may produce: (a) social, cognitive, and physiological costs that exceed the costs of suppressing the emotion, along with (b) few of the social, cognitive, and physiological benefits that typically follow from expressing emotion in communal contexts.

There are good reasons why humans have the abilities to: (a) express emotion conveying their needs to others, (b) suppress or override emotion expressions, and (c) distinguish between relationship contexts in which others care about their well-being. Optimally, people have relationships with others who assume communal responsibility for them; they trust those others, and they are willing to express emotion to those others. Optimally, such people typically suppress the expression of emotion conveying their needs outside the context of their supportive (or potentially supportive) relationships. People who have strong communal relationships and who also match their emotion expression according to relationship context, should, over time, reap many benefits of expressing emotion, avoid most costs of doing so, and minimize costs associated with suppressing emotion.

References

Ainsworth, M. D., Blehar, M. C., Waters, E., & Wall, S. (1978). *Patterns of attachment: Assessed in the strange situation and at home*. Hillsdale, NJ: Lawrence Erlbaum Associates.

Batson, C. D. (1991). *The altruism question: Toward a social-psychological answer*. Hillsdale, NJ: Erlbaum.

Batson, C. D., Turk, C. L., Shaw, L. L., & Klein, T. R. (1995). Information function of empathic emotion: Learning that we value the other's welfare. *Journal of Personality and Social Psychology, 68*, 300–313.

Bem, D. J. (1972). Self-perception theory. In L. Berkowitz (Ed.), *Advances in experimental social psychology* (Vol. 6; pp. 1–62). New York: Academic Press.

Booth, R. J., Petrie, K. J., & Pennebaker, J. W. (1997). Changes in circulating lymphocyte numbers following emotional disclosure: Evidence of buffering? *Stress Medicine, 13*, 23–29.

Clark, L. F. (1993). Stress and the cognitive-conversational benefits of social interaction. *Journal of Social and Clinical Psychology, 12*, 325–355.

Clark, M. S. (2002). We should focus on interpersonal as well as intrapersonal processes in our search for how affect influences judgments and behavior. *Psychological Inquiry, 13*, 32–36.

Clark, M. S., Dubash, P., & Mills, J. (1998). Interest in another's consideration of one's needs in communal and exchange relationships. *Journal of Experimental Social Psychology, 34*, 246–264.

Clark, M. S., & Finkel, E. J. (in press). Emotion expression as a function of communal orientation and relationship type. *Personal Relationships*.

Clark, M. S., Graham, S., & Helgeson, V. (2003). *Willingness to express emotions predicts the development of close relationships and intimacy within those relationships.* Unpublished manuscript.

Clark, M. S., & Mills, J. (1993). The difference between communal and exchange relationships: What it is and is not. *Personality and Social Psychology Bulletin, 19,* 684–691.

Clark, M. S., Mills, J., & Corcoran, D. (1989). Keeping track of needs and inputs of friends and strangers. *Personality and Social Psychology Bulletin, 15,* 533–542.

Clark, M. S., Mills, J., & Powell, M. (1986). Keeping track of needs in communal and exchange relationships. *Journal of Personality and Social Psychology, 51,* 333–338.

Clark, M. S., Ouellette, R., Powell, M., & Milberg, S. (1987). Relationship type, recipient mood, and helping. *Journal of Personality and Social Psychology, 53,* 94–103.

Clark, M. S., & Taraban, C. (1991). Reactions to and willingness to express emotion in communal relationships. *Journal of Experimental Social Psychology, 27,* 324–336.

Collins, N. L., & Read, S. J. (1990). Adult attachment, working models, and relationship quality in dating couples. *Journal of Personality and Social Psychology, 58,* 644–663.

Collins, R. L. (1994). Social support provision to HIV-infected gay men. *Journal of Applied Social Psychology, 24,* 1848–1869.

Collins, R. L., & Di Paula, A. (1997). Personality and the provision of support: Emotions felt and signaled. In G. R. Pierce, B. Lakey, I. G. Sarason, & B. R. Sarason (Eds.), *Sourcebook of social support and personality* (pp. 429–443). New York: Plenum.

Cottington, E. M., Matthews, K. A., Talbott, E. & Kuller, L. H. (1986). Occupational stress, suppressed anger, and hypertension. *Psychosomatic Medicine, 48,* 249–260.

Crowell, J. A., & Feldman, S. S. (1988). Mothers' internal models of relationships and children's behavioral and developmental status: A study of mother-child interaction. *Child Development, 59,* 1273–1285.

Cutrona, C. E., & Russell, D. W. (1987). The provisions of social relationships and adaptation to stress. In W. H. Jones & D. Perlman (Eds.), *Advances in personal relationships* (Vol. 1; pp. 37–67). Greenwich, CT: JAI Press.

Dawson, M. E., Schell, A. M., & Filion, D. (2000). The electrodermal system. In J. T. Cacioppo, L. G. Tassinary, & G. G. Berntson (Eds.), *Handbook of psychophysiology* (2nd Edition; pp. 200–223). Cambridge: Cambridge University Press.

Downey, G., & Feldman, S. I. (1996). Implications of rejection sensitivity for intimate relationships. *Journal of Personality and Social Psychology, 70,* 1327–1341.

Eisenberg, N., & Fabes, R. A. (1990). Empathy: Conceptualization, measurement, and relation to prosocial behavior. *Motivation and Emotion, 14,* 131–149.

Esterling, B. A., Antoni, M. H., Fletcher, M. A., Margulies, S., & Schneiderman, N. (1994). Emotional disclosure through writing or speaking modulates latent Epstein-Barr virus antibody titers. *Journal of Consulting and Clinical Psychology, 62,* 130–140.

Feeney, B. C., & Collins, N. L. (2001). Predictors of caregiving in adult intimate relationships: An attachment theoretical perspective. *Journal of Personality and Social Psychology, 81,* 972–994.

Feeney, J. A. (1995). Adult attachment and emotional control. *Personal Relationships, 2,* 143–159.

Feeney, J. A. (1999). Adult attachment, emotional control, and marital satisfaction. *Personal Relationships, 6*, 169–185.
Finkel, E. J., & Clark, M. S. (2003). Facilitated emotion expression: One pathway linking close relationships to health. Unpublished manuscript.
Fitness, J. (2000). Anger in the workplace: An emotion script approach to anger between workers and their superiors, co-workers and subordinates. *Journal of Organizational Behavior, 21*, 147–162.
Foa, E. B., & Kozak, M. J. (1986). Emotion processing of fear: Exposure to corrective information. *Psychological Bulletin, 99*, 20–35.
Frankl, V. E. (1955/1984). *Man's search for meaning: An introduction to logotherapy* (3rd Edition). New York: Vintage Books.
Frederickson, B. L. (1998). What good are positive emotions? *Review of General Psychology, 2*, 300–319.
Frijda, N. H. (1993). Moods, emotion episodes, and emotions. In M. Lewis and J. M. Haviland (Eds.), *Handbook of emotions* (pp. 381–404). New York: Guilford Press.
Gross, J. J., & Levenson, R. W. (1993). Emotion suppression: Physiology, self-report, and expressive behavior. *Journal of Personality and Social Psychology, 64*, 970–986.
Gross, J. J., & Levenson, R. W. (1997). Hiding feelings: The acute effects of inhibiting negative and positive emotion. *Journal of Abnormal Psychology, 106*, 95–103.
Hatfield, E., Cacioppo, J. T., & Rapson, T. L. (1991). Primitive emotional contagion. In M. S. Clark (Ed.), *Emotion and social behavior* (pp. 151–177). Newbury Park, CA: Sage.
Hill, M. G., Weary, G., & Williams, J. (1986). Depression: A self-presentation formulation. In R. F. Baumeister (Ed.), *Public self and private self* (pp. 213–240). New York: Springer-Verlag.
Hoffman, M. L. (1984). Interaction of affect and cognition in empathy. In C. E. Izard, J. Kagan, & R. Zajonc (Eds.), *Emotion, cognition, and behavior*. New York: Cambridge University Press.
Hoover-Dempsey, K. V., Plas, J. M., & Strudler-Wallston, B. (1986). Tears and weeping among professional women: In search of new understanding. *Psychology of Women Quarterly, 10*, 19–34.
Horowitz, M. J. (1975). Intrusive and repetitive thoughts after experimental stress: A summary. *Psychosomatic Medicine, 41*, 209–218.
Horowitz, M. J. (1979). *Stress response syndromes*. New York: Aronson.
Janoff-Bulman, R. (1992). *Shattered assumptions: Towards a new psychology of trauma*. New York: Free Press.
Jorgensen, R. S., Johnson, B. T., Kolodziej, M. E., & Schreer, G. E. (1996). Elevated blood pressure and personality: A meta-analytic review. *Psychological Bulletin, 120*, 293–320.
Julkunen, J. (1996). Suppressing your anger: Good manners, bad health? *Stress and Emotion: Anxiety, Anger, and Curiosity, 16*, 227–240.
Keltner, D., Ekman, P., Gonzaga, G. G., & Beer, J. (2003). Facial expression of emotion. In R. J. Davidson, K. R. Scherer, & H. H. Goldsmith (Eds.), *Handbook of affective sciences* (pp. 415–432). Oxford: Oxford University Press.
Klein, K. (2002). Stress, expressive writing, and working memory. In S. J. Lepore & J. M. Smyth (Eds.), *The writing cure: How expressive writing promotes health and emotional well-being* (pp. 135–155). Washington, DC: American Psychological Association.

Klein, K., & Boals, A. (2001). Expressive writing can increase working memory capacity. *Journal of Experimental Psychology: General, 130*, 520–533.

Kunce, L. J., & Shaver, P. R. (1994). An attachment-theoretical approach to caregiving in romantic relationships. In K. Bartholomew & D. Perlman (Eds.), *Advances in personal relationships* (Vol. 5; pp. 205–237). London: Jessica Kingsley.

Levenson, R. W. (1994). Human emotion: A functional view. In P. Ekman & R. K. Davidson (Eds.), *The nature of emotion: Fundamental questions* (pp. 123–126). New York: Oxford University Press.

Lippert, T., & Prager, K. J. (2001). Daily experiences of intimacy: A study of couples. *Personal Relationships, 8*, 283–298.

Mills, J., & Clark, M. S. (1982). Exchange and communal relationships. In L. Wheeler (Ed.), *Review of personality and social psychology* (Vol. 3; pp. 121–144). Beverly Hills, CA: Sage.

Mills, J., & Clark, M. S. (1986). Communications that should lead to perceived exploitation in communal and exchange relationships. *Journal of Social and Clinical Psychology, 4*, 225–234.

Mills, J., Clark, M. S., Ford, T. E., & Johnson, M. (in press). Measurement of communal strength. *Personal Relationships*.

Mills, J., Jellison, J. M., & Kennedy, J. (1976). Attribution of attitudes from feelings: Effect of positive or negative feelings when the attitude object is benefited or harmed. In J. Harvey, W. Ickes, & R. Kidd (Eds.), *New directions in attribution research* (Vol. 1; pp. 271–289). Hillsdale, NJ: Erlbaum.

Murray, S. L., Holmes, J. G., MacDonald, G., & Ellsworth, P. (1998). Through the looking glass darkly? When self-doubts turn into relationship insecurities. *Journal of Personality and Social Psychology, 75*, 1459–1480.

Parrott, W. G. (1993). Beyond hedonism: Motives for inhibiting good moods and for maintaining bad moods. In D. M. Wegner & J. W. Pennebaker (Eds.), *Handbook of mental control* (pp. 278–305). Englewood Cliffs, NJ: Prentice-Hall.

Pennebaker, J. W. (1989). Confession, inhibition, and disease. In L. Berkowitz (Ed.), *Advances in Experimental Social Psychology* (Vol. 22; pp. 211–244). New York: Academic Press.

Pennebaker, J. W. (1993). Putting stress into words: Health, linguistic, and therapeutic implications. *Behavioral Research and Therapy, 31*, 539–548.

Pennebaker, J. W., Hughes, C. F., & O'Heeron, R. C. (1987). The psychophysiology of confession: Linking inhibitory and psychosomatic processes. *Journal of Personality and Social Psychology, 52*, 781–793.

Pennebaker, J. W., Mayne, T. J., & Francis, M. E. (1997). Linguistic predictors of adaptive bereavement. *Journal of Personality and Social Psychology, 72*, 863–871.

Pennebaker, J. W., & Seagal, J. D. (1999). Forming a story: The health benefits of narrative. *Journal of Clinical Psychology, 55*, 1243–1254.

Pennebaker, J. W., Zech, E., & Rimé, B. (2001). Disclosing and sharing emotion: Psychological, social and health consequences. In M. S. Stroebe, R. O. Hansson, W. Stroebe, & H. Schut (Eds.), *Handbook of bereavement research: Consequences, coping, and care* (pp. 517–543). Washington, DC: American Psychological Association.

Petrie, K. J., Booth, R. J., Pennebaker, J. W., Davison, K. P., & Thomas, M. (1995). Disclosure of trauma and immune response to hepatitis B vaccination program. *Journal of Consulting and Clinical Psychology, 63*, 787–792.

Reilly, J., & Seibert, L. (2003). Language and emotion. In R. J. Davidson, K. R. Scherer, & H. H. Goldsmith (Eds.), *Handbook of affective sciences* (pp. 535–559). New York: Oxford University Press.

Richards, J. & Gross, J. (2000). Emotion regulation and memory: The cognitive costs of keeping one's cool. *Journal of Personality and Social Psychology, 79*, 410–424.

Rimé, B., Finkenauer, C., Luminet, O., Zech, E., & Philippot, P. (1998). Social sharing of emotion: New evidence and new questions. In W. Stroebe & M. Hewstone (Eds.), *European review of social psychology* (Vol. 9; pp. 145–189). Chichester, UK: John Wiley & Sons Ltd.

Rimé, B., Mesquita, B., Philippot, P., & Boca, S. (1991). Beyond the emotional event: Six studies on the social sharing of emotion. *Cognition and Emotion, 5*, 435–465.

Riskind, J. H. (1984). They stoop to conquer: Guiding and self-regulatory functions of physical posture after success and failure. *Journal of Personality and Social Psychology, 47*, 479–493.

Scherer, K. R., Johnstone, T., & Klasmeyer, G. (2003). Facial expression of emotion. In R. J. Davidson, K. R. Scherer, & H. H. Goldsmith (Eds.), *Handbook of affective sciences* (pp. 433–456). New York: Oxford University Press.

Shimanoff, S. B. (1988). Degree of emotional expressiveness as a function of face-needs, gender, and interpersonal relationship. *Communication Reports, 1*, 43–59.

Silver, R. L., Boon, C., & Stones, M. H. (1983). Searching for meaning in misfortune: Making sense of incest. *Journal of Social Issues, 39*, 81–102.

Silver, R. L., & Wortman, D. B. (1980). Coping with undesirable life events. In J. Garber & M. E. P. Seligman (Eds.), *Human helplessness* (pp. 279–340). New York: Academic Press.

Simon, H. A. (1967). Motivational and emotional controls of cognition. *Psychological Review, 74*, 29–39.

Simpson, J. A., Rholes, W. S., & Nelligan, J. S. (1992). Support seeking and support giving within couples in an anxiety-provoking situation: The role of attachment styles. *Journal of Personality and Social Psychology, 62*, 434–446.

Sommers, S. (1984). Reported emotions and conventions of emotionality among college students. *Journal of Personality and Social Psychology, 46*, 207–215.

Wegner, D. M. (1994). Ironic processes of mental control. *Psychological Review, 101*, 34–52.

Williamson, G., & Clark, M. S. (1989). Providing help and desired relationship type as determinants of changes in moods and self-evaluation. *Journal of Personality and Social Psychology, 56*, 722–734.

Williamson, G., & Clark, M. S. (1992). Impact of desired relationship type on affective reactions to choosing and being required to help. *Personality and Social Psychology Bulletin, 18*, 10–18.

Zeman, J., & Shipman, K. (1996). Children's expression of negative affect: Reasons and methods. *Developmental Psychology, 32*, 842–849.

PART II

THE INTRAGROUP CONTEXT

6

Emotional Contagion

Religious and Ethnic Hatreds and Global Terrorism

Elaine Hatfield and Richard L. Rapson

"Why can't the Palestinians and Israelis craft a peaceful solution to the current crisis?" political commentators ask. To many, the accords seem so straightforward. In the end – whether the peace process takes 1 year, 10 years, or 1,000 years – Palestinians and Israelis must find some way to share the Promised Land. Both will have to sacrifice the cherished conviction that they (and only they) are the rightful inheritors of the lands of the Ken'ites and the Ken'izites, the Kad'mon-ites and the Hittites, the Per'izzites and the Reph'aims, the Am'or-ites and the Canaanites, the Girgashites and the Jeb'u-sites... (for a discussion of prevailing views, see Bickerton & Klausner, 1998; Friedman, 1995; Said, 1979). And yet the killings go on.

The Palestinians and the Israelis are not the only peoples who find themselves swept up in "perplexing" political, religious, and ethnic conflicts. In the past decade, the world has witnessed a plethora of the horrific: suicide bombers, mass murder, genocide, crimes against humanity, and global terrorism. We have only to speak the names – "Serbia and Bosnia," "Northern Ireland," "Cambodia," "Rwanda," "Palestine and Israel," and the "World Trade Center" – to despair.

Social psychologists have devoted a great deal of thought to unraveling the mysteries of the "psycho-logic" that allows good people to commit staggering wrongs – to engage in orgies of torture and killing (see Reich, 1990). Theologians parse the promises of the *Bible*, the *Torah*, and the *Qur'an*. Social psychologists speak of cognitive transformations that allow people to interpret the Golden Rule and the Fifth Commandment that "Thou Shalt Not Kill" as meaning "God Is On Our Side" and "Victory At Any Price," and "By Any Means." In discussing how terrorists can so blithely invoke religious precepts in justifying moral atrocities, Albert Bandura (1990) observed:

> People see themselves as fighting ruthless oppressors who have an unquenchable appetite for conquest, protecting their cherished values and way of life, preserving

world peace, saving humanity from subjugation to an evil ideology, and honoring their country's international commitments. (p. 164)

Psychologists speak of cultural factors, "moral disengagement," "self-deception," "depersonalization," "splitting," and "externalization." The development of an "Us versus Them" mentality, of "denials of doubt," and a refusal to admit even the *possibility* of uncertainty (Newman & Erber, 2002; Rapson, 1978).

Yet these intellectual analyses seem pallid when confronting the stark enormities of suffering in conflicts such as those in the Middle East: The grief-stricken Israeli father whose daughter has died in a Tel Aviv car bombing; Palestinian militants mourning the death of Muhammad al-Dura; the twelve-year-old boy from Gaza, caught in a hail of Israeli gunfire; the Israeli settlers and "Millennialists," attempting to demolish the Islamic Holy of Holies; a Palestinian woman in Jenin, sitting amid the rubble of her home, bulldozed by Israeli "peace" forces; the constant fear in which Israeli and Palestinian children live. Nor do abstract psychological phrases quite capture the anger, grief, and confusion of Americans listening to Israelis and Arabs denouncing their rivals' cruelty, inhumanity, and intransigence as they contemplate these outrages.

We would argue that, although political policy makers and psychologists can best understand the white heat of conflicts (such as the Arab-Israeli clash) by considering: (1) the cultural, historical, and economic factors sparking such conflicts; and (2) the cognitive and rational calculations of combatants – we must not stop there. (3) We must grapple with peoples' emotions as well – facing up to the inner conflicts of people caught up in such "Holy" crusades and attempting to comprehend the nature of their shame, fear, rage, hatred, and despair.

We must be sensitive to the emotional lives of Arabs and Jews, of Serbs and Croats, of Irish Protestants and Irish Catholics. We should be aware that people experience both their own joys and sorrows *and* tend to "catch" the emotions (the joy, love, anger, fear, and sadness) of those around them. In an isolated group, when there is no real cross-cultural dialogue going on, when people spend their days with others who share their resentments and fury, feelings are sometimes like cancer cells – duplicating and dividing and dividing yet again, as time and hostilities go on.

Of the suffering that the conflict-riven have endured, we can hardly add anything new. Poets, writers, and social commentators have depicted that with greater power than we could (see Benarroch, 2001; Darwish, 1995). In this chapter, we will discuss a topic not commonly addressed: the process of primitive emotional contagion that shapes people's reactions in the best and worst of circumstances.

It is our hope to provide a few insights into the powerful forces that unite people and divide them from their fellows. We hope to provide a better understanding of the factors that provide a shared vision, push emotions to a fever pitch, and contribute to people's perplexing and unrelenting willingness to engage in Holy Wars – no matter how wasted the effort, horrendous the costs, and how devastated a suffering humanity. We begin by discussing emotional contagion and the psychological mechanisms that account for this ubiquitous phenomenon.

THE THEORY OF EMOTIONAL CONTAGION

Defining Emotional Contagion

Emotional contagion is defined as:

> The tendency to automatically mimic and synchronize expressions, vocalizations, postures, and movements with those of another person and, consequently, to converge emotionally (Hatfield, Cacioppo, & Rapson, 1993, p. 5).

The Emotional Contagion Scale is designed to assess people's susceptibility to catching joy-happiness, love, fear-anxiety, anger, and sadness-depression, as well as emotions in general (see Doherty, 1997).

Theory of Emotional Contagion

Psychologists point out that emotions can be caught in a variety of ways. Early investigators focused on the complex cognitive processes by which people come to know and feel what others are feeling. They speculated that conscious reasoning, analysis, and imagination accounts for such a knowing and feeling. As Adam Smith (1759/1966) observed:

> Though our brother is upon the rack... by the imagination we place ourselves in his situation, we conceive ourselves enduring all the same torments, we enter as it were into his body, and become in some measure the same person with him, and thence form some idea of his sensations, and even feel something which, though weaker in degree, is not altogether unlike them. (p. 9)

Other psychologists have argued that children and adults come to share others' emotions because they are taught to do so. By way of example, Justin Aronfreed (1970) pointed out that, if a father habitually lashes out at his son when he staggers home from work hot, tired, and upset, soon the sight of the distressed father will come to elicit a stab of anxiety in the son. A person's emotional behavior may also generate an *unconditioned* emotional response in bystanders. When some people are nervous, for example, their shrill, hysterical voices grate on us like chalk screeching on a blackboard.

We would agree that conscious cognitive processes, social conditioning, sympathy, and empathy (see Davis, this volume) all play a part in explaining "emotional contagion." But conscious and semiconscious processes are not the whole story. In conflict-riven situations – such as those in the Middle East, Serbia and Bosnia, and Northern Ireland – a third force shapes combatants' emotions: emotional contagion. Emotional contagion is a primitive process. It happens swiftly, automatically, and outside of conscious awareness – hence its startling power in shaping men and women's cognitive and emotional lives.

Mechanisms of Emotional Contagion

The process of emotional contagion is thought to involve three steps: (1) Mimicry, (2) Feedback, and, consequently, (3) the Experience of Emotional Contagion.

Step 1: Mimicry

Proposition 1: In conversation, people automatically and continuously mimic and synchronize their movements with the facial expressions, voices, postures, movements, and instrumental behaviors of others.

Scientists and writers have long observed that people tend to mimic the emotional expressions of others. As Adam Smith (1759/1966) observed:

> "When we see a stroke aimed, and just ready to fall upon the leg or arm of another person, we naturally shrink and draw back on our leg or our own arm." (p. 4)

Smith felt that such imitation was "almost a reflex." Since the 1700s, researchers have collected considerable evidence that people do indeed imitate others' facial, vocal, and postural expressions of emotion – with surprising speed and accuracy.

Social-psychophysiologists document that peoples' facial expressions [as measured by electromyographic (EMG) procedures] reflect the emotional expressions of those they observe. Ulf Dimberg (1982), for example, studied college students at the University of Uppsala, Sweden. He recorded participants' facial EMG activity as they observed targets displaying happy and angry facial expressions. Participants were found to display very different EMG response patterns when observing happy versus angry faces. Specifically, when subjects observed happy facial expressions, they showed increased muscular activity over the *zygomaticus major* (cheek) muscle region. When they observed angry facial expressions, they showed increased muscular activity over the *corrugator supercilii* (brow) muscle region.

People also mimic and synchronize vocal utterances. William Condon (1982) argues that such synchrony begins early:

> I think that infants from the first moment of life and even in the womb are getting the rhythm and structure and style of sound, the rhythms of their culture, so that they imprint to them and the rhythms become part of their very being. When they say the baby will babble French or babble Chinese, this may mean that the

> predominant rhythms are already laid into the neurological system, so that, when the child starts to talk, he incorporates the lexical items of the system right into these rhythms.
>
> As an infant hears his mother speaks in a certain pattern, he begins to move with her breathing rhythms, rhythmic heart beats, movements and so forth. Thus his rhythms become coordinated with hers early on. (pp. 66–67)

There is considerable evidence in controlled interview settings that people tend to mimic others' utterance durations, speech rate, and latencies of response. They have also been found to mimic and synchronize their postures and movements with others (see Hatfield et al., 1993, for a review of this voluminous research).

Researchers argue that such mimicry is *not* consciously mediated: The process is simply too complex and too fast to allow higher cognitive centers to be involved. An example: It took the lightning fast Muhammed Ali a minimum of 190 milliseconds to detect a light and 40 milliseconds more to throw a punch in response – a total of 230 milliseconds. Yet, William Condon and W. D. Ogston (1966) found that college students could "instinctively" synchronize their movements within 21 milliseconds (half the time of one film frame.) When we consider that, moment-to-moment, people are mimicking a plethora of facial, vocal, and postural actions, the idea that all this mimicry could be consciously mediated seems implausible. Mark Davis (1985) argued that microsynchrony occurs too fast and too ubiquitously to be a conscious process. More likely, it is mediated by brain structures at multiple levels of the neuraxis. Primitive emotional contagion, he argues, is "something you've got or something you don't." There is no way that one can deliberately "do it" (p. 69). Those who try consciously to mirror others, he speculates, are doomed to look "phony."

In any case, there is considerable evidence that: (1) people are capable of mimicking/synchronizing their faces, vocal productions, postures, and movements with startling rapidity; and (2) they are capable of automatically mimicking/synchronizing a startling number of emotional characteristics at a single instant.

Step 2: Feedback

Proposition 2: Subjective emotional experience is affected, moment-to-moment by the activation and/or feedback from facial, vocal, postural, and movement mimicry.

Emotions theorists point out that emotional experience may be influenced by three different processes: (1) the central nervous system commands that direct such mimicry/synchrony in the first place; (2) the afferent feedback from such facial, verbal, or postural mimicry/synchrony; or (3) conscious self-perception processes, wherein individuals make inferences about their own emotional states on the basis of their own expressive behavior. Given the functional redundancy that exists across levels of the neuraxis, all three processes may operate to ensure that emotional experience is shaped by facial, vocal, and postural mimicry and feedback.

Darwin (1872/1965) argued that emotional experience should be profoundly affected by feedback from the facial muscles:

> The free expression by outward signs of an emotion intensifies it. On the other hand, the repression, as far as is possible of all outward signs softens our emotions. He who gives way to violent gestures will increase rage; he who does not control the signs of fear will experience fear in a greater degree; and he who remains passive when overwhelmed with grief loses his best chance of recovering elasticity of mind. (p. 365)

Recent reviews of the literature on facial feedback document that emotions are tempered to some extent by facial feedback. What remains unclear is how important such feedback is (is it necessary, sufficient, or merely a small part of emotional experience?) and exactly how the two are linked.

Researchers have tested the facial feedback hypothesis – using three different strategies to induce subjects to adopt emotional facial expressions. (1) Sometimes, they simply ask subjects to exaggerate or to try to hide any emotional reactions they might have. (2) Sometimes, they try to "trick" subjects into adopting various facial expressions. (3) Sometimes, they try to arrange things so subjects will unconsciously mimic the emotional facial expressions of others. In all three types of experiments, researchers find that subjects' emotional experiences are affected by the facial expressions they adopt.

In a classic experiment, James Laird (1984) told subjects that he was interested in studying the action of facial muscles. The experimental room contained apparatus designed to convince anyone that complicated multichannel recordings were about to be made of facial muscle activity. Silver cup electrodes were attached to the subjects' faces between their eyebrows, at the corners of their mouths, and at the corner of their jaws. These electrodes were connected via an impressive tangle of strings and wires to electronic apparatus (which, in fact, served no function at all). The experimenter then proceeded surreptitiously to arrange the faces of the subjects into emotional expressions. Laird found that emotional attributions *were* shaped, in part, by changes in the facial musculature. Subjects in the "frown" conditions were less happy and more angry than those in the "smile" conditions. The subjects' comments give us some idea of how this process worked. One man said with a kind of puzzlement:

> When my jaw was clenched and my brows down, I tried not to be angry but it just fit the position. I'm not in any angry mood but I found my thoughts wandering to things that made me angry, which is sort of silly I guess. I knew I was in an experiment and knew I had no reason to feel that way, but I just lost control. (p. 480)

The link between emotion and facial expression appears to be quite specific. When people produced facial expressions of fear, anger, sadness, or disgust, they were more likely to feel the emotion associated with those *specific* expressions.

Paul Ekman and his colleagues (1983) argued that both emotional experience *and* autonomic nervous system activity are affected by facial feedback. They asked people to produce six emotions: surprise, disgust, sadness, anger, fear, and happiness. Participants were to do this either by reliving times when they had experienced such emotions or by arranging their facial muscles in appropriate poses. The authors found that the act of reliving emotional experiences or flexing facial muscles into characteristic emotional expressions produced effects on the autonomic nervous system (ANS) that would normally accompany such emotions. Thus, facial expressions seemed to be capable of generating appropriate ANS arousal.

Vocal feedback can also influence emotional experience. In one experiment, Elaine Hatfield and her colleagues (1995) asked subjects to reproduce one of six "randomly generated" sound patterns. Communications researchers have documented that emotions are linked with specific patterns of intonation, voice quality, rhythm, and pausing. (Klaus Scherer, 1982, for example, found that when people are happy they produce sounds with small amplitude variation, large pitch variation, fast tempo, a sharp sound envelope and few harmonics). The five tapes were designed to possess the sound characteristics associated with joy, love, anger, fear, and sadness. The authors found that individuals' emotions were affected by feedback from their vocal productions.

Finally, evidence exists suggesting that emotions are shaped by feedback from posture and movement. Interestingly enough, the theorist of theatre, Konstantin Stanislavski (in Moore, 1960), noticed the connection between posture and performance. He argued:

> Emotional memory stores our past experiences; to relive them, actors must execute indispensable, logical physical actions in the given circumstances. There are as many nuances of emotions as there are physical actions. (pp. 52–53)

Stanislavski proposed we may relive emotions anytime we engage in a variety of small actions that were once associated with these emotions. Whether or not Stanislavski is correct, there exists an array of evidence supporting the contention that subjective emotional experience is affected, moment-to-moment, by the activation and/or feedback from facial, vocal, postural, and movement mimicry.

Step 3: Emotional Contagion

Proposition 3: Consequently, people tend, from moment-to-moment, to "catch" others' emotions.

There is compelling evidence that people do indeed tend to catch the emotions of others. This evidence comes from social psychologists and sociologists, clinical researchers (exploring transference and counter-transference, and the impact that anxious, depressed, and angry people have on others), animal researchers, developmentalists (interested in primitive emotional contagion, empathy, and sympathy), and (most recently) historians (see Hatfield et al., 1993, for a review of this research.) Since in this paper we are focusing on the impact of contagion on religious and ethnic hatreds and global terrorism, we briefly review a sampling of the historical research on "hysterical contagion."

EMOTIONAL CONTAGION: A HISTORICAL APPROACH

Were our forebears as sensitive to others' emotions and as likely to "catch" others emotions as we are? Historians are currently debating this question. Before the eighteenth century Enlightenment, most people neither read nor wrote; thus, it is not easy for historians to answer such questions. Currently, most historians tend to argue that our forebears were surprisingly insensitive to the suffering that engulfed them.

Lawrence Stone (1977), in his trailblazing *The Family, Sex, and Marriage: In England 1500–1800*, for example, argued that in the preindustrial era, even in the closest of family relationships, people possessed little ability to "feel themselves into" the emotions of others. The English of that era, he insisted, tended to display "suspicion towards others, proneness to violence, and an incapacity to develop strong emotional ties to any one individual" (p. 409).

Stone's challenging explorations generated a whirlwind of debate among historians and many other scholars. Were people as remote, their emotions as crude and ugly, as Stone claimed? Some historians insist that people were far more compassionate in the preindustrial era than Stone admits (Gadlin, 1977; Ladurie, 1979; Taylor, 1989).

Nonetheless, there is considerable evidence in favor of Stone's contentions. Some examples follow.

In 1466, in Rome, for example, Pope Paul II initiated the February Carnival, a race run on the Corso, a narrow ribbon of road that ran from the Piazza del Popolo to the Piazza Venezia in the Holy City. To our eyes, the Carnival seems a barbaric celebration:

> The Carnival was, even after its most barbarous customs were suspended by fiat, a peculiar mixture of glamour and cruelty. Even some of its participants were terminally divided between believing the Carnival was an occasion of innocent vivacity and condemning it as the epitome of masked wickedness. Horses were at one time whipped by little boys, and donkeys and buffaloes viciously goaded by men on horseback; and cripples and hunchbacks, naked old men, and despised Jews were made to run for sport. (Harrison, 1989, pp. 227–228)

Four centuries later, in the same city, Charles Dickens attended a public execution. He reported that, at the beheading, the crowd "counted the drops of blood that spurted out of the neck of the executed man in order to bet that number on the lottery; [Dickens] was naturally appalled" (Harrison, 1989, p. 325). In cases like this – as in lynchings, cat massacres (Darnton, 1984), and guillotinings – contagion becomes complex! Spectators, though not catching the suffering of the executed, may well be picking up the pleasure, excitement, and anger of the mob around them. If people lacked empathy for the woe of others, contagion seemed plentiful enough when it came to the rougher and wilder emotions of fear, anger, and hatred.

Nonetheless – whether people in the sixteenth to the eighteenth centuries were as sensitive to others' feelings as they are in the twenty-first century or whether they were not – primitive emotional contagion did seem to be a common occurrence. Historians report that, in many societies and many eras, in times of stress, fear, hysterical grief, and anger have swept through rural communities (Rude, 1981). They attribute such social phenomenon to "emotional contagion" or "hysterical contagion."

The Dancing Manias of the Middle Ages

In the Middle Ages, in the wake of the Black Death, dancing manias, redolent of mass hysteria, swept throughout Europe. Harold Klawans (1990) set the scene of generalized "sorrow and anxiety" that drove people "to the point of hysteria":

> [The bubonic plague, the infamous Black Death] appeared [in the 12th century,] an illness far worse than any of the others.... It was an epidemic of unprecedented proportions that broke over Europe in a great wave. Entire villages were exterminated. Fields became neglected. Soon famine complicated the pestilence. And just as the plague receded and the population and economy began to recover, another wave struck.

From 1119 to 1340 – a period of 221 years – the plague ravaged Italy sixteen times. No words can fully describe its horrors, but the people who witnessed them, who lived in those days so full of the uncertainty of life, of sorrow, and of anxiety, were driven to the point of hysteria.

It was at that point that the dancing mania began and spread like a contagion. Today, most historians view this phenomenon as a form of mass hysteria (Klawans, 1990, pp. 236–237).

One writer (reported in Hecker, 1837/1970) described the twelfth-century scene this way:

> The effects of the *Black Death* had not yet subsided and the graves of millions of its victims were scarcely closed, when a strange delusion arose in Germany, which took possession of the minds of men, and, in spite of the divinity of our nature, hurried away body and soul into the magic circle of hellish superstition. It was a convulsion which in the most extraordinary manner infuriated the human frame,

and excited the astonishment of contemporaries for more than two centuries, since which time it has never reappeared. It was called the dance of St. John or of St. Vitus, on account of the Bacchantic leaps by which it was characterized, and which gave to those affected, while performing their wild dance, and screaming and foaming with fury, all the appearance of persons possessed. It did not remain confined to particular localities, but was propagated by the sight of the sufferers, like a demoniacal epidemic, over the whole of Germany and the neighboring countries to the northwest, which were already prepared for its reception by the prevailing opinions of the times.

So early as the year 1374, assemblages of men and women were seen at Aix-la-Chapelle who had come out of Germany, and who, united by one common delusion, exhibited to the public both in the streets and in the churches the following strange spectacle. They formed circles hand in hand, and appearing to have lost all control over their senses, continued dancing, regardless of the by-standers, for hours together in wild delirium, until at length they fell to the ground in a state of exhaustion. They then complained of extreme oppression, and groaned as if in the agonies of death, until they were swathed in cloths bound tightly round their waists, upon which they again recovered, and remained free from complaint until the next attack. This practice of swathing was resorted to on account of the tympany which followed these spasmodic ravings, but the by-standers frequently relieved patients in a less artificial manner, by thumping and trampling upon the parts affected. While dancing they neither saw nor heard, being insensible to external impressions through the senses, but were haunted by visions, their fancies conjuring up spirits whose names they shrieked out; and some of them afterward asserted that they felt as if they had been immersed in a stream of blood, which obligated them to leap so high. Others, during the paroxysm, saw the heavens open and the Saviour enthroned with the Virgin Mary, according as the religious notions of the age were strangely and variously reflected in their imaginations. Where the disease was completely developed, the attack commenced with epileptic convulsions. (pp. 1–2)

The dancing mania spread from town to town. In Cologne, 500 joined the wild revels; in Metz, 1,100 danced. Priests tried to exorcise the devils. Sufferers traveled to the Tomb of Saint Vitus in southern France to be cured. Paracelsus, a sixteenth-century physician and alchemist, devised a harsh but effective treatment for the dancing mania: He dunked the victims in cold water, forced them to fast, and condemned them to solitary confinement. The hysterical outbreaks began to subside.

The historical record abounds in descriptions of mass emotional effusions inspired by superstition and charismatic demagogues. (Modern-day tent and TV evangelists are masters of the art of contagion, as were such orators as Adolph Hitler.) However, even supposedly "reasonable" folk are not immune to the spread – witness the next case from "The Age of Reason."

The Great Fear of 1789

In the eighteenth century, the *philosophes* of the Enlightenment championed the cause of science and reason over ignorance, superstition, and tyranny.

Much intellectual leadership came from such French writers as Voltaire, Montesquieu, Rousseau, and Diderot, who challenged the traditional legal, moral, hierarchical, and religious foundations of French society. By 1789, large sections of France's professional and middle classes had been converted to these revolutionary ideas, and they became active in trying to achieve the changes in French society that they thought necessary. In fact, some of these advocates of reason began to try to force social change.

Reason and persuasion soon gave way to hate and terror. Rumors began to circulate that the Royal Court and aristocracy were plotting to take over Paris by counterforce. People fled Paris in fear. As they trudged along country roads on their way to the French countryside, they spread rumors of an impending assault on the provinces by a mercenary army of criminals and foreigners in the pay of the aristocracy.

France became gripped by an almost universal panic. Fear bred fear. Local authorities and citizens became convinced that the criminal army was not just on the march, but was at the door. This led to the breakdown of local government, the arming of the poor, and food riots, and furnished a dramatic impetus to revolution in the provinces (Bernstein, 1990; Cook, 1974; Headley, 1971; Lefebvre, 1973).

After the storming of the Bastille in 1789, historians described the years that later ensued as the Reign of Terror – a term suggesting that emotional contagion may have a life well beyond the walls of the laboratory.

The New York City Draft Riots of 1863

New York City, in the hot summer of 1863, was a place of extremes. The Civil War had brought ever greater wealth to a few and increasing poverty to many. Wartime inflation eroded the buying power of the poor. The city's struggling immigrant population lived in run-down, crowded tenements. Immigrants, especially the Irish, were outraged at the use of blacks to replace striking Irish longshoremen.

New York was an antiwar city, controlled by a local Democratic political machine, which had lost power and influence to the national Republican "war" party. The city's Democratic press and politicians skillfully played up the theme that Northern white workers were betraying their own best interests by fighting to free slaves who would then compete for their jobs.

In the midst of this, a national military draft commenced during the summer of 1863. The new law permitted a commutation of military service for anyone who could pay a $300 fee. This set the stage for viewing the draft as a symbol of Republican over Democrat, national over local government, native over immigrant, and rich over poor.

The first 1,236 names of New York City drafted men appeared in the morning papers at the same time that casualty lists from Gettysburg (the bloodiest battle ever fought on the North American continent) were posted around the city. Early the next morning, men, women, and boys began to move along streets carrying the weapons of the poor – crowbars and clubs. Mobs quickly formed and grew, caught up in and carried away with anger.

Four days of subsequent uncontrolled violence – including the lynching and burning of 12 blacks – left 119 persons dead and 306 injured. Forty-three regiments of union troops had to be stationed in and around the city to ensure order (Church, 1964; McCague, 1968).

The Era of Mass Media

Research on emotional contagion has focused on the effect of interpersonal interactions; there is, however, historical evidence to suggest that the dissemination of emotions does not always require direct physical contact or proximity. As rumors spread, emotions may accompany them. Mass communications – films, newspapers, radio, and (particularly) television – can transmit people's emotions far beyond their geographical perimeters. Our very image of the mob is linked inextricably with notions of the spread of anger, leading to the out-of-control behaviors of murder, lynchings, and large-scale destruction. We see daily on television the pictures of weeping and angry crowds mourning the death of a Palestinian guerrilla or an Israeli child, a murdered leader and her mournful followers, or the defiant and angry opposition. We replay the weekend of mourning by an entire nation (perhaps even the entire world) on the assassination of John F. Kennedy. Are these instances of emotional contagion, or are these phenomena too complicated to be so labeled? Historical examples cannot be tested in the laboratory, but they do hint at the reality of emotional contagion and suggest that it may have occurred on a large scale in many historical eras. They also suggest that the mass media of our day may possess power even greater than generally realized because of their potential to precipitate the spread not just of information and entertainment, but also of emotions.

Summing Up

In this chapter, we have considered evidence in favor of three propositions: (1) that people tend to mimic others; (2) that emotional experience is affected by such feedback; and (3) that people therefore tend to "catch" others' emotions. We also reviewed historical evidence that, throughout history, in times of stress, people in many societies have seemed vulnerable to emotional or hysterical contagion.

It is not wise to claim too much. We are *not* arguing that emotional contagion is always a cause, or is generally the prime cause of religious and ethnic hatreds or of tribal and national outbursts of anger and violence. We have no idea how often contagion plays a part, or of how much a part it generally plays in such outbursts. After all, the people swept up in the "hysterical contagion" movements of the past are all long dead. We cannot question them as to what they felt and why. But we would argue that the existing psychological and historical evidence is compelling enough that in addition to the usual "suspects" – the cultural, political, and economic factors thought to breed religious and ethnic hatreds and global terrorism – pundits might be aware that psychological factors, such as emotional contagion, may play a role as well. Naturally, more theorizing and research are needed to determine when it plays a role, how much of a role it plays, and how crucial this role may be.

CONCLUSIONS

One of the great ideas of the eighteenth-century Enlightenment, the "Age of Reason," was the notion of tolerance. Voltaire, Diderot, Jefferson, Locke, and a host of other thinkers argued in behalf of accepting that people can possess different beliefs and that such nonconformists need not be exiled, despised, castrated, or killed for them. But the idea of cherishing (or at least tolerating) differences is just that: an idea. It is not an emotion in itself, even though it can *lead* to feelings, such as the joy that can come when one discovers that an assumed enemy can be a friend.

But the idea of tolerance, like peace, remains a fragile flower, easily trampled underfoot. The conviction that cultural differences are to be accepted is oft times swept away in the anger, fear, and hate that is ignited and spread (via emotional contagion) to mobs joined in resentment. When faced with a sobbing Israeli father, with ululating mourners at the funerals of murdered children, with people fleeing burning buildings, or crowds running through the streets in panic or rage, it is a rare person who can resist getting lost in a morass of emotion. Passion takes a toll on logic and complex thinking. In troubled times, it is tempting to retreat into religious, national, familial, and tribal loyalties. Yet, it is just at these times that the world has the greatest need for intellectual *and* emotional intelligence. During outbreaks of the darker side of emotional contagion, we most need complex, nuanced thinking and emotional empathy for "the other." Can we find ways to give sufficient emotive power to the value of thoughtful contemplation so that it can match the force of feeling and emotional contagion, and hence help the world have a better chance of preventing contagion from becoming a plague? At the very least, we can be passionate about the value of mutual tolerance and can also try to plant a few seeds of understanding.

References

Aronfreed, J. (1970). The socialization of altruistic and sympathetic behavior: Some theoretical and experimental analyses. In J. Macaulay & L. Berkowitz (Eds.), *Altruism and helping behavior* (pp. 103–126). New York: Academic Press.

Bandura, A. (1990). Mechanisms of moral disengagement. In W. Reich (Ed.), *Origins of terrorism: psychologies, ideologies, theologies, states of mind* (p. 164). Washington, DC: Woodrow Wilson International Center for Scholars.

Benarroch, M. (2001). *The immigrant's lament*. Warner, NH: Minimal Press.

Bernstein, I. (1990). *The New York City draft riots*. New York: Oxford University Press.

Bickerton, I. J., & Klausner, C. L. (1998). *A concise history of the Arab-Israeli conflict* (3rd Edition). Upper Saddle River, NJ: Prentice Hall.

Church, W. F. (Ed.). (1964). *The influence of the enlightenment on the French revolution: Creative, disastrous or non-existent?* Lexington, MA: D. C. Heath.

Condon, W. S. (1982). Cultural microrhythms. In M. Davis (Ed.). *Interaction rhythms: Periodicity in communicative behavior* (pp. 53–76). New York: Human Sciences Press.

Condon, W. S., & Ogston, W. D. (1966). Sound film analysis of normal and pathological behavior patterns. *Journal Nervous Mental Disorders, 143*, 338–347.

Cook, A. (1974). *The armies of the streets: The New York City draft riots of 1863*. Lexington, KY: University of Kentucky Press.

Darnton, R. (1984). *The great cat massacre*. New York: Basic Books.

Darwin, C. (1965). *The expression of the emotions in man and animals* (p. 365). Chicago: University of Chicago Press. (Original work published in 1872.)

Darwish, M. (1995). *Memory for forgetfulness: August, Beirut, 1982*. Berkeley, CA: University of California Press.

Davis, M. H. (1985). Perceptual and affective reverberation components. In A. B. Goldstein and G. Y. Michaels (Eds.), *Empathy: Development, training, and consequences* (pp. 62–108). Hillsdale, NJ: Erlbaum.

Davis, M. H. (this volume). Empathy: Negotiating the border between self and other.

Dimberg, U. (1982). Facial reactions to facial expressions. *Psychophysiology, 19*, 643–647.

Doherty, R. W. (1997). The emotional contagion scale: A measure of individual differences. *Journal of Nonverbal Behavior, 21*, 131–154.

Ekman, P., Levenson, R. W., & Friesen, W. V. (1983). Autonomic nervous system activity distinguishes among emotions, *Science, 221*, 1208–1210.

Friedman, T. L. (1995). *From Beirut to Jerusalem*. New York: Anchor Books/Doubleday.

Gadlin, H. (1977). Private lives and public order: A critical view of the history of intimate relationships in the United States. In G. Levinger & H. L. Rausch (Eds.), *Perspectives on the meaning of intimacy* (pp. 33–72). Amherst: University of Massachusetts Press.

Harrison, B. G. (1989). *Italian days* (pp. 227–228, 325). New York: Ticknor & Fields.

Hatfield, E., Cacioppo, J. T., & Rapson, R. L. (1993). *Emotional contagion* (p. 5). New York: Cambridge University Press.

Hatfield, E., Hsee, C. K., Costello, J., Weisman, M. S., & Denney, C. (1995). The impact of vocal feedback on emotional experience and expression. *Journal of Social Behavior and Personality, 10*, 293–312.

Headley, J. T. (1971). *The great riots of New York 1712 to 1873*. New York: Dover.

Hecker, J. F. (1837/1970). *The dancing mania of the middle ages* (trans. B. G. Babington) (pp. 1–2). New York: Burt Franklin.

Klawans, H. L. (1990). *Newton's madness: Further tales of clinical neurology* (pp. 236–237). London: Headline Book Publishers.
Laird, J. D. (1984). The real role of facial response in the experience of emotion: A reply to Tourangeau and Ellsworth and others. *Journal of Personality and Social Psychology, 47,* 480, 909–917.
Ladurie, E. L. R. (1979). *Montaillou: The promised land of error.* New York: Vintage Press.
Lefebvre, G. (1973). *The great fear of 1789* (trans. J. White). New York: Pantheon.
McCague, J. (1968). *The second rebellion: The story of the New York City draft riots of 1863.* New York: Dial Press.
Moore, S. (1960). *The Stanislavski system* (pp. 52–53). New York: Viking Press.
Newman, L. S., & Erber, R. (2002). *Understanding genocide: The social psychology of the Holocaust.* Oxford, UK: Oxford University Press.
Rapson, R. L. (1978). *Denials of doubt: An interpretation of American history.* Lanham, MD: University Press of America.
Reich, W. (Ed.). (1990). *Origins of terrorism: Psychologies, ideologies, theologies, states of mind.* Washington, DC: Woodrow Wilson International Center for Scholars.
Rude, G. R. E. (1981). *The crowd in history: A study of popular disturbances in France and England, 1730–1848.* London: Lawrence and Wishart.
Said, E. W. (1979). *The question of Palestine.* New York: Vintage Books/Random House.
Scherer, K. (1982). Methods of research on vocal communication: Paradigms and parameters. In K. R. Scherer & P. Ekman (Eds.), *Handbook of methods in nonverbal behavior research* (pp. 136–198). New York: Cambridge University Press.
Smith, A. (1966). *The theory of moral sentiments* (pp. 4, 9). New York: Kelley. (Original work published in 1759.)
Stone, L. (1977). *The family, sex, and marriage: In England 1500–1800* (p. 409). New York: Harper & Row.
Taylor, C. (1989). *Sources of the self: The making of the modern identity.* Cambridge, MA: Harvard University Press.

7

The Emotional Convergence Hypothesis

Implications for Individuals, Relationships, and Cultures

Cameron Anderson and Dacher Keltner

Imagine the following scenario. Susan and Tom have just started dating and are dining at a local restaurant. The service has been slow, and as they wait for the check Tom is furious and wants to complain to the manager. Susan, on the other hand, notes how busy the restaurant has been, and feels sympathy for the overworked, harried waiter – if anything, she wants to leave a large tip. Susan and Tom argue about the matter and leave in a huff.

This sort of interpersonal problem, all too familiar to many of us, arises in part when people have different emotional reactions to events. When individuals' emotions diverge in social interactions, they are left to grapple with their different perceptions, action tendencies, and often uncharitable explanations for why they differ. Had Susan and Tom both felt sympathy for the waiter, they would have agreed on the reasons for the slow service, a course of action, and perhaps felt solidarity in their shared response.

Based on the idea that it is adaptive for relationship partners to have similar emotional reactions to events, we propose that people in close relationships develop increasing similarity in their emotional responses over time – a process we call *emotional convergence*. Furthermore, we propose that people with less power make more of the change necessary for emotional convergence to occur. In this chapter, we elaborate on the theoretical basis for these hypotheses and draw on recent longitudinal studies of relationships to provide supportive evidence. We then discuss the implications of these hypotheses at four levels of analysis: at the individual, relationship, group, and cultural levels.

EMOTIONAL SIMILARITY BETWEEN INDIVIDUALS

Theorists from a wide range of perspectives agree that it is beneficial for people to have similar emotional reactions to events (e.g., Barsade et al.,

2000; Bavelas et al., 1988; Cheney & Seyfarth, 1985; Hatfield, Cacioppo, & Rapson, 1994; Preston & de Waal, 2002; Schachter, 1951). In general, three reasons are cited.

First, emotional similarity coordinates the attention, thoughts, and behaviors across multiple individuals (e.g., Hatfield et al., 1994; Keltner & Kring, 1998). Emotional similarity thus helps individuals respond as a collective to potential opportunities or threats (Campbell, 1975; Festinger, 1951; Schachter, 1951; Sherif, 1936). For example, in many nonhuman species, group members emit alarm calls at the sight of predators, which prompts collective flight from danger (Cheney & Seyfarth 1985; Preston & de Waal, 2002). In humans, emotional similarity should guide collective action that would likely be more effective than the efforts of individuals acting alone (Campbell, 1975; Festinger, 1951; Schachter, 1951; Sherif, 1936). Shared anger might increase the chances that justice is redressed, collective sadness the chances that loss is replaced, collective awe the chances that leaders and collective principles are honored (Keltner & Haidt, 2001). In short, emotions coordinate cognitive and behavioral processes across individuals just as they coordinate cognitive and behavioral processes within individuals (Collins, 1990; Hatfield et al., 1994; Keltner & Haidt, 2001; Kemper, 1991).

Second, when two people feel similar emotions, they are better able to understand each other. People who experience similar emotions more easily take each other's perspective (Hatfield et al., 1994; Keltner & Kring, 1998), and thus are more likely to accurately perceive each other's perceptions, intentions, and motivations (Levenson & Ruef, 1994; Preston & de Waal, 2002). This greater understanding, in turn, should enable individuals to better predict each other's behaviors, which would lead to more cooperative and beneficial social interactions.

Third, people feel closer to and are more comfortable with others who experience similar emotions. Emotional similarity increases cohesion and solidarity, whereas emotional dissimilarity increases discomfort and the likelihood of interpersonal conflict (Barsade et al., 2000; Bell, 1978; Hatfield et al., 1994; Locke & Horowitz, 1990; Rosenblatt & Greenberg, 1988, 1991; Schachter, 1951; Wenzlaff & Prohaska, 1989). For example, in his well-known study of anxiety and affiliation, Schachter (1951) found that anxious participants preferred to be with others who were also anxious rather than others who felt calm. When two people feel similar emotions, their feelings, appraisals, and social dispositions are validated (Barsade et al., 2000; Locke & Horowitz, 1990; Rosenblatt & Greenberg, 1991; Schachter, 1951); they infer, often correctly, that they share a common stance (LaFrance & Ickes, 1981), and they feel understood by the other person (Hatfield et al., 1994; Locke & Horowitz, 1990).

HYPOTHESIS 1: EMOTIONAL CONVERGENCE OCCURS IN CLOSE RELATIONSHIPS

Given the benefits of emotional similarity and the problematic effects of emotional dissimilarity, people in close relationships should tend to become emotionally similar over time. Emotional convergence should be a part of successful, long-term bonds. Friends, romantic partners, family members, and close co-workers often spend a good deal of time with each other and thus face a number of emotionally relevant events together. Relationship partners who continue to emotionally respond differently to events would repeatedly encounter uncomfortable and potentially antagonistic situations, as the example that started this chapter illustrated. In contrast, relationship partners who begin to respond similarly to events would become more coordinated in their thoughts and behaviors and would be better equipped to respond collectively and effectively to problems and opportunities in the environment.

How would emotional convergence occur? One way relationship partners might become more similar over time is by coordinating their discrete emotional reactions to events on a situation-by-situation basis. That is, through processes such as emotional contagion (Hatfield et al., 1994) or empathy (Levenson & Ruef, 1994), relationship partners could observe each others' reactions to an event and modify their own emotional reaction to match their partner's. Indeed, studies have shown that individuals are more open to "catching" the emotions of others they know (Hatfield et al., 1994), and long-term romantic partners have more empathic matching of physiological responses to significant events than randomly paired individuals (Levenson & Ruef, 1994).

We propose, however, that relationship partners also achieve emotional coordination by developing similarity on a more stable, general level. That is, we argue relationship partners develop similarity in their emotional responsiveness, or their propensity to emotionally respond to events in certain ways (Watson, Clark, & Tellegen, 1988). In doing so, relationship partners would not need to observe each other's expressions in each and every situation to maintain emotional similarity – they would simply respond in a similar way automatically. Much previous work has shown how people in close relationships become similar in their enduring, stable patterns of thought and behavior, whether it be values and attitudes (Acitelli, Kenny, & Weiner, 2001), eating and drinking habits (Price & Vandenberg, 1980), or perceptions of others (Deutsch & Mackasy, 1985). Similarly, we contend that people in close relationships converge over time in their more global affectivity, or the way they emotionally respond to events. This raises the intriguing possibility that relationship-based emotional convergence generalizes to contexts in which the relationship partner is not even present. We come to acquire the emotional responses of our relationship partners, and this carries over to other contexts. This increased similarity could arise through conscious or unconscious processes, in that people might or might not be aware that they are starting to emotionally respond similarly to their relationship partner, but we suspect that it occurs largely on an unconscious level.

Longitudinal Study of Romantic Relationships

To examine whether emotional convergence occurs, we began by examining romantic relationships, which seemed the most likely relationship context in which emotional convergence would occur. We brought sixty heterosexual couples into the laboratory for an initial assessment, where we obtained measures of relationship satisfaction and relative power in the relationship. We assessed romantic partners' positive and negative emotional experiences within the context of three discussion tasks, in which they discussed events of their day, a recent success or good event, and a current concern or worry. Partners then reported privately their own emotional experiences. Six months later, thirty-eight couples were still together and participated in our follow-up assessment. We again obtained measures of relationship satisfaction and assessed positive and negative emotional experiences in the laboratory with the same discussion tasks.

We expected the partner's emotional experiences at Time 1 to already be somewhat similar, for two reasons. First, they had been dating for an average of six months, and thus some emotional similarity might have already developed. Second, these romantic partners may have chosen each other because they were emotionally similar, as predicted by the attraction/similarity hypothesis (Berscheid & Walster, 1983). However, we expected these similarity correlations to significantly increase by the second assessment, which would more strongly suggest convergence had occurred.[1]

As shown in Table 7.1, the within-couple similarity correlation was positive and significant for total emotional experience at Time 1, consistent with the idea that some emotional similarity had already developed. This effect held also for positive emotion and negative emotion. More important, six months later, the similarity correlation had become substantial for total emotional experience. This effect held for positive emotion, which one might expect; namely, romantic partners came to share their positive emotions more as their relationship developed. Perhaps more surprisingly, however, the effect held as well for negative emotion. Therefore, our first

[1] To assess whether dating partners became more similar in their emotional responses over time, the thirty-eight couples that participated in both sessions provided the relevant cross-time comparison. Thus, any increases in partners' emotional similarity would not be inflated by attrition effects (i.e., less emotionally similar couples breaking up and dropping out by Time 2).

TABLE 7.1. *Longitudinal Evidence for Emotional Convergence*

	Similarity Correlations Between Partners		
Relationship	**Time 1**	**Time 2**	**Increase**[a]
Romantic relationships			
Total emotion	.30*	.56**	.31**
Positive emotion	.32*	.51**	.23*
Negative emotion	.43**	.61**	.24*
Dormitory roommates			
Total emotion	.02	.55**	.54**
Positive emotion	.19	.47**	.31*
Negative emotion	.05	.38†	.34*

[a] Increases in r computed by Fisher r-to-z transformations, and tested for significance using a z-test (Raghunathan, Rosenthal, & Rubin, 1996, p. 179).

Note: $^{*}p < .05$; $^{**}p < .01$; $^{\dagger}p < .10$.

study provided strong evidence that emotional convergence occurs among romantic partners. Their emotional experiences during the laboratory tasks were somewhat similar in our initial assessment, but they became significantly more similar in the second assessment six months later.

Longitudinal Study of Same-Sex Roommates

We next examined whether this process occurs in other types of relationships. That is, we wondered whether emotional convergence is unique to romantic relationships, or does it occur in platonic relationships as well? Does it occur in same-sex as well as mixed-sex relationships? Moreover, the couples in the first study were already somewhat emotionally similar by our first assessment. Thus, we were interested in whether emotional convergence occurs among relationship partners who start out emotionally nonsimilar, as pressures toward uniformity might be less potent in relations between dissimilar individuals (Schachter, 1951).

To address these issues, we needed to examine same-sex platonic friends who, at the beginning of their relationship, were not similar to one another in their emotional dispositions or response tendencies. Given the fact that people often select others as relationship partners based on their similarity (for a review, see Berscheid & Walster, 1983), we had to study relationships whose partners did not select each other. Therefore, we examined dormitory roommates who were randomly assigned to live with one another by their university. The first laboratory assessment took place when the roommates had lived together for only two weeks, and most of them did not know each other well. The follow-up session took place nine months later at the end of the spring semester.

Using a design similar to the first study, we assessed positive and negative emotional experience in both sessions using laboratory procedures. For example, in one procedure, using a rigged lottery, each of the two roommates was ostensibly randomly chosen, and they in turn posed and held an embarrassing facial expression for one minute. In another procedure, participants were given a five-digit number and asked to subtract a second number from it aloud, repeatedly, for one minute (Tomaka et al., 1993). Following the tasks, roommates privately reported their emotional experiences during different stages of the session. To assess how close the roommates had become by the end of the year, we also obtained measures of closeness between roommates at the second session. Given roommates had only lived together for two weeks by the first session, we did not expect them to exhibit similarity in their emotional reactions. However, we expected their emotional reactions to become more similar over the course of the year, by the second assessment.

As shown in Table 7.1, the similarity correlations for total emotional experience, positive emotion, and negative emotion at Time 1 were not significant. Nine months later, the similarity correlation had become substantial for total emotional experience ($r = .55$); in fact, this similarity correlation is roughly equal to the similarity correlation among romantic partners. As in the study of romantic partners, this effect replicated for positive and negative emotion at Time 2. Therefore, these findings lend further support to the idea that emotional convergence occurs in close relationships – here, it even occurred in same-sex relationships whose partners did not choose each other.

Emotional Convergence When Relationship Partners Are Not Present

In a third study, we examined two issues. First, we wanted to show that relationship partners became more similar in their global affectivity. Second, we wanted to show that relationship partners would exhibit similarity in their emotional responses even when they are not in each other's company. If so, this would suggest that relationship partners in the first two studies were not just "catching" each other's emotional responses in the moment through processes such as emotional contagion or empathy. Thus, we separated relationship partners and assessed their emotional responses in different rooms, using film clips as emotion-induction stimuli.[2] Specifically, we used films from the Gross and Levenson (1995) film library.

[2] Given the fact that relationship partners might arrive to the laboratory in a similar mood, which would enhance the similarity of their emotional reactions, we controlled for their moods in all analyses testing emotional convergence.

TABLE 7.2. *Similarity in Emotion Between Roommates and Between Randomly Paired Participants*

	Similarity Correlations		
	Between Randomly Paired Participants	**Between Roommates**	**Difference**[a]
Emotional experience			
Total emotion	−.18	.29*	.45*
Positive emotion	−.05	.26*	.31*
Negative emotion	−.24	.35*	.54**

[a] Differences in r computed by Fisher r-to-z transformations, and tested for significance using a z-test (Cohen & Cohen, 1983).

Note: $^{*}p < .05$; $^{**}p < .01$.

We again examined dormitory roommates who did not know and choose each other at the beginning of the year. We measured their responses in one assessment, after they had lived together for seven months, with the assumption that any similarity observed would have been due to emotional convergence (and not selection effects). However, to reassure ourselves that the roommates were more similar to each other after seven months than when they were randomly paired together at the beginning of the year, we created a comparison group similar to the roommates at the beginning of the year. Specifically, we randomly paired participants with another roommate from the sample, and correlated participants' emotions with the emotions of these randomly chosen partners.

To measure roommates' global affectivity, we asked them to rate how much they felt a number of positive and negative emotions in general: amusement, anger, contempt, contentment, discomfort, disgust, fear, guilt, happiness, pride, sadness, and tension. After creating aggregates of total affectivity, positive affectivity, and negative affectivity, we found the similarity correlation between roommates was significant for total affectivity [$r = .25$ ($p < .05$)], for positive affectivity [$r = .46$ ($p < .01$)], and for negative affectivity [$r = .26$ ($p < .05$)]. In contrast, none of the similarity correlations was significant in the yoked-comparison group (rs = .07, −.11, and .20, respectively) for total, positive, and negative affectivity.

Table 7.2 shows the similarity correlations between roommates in their emotional responses to the films, as well as similarity correlations of the yoked-comparison group. As expected, for the yoked-comparison group, none of the similarity correlations was positive and significant. However, the similarity correlation between actual roommates was significant for total emotional experience, positive emotion, and negative emotion. Therefore, these findings suggest that relationship partner's emotional similarity was not due to emotional contagion or empathy. Instead, as these roommates were not in the same room when they responded to the films, they must have appraised the films in a similar way and thus reacted similarly emotionally.

Summary

Using longitudinal and cross-sectional design, as well as different measures of diverse emotions, our studies offered strong evidence that emotional convergence does occur both in romantic couples and in same-sex friendships. Moreover, our third study indicated that the effects of emotional convergence occur even when relationship partners cannot see each other's emotional reactions to events. Thus, the increasing emotional similarity we observed was not due to processes such as emotional contagion or empathy. Instead, relationship partners do seem to develop similar ways of emotionally responding to events on a general level over time.

HYPOTHESIS 2: EMOTIONAL CONVERGENCE BENEFITS RELATIONSHIPS

Earlier, we offered a functional account of emotional convergence, implying that there are benefits to the convergence we documented in our first two studies. Namely, we suggested convergent emotions coordinate relationship partners' mental states and beliefs, and they increase feelings of closeness and validation. Does convergence indeed benefit relationships? In the context of the studies described here, we examined two questions. First, were more emotionally similar couples more satisfied with their relationship and less likely to break up? Second, were more emotionally similar roommates closer to each other by the end of the year?

Among the couples, we did find that emotional similarity at Time 1 predicted later relationship satisfaction, measured six months later at Time 2. We also found that the couples who were less emotionally similar at Time 1 were more likely to break up within the six months of our study. As shown in Table 7.3, the couples who were still together at Time 2 were more emotionally similar at Time 1 ($r = .30$) than the couples who had broken up ($r = -.06$). This effect also held for positive emotion and negative emotion.

Among the roommates of our second study, we also found that roommates who became more emotionally similar over the year became closer; they trusted each other more, were more likely to disclose problems to each other, and expected to remain friends over the next ten years. Therefore, the evidence from those studies does suggest that emotional convergence occurs because the emotional similarity that develops over time benefits relationships. Of course, a next step in this line of investigation is to document how emotional convergence benefits relationships. We would expect

TABLE 7.3. *Emotional Similarity at Time 1 for Couples Who Broke Up or Were Still Together Six Months Later*

	Similarity Correlation Between Partners at Time 1	
Emotional Experience	**Couples Broken Up**	**Couples Still Together**
Total emotion	−.06	.30*
Positive emotion	−.05	.32*
Negative emotion	−.02	.43**

Note: *$p < .05$; **$p < .01$.

moments of emotional similarity to increase the coordination of relationship partners' actions, for example, as they work and play. We would expect these same partners to feel comfort and appreciation in contexts of convergence.

HYPOTHESIS 3: EMOTIONAL CONVERGENCE IS ASYMMETRICAL

Emotional convergence could develop over time in one of two very different ways. It could be a symmetrical process, in which both members equally influence each other's emotions over time. Thus, relationship partners' emotional experiences could end up at an average point of where they started. A mildly enthusiastic individual and a euphoric individual could form a friendship, for example; and, as they get close to one another, end up at some midpoint between each other.

Alternatively, one relationship partner might typically make more of the change required for emotional convergence to occur than the other. Here, one partner might evoke more change, and the other partner would be more receptive to that change. That is, one relationship partner would have more influence over the emotional convergence process – he or she would determine the emotional patterns of the relationship.

The determinants of asymmetry in emotional convergence are certain to be numerous. One might expect for example that more expressive relationship partners would evoke more convergence in their partners (Hatfield et al., 1994). One might also expect empathetic individuals to be more susceptible to convergence. Perhaps individuals more invested or committed to the relationship would converge more. In our own work, we focused on social power. Based on theory and research on social power (e.g., Keltner, Gruenfeld, & Anderson, 2003), we expected the emotional convergence process to be more asymmetrical in nature and that the relationship partner with more power will be more influential in the emotional convergence process. Stated another way, the relationship partner with less power should make more of the change necessary for emotional convergence to occur.

TABLE 7.4. *Power in the Emotional Convergence Process: Cross-Lagged Correlations Between Participants' Emotions at Time 2 and Their Partner's Emotions at Time 1 Separately for Participants High and Low in Power*

Relationship	Participants with More Power	Participants with Less Power
Romantic relationships		
Total emotion	.19	$.69^{**}$
Positive emotion	.12	$.50^{**}$
Negative emotion	.27	$.53^{**}$
Dormitory roommates		
Total emotion	−.10	$.40^{**}$
Positive emotion	.32	$.38^{*}$
Negative emotion	−.10	$.42^{**}$

Note: The correlations in the first column indicate how well the later emotions of the participants with more power were predicted by the prior emotions of the participant with less power. The correlations in the second column indicate how well the later emotions of the participants with less power were predicted by the prior emotions of the participants with more power. $^{*}p < .05$; $^{**}p < .01$.

Power is defined as the ability to provide or withhold resources or administer punishments in specific relationships (Emerson, 1962; Fiske, 1993; Thibaut & Kelley, 1959). Research from a variety of domains suggests that differences in power develop in virtually all relationships and groups, including romantic relationships, friendships, work groups, families, and communities (Anderson et al., 2001; Gray-Little & Burks, 1983; Owens & Sutton, 2001; Savin-Williams, 1979; Sulloway, 1996). Moreover, a growing body of work has shown that people with less power attend to those with high power more than vice-versa (e.g., Fiske, 1993; Keltner & Robinson, 1997). Thus, this suggests that people with less power should attend to and mimic the emotional styles of their partner more than vice-versa.

We examined whether people with less power made more of the change in the emotional convergence process in the two longitudinal studies described. Specifically, we measured each relationship partner's power and computed two cross-lagged correlations: (a) how well the emotions of the more powerful partner at Time 2 were predicted by the emotions of the less powerful partner at Time 1 and (b) how well the emotions of the less powerful partner at Time 2 were predicted by the emotions of the more powerful partner at Time 1.[3]

These cross-lagged correlations are presented in Table 7.4, for more and less powerful partners, between their own emotions at Time 2 and their

[3] To measure power among romantic partners, we asked each partner to rate each other's power in the relationship context. To measure power among dormitory roommates, we asked fellow dormitory members to rate each of the roommates' respect, prominence, and influence in the dormitory floor.

partners' emotions at Time 1. As shown in the table, the correlations between the more powerful partners' own emotion at Time 2 and their partners' emotion at Time 1 were not significant. These null findings emerged for positive and negative emotion. In contrast, the correlations between the emotions of the less powerful partner at Time 2 and their partners' prior emotions at Time 1 were substantial. Thus, these findings show that one relationship partner, who had less power more broadly, made more of the change necessary for emotional convergence to occur. That is, the emotions of the relationship partner with lower power or status were better predicted by their partners' prior emotions than vice-versa.

IMPLICATIONS AND QUESTIONS FOR FUTURE RESEARCH

In summary, our studies provided three major findings. First, emotional convergence occurs in close relationships. Relationship partners became more similar in their emotional reactions to events, and this similarity was exhibited even in contexts in which they were not in each others' company. Second, the emotional similarity that results from convergence benefits relationships; convergent couples are more likely to stay together and be satisfied; convergent friends are closer. Third, the relationship partner with less power makes more of the change necessary for emotional convergence to occur (stated another way, the relationship partner with more power had much more influence in the emotional convergence process than the relationship partner with less power). We now turn to the implications of these findings, organized by four levels of analysis: at the individual, relationship, group, and cultural levels.

Emotional Convergence and the Individual

On the individual level, our finding that emotional convergence occurs in close relationships indicates that individuals' emotions are strongly shaped by their relationships with others. At any moment in time, the individual's life is influenced by intrapsychic factors: appraisals of the environment, memories and associations, varying levels of arousal, and fatigue. At the same time, our findings indicate that a significant part of the individual's moods and emotions come from other people.

Perhaps what is most intriguing at the individual level of analysis about emotional convergence is that it occurs among people with low power much more than it does among people with high power. Our cross-lagged correlations showed that the emotions of the relationship partner with less power were extremely influenced by their partner's emotions, but that the emotions of the relationship partner with more power were almost unmoved by their partner's emotions. These findings paint a striking picture of the emotional lives of people with low power (see also Kemper, 1991;

Tiedens, 2001; Tiedens, Ellsworth, & Mesquita, 2000). Specifically, they suggest that the emotions of people with low power will be quite variable, changing across relationship contexts as they adapt to the different individuals in different contexts. For example, as they move from one relationship context to another (e.g., spending time with their friend to spending time with their spouse), they will change their emotional response to match that of the person they are with at that time.

We suggest that people with less power might develop something akin to relationship schemas, which guide their emotional responses in different relationship contexts. Relationship schemas are defined as cognitive structures representing regularities in patterns of interpersonal readiness (Baldwin, 1992). When individuals are with a friend, for example, or when they are primed to think of that friendship, a relationship schema is activated and guides them to think and behave according to the norms of that friendship (Baldwin, 1992). As evidence, college students primed to think about their relationship with their parents responded more conservatively to sexually explicit materials than students primed to think about their relationship with college friends (Baldwin, 1992). In similar fashion, individuals with low power might develop an implicit knowledge of the emotional regularities in each of their relationships, which can be activated to guide their emotional reactions in the context of those relationships and not others.

Emotional Convergence in Relationships

Our findings showed that emotional similarity benefited relationships. Romantic partners who became more emotionally similar over time were more satisfied with their relationship and were less likely to break up. Dormitory roommates who became more emotionally similar over time became closer to one another by the end of the academic year and reported a higher likelihood of remaining friends in the subsequent ten years.

This finding speaks not only to relationship maintenance, but also to how relationships are formed in the first place. Research on the similarity-attraction hypothesis has shown that people are attracted to others who are similar to them on a host of variables, ranging from their attitudes and values, to personality traits, to physical attributes, to socioeconomic status, to cognitive styles (Berscheid & Walster, 1983). Our findings suggest that these effects extend to the emotional domain as well, in that people are likely attracted to others who express emotions that are similar to their own. We have obtained preliminary evidence for this idea in our own work on coalition formation (Anderson, Thompson, & Choi, 2004). Specifically, we have found that, in competitive, multiparty environments, individuals tend to choose other people who are emotionally similar to them to form coalitions. Part of the reason why people choose emotionally similar others, it seems, is that they trust them more than people who are emotionally dissimilar to them. Thus, emotional similarity between individuals breeds the trust and attraction that leads to relationship formation, just as it fosters relationship cohesion after the relationship has formed.

Of course, there are times in which we expect emotional convergence to be more harmful than helpful – that is, there are many contexts in which emotional dissimilarity should be beneficial. One condition in which emotional convergence might actually harm relationships and individuals is when relationship partners converge on extreme and unhealthy levels of emotion. Studies of emotional disorders in relationships have provided evidence suggesting that emotional convergence can occur at extreme levels of emotion. Researchers of depressed parents have found that children of depressed parents often become depressed themselves (Field et al., 1990; Gaensbauer et al., 1984; Zahn-Waxler et al., 1984). Studies of high school classmates showed that students with chronic anxiety disorders were more likely to have friends suffering from the same disorder (Hogue & Steinberg, 1995). A study of college roommates also found that individuals who lived with a depressed person for three months were more likely to themselves become depressed (Howes, Hokanson, & Loewenstein, 1985). Although these studies suggest that emotional convergence can at times have harmful effects, they also imply something striking about the emotional convergence process itself. Namely, the effects of emotional convergence are so strong that they cause people to follow others' unhealthy patterns of emotionality. Individuals in close relationships seem open enough to changing their emotions that they do so even when it involves matching a partner's extreme and dysfunctional levels of emotion.

Emotional Convergence in Groups

As we have argued, emotional convergence should occur in any situation in which two or more individuals become close enough to influence each other's emotional response. Therefore, we expect emotional convergence to occur in larger social groups, as well as dyadic relationships. For example, emotional convergence should occur in families, social clubs, teams, or work groups – any group in which people spend a good deal of time together and whose members become close. Indeed, the process of emotional convergence might be the primary mechanism for why groups exhibit a "group emotion," or homogeneity in their emotions (Bartel & Saavedra, 2000; Kelly & Barsade, 2001).

Where would a group's emotion originate? We believe that the pattern of emotional convergence in any group will be tied to its hierarchy. Previous research has shown that hierarchies develop in virtually all social groups and that attention tends to be "directed upward" in groups' hierarchies, whereas influence tends to be directed downward (Fiske, 1993; French & Raven, 1959). People lower in the hierarchy pay more attention to, and are more influenced by, those higher in the hierarchy. Furthermore, people with less power are more motivated to maintain close relationships with powerful others than vice-versa. This suggests that leaders will have more influence over a group's emotions than other group members. Indeed, anecdotal evidence suggests that leaders' emotions can have an immediate and powerful influence over the emotions of subordinates (Hatfield et al., 1994). Our findings concerning power within dyadic bonds lend further support to this notion.[4]

Emotional convergence also has implications for how we understand the phenomena of socially shared cognition. One of the primary aims of social psychology has been to understand how people establish a common social reality (Festinger, 1951; Sherif, 1936; Thompson & Fine, 1999). How do individuals come to share perceptions of the environment, reason in similar ways, make similar decisions, and follow similar patterns of behavior? Although studies have typically focused on cognitive channels of interpersonal influence, our findings suggest that emotions might play a part as well. Emotions have been shown to influence a host of cognitive processes. They focus people's attention on certain aspects of the environment; change the way people interpret events; alter individuals' style of reasoning, probability estimates, and perceptions of fairness; and modify the way individuals interpret others' behavior (Ashby, Isen, & Turken, 1999; Forgas, 2002; Keltner, Ellsworth, & Edwards, 1993; Lerner & Keltner, 2001; Levenson, 1994). Therefore, if people in relationships emotionally converge over time, as our studies suggest, then this increasing emotional similarity should induce greater similarity in cognitive processes. In short, the transfer of emotions from one person to another over time should facilitate socially shared cognition, and the convergence of norms, values, and attitudes.

Just as emotional similarity benefits dyadic relationships, we also suggest that it benefits larger groups, in that groups whose members are more emotionally similar should be more cohesive and coordinated. This higher level of cohesion and coordination should, in turn, help groups work more

[4] One study by Hsee, Hatfield, Carlson, and Chemtob (1990) found that people with power were more susceptible to contagion than people low in power. However, this unexpected finding could have been due to two confounds. First, people in power were placed in "teacher" roles, which might have implied an expectation that they pay close attention to their "student." This higher attention paid to students might have in turn made them more susceptible to contagion. Second, people in the power roles were ostensibly going to give electric shocks to those with lower power; thus, they could have been empathizing with the low power others, making them more susceptible to contagion.

effectively toward their collective goals. The increased cohesion among emotionally similar group members would increase their commitment to the group and their motivation to work together on difficult tasks. The increased coordination among emotionally similar group members would increase their efficiency and effectiveness in working on complex tasks. In short, emotional similarity should make group members work harder and more effectively together. We have obtained some preliminary evidence for these ideas in a laboratory study in which we manipulated emotional similarity versus dissimilarity among individuals working together on a difficult task (Choi, Anderson, & Thompson, 2004). We found that people made to feel emotionally similar worked harder and more effectively together than people made to feel emotionally dissimilar. What was particularly striking, however, was that people made to feel similarly sad outworked and outperformed people who were made to feel emotionally dissimilar (happy and sad). Thus, it seemed as though people were at an advantage when they were feeling similarly badly than when they were feeling emotionally different from each other.

As we noted previously, however, there are likely to be contexts in which emotional dissimilarity is more beneficial than emotional similarity. For example, in the context of work groups, we expect emotional dissimilarity to increase performance on tasks that require divergent thinking or that are facilitated by diversity in cognitive styles. In such contexts, emotional dissimilarity might help foster differences in cognitions, which would lead to a wider range of ideas and perspectives. Furthermore, in contexts where groups are benefited by a devil's advocate, emotional dissimilarity might be more beneficial than emotional similarity and help avoid problems of groupthink (Janis, 1982).

Emotional Convergence and Cultural Variation in Emotion

The literature on culture and emotion has found consistencies across cultures in certain aspects of the emotional response – for example, in the link between the experience of emotion and facial displays (e.g., Ekman, 1973) – as well as a number of differences. In particular, many studies have found cultural variation in the way people appraise emotion-antecedent events (for a review, see Mesquita & Frijda, 1992). For example, in a study that involved respondents from 37 countries, Scherer (1997) found sizable differences across cultures in how individuals appraise events along the dimensions of immorality, unfairness, and external attribution. In summarizing the literature on culture and emotion, Mesquita and Frijda (1992) concluded that differences across cultures in appraisal propensities have been consistently found.

Given the evidence that people in different cultures appraise emotion-antecedent events differently, it is important to understand how these differences develop. Alternatively stated, how do people within cultures maintain similarity in their appraisal propensities? For example, how is it that individuals in the United States similarly use the "responsibility" dimension in appraising negative events much more than do individuals in Japan (Matsumoto et al., 1988)? How are such appraisal tendencies transmitted from one person to another in a given culture?

One idea is that the cultural transmission of appraisal styles occurs through emotional communication in everyday social interactions. When someone expresses emotion in response to an event, this expression communicates to others how they define the event, or how they appraised that event (Frijda & Mesquita, 1994; Keltner & Haidt, 2001). Thus, this provides the opportunity for the social transmission of appraisal styles. Others have the opportunity to adopt that appraisal, or to change their own appraisal of the event to match the expresser's. Frijda and Mesquita (1994) make a similar argument:

> emotional expressions "...indicate to others the emotional potential of the situation. Emotions tend to define events to other individuals as emotionally valent ones.... [T]hey show the event to possess emotion-arousing properties.... [E]motions are among the prime means for the transmission of socially shared meanings." (pp. 74–75)

The present research provides some evidence that people may in fact transmit appraisal styles between each other. In the current studies, we found that people in close relationships come to share similar styles of emotionally responding to events. This suggests that people might have been implicitly communicating and transmitting appraisal styles over the course of their relationship's development. Over many months, people in these relationships had many opportunities to observe each others' emotional expressions in reactions to events, to infer the meaning ascribed to those events by each other, and to modify their own appraisal of those events accordingly. Thus, cultural homogeneity in appraisal styles might develop out of the emotional convergence that transpires in close interpersonal relationships. Future studies, of course, need to examine more directly whether emotional convergence does involve a convergence in appraisal styles, and whether this might underlie homogeneity in group members' emotions.

CONCLUSIONS

Emotion researchers have long looked within the individual to understand the nature of experience, documenting relations between emotion components (e.g., emotional experience, expressive behavior, and physiological response). This intrapersonal focus made sense, as emotional experience is usually private, personal, and covert. However, as much of the work in this volume can attest, our understanding of emotional experience will be just as fruitfully advanced by looking outside of the individual, especially to the individual's relationships and groups. The findings we presented in this chapter suggest that the individual's emotions are intimately tied to the emotions of close others. Human experience may be even more social than we imagined, or that the prose of our private experience suggests.

References

Acitelli, L. K., Kenny, D. A., & Weiner, D. (2001). The importance of similarity and understanding of partners' marital ideals to relationship satisfaction. *Personal Relationships, 8*, 167–185.

Anderson, C., John, O. P., Keltner, D., & Kring, A. M. (2001). Who attains social status? Effects of personality and physical attractiveness in social groups. *Journal of Personality and Social Psychology, 81*, 116–132.

Anderson, C. Thompson, L., & Choi, H. S. (2004). *Emotional similarity and the formation of coalitions in multi-party competitive environments*. Manuscript in preparation.

Ashby, F. G., Isen, A. M., & Turken, A. U. (1999). A neuropsychological theory of positive affect and its influence on cognition. *Psychological Review, 106*, 529–550.

Baldwin, M. W. (1992). Relationship schemas and the processing of social information. *Psychological Bulletin, 112*, 461–484.

Barsade, S. G, Ward, A. J., Turner, J. D. F., & Sonnenfeld, J. A. (2000). To your heart's content: A model of affective diversity in top management teams. *Administrative Science Quarterly, 45*, 802–836.

Bartel, C. A., & Saavedra, R. (2000). The collective construction of work group moods. *Administrative Science Quarterly, 45*, 197–231.

Bavelas, J. B., Black, A., Chovil, N., Lemery, C. R., & Mullett, J. (1988). Form and function in motor mimicry: Topographic evidence that the primary function is communication. *Human Communication Research, 14*, 275–299.

Bell, P. A. (1978). Affective state, attraction, and affiliation: Misery loves happy company, too. *Personality and Social Psychology Bulletin, 4*, 616–619.

Berscheid, E., & Walster, E. (1983). *Interpersonal attraction*. Reading, MA: Addison-Wesley.

Campbell, D. T. (1975). On the conflicts between biological and social evolution and between psychology and moral tradition. *American Psychologist, 30*, 1103–1126.

Cheney, D. L., & Seyfarth, R. M. (1985). Vervet monkey alarm calls: Manipulation through shared information? *Behaviour, 94*, 150–166.

Choi, H. S., Anderson, C., & Thompson, L. (2004). *Emotional diversity and workgroup performance*. Manuscript in preparation.

Cohen, J., & Cohen, P. (1983). *Applied multiple regression/correlation analysis for the behavioral sciences*. Hillsdale, NJ: Lawrence Erlbaum.

Collins, R. (1990). Stratification, emotional energy, and the transient emotions. In T. D. Kemper (Ed.), *Research agendas in the sociology of emotions* (pp. 27–57). Albany, NY: State University of New York Press.

Deutsch, F., M., & Mackesy, M. E. (1985). Friendship and the development of self-schemas: The effects of talking about others. *Personality and Social Psychology Bulletin, 11*, 399–408.

Ekman, P. (1973). Universals and cultural differences in facial expressions of emotion. *Nebraska Symposium on Motivation*, 207–283.

Emerson, R. M. (1962). Power dependence relations. *American Sociological Review, 27*, 31–41.

Festinger, L. (1951). Architecture and group membership. *Journal of Social Issues, 7*, 152–163.

Field, T., Healy, B. T., Goldstein, S., & Guthertz, M. (1990). Behavior-state matching and synchrony in mother-infant interactions of nondepressed versus depressed dyads. *Developmental Psychology, 26*, 7–14.

Fiske, S. T. (1993). Controlling other people: The impact of power on stereotyping. *American Psychologist, 48*(6), 621–628.

Forgas, J. P. (2002). Feeling and doing: Affective influences on interpersonal behavior. *Psychological Inquiry, 13*, 1–28.

French, J., & Raven, B. (1959). The bases of social power. In D. Cartwright (Ed.), *Studies in social power* (pp. 150–165). Ann Arbor, MI: Institute for Social Research.

Frijda, N. H., & Mesquita, B. (1994). The social roles and functions of emotions. In S. Kitayama & H. R. Markus (Eds.), *Emotion and culture: Empirical studies of mutual influence* (pp. 51–88). Washington, DC: American Psychological Association.

Gaensbauer, T. J., Harmon, R. J., Cytryn, L., & McKnew, D. H. (1984). Social and affective development in infants with a manic-depressive parent. *American Journal of Psychiatry, 141*, 223–229.

Gray-Little, B., & Burks, N. (1983). Power and satisfaction in marriage: A review and critique. *Psychological Bulletin, 93*, 513–538.

Gross, J. J., & Levenson, R. W. (1995). Emotion elicitation using films. *Cognition and Emotion, 9*, 87–108.

Hatfield, E., Cacioppo, J. T., & Rapson, R. L. (1994). *Emotional contagion*. New York: Cambridge University Press.

Hogue, A., & Steinberg, L. (1995). Homophily in internalized distress in adolescent peer groups. *Developmental Psychology, 31*, 897–906.

Howes, M. J., Hokanson, J. E., & Loewenstein, D. A. (1985). Induction of depressive affect after prolonged exposure to a mildly depressed individual. *Journal of Personality and Social Psychology, 49*, 1110–1113.

Hsee, C. K., Hatfield, E., Carlson, J. G., & Chemtob, C. (1990). The effect of power on susceptibility to emotional contagion. *Cognition & Emotion, 4*, 327–340.

Janis, I. (1982) *Groupthink*. Boston, MA: Houghton Mifflin.

Kelly, J. R., & Barsade, S. G. (2001). Mood and emotions in small groups and work teams. *Organizational Behavior and Human Decision Processes, 86*, 99–130.

Keltner, D., Ellsworth, P. C., & Edwards, K. (1993). Beyond simple pessimism: Effects of sadness and anger on social perception. *Journal of Personality and Social Psychology, 64*, 740–752.

Keltner, D., Gruenfeld, D. H., & Anderson, C. (2003). Power, approach, and inhibition. *Psychological Review, 110*, 265–284.

Keltner, D., & Haidt, J. (2001). Social functions of emotions. In T. J. Mayne & G. A. Bonanno (Eds.), *Emotions: Current issues and future directions*. New York: Guilford.

Keltner, D., & Kring, A. M. (1998). Emotion, social function, and psychopathology. *Review of General Psychology, 2*, 320–342.
Keltner, D., & Robinson, R. J. (1997). Defending the status quo: Power and bias in social conflict. *Personality and Social Psychology Bulletin, 23*, 1066–1077.
Kemper, T. D. (1991). Predicting emotions from social relations. *Social Psychology Quarterly, 54*, 330–342.
LaFrance, M., & Ickes, W. (1981). Posture mirroring and interactional involvement: Sex and sex typing effects. *Nonverbal Behavior, 5*, 139–154.
Lerner, J. S., & Keltner, D. (2001). Fear, anger, and risk. *Journal of Personality and Social Psychology, 81*, 146–159.
Levenson, R. W. (1994). Human emotions: A functional view. In P. Ekman & R. J. Davidson (Eds.), *The nature of emotion: Fundamental questions*. New York: Oxford University Press.
Levenson, R. W., & Ruef, A. M. (1994). Empathy: A physiological substrate. *Journal of Personality and Social Psychology, 63*, 234–246.
Locke, K. D., & Horowitz, L. M. (1990). Satisfaction in interpersonal interactions as a function of similarity in level of dysphoria. *Journal of Personality and Social Psychology, 58*, 823–831.
Matsumoto, D., Kudoh, T., Scherer, K., & Wallbott, H. (1988). Antecedents of and reactions to emotions in the United States and Japan. *Journal of Cross-Cultural Psychology, 19*, 267–286.
Mesquita, B., & Frijda, N. H. (1992). Cultural variations in emotions: A review. *Psychological Bulletin, 112*, 179–204.
Owens, D. A., & Sutton, R. I. (2001). Status contests in meetings: Negotiating the informal order. In M. E. Turner (Ed.), *Groups at work: Advances in theory and research* (pp. 25–35). Mahwah, NJ: Lawrence Erlbaum and Associates.
Preston, S. D., & de Waal, F. B. M. (2002). Empathy: Its ultimate and proximal bases. *Brain and Behavioral Sciences, 25*, 1–72.
Price, R. A., & Vandenberg, S. G. (1980). Spouse similarity in American and Swedish couples. *Behavior Genetics, 10*, 59–71.
Raghunathan, T. E., Rosenthal, R., & Rubin, D. B. (1996). Comparing correlated but nonoverlapping correlations. *Psychological Methods, 1*, 178–183.
Rosenblatt, A., & Greenberg, J. (1988). Depression and interpersonal attraction: The role of perceived similarity. *Journal of Personality and Social Psychology, 55*, 112–119.
Rosenblatt, A., & Greenberg, J. (1991). Examining the world of the depressed: Do depressed people prefer others who are depressed? *Journal of Personality and Social Psychology, 60*, 620–629.
Savin-Williams, R. C. (1979). Dominance hierarchies in groups of early adolescents. *Child Development, 50*, 923–935.
Schachter, S. (1951). Deviation, rejection, and communication. *Journal of Abnormal and Social Psychology, 46*, 190–207.
Scherer, K. R. (1997). The role of culture in emotion-antecedent appraisal. *Journal of Personality and Social Psychology, 73*, 902–922.
Sherif, M. (1936). *The psychology of social norms*. New York: Harper.
Sulloway, F. J. (1996). *Born to rebel: Birth order, family dynamics, and creative lives*. New York: Pantheon Books.

Thibaut, J. W., & Kelley, H. H. (1959). *The social psychology of groups*. New York: Wiley.

Thompson, L., & Fine, G. A. (1999). Socially shared cognition, affect, and behavior: A review and integration. *Personality and Social Psychology Review, 3*, 278–302.

Tiedens, L. Z. (2001). Anger and advancement versus sadness and subjugation: The effect of negative emotion expressions on social status conferral. *Journal of Personality and Social Psychology, 80*, 86–94.

Tiedens, L. Z., Ellsworth, P. C., & Mesquita, B. (2000). Stereotypes about sentiments and status: Emotional expectations for high- and low-status group members. *Personality and Social Psychology Bulletin, 26*, 560–574.

Tomaka, J., Blascovich, J., Kelsey, R. M., & Leitten, C. L. (1993). Subjective, physiological, and behavioral effects of threat and challenge appraisal. *Journal of Personality and Social Psychology, 65*, 248–260.

Watson, D., Clark, L. A., & Tellegen, A. (1988). Development and validation of brief measures of positive and negative affect: The PANAS scales. *Journal of Personality and Social Psychology, 54*, 1063–1070.

Wenzlaff, R. M., & Prohaska, M. L. (1989). When misery prefers company: Depression, attributions, and responses to others' moods. *Journal of Experimental Social Psychology, 25*, 220–233.

Zahn-Waxler, C., Cummings, E. M., McKnew, D. H., & Radke-Yarrow, M. (1984). Altruism, aggression and social interactions in young children with a manic-depressive parent. *Child Development, 55*, 112–122.

8

Emotional Variation in Work Groups

Causes and Performance Consequences

Larissa Z. Tiedens, Robert I. Sutton, and
Christina T. Fong

The human tendency toward homogeneity is a cornerstone of social psychology. Classic studies going back to at least Asch (1955, 1956) and Sherif (1936) suggest that, when interacting with others, variance in human thought and action disappears as people conform to other group members and group norms. Convergence is considered to be a primary consequence of social interaction and group life. In fact, group life often becomes synonymous with uniformity and conformity among members. So, it is not surprising that research on emotion as a group-level construct focuses on homogeneity and on the mechanisms that propel group members to share emotional reactions (see Anderson & Keltner, this volume; Barsade & Gibson, 1998; Bartel & Saavedra, 2000; Hatfield, Cacioppo, & Rapson, 1994; Hatfield & Rapson, this volume).

Although group dynamics researchers have documented powerful pressures that drive out variance, variance within groups has also been a persistent, if less frequent, theme as well (Cartwright & Zander, 1960; Schein, 1965). Groups do not transform members into clones: Variance persists in even the most homogenous groups, and such variation can have important consequences. Some modern research on group cognition does imply the value of examining variation in groups. The widely studied notion of transactive memory, for example, is predicated on the heterogeneity of information held by group members – that group members know and remember different things (e.g., Liang, Moreland, & Argote, 1995; Moreland, 1999; Wegner, 1986).

A similar perspective can be used to examine group emotion. Group members can feel and express varied emotions, and doing so does not necessarily make them less of a group or the emotions less central to the group definition and experience. After all, every group is composed of people who feel and express distinct emotions. We argue that, for many emotions that group members feel and display, it is often just as important, sometimes more important, to consider the differences rather than the similarities.

This chapter focuses on groups organized to fulfill task-related goals, especially work groups. We consider the possibility and consequences of high emotional variance, or emotional heterogeneity. We discuss properties of work groups that influence whether groups are high or low in emotional variance, and how levels of emotional variance shape group outcomes. We also suggest that a group's emotional homogeneity or heterogeneity can result from specific and controllable decisions about group composition and structure, which can ultimately shape team performance.

Examining emotional variation in a group requires conceptualizing the relationship between individual and group emotions somewhat differently than has been done in the past. For example, George's (1990) research in twenty-six retail stores measured levels of individual disposition toward positive affectivity and negative affectivity and aggregated them to the group (i.e., store) level. She then treated group mean levels of positive and negative affectivity as a measure of group affective tone. George assumed, following prior methodological work on cross-level analysis, that within-group consistency in members' emotional dispositions indicated that emotion could be a group characteristic.

We propose that George's approach, while useful, oversimplifies the relationship of individual emotion and group emotion. Indeed, George's research showed that there was variance in affectivity, with some groups showing far more affective consistency than others. We suggest that such variance can be considered a meaningful group attribute. Consider, for example, customers who go to a store in which there is high emotional variance. During a typical visit, a customer might interact with a cheerful clerk, then a grumpy one, and then an indifferent one. Such inconsistency in expressed emotion (and customer experience) is at least as useful for describing and understanding the store as the mean level of expressed positive and negative affect expressed to customers.

SOURCES OF EMOTIONAL VARIANCE IN GROUPS

There are two primary kinds of emotional variance in groups. The first is the "bottom-up" variation that occurs through the aggregation of individual attributes, similarities, and differences, especially in terms of enduring characteristics that each member had before he or she joined the group. The second is "top-down" variation. Features of the group and its context can influence what group members think, feel, and do, regardless of individual member characteristics. For example, the two primary concepts examined by group dynamics researchers, norms and roles, reflect that some expectations are held for all members (thus typically driving out variance), and other expectations vary across members who hold different roles (thus typically inducing variance). We propose that basic properties of groups – including composition, norms, roles, and hierarchy – shape the degree to which the group is oriented toward emotion variation or convergence.

There are also two primary routes through which emotions are generated: a cognitive route and a behavioral route. The cognitive route refers to instances in which a person (either individually or through interaction with others) perceives and interprets the environment in some way, which affects felt or expressed emotions. For example, research on emotional homogeneity demonstrates that when people try to understand another person's perspective, such efforts to mentally "walk a mile in their shoes" causes them to experience the same emotions experienced by the person they are trying to understand (e.g., Davis, 1994; Hoffman, 1984). In this case, individuals in a group feel the same things because they think the same things. In the behavioral route, expressing an emotion influences a person's inner state, such that the actor comes to experience the emotion associated with its behavioral expression (Strack, Martin, & Stepper, 1988). This route has also been discussed in the literature that focuses on homogeneity. Specifically, research on emotion contagion has discussed how people mimic the nonverbal behaviors of others, which means they express the same emotions as those around them and then this leads them to experience the same emotions (Hatfield et al., 1994).

Field studies in groups and organizations suggest that both routes shape the emotions that members express and feel, and in fact, both are used explicitly in many settings. Research on brainstorming groups at IDEO, a product development firm, shows that new designers and clients are taught that brainstorming sessions are intellectually stimulating and fun. Subtle rewards and punishments are given based on emotional behaviors. Those who make jokes or take a funny perspective are considered valuable group members, whereas designers who appear to be bored or grouchy are sometimes pressured through gentle teasing to express the required good cheer, or to leave. So, IDEO uses a cognitive route to set expectations that fun will be had and to frame various events as funny, and also employs behavioral measures so that when people attend the sessions, "fun" is expressed and internalized (Sutton & Hargadon, 1996).

Most experimental and field research has focused on how these cognitive and behavioral routes can reduce emotional variance. Yet, these mechanisms can also promote variation in emotions, and, as we discuss, such variation reveals much about a group and may have important implications for group performance and related outcomes.

Variation Due to Individual Differences

Groups are aggregates of individuals. In general, we suggest that groups composed of people with varied dispositions to express or feel certain emotions will also achieve a group tone marked by emotional variation. These individual differences could relate to dispositional affect (e.g., Barsade et al., 2000), as well as other personality factors that are directly related to the experience and expression of emotions, such as individual differences in expressivity (Friedman et al., 1980), in proneness to empathy (Davis, 1994), and in the desire to regulate and suppress emotions (e.g., Gross & John, 1995; King, 1998). Furthermore, individual differences in emotional experience and expression have been linked to enduring social motives (McClelland, 1985; Zurbriggen & Sturman, 2002) and to the Big-5 personality traits (Diener et al., 1992; Larsen & Ketelaar, 1989; Rusting & Larsen, 1998). People who score high on the Neuroticism scale also report more negative feelings, whereas people who score higher in Extraversion report experiencing more positive emotion. In addition, certain personality types, like high empathetic individuals, are more prone to mimic and thus "catch" the emotions of others (Chartrand & Bargh, 1999). Variance in such personality variables can influence the range of emotional responses within a group. These arguments and findings imply that, to the extent that a group is composed of people with varied personalities, the more varied group emotion and behaviors linked to emotion we expect to observe.

Other individual differences are more specifically related to the group. For example, feelings of identification with the group influence both the intensity and kind of individual emotional reactions that group members have (Doosje et al., 1998; Mackie, DeVos, & Smith, 2000; Mackie, Silver, & Smith, this volume). This suggests that emotional experiences within a group may vary as a function of how many group members identify strongly (and weakly) with the group. People highly identified with a group are probably more likely to feel pride about the group's accomplishments, whereas group members with weaker identification might admire their team members as individuals, but not feel strongly attached to them or the group (Cialdini et al., 1976; Wann & Branscombe, 1993). Furthermore, Mackie and her colleagues argue that an individual's interpretations of the group's relative position will affect his or her emotional responses. Specifically, a person's interpretation of his/her group as strong versus weak can affect whether the individual feels emotions like anger or fear. Although the strength or weakness of a group may be an objective property of that group, it is also often a subjective assessment such that individual group members may differ in whether they believe that their group is strong or weak. In such cases, variation in emotional responses to group-related events can occur.

The effects of individual differences on groups are likely a result of both the cognitive and behavioral routes to emotion generation. Personality, culture, and perception of the group all affect the way in which people interpret the events that occur within a group, which means that different people can have very different feelings about the same events. For example, Cohen et al., (1996) conducted a study with male students who grew up in the northern versus the southern United States. A confederate bumped into each participant and called him an "asshole." Northerners were relatively unaffected by the insult, but southerners were more likely to view the insult as a threat to their masculine reputation, become upset, and engage in aggressive and dominant behavior. This research suggests that even when group members have the exact same experiences, personality and cultural differences can cause members to notice them to a different degree, to interpret the events differently, to remember different aspects of the event, and even to behave differently so they can end up feeling different emotions (also see Mesquita & Frijda, 1992).

Variation Due to Group Norms

All groups have norms that guide members' behavior. Groups (and the organizations they are embedded in) often socialize newcomers, and reward and punish all members, to help ensure that members will follow certain "display rules," so they will express certain emotions and suppress others. Similarly, groups also teach and enforce feeling rules, norms about which emotions they are expected to feel at which times. Similar to the logic of method acting in which performers try to experience the same thoughts and emotions as the characters they play (Moore, 1984), feeling rules are espoused and enforced, in part, to help members display more authentic emotions to customers and to each other.

As we suggested earlier, norms (including display and feeling rules) can and do drive out variation. Hochschild (1983), Van Maanen and Kunda (1989), and Sutton and Rafaeli (1988) have all discussed work settings and organizational cultures that demand that members feel and express happiness. All Mary Kay Cosmetics "beauty consultants" are expected to be enthusiastic (Ash, 1984), and all 7/Eleven clerks are expected to smile, establish eye contact, and offer polite social amenities to customers. Organizations also impact the cognitive route by teaching employees to think about situations in a way that produces the desired emotions. Hochschild (1983) describes, for example, how flight attendants at Delta were trained to think of unruly and drunk customers as "nervous fliers," with the hope that thinking about these customers in this light would help them to be friendly to such customers, or at least not become rude and hostile toward them.

Although feeling rules and display rules generally drive out variance in emotions, there is important variation in the way in which emotion rules are enacted, which allows ample potential for variation in emotion to exist. First, groups with lower cohesiveness, those with weaker social glue, will be less constrained by emotion rules. When groups are less cohesive, members interact with each other less, stand and sit farther apart, pay less attention to each other, show fewer signs of mutual affection, and are less likely to punish and expel deviants (Levine & Moreland, 1998). Therefore, in these groups, emotion rules will be followed less often and deviation from them will not be noticed or responded to; thus, there will be greater emotion variation.

Second, some groups have norms that are specifically focused on emotion. Bartel and Saavedra (2000) asked members of 70 work groups to indicate how strong the mood regulation norms were. Bartel and Saavedra found a great deal of variance on this measure and that higher levels of emotional regulation norms predicted greater similarity in arousal emotions observed among group members.

Third, whereas some groups have norms that press all members to feel the same emotion all the time, others have norms that advocate variation. For example, Mars and Nicod's (1984) ethnographic study of five hotel restaurants suggests that a narrower range of emotions is expected in more prestigious than less prestigious hotels. Mars and Nicod report that waiters in the most prestigious hotels were always expected to be charming, polite, and discreet during service encounters, but a much wider range of expressed emotions was acceptable in less prestigious hotels.

Groups may also have strong norms to express and feel widely varying emotions for different types of people or in different situations. Rafaeli and Sutton (1987) propose that the "emotion work" done by people and teams varies considerably in the diversity of emotional responses required. To the extent that groups require such constant shifting of emotional gears from members, we would expect a group to have more varied emotion. Denison and Sutton's (1990) observations of a team of surgical nurses, for example, revealed that their displays required them to constantly shift emotion, and this appeared to provoke a similarly broad range of inner feelings. These emotions ranged from being cool and solemn in the operating room, to expressing empathy and warmth to patients and families, to teasing and joking with surgeons during breaks, to expressing contempt and anger at the researchers for taking too much of their time.

Similarly, the telephone bill collectors that Sutton (1991) and Gibson and Fichman (2002) studied were trained, monitored, rewarded, and punished to help ensure that they constantly and rapidly "shifted emotional gears" in response to different debtor characteristics, especially the debtor's demeanor. For example, these bill collectors were trained and rewarded to convey anger toward relaxed and nice debtors; management believed that such people were not worried enough about the overdue payment, so conveying a bit of nastiness would help them become upset and motivated enough to pay the bill. In contrast, collectors were trained to express a calm demeanor and to utter soothing words to angry debtors because management believed they were upset enough about the overdue payment, but needed to calm down enough to realize that they would not have suffered such unhappiness any longer if they would just pay the bill!

Moreover, other norms not directly related to emotions can broaden or narrow the range of emotions felt and expressed in a group. To illustrate, some work groups encourage disagreement among members, whereas others stifle it (Pelled, Eisenhardt, & Xin, 1999). To ensure that members do not find their opinions stifled, such groups can provoke disagreement through the creation of particular roles or by providing status symbols or other rewards to those who disagree (Cialdini, Reno, & Kallgren, 1990). The Intel Corporation, for example, provides classes for all full-time employees in "constructive confrontation," which includes extensive role-playing; Intel employees are then evaluated and rewarded partly on the basis of their ability to engage in constructive confrontation. Groups that have norms that facilitate disagreement will likely be characterized by more emotional variation. In part, the disagreement itself is likely to generate emotion variation through the debates that ensue, but also group members will expect and be accustomed to thinking and behaving in ways that are different from one another and differently from the way they have in the past.

Variation Due to Group Roles

Most groups, especially work groups, organize themselves by assigning formal and informal roles and dividing labor among members (Cartwright & Zander, 1960; Bales, 1950; Schein, 1965). Individuals are given (or take) particular titles and responsibilities and, in doing so, split up their primary task into individual units. The role that a group member takes in a group can influence the emotions that they experience and express by affecting what people think and how people act. Consider Lieberman's (1956) classic study of the effects of roles on attitude change. Lieberman measured the initial attitudes toward the company, the union, and their jobs in a sample of factory workers. A few months later, some workers were promoted to supervisors, whereas other workers were elected to be union shop stewards. There were no significant differences between workers' attitudes in the three groups before they were promoted. But after they were promoted, and thus exposed to different information and asked to behave in different ways (including to express different emotions), the new supervisors developed more positive attitudes toward the company and less positive attitudes toward the union. Conversely, those promoted to shop stewards changed their attitudes in the exact opposite directions, and there were no significant changes among respondents who continued working in their old roles. The implication for emotional variance in a group is that, to the extent that the group is composed of people who hold different roles with different emotional perspectives and demands, emotional variance is likely to arise. Indeed, the supervisors, shop stewards, and regular factory workers that Liberman studied were members of the same work groups.

When roles are highly differentiated, and interdependence between roles is low, emotional variance in groups becomes particularly likely. Under such conditions, group members can become "component focused," directing their attention entirely on their own task, to the exclusion of the other group activities (Heath & Staudenmayer, 2000). When people devote attention to their own little worlds and ignore what is happening to fellow members, they experience different events than other group members who face different demands and do different jobs, which ought to produce differences in emotion. In addition, once people have a component focus, they are less likely to notice (and thus "catch") the frustration and joy experienced by others.

Furthermore, widely varying behaviors, including emotions, are expected in and provoked by different roles within the same group. Consider some common roles that group dynamics researchers identified, like task leaders, social-emotional leaders, clowns, and scapegoats (Bales, 1950; Cartwright & Zander, 1960). Even in groups with strong norms for convergent emotional expressions, there will be more warmth from the social-emotional leader than the task leader, and more laughing and joking from the clown than the scapegoat. Other common roles can also create emotional demands that vary across group members. A group organized around a particular product might, for example, consist of a sales person who is expected to be upbeat and excited about the product, but also a manager who finds that expressing cold disapproval helps dissuade her subordinates from missing deadlines (Huy, 2002).

Or, consider the *Saturday Night Live* cast. Lorne Michaels, executive producer of TV's *Saturday Night Live* for nearly three decades, has always pressed performers to accentuate and develop their personae. This means, in large part, developing a trademark demeanor, or role. Even though there were clear strong norms for being funny, distinct roles in the cast were evident from *Saturday Night Live's* first season. The differences rather than the similarities among the Not Ready for Prime Time Players' expressed emotions are most striking, ranging from the wildly impulsive and temperamental John Belushi, to the cool and detached Jane Curtin, to the bewildered Chevy Chase, to the silly and exuberant Gilda Radner (Shales &

Miller, 2002). And these emotional differences appeared to increase rather than decrease over time.

Groups doing work that entails persuasion, especially gaining compliance from unwilling people, sometimes use the good cop–bad cop approach. This technique is employed during interactions with outsiders, members in the "good cop" role adopt a caring, considerate, and generally positively affective tone, whereas the "bad cops" adopt an angry, bullying tone (Brodt & Tuchinsky, 2000). Qualitative research by Rafaeli and Sutton (1991) on bill collectors and police interrogators found that teams in both occupations used the good cop–bad cop method strategically and mindfully. A police interrogator reported, for example, that

> whenever we did the good guy, bad guy thing, we would plan and coordinate. The good guy would say "C'mon, leave him alone, let him calm down. He looks like a good guy to me, I think we should help him." Then the bad guy would say, "What is wrong with you. He is a piece of shit. . . . " (p. 759)

Other groups create "devil's advocate" roles in which a group member is expected to go out of his or her way to disagree with whatever seems to be the predominant opinion in the group (Schwenk & Cosier, 1980). Janis (1972) suggested using devil's advocates as an antidote to "groupthink," and there is at least anecdotal evidence that a few top executives intentionally recruit people who will argue with them and be unpleasant to offset the parade of pleasant and obsequious yes-men and women that most top executives encounter. Rey More, a senior vice-president at Motorola, reported one of the most important staff members was his harshest critic, because "He tells me I am wrong. He compensates for my blind spots. I need him desperately" (Sutton, 2002, p. 45). Roles like the devil's advocate and good cop–bad cop pairing create emotional variation in groups, both by influencing the behavior and the cognition of the people in these roles, as well as people who interact with them.

Variation Due to Social Hierarchies

Most groups, whether by accident or design, have social hierarchies (Lonner, 1980). The criteria used to rank members varies wildly, but in nearly all groups, some members are more valued and respected, which entitles them to certain status symbols and markers, whereas others are considered less valuable and denied such markers (Smith & Tyler, 1997). A person's absolute and relative ranking in the group hierarchy can shape the emotions that he or she is expected to display and is likely to feel.

High status members use "control moves" (Goffman, 1969) to keep members in their place, which can range from explicit aggression like glaring and shouting, to more subtle moves like smiling in a condescending way at lower status members or patting them on the head. In contrast, newcomers and other members at the bottom of a group's pecking order try to get or maintain a toehold in their precarious and powerless positions by expressing warmth, flattery, and deference to higher status members. In an ethnographic study at a research lab, for example, Owens and Sutton (2001) recorded an incident in which one of the lowest status members of a research team group warmly complimented one of the highest status members for developing a great idea, even though the idea was actually generated by numerous other members. The differences in the influence strategies available to and used by members at different hierarchical levels will create variation in the emotions expressed (and probably felt) in groups, because nearly all groups have pecking orders.

Hierarchies also produce varied emotions through the cognitive route. Tiedens (2001) argued that status shapes how people interpret group successes and failures, which, in turn, affects their emotional reactions. In groups in which the hierarchy is considered fair and legitimate, high status members are thought to be more competent and skilled than low status group members. Group members who are considered the most competent are prone to blame others for negative events, which is likely to enhance their feelings of anger. In contrast, group members considered to be less competent (low status members in legitimate hierarchies) may blame themselves, and when they do so, feel guilty. Similarly, the most skilled members (or high status members) typically feel pride in response to a positive event because they credit themselves; in contrast, members who consider themselves less skilled may credit others, provoking feelings of gratitude and appreciation.

Furthermore, hierarchies can produce emotions in group members because people tend to have attitudes and opinions about the hierarchies they are part of, particularly about the degree to which the hierarchy is fair and just (e.g., Sidanius & Pratto, 1999), and these attitudes are related to emotion. In general, perceptions of illegitimacy are related to negative feelings, particularly feelings of anger (Kappen & Branscombe, 2001). People can vary significantly in perceptions of whether a particular hierarchy is legitimate or not, which, in turn, can produce varied emotional responses.

Status may also influence the behavioral generation of group emotions. Preliminary evidence for this comes from a study by Tiedens and Fragale (2003), who found that when a person displays a nonverbal behavior associated with status, it is not mimicked, but rather it is "complemented"; nonverbal behaviors that convey high status are responded to with low status behaviors, and low status behaviors are responded to with high status behaviors. Although the tests of this complementing effect in this study involved a nonverbal behavior that is not directly related to emotional experience (body span), the same principle could be in effect for emotions associated with status positions. Specifically, emotional expressions that convey the claiming of status for oneself, such as anger or pride (Tiedens,

Ellsworth, & Mesquita, 2000) could be responded to with complementary emotional responses that sacrifice or reject status, such as sadness, fear, guilt, or gratitude.

PERFORMANCE CONSEQUENCES

Our review suggests that numerous factors determine the level of emotional variance within a group. But does it make any difference? Does such variation affect a group's ability to achieve its goals? Many researchers have examined the effects of diversity (informational, demographic, or otherwise) on group performance. Some of these scholars have emphasized the need for diversity in groups and shown empirically that the wider range of perspectives, opinions, and information in the group, the better it will perform (Bantel & Jackson, 1989; Cox, Lobel, & McLeod, 1991; Milliken & Martins, 1996; Nemeth, 1986, 1994). Yet other research reveals that diversity can have costs. Differing perspectives are often accompanied by different values, and value conflict can undermine the group's ability to achieve its goals (Jehn, 1994, 1997; Jehn, Chadwick, & Thatcher, 1997). Such conflict is problematic because one of a group's fundamental tasks is to coordinate member behavior (Heath & Staudenmayer, 2000), and coordination requires consensus about how to do things (Ancona & Caldwell, 1992).

Direct evidence about the virtues and drawbacks of emotional diversity is rare. But a recent study of sixty-two top management teams raises doubts about the benefits of high emotional variation for performance (Barsade et al., 2000). Members of these teams reported their dispositional affect on the Well-Being Scale from the Multidimensional Personality Questionnaire (Tellegen, 1982). Barsade and her colleagues also collected information from publicly available databases about the financial success of the companies led by these executive teams. They found that, although teams composed of members with more diverse functional backgrounds led higher performing firms, diversity in positive affectivity in top executive teams was associated with lower firm performance.

These findings raise important questions for future research. In particular, as the authors acknowledge, this cross-sectional study cannot untangle the causal relationship observed between emotional diversity and performance. The causality could easily be reversed, because group performance information has powerful and dramatic effects on self-report data, including reports about group dynamics, individual behavior, self-assessments of individual ability, and emotion (Staw, 1975).

The study by Barsade and her colleagues is a useful early step, but leaves open the question of how emotional variation affects performance, and it suggests some of the difficulties in assessing that question. It is clear that group emotion and performance have reciprocal relations, and studies need to be designed so that such causal relationships can be untangled.

More generally, the problems associated with defining and measuring group performance have troubled researchers for decades. There is agreement among most researchers, however, that group performance is a multidimensional construct, and there are certain constructs that have proven useful in multiple studies (see Cohen & Bailey, 1997; Hackman, 1987; McGrath, 1984). We consider the effects of emotional variation on four aspects of performance: creativity, decision quality, efficiency, and persuasion.

We derive our ideas about these performance outcomes from several sources. First, we consider those rare studies that provide direct evidence on the relationship between emotional diversity and performance. Second, we consider recent research on what happens when individuals feel a mix of emotions rather than a single emotion, because such evidence and research may apply at higher levels of analysis. Third, we seek guidance and inspiration from nonacademic sources (such as biographies and case studies) to fuel our speculations about the effects of emotional variation.

Creativity

The link between emotional experience and creativity has received much attention at both the individual and group levels. At the individual level, much research suggests that positive emotions enhance creativity (Isen & Baron, 1991; Isen, Daubman, & Nowicki, 1987; Isen et al., 1985). Recent research has, however, called these findings into question and suggested that negative emotions can also increase creativity (George & Zhou, 2002; Kaufmann & Vosburg, 1997). Indeed, a blend of both positive and negative emotions might be the best way to spark creativity. C. T. Fong's (unpublished data) recent research supports this conclusion. Her experimental and field studies demonstrate that people who experience emotional ambivalence (the simultaneous experience of positive and negative emotion) are more creative than those who experience just positive emotion, negative emotion, or neutrality.

There are several reasons that high emotional variation might increase group creativity as well. First, research has demonstrated that people who experience positive emotions are more cognitively flexible (Murray et al., 1990), but people who experience negative emotions are better at analytical thinking (Schwarz & Bless, 1991). Creativity results from a combination of unusual and analytical thinking (Amabile, 1996; Staw, 1995), so groups in which some people experience positive emotions and others experience negative emotions may receive the combined benefits of both types of thinking, and demonstrate increased creativity.

Emotional variance within groups may be associated with increased creativity because creativity is sparked when people or groups see the same ideas in different and ever-shifting ways. Numerous historical accounts and case studies suggest that creativity depends on seeing the same old things in new ways (Sutton, 2002). This point has been made by many famous creators, including Nobel Prize-winning biochemist Albert Szent-Gyorgi, the first scientist to isolate vitamin C: "Discovery consists of looking at the same thing as everyone else and thinking something different" (Good, 1963, p. 192). Emotional variation could provide this variation in perspective.

The value of such emotional variation is especially clear in art and music. Arguably, the optimistic and relatively modest Paul McCartney and the grumpy and often wildly arrogant John Lennon wrote great songs, in part, because their widely disparate (and often clashing) emotional reactions caused them to see the same things in such different ways. Similarly, the venerable rock star Neil Young talks openly about the value of surrounding himself with people of varying personalities, who fight with him and each other constantly. As Young explained to his long-time producer, David Briggs, "If you agreed with me all the time, there wouldn't be any need for one of us. Guess which one?" (McDonough, 2002, p. 265). These mixed emotions, the simultaneous love and hate that Young, his fellow musicians, and his managers seem to have toward everything, along with the mood swings they seem to provoke in everyone around them, may have a silver lining, at least when it comes to creativity.

Decision Quality

There are numerous obstacles to quality decision-making in groups, many of which stem from flaws in how humans and human groups process information. Researchers have identified a number of group-level decision biases, including conformity (Asch, 1955, 1956), group polarization (Myers & Lamm, 1976), pluralistic ignorance (Miller & Prentice, 1994), the common knowledge problem (Holtz & Miller, 1985), and groupthink (Janis, 1972), which are all related to the inability to adequately consider the pros and cons of alternatives. In each of these situations, a group reaches consensus about the wrong decision, and analyses of their conversations show that they have not fleshed out pertinent arguments (Nemeth, 1986; Nemeth & Kwan, 1987).

Group biases may be due to some of the same processes involved in individual biases. The dual process framework (often applied to the study of individual biases) asserts that, when people think in a thorough, systematic, and central way, they are unlikely to fall prey to biases, but when they think in a heuristic and peripheral way, they likely fall prey to biases (e.g., Eagly & Chaiken, 1993; Petty & Cacioppo, 1996). Research on emotion and cognition has demonstrated that, whereas some emotions (such as sadness) lead people to process thoroughly and leave the individual relatively immune to cognitive biases, others (such as anger) result in more spontaneous processing and increase the likelihood of decision-making errors (Bodenhausen, 1993; Tiedens & Linton, 2001).

Recent research shows that feeling a blend of emotions might also affect depth of processing. Specifically, C. T. Fong and L. Z. Tiedens (unpublished data) induced feelings of happiness, sadness, neutrality, or a mixture of happiness and sadness in participants. Participants who felt simultaneously happy and sad were better able to distinguish between weak and strong arguments and were less prone to some biases than people in any of the other conditions. One interpretation of these studies is that participants who felt simultaneous positive and negative affect were better able to consider all sides of the arguments. The dual nature of the emotional state that these individuals were experiencing may have served as a vivid reminder that complex answers and multiple perspectives are possible and perhaps even necessary.

Variation in group emotion might accomplish the same thing. Members who are provoked or disposed to feel positive emotions might focus on the strengths of a position, whereas members experiencing negative emotions may focus on its weaknesses. A discussion between people with these disparate feelings might produce best and worst case scenarios, resulting in thorough and complex analysis of the problem and possible solutions. We do not know of any systematic research on this point, but case studies that compare top executive teams that make good versus bad decisions are suggestive. In the 1970s, 1980s, and early 1990s, Intel was led primarily by a trio of executives: Bob Noyce, Gordon Moore, and Andy Grove. In addition to having differing skills and job responsibilities, the stark contrast between the calm Noyce and Moore versus the hotter-tempered Grove may have helped the team see different aspects of problems they faced and decisions they made. As research on emotion and decision making implies they might, the trio was constantly challenged to balance Noyce's and Moore's proclivity to analyze pros and cons with Grove's impulse to take action (O'Toole, Galbraith, & Lawler, 2002).

Finally, the expression of diverse emotions might have communicative value that attenuates group biases. Many poor decisions are made by groups because the mere existence of similarity creates the sense of objective truth, even when the decisions are in the realm of subjectivity and uncertainty (e.g., Janis, 1972). Varied emotional reactions could remind group members that there are many ways to see any issue, which could puncture any illusion that the group sees as the one true objective reality. This speculation is consistent with research by Nemeth and her colleagues, who demonstrated that exposure to minority viewpoints prompts people to think in divergent ways, and consider problems from varying viewpoints (Nemeth, 1986; Nemeth & Kwan, 1987).

Efficient Execution

Once groups have considered their options and chosen a course of action, they need to implement their decision. Emotions function to prepare individuals to act quickly and efficiently, so when an emotion is appropriate to the task at hand, it could result in greater efficiency. However, to function efficiently, group members must coordinate their actions. Coordination entails dividing the labor and then determining how the planned actions will be articulated in time and space. Groups typically excel at the dividing-up tasks, but often do not devote sufficient attention to weaving together the elements (Heath & Staudenmayer, 2000). Doing so requires that individuals think beyond their own tasks and consider how their actions are interdependent with others. When people experience emotions that differ from fellow team members, they experience psychological separation from each other, which reduces their construed interdependence with fellow members (Bartel & Saavedra, 2000). In contrast, group members probably feel the greatest amount of interdependence when they are experiencing the same emotions (Anderson & Keltner, 2004, this volume). So, emotional variance may add to the difficulties that groups face in coordinating activities.

Moreover, high levels of emotional variance can be viewed as a type of emotional complexity. At the individual level, higher levels of integrative complexity have been associated with tendencies toward paralysis and indecision (Suedfeld, 1992). This sort of cognitive complexity may be associated with emotional complexity, thus suggesting that complex emotional reactions may lead to this type of paralysis. In support of this idea, others have also suggested that conflicting emotions may lead to action blockage (Peterson, 1987). Similarly, groups experiencing high levels of emotional conflict could become overwhelmed by this type of conflict or feel uncertain about the best way to proceed, which could cause inaction.

Field research on this point is limited, but there are tantalizing hints that variation in emotions can inhibit decision execution. To return to the Intel example, a crucial part of the training that employees are given in "constructive confrontation" is that, although disagreement is encouraged during the decision-making stage, once a decision is made, everyone is responsible for enthusiastically committing to the decision and doing everything possible to make it successful. Moreover, employees who start complaining about how bad a decision is during the implementation phase are viewed as especially destructive. Intel describes this process as "disagree and then commit," which is consistent with the view that mixed emotions in a group helps decision-making, but hampers decision implementation. In other words, Intel expects high emotional and cognitive complexity before a decision is made, and low emotional and cognitive complexity after it is made, and the focus has turned to implementation.

Finally, if shared emotions do facilitate implementation, literature on the strength of norms and deviance suggests a paradoxical twist. It turns out that espoused norms are more likely to guide behavior when they are occasionally violated and other members notice those violations. This conclusion is implied in Erving Goffman's classic *Relations in Public*. Goffman (1971) points out that, when something is missing or is done wrong in a setting, it reminds people how things are "supposed to be." Cialdini and his colleagues (1990) have conducted research on littering norms that lends credence to this view. They found that people were significantly less likely to litter in parking lots, walkways, and other settings that contained one-piece trash than in settings that were completely clean; their interpretation of this finding was that a single piece of trash in an otherwise pristine setting made the norm against littering more vivid than if it contained no trash at all. Of course, we need research directly on the effects of "emotional deviants" or occasional acts of "emotional deviation" on other members. But existing theory and research implies that, although a wide range of felt and expressed emotions in a group would likely hamper efficient execution, keeping (rather than expelling or retraining) members who occasionally violate feeling and expression rules may actually strengthen the hold of expression norms over everyone else, which, in turn, just might help the group execute decisions more efficiently.

Persuasion and Compliance

Finally, expressing varied emotions may facilitate persuasion and compliance, which is the primary task for some work groups and an important task for most others. Some evidence and theory suggests that strategic variation in the emotions presented by different members, at different times, and to different kinds of outsiders may help convince recalcitrant targets to do as they are asked. The research that we introduced earlier on the good cop–bad cop technique is pertinent. Rafaeli and Sutton (1987) proposed that the psychological contrast created between the provoked negative and positive emotions accentuate the persuasive power of each emotion: "Targets" experienced greater fear in response to the bad cop and greater relief in response to the good cop (as well as greater liking of the good cop).

Direct tests of the emotional components of the good cop–bad cop technique have not been made, but two laboratory studies of negotiation situations did examine the persuasive power of teaming a tough negotiator (who makes extreme demands) with a more reasonable negotiator (who makes less extreme demands). These studies suggest that a more reasonable negotiator will convince his or her opponent to give up more money than when the opponent bargains only with a reasonable negotiator or a series of reasonable negotiators (Brodt & Tuchinsky, 2000; Hilty & Carnevale, 1993). These findings can be explained by psychological contrast effects, in which the "reasonable" negotiator seems even more reasonable after the opponent hears the unreasonable demands, and thus is likely to give up a bit more money.

INTENTIONAL EMOTIONAL VARIATION

Research on emotional contagion has been most concerned with the unconscious processes that support it. As a result, emotional conformity often is presented as the default consequence of interpersonal interaction. Yet our discussion of the causes of emotional variation suggests that variation occurs in most groups. Furthermore, our discussion of the performance consequences of variation suggests that neither emotion conformity nor emotion variation is completely good or completely bad. Emotion variation may serve some group goals, but hinder others. For example, if superior creativity, decision making, and the ability to persuade outsiders are valued, then variation is probably superior to convergence. Yet variation may hinder term execution, as well as cohesion and liking in groups.

Our review also suggests ways in which members can influence emotional variation in their groups. Groups desiring heterogeneity, for example, should use selection and formation processes that encourage diversity in background, experience, personality, and relationship with the group. Furthermore, structures such as roles and hierarchies can be used to differentiate members from one another and to make such differentiation salient. Norms should emphasize the value of disagreement within the group, and should pressure different members to feel and express different emotions at different times with different people.

Our perspective also suggests that neither emotional convergence nor divergence is inherently more automatic or natural. Although there is a human tendency to select similar others (a characteristic that will facilitate homogeneity), there are also tendencies to create hierarchies and divide labor (characteristics that facilitate heterogeneity). Emotional heterogeneity and homogeneity are consequences of choices that people make about how groups are designed and managed, rather than natural by-products of group life. As such, group members and group researchers would be well-served to pay attention to the variance, as well as to the central tendency of emotions within groups. This variance can be the defining characteristic of the group and can impact its performance.

References

Amabile, T. M. (1996). The meaning and measurement of creativity. In T. M. Amabile (Ed.), *Creativity in context* (pp. 19–40). Boulder, CO: Westview Press.

Ancona, D. G., & Caldwell, D. F. (1992). Bridging the boundary: External activity

and performance in organizational teams. *Administrative Science Quarterly, 37*, 634–655.
Anderson, C., & Keltner, D. (this volume). The emotional convergence hypothesis: Implications for individuals, relationships, and cultures.
Asch, S. E. (1955). Opinions and social pressure. *Scientific American, 193*, 31–35.
Asch, S. E. (1956). Studies of independence and conformity. I. A minority of one against a unanimous majority. *Psychological Monographs, 70*, 70.
Ash, M. K. (1984). *Mary Kay on people management*. New York: Warner Books.
Bales, R. F. (1950). *Interaction process analysis: A method for the study of small groups*. Cambridge, MA: Addison-Wesley.
Bantel, K. A., & Jackson, S. E. (1989). Top management and innovations in banking – Does the composition of the top team make a difference? *Strategic Management Journal, 10*, 107–124.
Barsade, S., & Gibson, D. (1998). Group emotion: A view from top and bottom. In D. Gruenfeld (Ed.), *Research on managing groups and teams* (Vol. 1; pp. 81–102). Stamford, CT: JAI Press.
Barsade, S., Ward, A. J., Turner, J. D. F., & Sonnenfeld, J. (2000). To your heart's content: A model of affective diversity in top management teams. *Administrative Science Quarterly, 45*, 802–836.
Bartel, C., & Saavedra, R. (2000). The collective construction of work group moods. *Administrative Science Quarterly, 45*, 197–231.
Bodenhausen, G. V. (1993). Emotions, arousal and stereotypic judgments: A heuristic model of affect and stereotyping. In D. M. Mackie & D. L. Hamilton (Eds.), *Affect, cognition and stereotyping: Interactive processes in group perception* (pp. 13–38). San Diego, CA: Academic Press.
Brodt, S. E., & Tuchinsky, M. (2000). Working together but in opposition: An examination of the "good-cop/bad-cop" negotiating team tactic. *Organizational Behavior and Human Decision Processes, 81*, 155–177.
Cartwright, D., & Zander, A. (Eds.). (1960). *Group dynamics: research and theory* (2nd Edition). Evanston, IL: Row, Peterson.
Chartrand, T. L., & Bargh, J. A. (1999). The chameleon effect: The perception behavior link and social interaction. *Journal of Personality and Social Psychology, 76*, 893–910.
Cialdini, R. B., Borden, R. J., Thorne, A., Walker, M. R., Freeman, S., & Sloan, L. R. (1976). Basking in reflected glory: Three (football) field studies. *Journal of Personality and Social Psychology, 34*, 366–375.
Cialdini, R. B., Reno, R. R., & Kallgren, C. A. (1990). A focus theory of normative conduct: Recycling the concept of norms to reduce littering in public places. *Journal of Personality and Social Psychology, 58*, 1015–1026.
Cohen, D., Nisbett, R. E., Bowdle, B. F., & Schwarz, N. (1996). Insult, aggression, and the Southern culture of honor: An "experimental ethnography." *Journal of Personality and Social Psychology, 70*, 945–960.
Cohen, S. G., & Bailey, D. E. (1997). What makes teams work: Group effectiveness research from the shop floor to the executive suite. *Journal of Management, 23*, 239–290.
Cox, T. H., Lobel, S. A., & McLeod, P. L. (1991). Effects of ethnic group cultural differences on cooperative and competitive behavior on a group task. *Academy of Management Journal, 34*, 827–847.

Davis, M. H. (1994). *Empathy: A social psychological approach*. Boulder, CO: Westview Press.

Denison, D. R., & Sutton, R. I. (1990). Operating room nurses. In J. R. Hackman (Ed.), *Groups that work* (pp. 293–308). San Francisco: Jossey Bass.

Diener, E., Sandvik, E., Pavot, W., & Fujita, F. (1992). Extroversion and subjective well-being in a United States national probability sample. *Journal of Research in Personality, 26*, 205–215.

Doosje, B., Branscombe, N. R., Spears, R., & Manstead, A. S. R. (1998). Guilty by association: When one's group has a negative history. *Journal of Personality and Social Psychology, 75*, 872–886.

Eagly, A. H., & Chaiken, S. (1993). *The psychology of attitudes*. Orlando, FL: Harcourt Brace Jovanovich College Publishers.

Friedman, H. S., Prince, L. M., Riggio, R. E., & DiMatteo, M. R. (1980). Understanding and assessing nonverbal expressiveness – The Affective Communication Test. *Journal of Personality and Social Psychology, 39*, 333–351.

George, J. M. (1990). Personality, affect, and behavior in groups. *Journal of Applied Psychology, 75*, 107–116.

George, J. M., & Zhou, J. (2002). Understanding when bad moods foster creativity and good ones don't: The role of context and clarity of feelings. *Journal of Applied Psychology, 87*, 687–697.

Gibson, F. P., & Fichman, M. (2002). *Emotions as information in bargaining: What happens when the credit collector calls?* Working paper, The University of Michigan, Graduate School of Business.

Goffman, E. (1969). *Strategic interaction*. Philadelphia: University of Pennsylvania Press.

Goffman, E. (1971). *Relations in public*. New York: Harper & Row.

Good, I. J. (1963). The social implications of artificial intelligence. In I. J. Good, A. J. Mayne, & J. Maynard Smith (Eds.), *The scientist speculates* (pp. 192–198). New York: Basic Books.

Gross, J. J., & John, O. P. (1995) Facets of emotional expressivity: Three self-report factors and their correlates. *Personality and Individual Differences, 19*, 555–568.

Hackman, J. R. (1987). The design of work teams. In J. W. Lorsch (Ed.), *Handbook of organizational behavior* (pp. 315–342). Englewood Cliffs, NJ: Prentice-Hall.

Hatfield, E., Cacioppo, J. T., & Rapson, R. L. (1994). *Emotional contagion*. New York: Cambridge University Press.

Hatfield, E., & Rapson, R. L. (this volume). Emotional contagion: Religious and ethnic hatreds and global terrorism.

Heath, C., & Staudenmayer, N. (2000). Coordination neglect: How lay theories of organizing complicate coordination in organizations. *Research in Organizational Behavior, 22*, 153–191.

Hilty, J. A., & Carnevale, P. A. (1993). Black hat/white hat strategy in bilateral negotiations. *Organizational Behavior and Human Decision Processes, 55*, 444–469.

Hochschild, A. (1983). *The managed heart: The commercialization of human feeling*. Berkeley, CA: University of California Press.

Hoffman, M. L. (1984). Interaction of affect and cognition in empathy. In C. E. Izard, J. Kagan, & R. B. Zajonc (Eds.), *Emotions, cognition, and behavior* (pp. 103–131). Cambridge: Cambridge University Press.

Holtz, R., & Miller, N. (1985). Assumed similarity and opinion certainty. *Journal of Personality and Social Psychology, 48*, 890–898.
Huy, Q. N. (2002). Emotional balancing of organizational continuity and radical change: The contribution of middle managers. *Administrative Science Quarterly, 47*, 31–69.
Isen, A. M., & Baron, R. A. (1991). Positive affect as a factor in organizational behavior. *Research in Organizational Behavior, 13*, 1–53.
Isen, A. M., Daubman, K. A., & Nowicki, G. P. (1987). Positive affect facilitates creative problem solving. *Journal of Personality and Social Psychology, 52*, 1122–1131.
Isen, A. M., Johnson, M. M. S., Mertz, E., & Robinson, G. F. (1985). The influence of positive affect on the unusualness of word associations. *Journal of Personality and Social Psychology, 48*, 1413–1426.
Janis, I. L. (1972). *Victims of groupthink*. Boston: Houghton Mifflin.
Jehn, K. A. (1994). Enhancing effectiveness: An investigation of advantages and disadvantages of value-based intragroup conflict. *International Journal of Conflict Management, 5*, 223–238.
Jehn, K. A. (1997). Affective and cognitive conflict in work groups: Increasing performance through value-based intragroup conflict. In C. K. DeDreu & E. Van de Vliert (Eds.), *Using conflict in organizations*. Thousand Oaks, CA: Sage.
Jehn, K. A., Chadwick, C., & Thatcher, S. M. B. (1997). To agree or not to agree: The effects of value congruence, individual demographic dissimilarity, and conflict on workgroup outcomes. *International Journal of Conflict Management, 8*, 287–305.
Kappen, D. M., & Branscombe, N. R. (2001). The effects of reasons given for ineligibility on perceived gender discrimination and feelings of injustice. *British Journal of Social Psychology, 40*, 295–313.
Kaufmann, G., & Vosburg, S. K. (1997). "Paradoxical" mood effects on creative problem-solving. *Cognition & Emotion, 11*, 151–170.
King, L. A. (1998). Ambivalence over emotional expression and reading emotions in situations and faces. *Journal of Personality and Social Psychology, 74*, 753–762.
Larsen, R. J., & Ketelaar, T. (1989). Extraversion, neuroticism and susceptibility to positive and negative mood induction procedures. *Personality & Individual Differences, 10*, 1221–1228.
Levine, J. M., & Moreland, R. L. (1998). Small groups. In D. T. Gilbert, S. T. Fiske, & G. Lindzey (Eds.), *The handbook of social psychology* (4th Edition; Vol. II; pp. 415–469). New York: McGraw-Hill.
Liang, D. W., Moreland, R., & Argote, L. (1995). Group versus individual training and group performance: The mediating factor of transactive memory. *Personality & Social Psychology Bulletin, 21*, 384–393.
Liberman, S. (1956). The effects of changes in roles on the attitudes of role occupants. *Human Relations, 9*, 385–402.
Lonner, W. J. (1980). The search for psychological universals. In H. C. Triandis & W. W. Lambert (Eds.), *Handbook of cross-cultural psychology* (Vol. 1; pp. 143–204). Boston: Allyn and Bacon.
Mackie, D. M., DeVos, T., & Smith, E. R. (2000). Intergroup emotions: Explaining offensive action tendencies in an intergroup context. *Journal of Personality and Social Psychology, 79*, 602–616.

Mackie, D. M., Silver, L., & Smith, E. R. (this volume). Intergroup emotions: Emotions as an intergroup phenomenon.

Mars, G., & Nicod, M. (1984). *The world of waiters.* London: George Allen & Unwin Ltd.

McClelland, D. C. (1985). How motives, skills, and values determine what people do. *American Psychologist, 40,* 812–825.

McDonough, J. (2002). *Shakey: Neil Young's biography* (p. 265). New York: Random House.

McGrath, J. E. (1984). *Groups: Interaction and performance.* Englewood Cliffs, NJ: Prentice-Hall.

Mesquita, B., & Frijda, N. (1992). Cultural variations in emotions: A review. *Psychological Bulletin, 112,* 179–204.

Miller, D. T., & Prentice, D. A. (1994). Collective errors and errors about the collective. *Personality and Social Psychology Bulletin, 20,* 541–550.

Milliken, F. J., & Martins, L. L. (1996). Searching for common threads: Understanding the multiple effects of diversity in organizational groups. *Academy of Management Review, 21,* 402–433.

Moore, S. (1984). *The Stanislavski system.* New York: Penguin.

Moreland, R. L. (1999). Transactive memory: Learning who knows what in work groups and organizations. In Thompson, L. L., Levine, J. M. (Eds). *Shared cognition in organizations: The management of knowledge.* (pp. 3–31). Mahwah, NJ: Lawrence Erlbaum Associates.

Murray, N., Sujan, H., Hirt, E. R., & Sujan, M. (1990). The influence of mood on categorization: A cognitive flexibility interpretation. *Journal of Personality and Social Psychology, 59,* 411–425.

Myers, D. G., & Lamm, H. (1976). The group polarization phenomenon. *Psychological Bulletin, 83,* 602–627.

Nemeth, C. J. (1986). Differential contributions of majority vs. minority influence. *Psychological Review, 93,* 23–32.

Nemeth, C. J. (1994). The value of minority dissent. In S. Moscovici & A. Mucchi-Faina (Eds.), *Minority influence* (pp. 3–15). Chicago: Nelson-Hall Publishers.

Nemeth, C. J., & Kwan, J. L. (1987). Minority influence, divergent thinking and detection of correct solutions. *Journal of Applied Social Psychology, 17,* 788–799.

O'Toole, J., Galbraith, J., & Lawler, E. E., III (2002). When two (or more) heads are better than one: The promise and pitfalls of shared leadership. *California Management Review, 44,* 65–83.

Owens, D. A., & Sutton, R. I. (2001). Status contests in meetings: Negotiating the informal order. In M. E. Turner (Ed.), *Groups at work: Theory and research* (pp. 299–316). Mahwah, NJ: Lawrence Erlbaum Associates.

Pelled, L. H., Eisenhardt, K., & Xin, K. R. (1999). Exploring the black box: An analysis of work group diversity, conflict, and performance. *Administrative Science Quarterly, 44,* 1–28.

Peterson, C. (1987). To be or not to be: A study of ambivalence. *Journal of Analytical Psychology, 32,* 79–92.

Petty, R. E., & Cacioppo, J. T. (1996). *Attitudes and persuasion: Classic and contemporary approaches.* Boulder, CO: Westview Press.

Rafaeli, A., & Sutton, R. I. (1987). Expression of emotion as part of the work role. *Academy of Management Review, 12,* 23–37.

Rafaeli, A., & Sutton, R. I. (1991). Emotional contrast strategies as means of social influence: Lessons from criminal interrogators and bill collectors. *Academy of Management Journal, 34*, 749–775.

Rusting, C. L., & Larsen, R. J. (1998). Diurnal patterns of unpleasant mood: Associations with neuroticism, depression, and anxiety. *Journal of Personality, 66*, 85–103.

Schein, E. H. (1965). *Organizational psychology*. Englewood Cliffs, NJ: Prentice-Hall.

Schwarz, N., & Bless, H. (1991). Happy and mindless, but sad and smart? The impact of affective states on analytic reasoning. In J. P. Forgas (Ed.), *Emotion and social judgments, International Series in Experimental and Social Psychology* (pp. 55–71). Oxford, UK: Oxford.

Schwenk, C. R., & Cosier, R. A. (1980). Effects of the expert, devil's advocate, and dialectical inquiry methods on prediction performance. *Organizational Behavior and Human Decision Processes, 26*, 409–424.

Shales, T., & Miller, J. A. (2002). *Live from New York*. New York: Little, Brown.

Sherif, M. (1936). *The psychology of social norms*. Oxford: Harper.

Sidanius, J., & Pratto, F. (1999). *Social dominance: An intergroup theory of social hierarchy and oppression*. New York: Cambridge University Press.

Smith, H. J., & Tyler, T. R. (1997). Choosing the right pond: The impact of group membership on self-esteem and group-oriented behavior. *Journal of Experimental Social Psychology, 33*, 146–170.

Staw, B. M. (1975). Attribution of the "causes" of performance: An alternative interpretation of cross-sectional research on organizations. *Organizational Behavior and Human Performance, 13*, 414–432.

Staw, B. M. (1995). Why no one really wants creativity. In C. M. Ford & D. A. Gioia (Eds.), *Creative action in organizations* (pp. 161–166). Thousand Oaks, CA: Sage.

Strack, F., Martin, L., & Stepper, S. (1988). Inhibiting and facilitating conditions of the human smile: A nonobtrusive test of the facial feedback hypothesis. *Journal of Personality and Social Psychology, 54*, 768–777.

Suedfeld, P. (1992). Cognitive managers and their critics. *Political Psychology, 13*, 435–453.

Sutton, R. I. (1991). Maintaining norms about emotional expression: The case of bill collectors. *Administrative Science Quarterly, 36*, 245–68.

Sutton, R. I. (2002) *Weird ideas that work* (p. 45). New York: The Free Press.

Sutton, R. I., & Hargadon, A. (1996). Brainstorming groups in context: Effectiveness in a product design firm. *Administrative Science Quarterly, 41*, 685–718.

Sutton, R. I., & Rafaeli, A. (1988). Untangling the relationship between displayed emotions and organizational sales: The case of convenience stores. *Academy of Management Journal, 31*, 461–487.

Tellegen, A. (1982). *Brief manual for the differential personality questionnaire*. Department of Psychology, University of Minnesota, Minneapolis, Minnesota.

Tiedens, L. Z. (2001). Powerful emotions: The vicious cycle of social status positions and emotions. In N. Ashkanasy, W. Zerbe, & C. Hartel (Eds.), *Emotions in the workplace: Research, theory, and practice*. (pp. 71–81). Westport, CT: Quorum Books.

Tiedens, L. Z., Ellsworth, P., & Mesquita, B. (2000). Stereotypes of sentiments and status: Emotional expectations for high and low status group members. *Personality and Social Psychology Bulletin, 26*.

Tiedens, L. Z., & Fragale, A. R. (2003). Power moves: Complementarity in submissive and dominant non-verbal behavior. *Journal of Personality and Social Psychology. 84*, 558–568.

Tiedens, L. Z., & Linton, S. (2001). Judgment under emotional certainty and uncertainty: The effects of specific emotions on information processing. *Journal of Personality and Social Psychology, 81*, 973–988.

Van Maanen, J., & Kunda, G. (1989). "Real feelings": Emotional expression and organizational culture. In L. Cummings & B. Staw (Eds.), *Research in organizational behavior* (Vol. 11; pp. 43–104). Greenwich, CT: JAI Press.

Wann, D. L., & Branscombe, N. R. (1993). Sports fans: Measuring degree of identification with their team. *International Journal of Sport Psychology, 24*, 1–17.

Wegner, D. M. (1986). Transactive memory: A contemporary analysis of the group mind. In B. Mullen & G. R. Goethals (Eds.), *Theories of group behavior* (pp. 185–208) New York: Springer-Verlag.

Zurbriggen, E. L., & Sturman, T. (2002). Linking motives and emotions: A test of McClelland's hypotheses. *Personality and Social Psychology Bulletin, 28*, 521–535.

9

Inside the Heart of Emotion: On Culture and Relational Concerns

Patricia M. Rodriguez Mosquera, Agneta H. Fischer, and Antony S. R. Manstead

Culture lies at the heart of emotion. Emotions are primarily relational processes that shape and are shaped by our relations with other people. Social life is the stage on which our emotions acquire significance and meaning. Cultures vary with respect to the relational, interpersonal themes that are promoted in social life. Some cultures emphasize the importance of maintaining one's independence and autonomy in social relations. Social interactions in other cultures are centered around the avoidance of conflict and the maintenance of harmony. Yet, other cultures promote the protection of reputation and face as a central interpersonal concern. This diversity in relational concerns across cultures should influence emotional processes in important ways, from the situations that most commonly are the object of emotional experiences to the ways in which emotions are communicated to others.

In this chapter, we address the question of how culture shapes emotion. We present a theoretical approach that aims to "unpackage" the role of culture in emotion. One of the major challenges that the rapidly developing field of culture and emotion faces is quite simply how best to explain cultural variation in emotion. "Unpackaging" here refers to the importance of including measures of culture-related variables in (cross-) cultural studies on emotion. We believe that cultural variation in relational concerns is central to understanding and explaining cultural variation in emotion. We argue that relational concerns are central motivational forces in social interactions, because they signal to the individual those behaviors that should be expressed or avoided when relating to others in a certain cultural context. The emotions that are elicited when relational concerns are advanced or threatened therefore play a central role in the management of interpersonal relations. In the present chapter, we focus on a specific type of relational concerns, namely honor concerns.

We start by describing what it means to adopt an unpackaging approach when doing culture and emotion research and why this approach is essential for the advancement of the field. Next, we review the existing theoretical and empirical literature on concerns. Concern is a central concept in emotion theory, and we believe such a review is necessary to clarify the ways in which our view on concerns converges and diverges with earlier work on this construct. We then illustrate the theoretical arguments advanced in relation to unpackaging culture and relational concerns with a discussion of our own research on honor and emotions.

UNPACKAGING CULTURE: ON HOW TO DO THEORY AND RESEARCH ON CULTURE AND EMOTION

Culture is a "packaged" variable (Whiting, 1976). Cultures are complex systems of shared beliefs, values, norms, and expectations. This shared system of meanings shapes the social environment by influencing social structures, traditions, informal and institutionalized practices, thereby also influencing individuals' psychological processes and social behavior. When differences in emotion are found between two or more cultures, it is of central importance to understand what it is about the cultures involved that can account for the observed differences. Stating that observed differences in emotion between culture A and culture B are cultural differences without having taken any measures of culture-related variables (e.g., values) is an empty statement. Unpackaging refers to the "unwrapping" (i.e., operationalization and measurement of culture in psychological research) (Bond, in press; Bond & Tedeschi, 2001).

Central to "unpackaging" culture is the translation of features or aspects of the culture assumed to be important in a certain social behavior into psychological constructs that can be operationalized and measured. The process of unpackaging culture is supposed to start at the moment at which a theory concerning the role of culture in a given social behavior is being generated. This requires knowledge of which aspects of the cultural context should have an impact on the behavior in question. Once those aspects have been identified, the next step is to operationalize them in the form of measurable variables that can be included in research designs. In short, unpackaging culture refers to the development of measures for *psychological predictors* or *mediators* of cultural variation in social behavior.

Applying this approach to the cross-cultural study of emotions entails conceiving of culture in a way that can provide a satisfying theoretical and empirical explanation of cultural variation in emotion. It leads to elaborate theorizing about those aspects or features of cultures that are important for emotional processes, their definition, operationalization, and measurement. In our view, an unpackaging approach to culture and emotion research is essential for the advancement of the field. This is because comparative research on emotion within psychology can be characterized as focusing on the *description* rather than on the explanation of cultural variation in emotion.

This focus on describing rather than explaining observed cultural differences in emotion is partly a consequence of the type of research questions that marked the beginning of cross-cultural research on emotion more than thirty years ago. The so-called universality studies by Paul Ekman and Wallace Friesen were focused on the search for universals in emotion and, especially, in facial expression of emotions (see Ekman, 1973, for a review). The universality studies endorsed a conception of culture as a moderator of a basically innate emotion or affect program. Culture was of interest to the extent that it inhibited, promoted, or "masked" what would otherwise be universal facial expressions of emotion. This conception of culture was embodied in the well-known concept of display rules (Ekman, 1972; Ekman & Friesen, 1969; Friesen, 1972). Culture was therefore attributed a minimal role in the emotion process, and cross-cultural research was seen as the means to try to validate a theory that advocated the universality of human emotions.

This emphasis on universality inhibited the development of theories on cultural variation in emotion in the two decades following Ekman and Friesen's studies. Research efforts during this period were mainly concentrated on the description of differences and similarities in emotions across cultural groups (for a review, see Mesquita & Frijda, 1992). Observed differences in emotion were often labeled ad hoc as cultural differences. Measures of potential cultural determinants of emotion were, however, rarely taken. Despite this lack of theoretical clarity on the role of culture in explaining variation in emotion, the conclusions reached by these studies led to a significant change in the type of questions that became relevant for emotion and culture researchers. In particular, the bulk of the research evidence generated by these studies demonstrated that there is evidence of both cross-cultural differences and similarities in emotions. This implied that emotions are neither universal nor culture-specific, and that the influence of culture on emotion can be best understood in terms of *degree of variation*: The degree of cultural variation in emotion depends on the cultures, emotions, and emotion components (e.g., antecedents or social sharing of emotion) under study. It therefore became important to identify the *extent* to which and the *way* in which culture shapes emotions.

Research in the past decade has tried to address these latter issues by comparing cultures that differ with respect to specific culture-related dimensions, such as values or the nature of the self-concept (e.g., Kitayama & Markus, 1994; Kitayama, Markus, and Matsumoto, 1995; Manstead & Fischer, 2002; Markus & Kitayama, 1991; Mesquita, 2001). By comparing cultures that differ in the significance attached to certain ideals or dimensions of self-definition, research has gone beyond the mere description of group differences and toward the development of more elaborated theoretical frameworks for conducting research on culture and emotion. Nevertheless, it has not yet become common practice to include measures of culture-related dimensions or variables when doing comparative research on emotion. Adopting an unpackaging approach is therefore a necessary and essential next step if we wish to unravel the processes by which the cultural context shapes emotion.

In sum, unpackaging represents a way to do theory and research on culture and emotion. Because it implies the development of psychological predictors or mediators of cultural variation in emotion and therefore their measurement at the individual level, it may be thought that such an approach would either lead to the "psychologization" of culture in emotion theory (i.e., the simplification or reduction of the richness and complexity of cultural systems) or to an excessive focus on internal variables rather than on the social context of emotion. However, this would be a misinterpretation of what this approach entails. Unpackaging culture implies placing culture at the heart of social and emotional processes. Such an approach is based on the theoretical position that culture is constitutive of emotional processes and of the social context of emotion. Culture shapes the social environment in which individuals grow up and live by influencing social structures and practices. Emotional processes are shaped by culture through individuals' participation in cultural practices. If culture is constitutive of emotion, we should define which aspects, components, or dimensions of culture are relevant for emotional processes and how they translate into psychological tendencies, dispositions, or sensitivities. Moreover, such an approach prevents us from making what it is called the ecological fallacy in cross-cultural psychology, a common mistake in comparative research on social behavior (Hofstede, 2001). The ecological fallacy refers to the explanation of individual behavior (e.g., emotional reactions to a certain situation) by culture-level dimensions, such as level of individualism or collectivism of a nation.

We believe that a fruitful way in which culture can be unpackaged in relation to emotion is by focusing on the relational concerns that are promoted by cultures. We turn now to an explanation of what relational concerns are and how they relate to culture and emotion.

EMOTION, CULTURE, AND RELATIONAL CONCERNS

Concern is a popular concept in emotion theory. It refers to what an individual cares about. Most emotion researchers would agree that emotions arise from the evaluation that a certain event advances or threatens an individual's concerns. A systematic analysis of the concept of psychological concerns was first introduced by Nico Frijda (1986) in his seminal work *The Emotions*. We first review the existing literature on concerns and then present our own approach to concerns, culture, and emotion.

A Brief Journey into the History of Concerns in Emotion Theory

Concerns were defined by Nico Frijda as dispositions or sensitivities to certain types of events. In Frijda's own words: "Concern is defined as a disposition to desire occurrence or nonoccurrence of a given kind of situation" (Frijda, 1986, p. 335). Frijda conceived of concerns as central to the elicitation of emotion and to the evaluation of the affective significance of an event. Emotions are elicited by those situations that advance or threaten an individual's concerns. Events are not in themselves "emotional." The probability that a given event will elicit emotion depends on its significance to the individual's concerns, that is, on the extent to which the individual desires the occurrence and nonoccurrence of the event. Those events that advance an individual's concerns should have a positive affective balance and lead to positive emotions. In contrast, events that threaten an individual's concerns should be evaluated as having a negative affective balance and lead to negative emotions.

Frijda proposed two important dimensions for the classification of concerns. Concerns can be characterized by whether they are "source" or "surface" concerns. Source concerns are general states that are desired by the individual, such as having security, sexual satisfaction, or affection. Surface concerns, by contrast, are object-oriented desires, such as attraction to a certain person. These latter sorts of concerns are instantiations of source concerns. A second important dimension for the classification of concerns is the extent to which they are "conscious" or "unconscious."[1] This refers to the extent to which individuals are consciously aware of the significance of a given concern. A given situation can be relevant to a multiplicity of concerns, and to both source and surface concerns simultaneously. Moreover, it is assumed that the intensity of the emotions elicited in a given situation depends on the significance of the underlying concerns for the individual: The greater the significance of these concerns, the greater the intensity of the elicited emotions.

The influence of culture on the relationship between concerns and emotion was elaborated in subsequent work by Nico Frijda, Batja Mesquita and colleagues (Frijda & Mesquita, 1994; Mesquita, 2001; Mesquita, Frijda, & Scherer, 1997; Mesquita & Karasawa, 2002). In these publications, concerns were described as constituting a source of intercultural variation in emotion due to the existence of cultural differences in focal concerns (i.e., in the kinds of concern that would be relevant to emotion in different cultures). "Focality" in this context therefore refers to the cultural significance or centrality of a given concern. The focality of a concern in a given culture

[1] Frijda originally used the terms "awaken" and "latent" to refer to concerns the individual is either conscious or not conscious about, respectively (Frijda, 1986). We use here the terms "conscious" and "unconscious" to refer to awaken and latent concerns for the sake of clarity.

influences the emotion process in two fundamental ways. First, focal concerns should attract attention to the events that could potentially advance or threaten them. Focal concerns are therefore seen as guiding attentional resources to or focusing attentional resources on certain type of situations. Second, focal concerns should lead to cultural expertise on events relevant to them. Events that are relevant to concerns are called "focal event types" and typically there are clear scripts regarding their interpretation and emotional responses to them. The existence of clear norms about how to react to focal event types leads to a sense of "obviousness" (see also Mesquita, 1993) among members of the culture in question with regard to how to interpret a given event and how to respond to it.

This research by Nico Frijda, Batja Mesquita and colleagues represents the extent of the work to date on concerns that has been carried out in emotion psychology. This work has established that concerns are a core feature of emotional life. By giving a central role to concerns in his emotion theory, Frijda stressed the motivational character of the emotion process. Furthermore, the work by Batja Mesquita and colleagues has demonstrated that the cultural context importantly influences the types of concern that become focal or significant for the individual. Although we believe that this work has been of major importance for the advancement of emotion theory, we also believe that the concept of concern, as it has been described in previous research, lacks definitional consistency and clarity. More specifically, the concept of concern has been defined in four different ways.

First, concerns have been described as general goals or values. In Frijda's (1986) emotion theory, concerns were explicitly defined as general issues the individual cares about (e.g., source concerns such as affiliation or security). This way of defining concerns is similar to the construct of values as defined in cross-cultural psychology (i.e., as desirable, transsituational goals that serve as guiding principles in one's life) (see, e.g., Schwartz, 1992, 1999; Schwartz & Bilsky, 1990). Second, concerns have also been defined in situational terms, as being represented in the individual's mind as desired or undesired kinds of situations that serve as standards when evaluating newly encountered events (Frijda, 1986). Third, concerns have also been conceptualized as the evaluation of situations. In the study by Mesquita and Karasawa (2002), American and Japanese college students were asked to evaluate autobiographically recalled situations along dimensions relevant to either independent (e.g., the extent to which the self can cope with the situation) or interdependent (e.g., the extent to which the situation brings you closer or further away from other people) concerns. This way of conceptualizing and measuring concerns comes close to current definitions of appraisal (Scherer, Schorr, & Johnstone, 2001). Fourth, concerns seem also to be a mixture of "goals, motives, values, and expectations about oneself or others and about the world in which one lives" (Mesquita,

2001, p. 69). In short, there is a lack of clarity about what concerns really are and about the role that they play in the emotion process.

In the next section, we seek to resolve this definitional problem and also to expand the existing conceptualization of concerns and emotion. We place concerns at the center of individuals' interpersonal relations. In our view, the work reviewed in the present section has adopted a rather "individualistic" view on concerns and emotions. All four definitions of concerns discussed refer to concerns as intrapsychic entities, and the most important function ascribed to emotions is the protection of an individual's concerns and the preservation of an individual's intrapsychic balance. Emotions, however, arise predominantly in the context of interpersonal relations (Parkinson, 1995; Tangney & Dearing, 2002; Tangney & Fischer, 1995), and we believe that those concerns that entail social, cultural prescriptions about how the self should relate to others are the most important for emotional processes. In our view, concerns can best be described as relational sensitivities.

Relational Concerns

Relationships are central to human life throughout the world. However, cultures vary with respect to beliefs, values, and norms about how the self should relate to others. The well-known cultural dimensions of individualism-collectivism (Kim et al., 1994; Triandis et al., 1988; Triandis, 1989, 1994) and independence-interdependence (Markus & Kitayama, 1991, 1994) capture two different cultural conceptions of relationships. The core characteristic of collectivist and interdependent cultures is their emphasis on interpersonal closeness, whereas individualist and independent cultures promote interpersonal distance and separateness. The majority of cross-cultural research on emotion has been carried out in relation to these dimensions by comparing collectivist (or interdependent) with individualist (or independent) cultures (see, e.g., Kitayama et al., 1995; Manstead & Fischer, 2002; Markus & Kitayama, 1994; Mesquita, 2001). More recently, research on culture and emotion has started to focus on honor cultures. Social interactions in honor cultures revolve around the avoidance of dishonor through the protection of reputation (Cohen & Nisbett, 1994; Cohen et al., 1996; Cohen & Nisbett, 1997; Cohen, Vandello, & Rantilla, 1998; Rodriguez Mosquera, Manstead, & Fischer, 2000, 2002a). Interdependence, independence, and reputation can be described as different *interpersonal themes* around which relationships are construed and maintained.

Cultures socialize individuals to become sensitive and attach significance to certain interpersonal themes. This would translate at the individual level into certain dispositions or sensitivities that we label relational concerns. We define relational concerns as *psychological tendencies* or *sensitivities* to (1) behave in a way that advances or does not threaten culturally predominant interpersonal themes, and (2) attend or attune to certain behaviors of others that signal that such themes are at stake. Furthermore, behaviors and personal characteristics that advance relational concerns should be promoted by the cultural context as central for self-definition and feelings of self-worth; in other words, as central to one's own identity. In this way, relational concerns play a central role not only in the management of interpersonal relations, but also in the maintenance of a positive identity in a certain cultural context.

The cultural environment influences emotions partly through relational concerns. Those situations and behaviors (of oneself and others) that advance or threaten culturally promoted relational concerns should become core emotional events in a given culture. In other words, such situations and behaviors should often be the object of emotional experiences in the culture in question. Moreover, to the extent that there is some degree of within-culture consistency in emotional responses to core emotional events, driven by shared relational concerns, this commonality of emotional response will come to be seen as normative, thereby reinforcing (and perhaps even constituting) the culture in question. In this way, the cultural environment and emotions constitute and reproduce each other.

We propose culturally promoted relational concerns as central to the unpackaging of culture in emotion. We now turn to a discussion of our own research on the role of honor concerns in explaining cultural variation in emotion between honor and non-honor cultures.

HONOR AND EMOTION

Honor Cultures: The Threat of Dishonor

Social interactions in honor cultures are centered around the avoidance of dishonor. Avoiding dishonor can be achieved by behaving and maintaining a reputation in accordance with the honor code. The honor code involves a set of values that define normative standards for what is considered honorable and dishonorable, disgraceful behavior. The values embodied in the honor code can be divided into four major domains on the basis of the common theme each group of values shares: family honor, social interdependence, feminine honor, and masculine honor (Gilmore, 1987, 1990; Gilmore & Gwynne, 1985; Jakubowska, 1989; Nisbett & Cohen, 1996; Peristiany, 1965; Pitt-Rivers, 1977; Rodriguez Mosquera, Manstead, & Fischer, 2002a, 2002b; Stewart, 1994).[2]

[2] Honor cultures can best be characterized as a type of collectivist culture due to the importance placed on collectivist types of values. In particular, honor cultures promote a construal

In honor cultures, the family is conceptualized as a social unit that shares a common identity. This common or group-based identity is expressed in the notion of family honor (i.e., the value and status of the family in the eyes of others). Being concerned with family honor entails caring about social evaluations of one's family, about the impact of one's behavior on one's family honor, and about the defense of one's family's name. Honor is thus both a personal attribute and an attribute shared with one's own family, which implies a strong interdependence between personal and family honor. Feelings of self-worth in honor cultures are therefore strongly dependent on the actions of one's intimates, how they are evaluated, and the capacity of the self not to dishonor the family's collective reputation. Interdependence is also highly valued in honor cultures in the context of social relations outside the family. Social interdependence can be understood as a desire to express one's integrity in interpersonal relations. It refers to values that focus on the strengthening of social bonds and the maintenance of interpersonal harmony, such as generosity, honesty, or hospitality.

The task of upholding family honor and social interdependence is equally important for maintaining men's and women's honor. Feminine and masculine honor, by contrast, refer to behaviors and attributes relevant for the maintenance of women's or men's honor, respectively. The central ideal in the feminine honor code is sexual shame or chastity. Sexual shame is expressed in the form of virginity before marriage, restraint in sexual relations, *pudeur* in social relations with men, and decorum (e.g., wearing discreet clothing). Conforming to authority (usually male authority) within the family context is also central to the maintenance of feminine honor. This is due partly to the strong dependence of family honor on female relatives' sexual shame, and partly to the fact that men are usually regarded in honor cultures as the guardians of family reputation. Apart from the importance of protecting family honor, masculine honor centers on notions of virility and a reputation for "being tough." A reputation for "being tough" translates in behavioral terms into the need to appear strong and capable of responding to offenses that undermine one's manhood, one's own honor, or one's family honor.

We assume that the core values of the honor code are internalized to different degrees at the individual level, leading to individual differences in the extent to which an individual is attached to the honor code. Thus, there will be individual differences in the extent to which one is concerned

of the self based on the seeking of social approval. Furthermore, honor cultures promote the subordination of individual needs and desires to those of important ingroups, such as the family. However, honor cultures cannot simply be equated with collectivist cultures because they emphasize a particular set of values centered around the maintenance of honor and the avoidance of dishonor (i.e., the honor code). The notion that collectivist cultures differ in the aspect of collectivism they emphasize has already been advanced by Triandis et al. (1988).

with family honor, social interdependence, masculine honor and feminine honor. These relational concerns promoted in honor cultures will be referred to from now on simply as honor concerns. Those situations that threaten honor concerns and therefore have the potential to lead to dishonor are likely to be the object of intense emotional experiences in honor cultures. The social contexts that seem to be especially threatening for an individual's honor are those related to the *withdrawal of social respect*, as in the case of offenses. Offenses can therefore be described as core emotional events in honor cultures.

Offenses, Honor Concerns, Anger, and Shame

Research in both cultural anthropology and social psychology has shown that offenses, such as humiliations and insults, are responded to with intense emotional reactions, especially of anger, in honor cultures (Cohen & Nisbett, 1994, 1997; Cohen et al., 1996; Miller, 1993; Murphy, 1983; Nisbett & Cohen, 1996; Peristiany, 1965; Pitt-Rivers, 1977; Stewart, 1994). This impact of offenses on emotion is related to the keen sensitivity to social approval and disapproval of one's behavior and personality that exists in honor cultures. One's identity as an honorable person is dependent on other's recognition of one's claim to honor.

Empirical research on honor, offenses, and emotion has to date focused mainly on the characteristics of offense situations that lead to emotion, particularly to anger, in honor cultures. This research has documented that offenses that (1) threaten masculinity, (2) question the reputation of one's female relatives with respect to sexual shame, or (3) take place in public lead to intense anger in honor cultures (see, e.g., Nisbett & Cohen, 1996; Peristiany, 1965; Stewart, 1994). It is reasonable to assume that emotional reactions to offenses should be mediated by honor concerns. Although a psychological concern for maintaining honor is usually assumed to be the factor underlying emotional responses to offenses in honor cultures, its role in emotion has mostly been inferred on the basis of the strength of an emotional response (such as anger). The stronger the response, the greater is the presumed concern for honor. Previous research on honor and emotion has therefore never directly assessed honor concerns. This was our motivation for carrying out a study on the role of honor concerns in emotional reactions to offenses (Rodriguez Mosquera et al., 2002b). In this study, we focused on a specific type of offense, namely verbal insults, and on two emotions that are closely related to the loss of honor, namely anger and shame (see, e.g., Gilmore, 1987; Nisbett & Cohen, 1996; Rodriguez Mosquera et al., 2000).

The participants in this research were young, middle-class populations living in two countries that differ with respect to the significance attached to honor: Spain and the Netherlands. Previous cross-cultural studies on values in these countries have established that honor is more important in Spain than in the Netherlands (Fischer, Manstead, & Rodriguez Mosquera, 1999, Study 1; Rodriguez Mosquera, 1999). This significance of honor in Spain is in line with ethnographic research on honor in that country (Gilmore, 1987; Gilmore & Gwynne, 1985; Murphy, 1983; Pitt-Rivers, 1965, 1977). By contrast, individualistic values that emphasize independence, autonomy, and the capacities and achievements of the self (e.g., ambition, capability) are more significant in the Netherlands than in Spain.

One hundred and twenty-five Dutch (61 females, 64 males) and 135 Spanish (62 females, 73 males) university students completed a questionnaire that included two sets of measures. The first assessed the four types of relational concerns that we expect to be promoted in honor cultures: a concern for integrity in social relations (i.e., interdependence), a concern for group-based or family honor, a concern for masculine honor, and a concern for feminine honor. Honor concerns were operationalized in the form of items describing either a behavior or a reputation that violates the concern in question (see Appendix for examples of items for each domain of honor concern). This was intended to reflect the fact that the maintenance of honor is dependent on both one's actions and one's reputation (see, e.g., Peristiany, 1965). Because we proposed that relational concerns should be central to self-definition and identity, participants in this study were asked to rate the extent to which the behavior or reputation described in each item would damage their feelings of self-worth on 7-point scales, ranging from "not at all" (0) to "very much" (6).

The second set of measures in the questionnaires involved responses to vignettes in which verbal insults that threaten honor themes were described: being depicted as a disgraceful member of one's family (threat to family honor); as unable to protect an intimate other in a threatening situation (threat to masculine honor); and as having various sexual partners (threat to sexual shame).[3] Participants were asked to report the extent to which they would feel anger and shame in reaction to the verbal insults.

[3] We expected the type of threat posed by a vignette to moderate the impact of nationality on emotional reactions to verbal insults. On the one hand, shame and anger should not be elicited by *any* offense in honor cultures, but rather in response to those offenses in which honor issues are at stake. On the other hand, it is reasonable to assume that offenses that carry a threat to individualism would be appraised as a threat in the Netherlands. To test the moderating factor of threat in emotional responses, we varied the type of threat posed by the insult described in the vignettes. In addition to the three vignettes that posed threats to honor, three vignettes that posed threats to individualism (i.e., threat to assertiveness, threat to autonomy, threat to competence) were also presented to participants. Dutch participants reported more intense anger and shame in reaction to the individualism-related vignettes. Furthermore, we found a significant interaction between country and gender: Male Dutch participants seem to be especially sensitive to situations in which their autonomy or competence is questioned. For more information on these results, see Rodriguez Mosquera et al. (2002b).

Three questions assessed the extent to which a vignette would elicit angry feelings, namely "To what extent would you feel insulted?," "To what extent would you feel enraged?," and "To what extent would this (i.e., the verbal insult) hurt your pride?" Two questions assessed the extent to which a vignette would elicit feelings of shame: "To what extent would you feel shame?" and "To what extent would this (i.e., the verbal insult) damage your self-esteem?" These questions were answered on 7-point scales ranging from *not at all* (0) to *very much* (6).

The most important prediction in this study was that the strength of honor concerns should mediate the effect of nationality on emotional reactions to the vignettes. For this purpose, mediational analyses were performed following Baron and Kenny's (1986) procedure. We found good support for this prediction with regard to *family honor*.[4] Spanish participants ($M = 5.35$) rated injuries to family honor, such as being unable to defend one's family's reputation, as more damaging to their feelings of self-worth than Dutch participants did ($M = 4.51$). Spanish participants ($M = 4.14$) also reported more intense shame in response to being depicted by an insult as a disgraceful member of the family than Dutch participants did ($M = 3.53$). Most importantly, greater shame among the Spanish was explained by their greater concern for family honor. This study therefore provides initial evidence for the proposed role of individual differences in relational concerns as mediators of cultural differences in emotion.

CONCLUSIONS

Emotions are anchored in social life. Social life varies across cultures. Cultures vary in the types of interpersonal theme they emphasize, such as the avoidance of conflict or the defense of reputation in interpersonal relations. In this chapter, we have presented a theoretical approach to the study of culture and emotion that accords a central role to culturally promoted relational concerns. Relational concerns were defined as sensitivities to behaviors (of oneself and others) and situations that advance or threaten core interpersonal themes in a given culture.

Two theoretical arguments were advanced. First, we believe that unpackaging culture is essential for the advancement of culture and emotion research. "Unpackaging" here refers to the replacement of the abstract, global, and often dichotomous (i.e., nationality) concept of culture that has

4 No cultural differences were found for our measures of concern for integrity, concern for masculine honor, and concern for feminine honor. However, a gender difference was found with regard to concern for feminine honor: Both Spanish and Dutch female participants rated behaviors and attributes that violate the sexual shame ideal as more negative to their feelings of self-worth than male participants did. Similar results were obtained for the vignette that expressed a threat to feminine honor. For more information on these results, see Rodriguez Mosquera et al. (2002b).

frequently been used in cross-cultural research on emotion by theoretically driven, measurable psychological constructs. Second, we proposed that culturally promoted relational concerns are central to unpackaging culture in emotion. These two theoretical arguments were illustrated by a discussion of our own research on honor, offenses and emotion.

Culture lies at the heart of emotion. It should not be reduced to the role of a moderator of emotional experiences and behavior. It is not only manifested in the form of contextual norms about the extent to and manner in which emotions should be felt and expressed to others. Cultures shape what we are sensitive to in interpersonal relations and the core of who we are.

APPENDIX

Example of Items for Each Domain of Honor Concern

Concern for Family Honor

"One's family having a bad reputation," "Self-damaging one's family's reputation," "Letting others insult your family."

Concern for Integrity

"Betraying other people," "Not keeping up one's word," "Having the reputation of being dishonest with others."

Concern for Feminine Honor

"Changing partners often," "Wearing provocative clothes," "Being known as having different sexual contacts."

Concern for Masculine Honor

"Not defending oneself when others insult you," "Being unable to maintain one's family," "Being known as someone who does not have authority over family."

References

Baron, R. M., & Kenny, D. A. (1986). The moderator-mediator variable distinction in social psychological research: Conceptual, strategic, and statistical considerations. *Journal of Personality and Social Psychology, 51*, 1173–1182.

Bond, M. H. (in press). Culture and aggression. From context to coercion. In C. D. Spielberger (Ed.), *The handbook of applied psychology*. New York: Academic Press.

Bond, M. H., & Tedeschi, J. T. (2001). Polishing the jade: A modest proposal for improving the study of social psychology across cultures. In D. Matsumoto (Ed.), *The handbook of culture and psychology* (pp. 309–324). Oxford, UK: Oxford University Press.

Cohen, D., & Nisbett, R. E. (1994). Self-protection and the culture of honor: Explaining southern violence. *Personality and Social Psychology Bulletin, 20*, 551–567.

Cohen, D., & Nisbett, R. E. (1997). Field experiments examining the culture of honor: The role of institutions in perpetuating norms about violence. *Personality and Social Psychology Bulletin, 23*, 1188–1199.

Cohen, D., Nisbett, R. E., Bowdle, B. F., & Schwarz, N. (1996). Insult, aggression and the southern culture of honor: An "experimental ethnography." *Journal of Personality and Social Psychology, 70*, 945–960.

Cohen, D., Vandello, J., & Rantilla, A. K. (1998). The sacred and the social: Cultures of honor and violence. In P. Gilbert & B. Andrews (Eds.), *Shame: Interpersonal behavior, psychopathology, and culture*. (pp. 261–282). London: Cambridge University Press.

Ekman, P. (1972). Universals and cultural differences in facial expressions of emotion. In J. Cole (Ed.), *Nebraska symposium of motivation* (Vol. 19; pp. 207–283). Lincoln, NE: University of Nebraska Press.

Ekman, P. (1973). *Darwin and facial expression*. New York: Academic Press.

Ekman, P., & Friesen, W. V. (1969). Nonverbal leakage and clues to deception. *Psychiatry, 32*, 88–106.

Fischer, A. H., Manstead, A. S. R., & Rodriguez Mosquera, P. M. (1999). The role of honor-related versus individualistic values in conceptualizing pride, shame and anger: Spanish and Dutch cultural prototypes. *Cognition and Emotion, 13*, 149–179.

Friesen, W. V. (1972). *Cultural differences in facial expressions in a social situation: An experimental test of the concept of display rules*. Unpublished doctoral dissertation, University of California, San Francisco.

Frijda, N. H. (1986). *The emotions* (p. 335). Cambridge: Cambridge University Press.

Frijda, N. H., & Mesquita, B. (1994). The social roles and functions of emotions. In S. Kitayama & H. R. Markus (Eds.), *Emotion and culture: Empirical studies of mutual influence* (pp. 51–87). Washington, DC: American Psychological Association.

Gilmore, D. D. (1987). *Honor and shame and the unity of the Mediterranean*. Washington, DC: American Anthropological Association.

Gilmore, D. D. (1990). *Manhood in the making: Cultural concepts of masculinity*. New Haven, CT: Yale University Press.

Gilmore, D. D., & Gwynne, G. (Eds.). (1985). Sex and gender in Southern Europe [Special Issue]. *Anthropology, 9*.

Hofstede, G. (2001). *Culture's consequences. Comparing values, behaviors, institutions, and organizations across nations*. London: Sage.

Jakubowska, L. (1989). A matter of honor. *The world and I, April*, 670–677.

Kim, U., Triandis, H. C., Kâgitçibasi, Ç., Choi, S., & Yoon, G. (1994). *Individualism and collectivism. Theory, method, and applications*. London: Sage.

Kitayama, S., & Markus, H. R. (1994). *Emotion and culture: Empirical studies of mutual influence*. Washington, DC: American Psychological Association.

Kitayama, S., Markus, H. R., & Matsumoto, H. (1995). Culture, self and emotion: A cultural perspective on "self-conscious" emotions. In J. P. Tangney & K. W. Fischer (Eds.), *Self-conscious emotions: The psychology of shame, guilt, embarrassment and pride* (pp. 439–464). New York: Guilford Press.

Manstead, A. S. R., & Fischer, A. H. (Eds.). (2002). Culture and emotion [Special Issue]. *Cognition and Emotion, 16*.

Markus, H. R., & Kitayama, S. (1991). Culture and the self: Implications for cognition, emotion and motivation. *Psychological Review, 98*, 224–253.

Markus, H. R. & Kitayama, S. (1994). The cultural construction of self and emotion: Implications for social behavior. In S. Kitayama & H. R. Markus (Eds.), *Emotion and culture: Empirical studies of mutual influence* (pp. 89–130). Washington, DC: American Psychological Association.

Mesquita, B. (1993). *Cultural variations in emotions. A comparative study of Dutch, Surinamese and Turkish people in the Netherlands*. Unpublished doctoral dissertation, University of Amsterdam.

Mesquita, B. (2001). Emotions in collectivist and individualist contexts. *Journal of Personality and Social Psychology, 80*, 68–74.

Mesquita, B., & Frijda, N. H. (1992). Cultural variations in emotions: A review. *Psychological Bulletin, 112*, 179–204.

Mesquita, B., Frijda, N. H., & Scherer, K. R. (1997). Culture and emotion. In J. W. Berry, P. R. Dasen, & T. S. Saraswathi (Eds.), *Handbook of cross-cultural psychology. Basic processes and human development* (Vol. 2; pp. 255–299). Boston: Allyn & Bacon.

Mesquita, B., & Karasawa, M. (2002). Different emotional lives. In A. S. R. Manstead & A. H. Fischer (Eds.), *Culture and emotion* [Special Issue of Cognition and Emotion] (pp. 127–142).

Miller, W. I. (1993). *Humiliation and other essays on honor, social discomfort, and violence*. Ithaca, NY: Cornell University Press.

Murphy, M. (1983). Emotional confrontations between Sevillano fathers and sons. *American Ethnologist, 10*, 650–664.

Nisbett, R. E., & Cohen, D. (1996). *Culture of honor: The psychology of violence in the South*. Boulder, CO: Westview.

Parkinson, B. (1995). *Ideas and realities of emotion*. New York: Routledge.

Peristiany, J. G. (Ed.). (1965). *Honour and shame: The values of Mediterranean society*. London: Weidenfeld and Nicolson.

Pitt-Rivers, J. (1965). Honor and social status. In J. G. Peristiany (Ed.), *Honour and shame: The values of Mediterranean society* (pp. 18–77). London: Weidenfeld and Nicolson.

Pitt-Rivers, J. (1977). *The fate of Shechem or the politics of sex: Essays in the anthropology of the Mediterranean*. Cambridge: Cambridge University Press.

Rodriguez Mosquera, P. M. (1999). *Honor and emotion: The cultural shaping of pride, shame and anger*. Doctoral dissertation, University of Amsterdam.

Rodriguez Mosquera, P. M., Manstead, A. S. R., & Fischer, A. H. (2000). The role of honor-related values in the elicitation, experience and communication of pride, shame and anger: Spain and the Netherlands compared. *Personality and Social Psychology Bulletin, 26*, 833–844.

Rodriguez Mosquera, P. M., Manstead, A. S. R., & Fischer, A. H. (2002a). Honor in the Mediterranean and Northern Europe. *Journal of Cross-Cultural Psychology, 33*, 16–36.

Rodriguez Mosquera, P. M., Manstead, A. S. R., & Fischer, A. H. (2002b). The role of honor concerns in emotional reactions to offenses. In A. S. R. Manstead & A. H. Fischer (Eds.), *Culture and emotion* [Special Issue of Cognition and Emotion] (pp. 143–164).

Scherer, K. R., Schorr, A., & Johnstone, T. (2001). *Appraisal processes in emotion. Theory, methods, research*. Oxford: Oxford University Press.

Schwartz, S. H. (1992). Universals in the structure and content of values: Theoretical advances and empirical tests in 20 countries. In M. P. Zanna (Ed.), *Advances in experimental social psychology* (Vol. 25; pp. 1–65). Orlando, FL: Academic Press.

Schwartz, S. H. (1999). A theory of cultural values and some implications for work. *Applied Psychology: An International Review, 48*, 23–47.

Schwartz, S. H., & Bilsky, W. (1990). Toward a theory of the universal structure and content of values: Extensions and cross-cultural replications. *Journal of Personality and Social Psychology, 58*, 878–891.

Stewart, F. H. (1994). *Honor*. Chicago, IL: Chicago University Press.

Tangney, J. P., & Dearing, R. L. (2002). *Shame and guilt*. New York: Guilford Press.

Tangney, J. P., & Fischer, K. W. (1995). *Self-conscious emotions: The psychology of shame, guilt, embarrassment and pride*. New York: Guilford Press.

Triandis, H. C. (1989). The self and social behavior in differing cultural contexts. *Psychological Review, 96*, 506–520.

Triandis, H. C. (1994). *Culture and social behavior*. New York: McGraw-Hill.

Triandis, H. C., Botempo, R., Villareal, M. J., Asai, M., & Lucca, N. (1988). Individualism and collectivism: Cross-cultural perspectives on self-ingroup relationships. *Journal of Personality and Social Psychology, 54*, 323–338.

Whiting, B. (1976). The problem of the packaged variable. In K. F. Riegel & J. A. Meacham (Eds.), *The developing individual in a changing world* (Vol. 1; pp. 303–309). The Hague: Mouton.

10

Objectification Theory and Emotions

A Feminist Psychological Perspective on Gendered Affect

Laura B. Citrin, Tomi-Ann Roberts, and
Barbara L. Fredrickson

In February 2002, the U.S. Food and Drug Administration approved the drug Botox, a diluted version of the neurotoxin that causes botulism, for the cosmetic purpose of removing wrinkles. Long in use by a mostly female consumer group – actresses and female TV personalities – as a quicker and easier way than plastic surgery to erase the signs of aging, Botox injections are now considered legally safe and can be marketed en masse to aging Americans in a fashion similar to the recent promotion of Viagra or Claritin. What is alarming about the potential widespread use, and the current popularity of it among women in the public eye, is its unavoidable side effect: loss of the ability to effectively communicate emotions via facial expression, particularly anger (see Friedman, 2002; Kuczynski, 2002).

Botox works by injection into the muscle behind one's wrinkles, and through local paralysis of that muscle, the wrinkles are smoothed. But because of that paralysis, one also can no longer use the muscles that caused the wrinkles – the lasting marks of repeated facial expressiveness – in the first place. So, in effect, having a Botox treatment not only makes it difficult for the recipient to demonstrate emotional feeling on the face, it also eliminates the evidence of years of emotions. About the common use of Botox by some women, *The New York Times* stated, "In a variation on '*The Stepford Wives*' [a 1975 film in which "perfect"[1] wives are revealed to be machines wearing mask-like disguises], it is now rare in certain social enclaves to see a woman over the age of 35 with the ability to look angry"

[1] The concept of "perfect" as it is utilized in the film is worth examining because it represents an ideal version of traditional femininity, one that depicts all other ways of being a woman as "flawed." The wives, who are actually robots, not only look flawless, but they also are flawless housekeepers, cooks, dressers, entertainers, and lovers; they do not complain or make undue demands of their husbands. Most importantly, they smile and act pleasantly content all of the time. The fact that the wives are robots is interesting in that it points out how impossible it is for a human being to meet this sort of ideal.

(Kuczynski, 2002, p. A1). Having one's wrinkles removed, and then, in effect, transforming one's face into a smooth, expressionless mask, may be the ultimate act of what has been termed "self-objectification" (Fredrickson & Roberts, 1997), because one literally becomes unable to use part of the body in an active, subjective fashion. Through paralysis of emotive muscles, one's face becomes a pretty *object*, a work of art, to be admired for *its* beauty and perfection, rather than a body part with a specific function – in this case, to communicate emotions.

Our concern is not with the specific reasons why an individual woman might choose to have a Botox treatment; rather, our focus is on the cultural environment in which women are objectified that creates fertile ground for a practice such as Botox to thrive. Many cultural pressures encourage women's preoccupation with their appearance, and the array of life benefits that physically attractive women receive in American culture abound, from popularity and marriage opportunities (e.g., Berscheid et al., 1971) to educational and economic rewards (e.g., Wooley & Wooley, 1980). Thus, according to Objectification Theory, as proposed by Fredrickson and Roberts (1997), many girls and women develop a habitual self-conscious body monitoring – they self-objectify, or take an observer's perspective on the physical self – to help determine how they will be treated in the world. This is not a trivial habit, and, as we shall discuss, it has significant consequences for women's subjective experiences.

The example of Botox is raised here because it illustrates the connections we would like to propose in this chapter between gender and emotion in the societal context of the objectification of women. Looking through the lens of Objectification Theory, we first discuss how gender, as a social construct that is heavily influenced by objectifying cultural discourses, shapes emotional experience and expression in women and men. Second, we examine the converse of this relationship – the ways in which emotional differences between men and women reinforce and reproduce gendered ways of being and behavior. Together, these two relationships function as a self-perpetuating cycle wherein emotions and social norms for gendered behavior and traits are intimately and reciprocally connected.

In the case of Botox, cultural values about beauty, femininity, and youth lead women to alter their appearance in ways that have a direct bearing on their emotional expression. This is one of the most literal examples of how *gender shapes emotion*. Imagine, then, a world in which women did not look angry, one in which it was normative to erase the visible signs of anger from a female face. What impact would this lack of anger expression have on people's ideas about women, about femininity, and about gender more generally? This is the type of question we ask in the second part of the chapter on the ways in which *emotion shapes gender*.

GENDER AS A SOCIAL CONSTRUCT

Critical to our inquiry here is an understanding of the concept of gender that is somewhat atypical in the mainstream social and personality psychology literature. Many feminist social scientists find it useful to distinguish between the concepts of sex and gender (Sherif, 1982; Unger, 1979; Unger & Crawford, 1993). *Sex* is most often defined as biological differences in anatomy and function (Crawford & Unger, 2000). *Gender* is distinct from biological sex and refers to the social expectations, social roles, and social traits associated with being a man or a woman. It is what the culture makes out of biological sex, and is a process that begins at birth, based on the fact that biological sex is an important social marker (Crawford & Unger, 2000). Gender has been argued, in fact, to be something one "does," or puts on (like a costume), and performs regularly in one's daily life either consciously or unconsciously (Butler, 1990; West & Zimmerman, 1987). Therefore, stating that emotions are *gendered* is more than a simple reference to differences in the ways men and women experience or express emotions; it is also a reference to the underlying set of social rules – both explicit and implicit – that govern the way emotion is "performed" by men and women. Being an anatomical male or female does not likely cause one to emote or not emote, or to express or not express particular emotions. Rather, it is gender – the set of social expectations that are affiliated with being male or female – that leads one to emote in particular ways.

Thinking about gender as a social construct – an idea of how women and men should think, act, and feel – rather than as a biological distinction, steers an analysis of the relationship between gender and emotion away from the debate about whether or not women experience or express emotions differently from men. Although we think it is important to tease apart sex differences in emotional *experience* from sex differences in emotional *expression* (which could be conceived of as self-censorship to meet gender norms), substantial critical review and analysis in this area has already been done, and we will not repeat that work here (for excellent reviews of this literature, see Brody, 1999; Brody & Hall, 2000; Fischer, 2000).

Instead, our approach to thinking about gender and emotions presupposes that there are sex differences in the experience and expression of certain emotions, and continues from there to look at how the relationship between gender and emotions is constituted. It is not that the distinction one might make between allegedly "real" sex differences in emotional experience and "performed" sex differences in emotional expression is beside the point. The fact that there are gender norms that might cause sex differences in emotional expression is exactly the point of this chapter as we turn our attention to the social values, demands, and expectations that shape the way men and women emote.

HOW GENDER SHAPES EMOTION

In this section, we lay the theoretical groundwork for understanding how gender shapes emotion. First, thinking about gender as a social construct necessitates a discussion of power and status differences between men and women, and the role of power in determining the relationship between gender and emotion. Second, we move from a general analysis of gendered power differentials to one that focuses specifically on the body, including the face, as the site of not only much expression or nonexpression, but also as a primary site on which gendered power dynamics are inscribed. Third, we describe in detail the ways in which our gendered world, one specifically in which women are sexually objectified, leads to particular consequences for women's emotional experience and expression. And last, we discuss the consequences of transgressing gender rules for emotional expression and the ways in which sanctions reinforce the rules of gender within an objectifying culture.

Power and Gender

There is a long-standing belief in the West about gender and emotions – namely, that women are emotional, ruled by their passions, and irrational, and that men are ruled by logic and rationality rather than their emotions. The belief that women are emotional and men are not has many societal consequences. If women are ruled by their passions, they cannot be trusted to be rulers or have too much control over business or other matters in which a "cool head" is required. If men are not particularly emotional, they are not well suited to be the primary caregiver of children or the elderly. The belief that men are rational and women are emotional is also partly the consequence of different social roles for men and women. Being a primary caregiver to children or a nurse or a teacher requires one to express a lot of positive, encouraging, nurturing emotions toward others (Eagly, 1987). Being a business manager requires one to express powerful emotions like anger and pride if one wants to be a respected and effective leader (see Tiedens, 2001; Tiedens, Ellsworth, & Mesquita, 2000). Thus, people express whatever emotions are appropriate for their social role (Alexander & Wood, 2000; Eagly, 1987). Social roles are not neutral; they always have a corresponding status marker in that certain roles carry more power than others.

Much research exists to demonstrate that status differences between individuals engender behavioral – both verbal and nonverbal – differences. For example, high-status people show different eye gaze and facial expression patterns than low-status people (Henley, 1977; Ridgeway, 1987). These differences appear to be both an outcome of social status, as well as a reflection of others' expectations of how individuals of differing status ought to behave. Women and men of course occupy different status positions in nearly all societies, with women being lower status than men. Indeed, many of the gender differences in verbal and nonverbal behaviors that have been demonstrated cross-culturally have been shown to be reflections of status differences between men and women (Hall, 1984; Henley, 1977).

The question of whether status and power influence emotion has been relatively less explored. However, some evidence does suggest that indeed people of different status levels experience and display different emotions (Keltner et al., 1998; Tiedens et al., 2000), with, for example, anger and pride being associated more with high-status people, and embarrassment, sadness, and guilt being associated more with low-status people. Obviously many of the facial and postural expressions (e.g., direct stare with no smile vs. gaze-avert with smile) that vary between status-unequals are reflections of emotions (anger vs. embarrassment or shame). Furthermore, gender differences abound with respect to the display of such expressions and in the culture's expectations of who ought to display such expressions.

So, gender differences in expressions of emotion are undoubtedly deeply infused with expectations regarding power and status. Indeed, Snodgrass (1985, 1992) found that subordinate individuals in any dyad, regardless of gender, are better able to decipher and understand facial expressions of emotion. The advantage in facial cue-reading accuracy was greatest, however, when the subordinate was a woman and the dominant member of the dyad was a man. Fischer (1993) found that the emotions of fear and sadness are described as expressions of vulnerability and powerlessness, and argued that women's greater tendency toward these emotions may reflect their lower status and power. In contrast, men's expressions of anger may be a reflection of their greater power. So, women's greater tendency to experience and express emotions such as shame, disgust toward the self, sadness, fear, and anxiety (as opposed to anger, pride, or contempt) is likely at least in part because such emotions are considered appropriate for lower status individuals.

Objectification Theory Puts the Body in the Analysis of Gendered Power Dynamics

A feminist analysis of status and power explores gender socialization in the context of the dominant patriarchal culture. Henley (1977) argued that socialization of subordinates in a dominant culture achieves a kind of colonization of the mind that ensures self-imposed powerlessness. Objectification Theory (Fredrickson & Roberts, 1997) also uses a feminist analysis of power, but it particularizes status differences between men and women by placing the *body* front and center in the analysis.

Objectification Theory argues that the United States is a culture in which women are sexually objectified, and this is a primary source of their relative powerlessness. Women are treated as physical objects to gaze at, scrutinize, and admire. In this context, in which the sexualized evaluation of girls' and women's bodies is normative, girls and women can come to treat themselves on some level as objects to be looked at and evaluated. Females learn, both directly and vicariously, that their "looks" matter, that other people's evaluations of their physical appearance can determine how they are treated and, ultimately, affect their social and economic life outcomes. The theory argues that women can adopt a "third-person" or "looking-glass" perspective on their physical selves as a way of anticipating and controlling their treatment – an effect termed "self-objectification" – which may in part supplant a more "first-person" point-of-view. This practice brings rewards, as evidenced by the greater life outcomes of women deemed "attractive." That is, physical beauty can function as a kind of power for women. But it also has costs – both for women individually, and for society as a whole, because it supports and maintains women's lower status position. Furthermore, the practices of self-objectification, we argue, "engender" emotional differences between men and women.

Looking through the lens of Objectification Theory, we can make some specific predictions about how gender – the social norms and expectations for women and men – shapes emotion. According to Objectification Theory, the objectification of women, and the subsequent self-objectification that many women engage in, has particular affect-related outcomes: increased states of shame, disgust, and anxiety; and decreased happiness, interest, and "flow" (Csikszentmihalyi, 1982, 1990), a highly positive state (Fredrickson & Roberts, 1997).

Emotional Consequences of Self-Objectification

Shame

As described earlier, when women internalize an observer's perspective on the self, they treat themselves as objects to be evaluated. As such, they adopt a peculiar form of self-consciousness characterized by habitual monitoring of the body. This psychological state may not only lead to disruptions in one's flow of consciousness, but it also makes one vulnerable to a very negative emotion – shame. Shame occurs when one evaluates oneself according to a particular ideal – in this case a cultural ideal of women's beauty (and perhaps simply just being "normal") – and then falls short of meeting that ideal (Darwin, 1872/1965; M. Lewis, 1992). Shame is the result of attributing one's shortcomings to the self ("I am a bad person") rather than a specific action ("I did something bad") (H. Lewis, 1971).

Empirical research has shown that women experience more shame than men (Ferguson & Crowley, 1997; H. Lewis, 1971; Silberstein,

Striegel-Moore, & Rodin, 1987; Stapley & Haviland, 1989). From the perspective of Objectification Theory, one important explanation lies in the nearly ubiquitous images of idealized female bodies that women are exposed to. Whether it is images of youth, slimness, or whiteness, very few women can actually meet this ideal. Therefore, women are regularly faced with the failure of meeting up with this idealized female image. Given that the ideal female body is a myth, as it is largely unrealistic and virtually impossible to attain (Wolf, 1991), Fredrickson and Roberts have argued that "the continual comparison that a woman may make between her actual body and the mythic ideal is a recipe for shame" (1997, p. 181). Because shame is considered a moral emotion, it can also be used to socialize societal standards (Citrin, 2003; Fredrickson, 1998; H. Lewis, 1989; M. Lewis, 1992).

Disgust

The emotion of disgust is intimately connected to the creation of culture (Miller, 1997). Social judgments create boundaries between clean and filthy, pure and tarnished, and those boundaries are reflected in the culture's social standards. Hence, people might find actions such as public urination or chewing food with one's mouth open "disgusting" precisely because they are "uncivilized." Self-disgust, then, is similar to shame in this sense; it can be prompted by a feeling that one has violated certain socio-moral standards. In fact, both self-disgust and shame can evoke the feeling of exposure and the desire to hide (Miller, 1997).

So disgust can play a positive role in the development of a civilized society by internalizing norms for cleanliness, restraint, and reserve (Miller, 1997). Unfortunately, it can also become a negative reaction to violations of these predetermined social standards. Insofar as many women experience a discrepancy between their actual body size and their ideal body size (Fallon & Rozin, 1985), women may become disgusted with their own bodies because they have violated a social standard by being unattractive or overweight, and hence "gross." Overweight individuals are perceived as lacking in self-control and moral discipline (Crandall, 1994). This perception appears to be especially true for overweight women (Quinn & Crocker, 1999). Indeed, it might be argued that the higher standards of cleanliness, hairlessness, odorlessness, and beauty held for women in our culture are a reflection of the greater burden placed on them to "civilize" their bodies lest they be seen as "disgusting" by others (Citrin, 2003; Roberts et al., 2002).

Research shows that people can feel a type of moral self-disgust when they fail at something, are criticized by superiors, or ignored and cut off from society (Haidt et al., 1997). The experience of self-disgust has been demonstrated to be an outcome of self-objectification. Fredrickson et al. (1998) found that women wearing swimsuits reported feeling more disgust, distaste, and revulsion than men, who, in contrast, reported more lighthearted self-conscious feelings of awkwardness, silliness, and foolishness. Higher self-objectification in women has also been correlated with greater feelings of disgust toward menstruation, one of the body's more "creaturely" physical functions (Roberts, in press). Roberts, Gettman, Konik, and Fredrickson (2001) found that priming women with self-objectifying words (e.g., weight, attractive), as opposed to neutral or body-competence words (e.g., health, vitality), led to greater feelings of self-disgust, whereas men were unaffected by the prime.

Anxiety

A culture of objectification also increases women's opportunities to experience anxiety. Anxiety, with its accompanying motor tension, vigilance, and scanning, occurs when people anticipate danger or threats to self; distinct from fear, however, these threats often remain ambiguous (Lazarus, 1991; Öhman, 2000). Objectification Theory highlights two forms of gendered anxiety: appearance anxiety and safety anxiety. Appearance anxiety results from not knowing exactly when and how one's body will be looked at and evaluated. Indeed, empirical studies document that women experience more anxiety about their appearance than do men (Dion, Dion, & Keelan, 1990). Appearance anxiety is often manifested by concerns for checking and adjusting one's appearance (Keelan, Dion, & Dion, 1992), a vigilant state that is often compounded by certain fashions marketed to women. Yet appearance anxiety is not just about so-called vanity. It is also fused with concerns about safety. For instance, those who suggest that a female victim of sexual assault "asked for it" often refer to her physical appearance as "provocative." Empirical studies demonstrate that more attractive rape victims are assigned greater blame for their own rape than less attractive victims (e.g., Jacobson & Popovich, 1983). This underscores the notion that sexual objectification is a key component of sexual violence. Because to some degree all women in our culture face the possibility of sexual victimization, they need to be attentive to the potential for sexually motivated bodily harm (Beneke, 1982; Brownmiller, 1975; Griffin, 1979; Pollitt, 1985). This attentiveness is a chronic and daily source of anxiety for many women, affecting both their personal and work lives (Gordon & Riger, 1989; Rozee, 1988). In fact, some feminists have argued that vigilance to safety may be the most fundamental difference between women's and men's subjective emotional experiences (Griffin, 1979; Pollitt, 1985).

Flow

Similarly, Objectification Theory posits that a culture of objectification diminishes women's opportunities to experience genuine positive emotions, in particular, states of flow. Flow is characterized by being fully absorbed in challenging mental or physical activity. Csikszentmihalyi (1990) identifies flow as a prime source of optimal experience, those rare moments during which we feel we are truly living, uncontrolled by others, creative and joyful. Maximizing such experience, he argues, improves the quality of life.

According to Objectification Theory, women's experiences of flow are diminished in two ways. First, and most obviously, a woman's activities are interrupted when actual others call attention to the appearance or functions of her body. As early as elementary school, in classrooms and on playgrounds, observational research shows that girls' activities and thoughts are more frequently disrupted by boys than vice versa (Thorne, 1993). As girls mature physically, these interruptions often draw attention to a girl's appearance, weight, or breast development (Brownmiller, 1984; Martin, 1996; Thorne, 1993). Second, Csikszentmihalyi (1990) argues persuasively that a person must necessarily lose self-consciousness to achieve flow, and laboratory experiments have shown that pleasurable absorption is reduced when individuals are made self-aware, either by the presence of a mirror or a video camera (Plant & Ryan, 1985). Women's internalization of an observer's perspective on their bodies, by definition, creates a form of self-consciousness that thwarts or limits their experiences of flow. Indeed, recent research shows that girls who hold a more self-objectifying view of their physical selves demonstrate less effective, less "free," or open arm-swing when throwing a softball (Fredrickson & Harrison, in press). Presumably, then, the much-maligned phenomenon of "throwing like a girl" (Young, 1991), in which one utilizes only part of the arm rather than putting the entire body into the throw, reflects the self-consciousness engendered by objectification.

Smiling

Even while cultural practices that objectify female bodies increase women's opportunities to experience certain negative emotions, and decrease their opportunities to experience certain positive emotions, these same practices appear to create opposite pressures on the expression of emotion. Women smile more frequently than men (Hall, Carter, & Horgan, 2000; LaFrance & Hecht, 2000). Although a number of nuanced explanations for this sex difference have been offered (see Hall, Carter, & Horgan, 2000; LaFrance & Hecht, 2000), we highlight the link between smiling and objectification. Smiling is, no doubt, a component of "looking pretty." As such, women are both expected and compelled to smile to be "good" women. It is not uncommon, for instance, for a woman to walk down the street and have a stranger ask her to "Smile!" When the stranger on the street asks a woman who is not smiling to smile, he or she is offering prescriptive, disciplinary advice about how to be a good woman. This cultural prescription to smile, however, erodes the communicative value of women's smiles. Shrout and Fiske (1981) found that judges gave higher positive ratings to men who smiled than men who did not, but did not rate women higher when they smiled, suggesting that smiling is so normative for women it loses its impact. Furthermore, an early study found that, although children were very responsive to their fathers' smiles, they virtually ignored their mothers' smiles, presumably because mothers smiled so often that their smiles had become nondiagnostic of their inner states (Bugental, Love, & Gianetto, 1971).

Women's smiling comes to reinforce their lower status position in society. Women anticipate greater costs in not smiling than do men, for example (LaFrance, 1998). Specifically, women believe they will be regarded less positively if they do not smile. However, there is a status trade-off: while women are *liked more* if they smile, they are often regarded as *less competent*, and are more likely to be interrupted (Coates & Feldman, 1996; Hecht & LaFrance, 1998). More sobering, research has found that men are far more likely than women to mistake a friendly smile from the opposite sex for a smile of sexual interest (Abbey, 1982).

Expressing Anger

On the opposite side of the coin from smiling, studies show that femininity is related to the suppression of anger (Kopper & Epperson, 1991, 1996). Alongside other viable explanations for this difference (see Kring, 2000), we suggest that angry faces are construed as "ugly" faces, inappropriate for good women to display. Indeed, this may be why losing the ability to express anger is not taken as a serious side effect of using Botox to reduce wrinkles. Anger, by definition, communicates expectations of power and just behavior. Angry women are often dubbed "bitches," perhaps because they raise the specter of a powerful woman who is stepping out of line. The normative mandate that women should not display anger is a disciplinary and a divisionary tactic. First, it is disciplinary in that it punishes women who do not conform, and it discourages women from ever transgressing in the first place. Second, it is divisionary because it divides groups of women into those who can control their anger and those who cannot or choose not to do so. Those who control their anger, at least in public, are described as "dignified," "sophisticated," or "mature," pointing to the role of power (via class distinctions) in the cultural ideology about gender and emotion.

Recognizing Emotional States

Finally, although long-standing stereotypes characterize women as more "in tune" with their own emotions than men, recent theory and empirical work call this view into question. Feminist writers have long described the ways in which a sexist culture yields women who are alienated and distant from their own bodies, and a significant part of the feminist movement of the 1970s involved educational efforts to reconnect women with their physical selves (e.g., Lerner, 1993; Rich, 1976). From the perspective of Objectification Theory, we argue that one significant path to this alienation is women's engagement in self-objectifying practices, which may carry negative consequences for women's ability to attend to internal, body cues of emotion. There is, indeed, empirical evidence that women are less attuned to internal physiological information (such as heart rate, stomach contractions, genital vasodilatation) than men and make relatively less use of such bodily cues than men in determining their subjective feeling and emotional states (see Roberts & Pennebaker, 1995, for a review of these studies). One possible path through which self-objectification practices might lead to this insensitivity is through the self-conscious body monitoring we have argued occupies women in a sexually objectifying culture. Because many women are vigilantly attuned to their bodies' outward appearance, they may have limited perceptual resources to attend to inner body experience.

So, living in an objectifying culture may not only impact women's expression of emotion, but also their experience of it. Our argument here is that women's chronic vigilance to their external appearance and to others' evaluations of their bodies leads to a general lack of the normally privileged access one has to internal, body-based cues to emotion. We do not mean to argue that women therefore feel fewer emotions overall. If one subscribes to an ecological approach (e.g., Gibson, 1979) to the self-perception of emotion and feeling states, there are ample other cues available in the external environment relative to emotions. In a sexually objectifying culture, women are likely using such external, situational cues (e.g., others' facial expressions and evaluations) to a greater extent in determining their own emotional states (Roberts & Pennebaker, 1995).

But perhaps one *could* take this argument about gender impacting the experience of emotion a step further. Consider our opening example of Botox. This self-objectifying practice may in a very real way not only limit women's ability to express such emotions as anger, but it may also profoundly affect their ability to *feel* them. Research on the Darwinian theory of facial feedback has convincingly demonstrated that the movements of our facial muscles significantly impact our felt emotional states (Ekman, Levenson, & Friesen, 1983; Stepper & Strack, 1993). Is it far-fetched to predict that women whose corrugator muscles cannot contract properly might not experience anger to the same degree as those whose can? Looking-glass selves, then, may not only express emotions differently, they may also come to experience some of them differently (especially those with gender-stereotyped expectations surrounding them, such as anger).

Consequences of Transgressing Gendered Emotion Norms

What happens when a man or woman breaks emotion norms (e.g., a woman expresses a lot of anger or a man cries in public)? The result of this type of gender transgression is often social sanction. It might be in the form of name-calling, social ostracism, or more tangible effects like being fired or not promoted. Take the case of anger, for example. In her review of the literature on the gendering of anger displays, Kring (2000) reported the following findings: Women who display anger feel more shame and embarrassment (Deffenbacher et al., 1996); worry about being denounced by male partners for their anger display (Campbell & Muncer, 1987; Fehr & Baldwin, 1996); and are more likely to be called "bitchy" or "hostile" (Tavris, 1989).

In a world in which being successful, especially in the business sector, is defined by so-called masculine traits – ambition, aggression, and toughness – it is difficult for a woman to display emotions appropriately and still be "successful." For an example of this sort of bind that some women find themselves in today, Susan Fiske described a sexual discrimination case against Price Waterhouse, one of the top accounting firms in the nation (Fiske, 1993). The case revolved around a female manager who was denied partnership in the accounting firm despite the fact that she made millions of dollars for the company, billed more hours than anyone in her cohort, and was well liked by her clients. She was also described as "aggressive, hard-working, and ambitious." According to Price Waterhouse, she did not make partner due to her "interpersonal skills problems." These "problems," she was told, could be corrected if she "walked, talked, and dressed more femininely" (p. 622). Although the issue of emotions did not arise explicitly, the specific traits at hand – aggressiveness, acting tough, not walking or talking femininely – implicate emotions implicitly. To be a successful manager, which this accountant was, one needs to act powerful, which in many ways means that one needs to express powerful (not powerless) emotions. However, taking on these powerful traits, a basic requirement to fit into this type of field, was seen as violating her gender prescriptive to be feminine, submissive, and passive, and hence, she was punished for her departure from feminine norms. Significantly, from our Objectification Theory perspective, her gender-nonconforming emotional behavior was construed as being *unattractive*. This is an example of the way gender can shape emotions in a coercive way, compelling us to conform to gender norms or be punished for transgressing.

HOW EMOTIONS SHAPE GENDER

In this section, we discuss the ways in which emotions shape our ideas about gender. First, we examine the socializing influence of seeing men and women express emotions differently – *who* expresses *what* emotions matters. Next, we look at the way certain emotions are particularly effective at socializing gender norms.

Emotional Expression: *Who Expresses What*

The issue of gender transgressions, as discussed in the previous section, highlights the *cyclical* relationship between gender and emotions, one in which gendered norms influence emotional expression (and perhaps experience) and emotional expression influences our ideas about gender. One way this works is that people avoid transgressing gender norms for fear of being punished, and the consequence is that *very few people actually do transgress*. This creates an environment in which children rarely see a woman or a man acting outside of gender prescriptions for emotional expression. The expression, or lack of expression, of emotions leads boys and girls to believe that women do not get angry and men do not cry, that this is inherently part of being male or female rather than the result of social expectations fulfilled. One can only imagine the socializing impact of a post-Botox, smooth-faced, always-"happy" *Stepford Wives* world in which it truly is a rarity to see a grown woman look angry.

Emotions, then, have the potential for shaping our conception of gender. Gender norms about emotions limit our options to express ourselves, and this constraint then influences the way others perceive us as gendered subjects. Thus, emotions, perhaps, both convey and reproduce social relationships. Tiedens et al. (2000) showed that people learn about an actor's status from observing his or her emotional reactions. Specifically, observers inferred that those who express anger and pride are higher status, whereas those who express sadness, guilt, and appreciation are lower status. This finding mirrors normative gender differences in emotions in our culture: Men (who are higher status than women) act more angry than women, and women (who are lower status than men) express sadness more than men. Of course, there are always exceptions to this generalization, but the exceptions – a man who cries a lot in public, a woman who does not hide her anger – are just that, exceptions, and are often punished in one way or another. When men and women conform to their gender roles, this maintains the status quo in terms of gender and power. So, when we observe men acting angry or proud and women acting sad or appreciative, we learn about their relative status in our society and come to think of it as "the way it is."

Tiedens et al. (2000) argued that emotion stereotypes about high- and low-status individuals are due to differences in the inferred abilities of people in high- and low-status positions. Similarly, we believe that the process of inferring status from emotions leads to a greater *acceptance* that the status positions held by each group – in this case, men and women – are acquired legitimately and justly. In a culture in which men have more power than women, emotions teach us particular lessons about gender, ones that reinforce the seemingly inherent "naturalness" of the gender hierarchy.

This seeming naturalness is facilitated by the fact that emotions are experienced *in the body* and, as such, they are more likely to be experienced as *naturally* occurring. When we feel disgust, for example, we are more likely to believe that the object of our disgust is *inherently* disgusting, because if it were not, we would not be experiencing/sensing it in our bodies. When we feel shame, the sensation is so bodily felt and so punitive that it is difficult to imagine that our actions were not inherently shameful. This visceral component of emotions aids in social learning as we come to conceive of socio-cultural norms and values as part of our individual selves rather than as a set of rules imposed on us (Citrin, 2003).

Particular Emotions Are Effective Gender Socializing Agents

Self-conscious emotions (shame, embarrassment, guilt, pride; Lewis, 2000) and moralizing emotions (contempt, anger, disgust; Shweder, Much, Mahapatra, & Park, 1997) seem to be particularly effective at both facilitating learning about social norms and conformity to those norms. Self-conscious and moralizing emotions keep women in their lower status place, as it were, by stopping them from being too fat, too hairy, too sexual, too loud, too aggressive, too powerful, and too "masculine." Research shows that individuals do respond with moralizing emotions such as disgust to women who violate gendered body norms. For example, Roberts et al. (2002) showed that people derogated the competence of a woman who dropped a wrapped tampon out of her bag, as well as distanced themselves psychologically and physically from her. Here, the cultural mandate to conceal all evidence of menstruation teaches us that women's menstruating bodies are "disgusting," which implicates women more generally. Similarly, we learn that a woman who is overtly sexual is shameful through seeing others' contempt. We learn that women's secondary sex characteristic of body hair is unacceptable when people react with disgust or shame at the sight of an unshaven leg or underarm (Citrin, 2003). We learn *what* is valued and not valued, *who* is not valued and who is, by both experiencing ourselves and seeing others' emotional reactions. In the examples listed, we learn that women's reproductive capacities are disturbing or dangerous, that women should not be sexual subjects, and that women's "natural" bodies are not acceptable without modification. Of course, we learn a lot about men, too, via the same type of process: The fact that their sexuality and their bodies (as they naturally occur) are less shameful or disgusting tells us something about who is more valued in our society.

Feeling a negative self-conscious emotion, particularly shame, is a punishing sensation. Being the object of someone else's disgust (or one's own self-directed disgust) is also shaming, because it brings into question not only one's worth as a human being, but also one's humanity itself. Moreover, as Objectification Theory has argued, feeling shame, disgust, and anxiety about meeting cultural expectations of femininity can produce particular mental health consequences. As these emotional experiences accumulate and compound, they contribute to women's disproportionate experiences of disordered eating, depression, and sexual dysfunction (Fredrickson & Roberts, 1997). Fredrickson et al. (1998) showed that inducing self-objectification in women led to greater feelings of body shame, which in turn led to restrained eating. Notably, this link between shame and eating was completely absent for men.

Eating disorders, depression, and sexual dysfunction are in fact so gendered (the cultural conceptions of these "disorders" are shaped by ideas about women) that they have come to be understood as aspects of femininity itself. As such, feeling depressed, or having ambivalent relations with food and one's own sexuality, are indeed ways of "doing gender" for many women. So, the transient emotions that were perhaps initially triggered by practices of objectification begin to shape how femininity is enacted on a more lasting basis. This produces a self-sustaining cycle between gender and emotions, with certain gendered ways of reinforcing particular emotions, and particular emotions reinforcing certain gendered ways of being.

CONCLUSIONS

This chapter approached the topic of gender differences in emotions by discussing two distinct, yet related, issues: (1) how gender norms in the United States shape the ways in which we express, and perhaps experience, emotions; and (2) the role emotions play in facilitating gender-related social norms. We proposed that gendered emotional responses are not only the *result* of particular cultural practices, but also that emotions can play the role of socializing *agent*, teaching us how to appropriately behave and interpret others' behaviors.

We focused specifically on one of the enduring aspects of American culture – the sexual objectification of women – and examined the ways in which living in an objectifying society results in certain affect-related outcomes for women, outcomes that in some ways reproduce opportunities for further objectification. Gender norms produce gender differences in emotional states, and these emotional differences reinforce and reproduce gender differences, creating a self-perpetuating cycle wherein emotions and social norms for gendered behavior and traits are intimately connected.

The analytic framework we utilized to think about gender and emotion, one in which power, and particularly power that is inscribed on the body, is central to the analysis, can also be utilized to think about the relationship between emotions and race, emotions, and class. Like gender, race and class are not only "identities" that reflect particular group memberships, but are also social concepts instilled with much cultural meaning. Cultural discourse on emotional control – controlling one's allegedly less *civilized* characteristics – is tied with cultural values not only about gender, as described earlier, but also about race and class. As a signifier of "civility," emotional control has been used to distinguish between groups – men from women, whites from blacks, North Americans from South Americans, Northern Europeans from Southern Europeans, and the rich or middle class from the poor. Historians of emotions, Lewis and Stearns, have pointed to the importance of these group comparisons for understanding social norms for emotional expression, stating "mainstream efforts at emotional control are *inexplicable* [emphasis added] without reference to the perceived emotionality of women, poor whites, and blacks" (1998, p. 11). All of these alleged intergroup distinctions point to the role of *power* in defining *what* is appropriate emotionality and *for whom*. How emotions are expressed, who expresses them, and how they are controlled – these questions are infused with the politics of power.

Although understanding power dynamics is essential for understanding differences among groups in emotion experience and expression, we believe the particular ways power is inscribed matters in making specific predictions about emotions. For women, sexualized evaluation of the body has been argued to occur with both "endless variety and monotonous similarity" (Rubin, 1975), and is a primary source of women's lower status. Within this cultural milieu, girls and women are coaxed to adopt an observer's perspective on their physical selves. "Doing" their gender in this way brings certain emotional consequences. These emotions, in turn, serve to reinforce their femininity and ultimately their lower status position in society. We encourage others to explore the particular ways power is inscribed for other marginalized groups (race, class, sexuality) to more fully understand the ways this impacts the emotional lives of members of those groups. Moving beyond simple "differences" models to ones that center around the social construction of gender (or race, or class, or sexuality) is key to broadening our understanding of the emotional lives of men and women in social context.

References

Abbey, A. (1982). Sex differences in attributions for friendly behavior: Do males misperceive females' friendliness? *Journal of Personality and Social Psychology, 42*, 830–838.

Alexander, M. G., & Wood, W. (2000). Women, men, and positive emotions. In A. H. Fisher (Ed.), *Gender and emotion: Social psychological perspectives* (pp. 189–210). New York: Cambridge University Press.

Beneke, T. (1982). *Men on rape*. New York: St. Martin's Press.

Berscheid, E., Dion, K., Walster, E., & Walster, G. W. (1971). Physical attractiveness and dating choice: A test of the matching hypothesis. *Journal of Experimental Social Psychology, 7*, 173–189.
Brody, L. R. (1999). *Gender, emotion, and the family*. Cambridge, MA: Harvard University Press.
Brody, L. R., & Hall, J. A. (2000). Gender, emotion, and expression. In M. Lewis & J. M. Haviland-Jones (Eds.), *Handbook of emotions* (2nd Edition; pp. 338–349). New York: Guilford Press.
Brownmiller, S. (1975). *Against our will: Men, women and rape*. New York: Simon & Schuster.
Brownmiller, S. (1984). *Femininity*. New York: Linden Press/Simon and Schuster.
Bugental, D. E., Love, L. R., & Gianetto, R. M. (1971). Perfidious feminine faces. *Journal of Personality and Social Psychology, 17*, 314–318.
Butler, J. (1990). *Gender trouble: Feminism and the subversion of identity*. New York: Routledge.
Campbell, A., & Muncer, C. (1987). Models of anger and aggression in the social talk of women and men. *Journal for the Theory of Social Behaviour, 17*, 498–511.
Citrin, L. B. (2003). *Disgust and the female body*. Manuscript under review.
Coates, E. J., & Feldman, R. S. (1996). Gender differences in nonverbal correlates of social status. *Personality and Social Psychology Bulletin, 22*, 1014–1022.
Crandall, C. S. (1994). Prejudice against fat people: Ideology and self-interest. *Journal of Personality and Social Psychology, 66*, 882–894.
Crawford, M., & Unger, R. K. (2000). *Women and gender: A feminist psychology* (3rd Edition). Boston: McGraw Hill.
Csikszentmihalyi, M. (1982). Toward a psychology of optimal experience. In L. Wheeler (Ed.), *Review of personality and social psychology*. Beverly Hills, CA: Sage.
Csikszentmihalyi, M. (1990). *Flow*. New York: Harper Perennial.
Darwin, C. (1965). *The expression of emotion in man and animals*. Chicago: University of Chicago Press. (Original work published 1872.)
Deffenbacher, J. L., Oetting, E. R., Lynch, R. S., & Morris, C. A. (1996). The expression of anger and its consequences. *Behavior Research and Therapy, 34*, 575–590.
Dion, K. L., Dion, K. K., & Keelan, J. P. (1990). Appearance anxiety as a dimension of social-evaluative anxiety: Exploring the ugly duckling syndrome. *Contemporary Social Psychology, 14*, 220–224.
Eagly, A. H. (1987). *Sex differences in social behavior: A social role interpretation*. Hillside, NJ: Erlbaum.
Ekman, P., Levenson, R. W., & Friesen, W. V. (1983). Autonomic nervous system activity distinguishes between emotions. *Science, 221*, 1208–1210.
Fallon, A. E., & Rozin, P. (1985). Sex differences in perception of desirable body shape. *Journal of Abnormal Psychology, 94*, 102–105.
Fehr, B., & Baldwin, M. (1996). Prototype and script analyses of laypeople's knowledge of anger. In G. J. O. Fletcher & J. Fitness (Eds.), *Knowledge structures in close relationships: A social psychological approach* (pp. 219–245). Mahwah, NJ: Lawrence Erlbaum.
Ferguson, T. J., & Crowley, S. L. (1997). Measure for measure: A multitrait-multimethod analysis of guilt and shame. *Journal of Personality Assessment, 69*, 425–441.

Fischer, A. H. (1993). Sex differences in emotionality: Fact or stereotype. *Feminism and Psychology, 3*, 303–318.

Fischer, A. H. (Ed.). (2000). *Gender and emotion: Social psychological perspectives*. New York: Cambridge University Press.

Fiske, S. T. (1993). Controlling other people: The impact of power on stereotyping. *American Psychologist, 48*(6), 621–628.

Fredrickson, B. L. (1998). Cultivated emotions: Parental socialization of positive emotions and self-conscious emotions. *Psychological Inquiry, 9*(4), 279–281.

Fredrickson, B. L., & Harrison, K. (in press). "Throwing like a girl": Self-objectification predicts adolescent girls' motor performance. *Journal of Sport and Social Issues*.

Fredrickson, B. L., & Roberts, T.-A. (1997). Objectification theory: Toward understanding women's lived experiences and mental health risks. *Psychology of Women Quarterly, 21*, 173–206.

Fredrickson, B. F., Roberts, T.-A., Noll, S. M., Quinn, D. M., & Twenge, J. M. (1998). That swimsuit becomes you: Sex differences in self-objectification, restrained eating, and math performance. *Journal of Personality and Social Psychology, 75*(1), 269–284.

Friedman, R. A. (2002, August 6). A peril of the veil of Botox. *The New York Times*, p. D5.

Gibson, J. J. (1979). *The ecological approach to visual perception*. Boston: Houghton-Mifflin.

Gordon, M. T., & Riger, S. (1989). *The female fear: The social cost of rape*. New York: Free Press.

Griffin, S. (1979). *Rape: The power of consciousness*. San Francisco: Harper & Row.

Haidt, J., Rozin, P., McCauley, C. R., & Imada, S. (1997). Body, psyche, and culture: The relationship between disgust and morality. *Psychology and Developing Societies, 9*, 107–131.

Hall, J. A. (1984). *Nonverbal sex differences: Communication accuracy and expressive style*. Baltimore: The Johns Hopkins University Press.

Hall, J. A., Carter, J. D., & Horgan, T. G. (2000). Gender differences in nonverbal communication of emotion. In A. Fischer (Ed.), *Gender and emotion: Social psychological perspectives* (pp. 97–117). New York: Cambridge University Press.

Hecht, M. A., & LaFrance, M. (1998). License or obligation to smile: Power, sex and smiling. *Personality and Social Psychology Bulletin, 24*(12), 1332–1342.

Henley, N. M. (1977). *Body politics: Power, sex and nonverbal communication*. Englewood Cliffs, NJ: Prentice-Hall.

Jacobson, M. B., & Popovich, P. M. (1983). Victim attractiveness and perceptions of responsibility in an ambiguous rape case. *Psychology of Women Quarterly, 8*, 100–104.

Keelan, J. P., Dion, K. K., & Dion, K. L. (1992). Correlates of appearance anxiety in late adolescence and early adulthood among young women. *Journal of Adolescence, 15*, 193–205.

Keltner, D., Young, R. C., Heerey, E. A., Oemig, C., & Monarch, N. D. (1998). Teasing in hierarchical and intimate relations. *Journal of Personality and Social Psychology, 75*, 1231–1247.

Kopper, B. A., & Epperson, D. L. (1991). Women and anger: Sex and sex-role comparisons in the expression of anger. *Psychology of Women Quarterly, 15*, 7–14.
Kopper, B. A., & Epperson, D. L. (1996). The experience and expression of anger: Relationships with gender, gender role socialization, depression, and mental health functioning. *Journal of Counseling Psychology, 43*, 158–165.
Kring, A. M. (2000). Gender and anger. In A. Fischer (Ed.), *Gender and emotion: Social psychological perspectives* (pp. 211–231). New York: Cambridge University Press.
Kuczynski, A. (2002, February 7). F. D. A. plans to approve a drug long endorsed by the vainer set. *The New York Times*, pp. A1, A18.
LaFrance, M. (1998). Pressure to be pleasant: Effects of sex and power on reactions to not smiling. *International Review of Social Psychology, 2*, 95–108.
LaFrance, M., & Hecht, M. (2000). Gender and smiling: A meta-analysis. In A. Fischer (Ed.), *Gender and emotion: Social psychological perspectives* (pp. 118–142). New York: Cambridge University Press.
Lazarus, R. S. (1991). *Emotion and adaptation*. New York: Oxford University Press.
Lerner, H. G. (1993). *The dance of deception: Pretending and truth-telling in women's lives*. New York: HarperCollins.
Lewis, H. B. (1971). *Shame and guilt in neurosis*. New York: International Universities Press.
Lewis, H. B. (1989). Some thoughts on the moral emotions of shame and guilt. In L. Cirillo, B. Kaplan, & S. Wapner (Eds.), *Emotions in ideal human development* (pp. 35–51). Hillsdale, NJ: Erlbaum.
Lewis, J., & Stearns, P. N. (1998). Introduction. In P. N. Stearns, & J. Lewis (Eds.), *An emotional history of the United States* (pp. 1–15). New York: New York University Press.
Lewis, M. (1992). *Shame: The exposed self*. New York: Free Press.
Lewis, M. (2000). Self-conscious emotions: Embarrassment, pride, shame, and guilt. In M. Lewis & J. M. Haviland-Jones (Eds.), *Handbook of emotions* (2nd Edition; pp. 623–636). New York: Guilford Press.
Martin, K. (1996). *Puberty, sexuality, and the self: Boys and girls at adolescence*. New York: Routledge.
Miller, W. I. (1997). *The anatomy of disgust*. Cambridge, MA: Harvard University Press.
Öhman, A. (2000). Fear and anxiety: Evolutionary, cognitive, and clinical perspectives. In M. Lewis & J. M. Haviland-Jones (Eds.), *Handbook of emotions* (2nd Edition; pp. 573–593). New York: Guilford Press.
Plant, R. W., & Ryan, R. M. (1985). Intrinsic motivation and the effects of self-consciousness, self-awareness, and ego-involvement: An investigation of internally controlling styles. *Journal of Personality, 53*, 435–449.
Pollitt, K. (1985, December 12). Hers. *New York Times*. p. C-2.
Quinn, D. M., & Crocker, J. (1999). When ideology hurts: Effects of belief in the Protestant ethic and feeling overweight on the psychological well-being of women. *Journal of Personality and Social Psychology, 77*, 402–414.
Rich, A. (1976). *Of woman born*. New York: Bantam.
Ridgeway, C. L. (1987). Nonverbal behavior, dominance, and the basis of status in task groups. *American Sociological Review, 52*, 683–694.

Roberts, T.-A. (in press). Female trouble: The menstrual self-evaluation scale and women's self-objectification. *Psychology of Women Quarterly.*

Roberts, T.-A., Gettman, J., Konik, J., & Fredrickson, B. L. (2001, August). *"Mere exposure:" Gender differences in the negative effects of priming a state of self-objectification.* Paper presented at the annual American Psychological Association Convention, San Francisco, CA.

Roberts, T.-A., Goldenberg, J. L., Power, C., & Pyszczynski, T. (2002). "Feminine protection": The effects of menstruation on attitudes toward women. *Psychology of Women Quarterly, 26,* 131–139.

Roberts, T.-A., & Pennebaker, J. W. (1995). Gender differences in perceiving internal state: Toward a his and hers model of perceptual cue use. *Advances in Experimental Social Psychology, 27,* 143–175.

Rozee, P. (1988, August). *The effects of fear of rape on working women.* Paper presented at the meeting of the American Psychological Association, Atlanta, GA.

Rubin, G. (1975). The traffic in women: Notes on the political economy of sex. In R. Reiter (Ed.), *Toward an anthropology of women* (pp. 157–210). New York: Monthly Review Press.

Sherif, C. W. (1982). Needed concepts in the study of gender identity. *Psychology of Women Quarterly, 6,* 375–398.

Shrout, P. E., & Fiske, D. W. (1981). Nonverbal behaviors and social evaluation. *Journal of Personality, 49,* 115–128.

Shweder, R. A., Much, N. C., Mahapatra, M., & Park, L. (1997). The "Big Three" of morality (autonomy, community, divinity) and the "Big Three" explanations of suffering. In A. Brandt & P. Rozin (Eds.), *Morality and health* (pp. 119–169). New York: Routledge.

Silberstein, L. R., Striegel-Moore, R., & Rodin, J. (1987). Feeling fat: A woman's shame. In H. B. Lewis (Ed.), *The role of shame in symptom formation* (pp. 89–108). Hillsdale, NJ: Erlbaum.

Snodgrass, S. E. (1985). Women's intuition: The effect of subordinate role on interpersonal sensitivity. *Journal of Personality and Social Psychology, 49,* 146–155.

Snodgrass, S. E. (1992). Further effects of role versus gender on interpersonal sensitivity. *Journal of Personality and Social Psychology, 62,* 154–158.

Stapley, J. C., & Haviland, J. M. (1989). Beyond depression: Gender differences in normal adolescents' emotional experiences. *Sex Roles, 20,* 295–308.

Stepper, S., & Strack, F. (1993). Proprioceptive determinants of emotional and nonemotional feelings. *Journal of Personality and Social Psychology, 64,* 211–220.

Tavris, C. (1989). *Anger: The misunderstood emotion.* New York: Simon & Schuster.

Thorne, B. (1993). *Gender play: Girls and boys in school.* New Brunswick, NJ: Rutgers University Press.

Tiedens, L. Z. (2001). Anger and advancement versus sadness and subjugation: The effect of negative emotion expressions on social status conferral. *Journal of Personality and Social Psychology, 80*(1), 86–94.

Tiedens, L. Z., Ellsworth, P. C., & Mesquita, B. (2000). Stereotypes about sentiments and status: Emotional expectations for high- and low-status group members. *Personality and Social Psychology Bulletin, 26*(5), 560–574.

Unger, R. K. (1979). Toward a redefinition of sex and gender. *American Psychologist, 34,* 1085–1094.

Unger, R. K. & Crawford, M. (1993). Commentary: Sex and gender – The troubled relationship between terms and concepts. *Psychological Science, 4,* 122–124.

West, C., & Zimmerman, D. H. (1987). Doing gender. *Gender and Society, 1,* 125–151.

Wolf, N. (1991). *The beauty myth: How images of beauty are used against women.* New York: William Morrow and Company.

Wooley, S. C., & Wooley, O. W. (1980). Eating disorders: Anorexia and obesity. In A. M. Brodsky & R. Hare-Mustin (Eds.), *Women and psychotherapy* (pp. 135–158). New York: Guilford Press.

Young, I. M. (1991). *Throwing like a girl and other essays in feminist philosophy and social theory.* Bloomington, IN: Indiana University Press.

PART III

THE INTERGROUP CONTEXT

11

Intergroup Emotions

Emotion as an Intergroup Phenomenon

Diane M. Mackie, Lisa A. Silver, and Eliot R. Smith

That emotions arise in intergroup contexts is of course uncontroversial. We are thrilled when our national team wins the World Cup against stiff competition, angry when protesters in another country burn our flag, excited as the party we voted for wins the election, and disgusted when local college students brawl drunkenly with a neighboring school. Despite the obvious impetus that intergroup behavior is to emotions, the idea that emotions may actually be intergroup phenomena is not so much controversial as it is, at least in social psychology, unconsidered. Emotion is typically assumed to be an individual phenomenon, triggered when an individual interprets events as either favoring or harming his or her personal goals or desires in the context of whether he or she has the personal resources to cope or not. Yet such approaches do not seem to fully capture the kinds of emotions evoked by our examples. Unless we are a member of the national team, caught by mistake in the demonstration, up for election, or one of those actually involved in the brawl, none of these events may impact us directly or personally. Yet because these events touch those we are close to, those we identity with, those we feel part of or one with, we, too, experience emotion.

Our attempts to explain such emotional experiences have led us to consider emotion as an intergroup phenomenon. That is, we consider intergroup emotions as depending on psychological identification with a group, as arising as a result of events and interactions that reflect the relative well-being of that group independent of our personal involvement in those events and interactions, and as functionally directed at regulating intergroup behavior toward those other groups. In this chapter, we first describe a theoretical approach, intergroup emotions theory (IET), which we have developed to try to capture the intergroup nature of emotions. We then consider the qualities that an emotional experience might have to include to qualify it as intergroup emotion and describe empirical evidence from our own and others' work relevant to these qualities. Finally, we speculate about some other possible implications engendered by the view of emotion as an intergroup phenomenon.

INTERGROUP EMOTIONS THEORY

We developed IET (Mackie, Devos, & Smith, 2000; Mackie & Smith, 1998; Smith, 1993, 1999; Smith & Ho, 2002) in an attempt to better explain intergroup behavior, especially negative forms of discrimination. Traditional models typically view discrimination as behavior consistent with prejudice defined as the positive or (usually) negative evaluation of a particular social group. These evaluations are assumed, in turn, to arise from the positive or negative attributes associated with the group. In this view, stereotypes and evaluation are features of or adhere to the group itself. A group has good or bad features and is, as a consequence, likable or unlikable. Favoring or disfavoring the group follows directly from its inherent characteristics. Despite the many theoretical and empirical advances fostered by this view (see Brewer & Brown, 1998; Brown & Gaertner, 2001; Fiske, 1998; Mackie & Smith, 1998; Sedikides, Schopler, & Insko, 1998, for reviews), it seems to deflect attention away from the context dependent, the interactional, the relational, in short, the intergroup nature of much prejudice and discrimination. Consider, for example, the minority group whose positive qualities of hard work and ambition make it a threat to the majority's position, the members of outgroups who are crucial helpmates in the workplace but excluded socially outside it, the bitter national enemy who in less than a generation becomes a trusted ally, or the intensity of hatred for the group most objectively similar to our own.

IET was thus developed to provide an account of intergroup behavior more closely rooted in intergroup relations. IET proposes that distinct reactions (both psychological and behavioral) to social groups are determined by differentiated emotional reactions to those groups based on appraisals of the ingroup vis-à-vis other groups. IET also assumes that, just as individual emotions are central parts of self-regulatory systems, social and intergroup regulation are crucial functions of intergroup emotions. From this perspective, intergroup emotions involve the impulse, desire, or tendency to take action aimed at bringing groups closer together, moving them further apart, changing or justifying a status hierarchy, eliminating a competitor, or nurturing an ally – all in the service of maintaining the ingroup. Obviously, such action tendencies, just like the many other cognitive and affective reactions that are triggered by intergroup emotions, are not always able to be executed, for a variety of reasons. Nevertheless, the specificity of the link between emotions and action tendencies allows the prediction of which among a range of behavioral options group members are, all else being equal, more likely to choose. Importantly, these action tendencies are not just predicted by specific antecedent conditions, but are assumed to be mediated by the experience of a particular emotion.

How do such emotions arise? Intergroup emotions come about on the basis of appraisals of distinct and changing situations and events for the benefit or harm of the groups to which we belong (particularly vis-à-vis other groups). Intergroup appraisals bear on group, rather than personal, concerns; such events do not necessarily directly affect individuals, but may help or hurt the groups to which they belong. In this broad sense, IET is an extension and integration of appraisal approaches to emotion into the intergroup relations domain (Mackie & Smith, 1998; Smith, 1993). According to a number of different appraisal approaches, specific patterns of appraisals will trigger specific emotions (Smith, 1993). IET borrows broadly from such theories. It draws more particularly on Lazarus' (Lazarus & Folkman, 1984; Lazarus, 1991) general focus on appraised outcomes and the ability to cope, perhaps because this latter aspect seems to capture best the relativistic nature of intergroup hierarchies and fits with the regulatory and adaptational approach we favor. For example, in our approach, an action that harms the ingroup and is perpetrated by a strong outgroup (perhaps suggesting that the ingroup does not have the resources to cope with the threat) should invoke fear. On the other hand, when the ingroup is appraised as having the resources (in terms of numbers, power, or legitimacy) to deal with an outgroup's negative action, anger is the theoretically more likely emotion to be triggered. Rather than being purely individual reactions, however, such emotional reactions depend on psychological identification with a group. The process of social identification leads ingroups and ingroup memberships to become part of the self and thereby acquire affective and emotional significance (Smith, 1993, 1999; Smith & Henry, 1996; Tajfel, 1982).

In sum, the experience of intergroup emotion is predicated on social identification. When social identification occurs, appraisals are intergroup-related rather than personally concerned. When appraisals occur on a group basis, intergroup emotions are experienced: Emotions are experienced on behalf of the ingroup, and the ingroup and outgroup become the targets of emotion. Specific intergroup emotions lead to differentiated intergroup action tendencies and behavior. Such differentiated intergroup behavior occurs because of and is mediated by specific intergroup emotions that have been triggered by particular appraisals of situations or events related to social identity.

When we use the term intergroup emotion, what is it about emotion that we believe to be intergroup in nature? First, we consider intergroup emotions as depending on psychological identification with a group. That is, such emotion arises only because the self is considered part of an ingroup that is inherently defined by reference to a salient or typical outgroup. Thus, evidence that the process of identification, and the quality of that identification, affects emotions experienced in an intergroup context provides support for the idea that emotion is an intergroup phenomenon.

Second, we see intergroup emotion as arising as a result of events and interactions that reflect the relative well-being of the groups to which people belong, independent of their personal involvement in those events and interactions. That is, intergroup emotion is experienced on behalf of the group even if the circumstances that engender it have no consequences for individual well-being. We believe that emotional experiences rooted in group outcomes, independent of personal involvement, provide some of the strongest evidence that emotion can be an intergroup phenomenon.

Third, we see intergroup emotion as functionally directed at regulating intergroup reactions toward ingroups and outgroups. In just the same way that individual emotion is self-regulatory in affecting self-knowledge, self-evaluation, and individual behavior, intergroup emotions regulate the cognitive, evaluative, and behavioral reactions that one group has regarding another. When experienced emotion promotes some forms of intergroup behavior and prevents others, we argue that emotion is an intergroup event.

EMPIRICAL EVIDENCE SUPPORTING IET

We now consider the empirical evidence from our work and others' that indicates that intergroup emotion has these three qualities.

The Role of Social Identification

The nature of the experience of intergroup emotion is predicated on social identification. It is only when we see ourselves as interchangeable members of a group, rather than as unique individuals, that the world can be appraised in terms of group rather than individual outcomes, and emotions can be experienced on behalf of fellow group members. The idea that emotional experience might depend on social categorization was tested in a study that focused participants on either their similarities to or differences from victims of harm from a third party (Gordijn et al., 2001). They found that participants were angrier and less happy when they saw themselves as belonging to the same rather than a different social category as the harmed group (although the basis for that feeling was not made clear). These results thus demonstrated that an emotional experience in the face of harm depended on, at the very least, categorization with the victims.

Important as the demonstration of categorization effects is for IET, it is not clear that categorization effects alone are capable of activating intergroup emotion. Membership in a group is not the same thing as identification with the group (see Hogg & Abrams, 1988, for a review), which we define, following Tajfel (1982), as knowledge about one's ingroup *plus its affective significance*. Many studies that make group membership salient, for example, may or may not also manipulate identification [indeed, it is likely that Gordijn and colleagues (1999) did manipulate identification with an important ingroup as well]. Different group members may be differentially identified with the group and to the extent that IE depends on identification, IET suggests that the more highly identified the member, the more easily, frequently, and intensely intergroup emotions should be generated.

As an initial assessment of this idea, shortly after the September 2001 attacks on the United States, we (D. M. Mackie, L. A. Silver, A. Maitner, & E. R. Smith, unpublished data) examined the relationship between identification and emotions in reaction to hypothetical terrorist attacks. In late September, we had the opportunity to measure the University of California Santa Barbara (UCSB) students' identification with "Americans" and to assess the extent to which they felt a series of emotions in reaction to a hypothetical terrorist attack on their country (not the 9–11 events in particular, although we can be sure that these were most salient). Of particular interest was the relationship between students' identification with their country, and their feelings of fear and anger about terrorist attacks on their country.

Fifty-six male and 121 female participants filled out the Five Factor Identification Scale (FFIS), a 25-item questionnaire (M. Silver, 2002). Exploratory and confirmatory factor analyses of responses to the FFIS across multiple samples and for multiple large ingroups have established five subcomponents of the overall identification score, described by M. Silver (2001) as measuring: "1) feelings of oneness with the group, 2) affective feelings about being a member of the group, 3) perceived similarity with/typicality as a group member, 4) importance of membership in the group to the self, and 5) emotional bond with the group." Correlational analyses supported the convergent and discriminant validities of these five subcomponents. The five subscales were all positively correlated with each other, but related differentially to group entitativity and loyalty. Interestingly, the similarity/typicality subscale consistently showed the lowest correlational relationships with other measured variables. Finally, the mean patterns supported predictions from social dominance theory (M. Silver, 2001). Use of the FFIS thus allowed us to consider the impact of multiple aspects of identification on intergroup emotions in addition to a single global measure.

After completing a series of unrelated questionnaires, participants reported their emotional reactions to various situations, including reactions to an attack on their country from a terrorist group from another country that killed thousands of innocent civilians. Participants were asked to indicate how angry, furious, and irritated (averaged to create an anger index, alpha = .77) they felt, and how fearful and worried (averaged to create a fear index, alpha = .88) they felt, on a 7-point scale from not at all to extremely.

As predicted by IET, we found that identification (as measured by a total average FFIS score) strongly predicted reports of both fear and anger. The more strongly participants identified as Americans, the more anger and the more fear they reported about terrorist attacks on their country (*B*'s = .324 and .232, for anger and fear respectively). Although a composite identification score significantly predicted emotions, we hoped to better understand which specific aspects of identification led to these relationships. Therefore, we also examined the relationship between the subscales of the identification measure and reported anger and fear.

A series of hierarchical regressions revealed that the experience of anger was significantly predicted by the membership importance subscale ($B = .157$, $p = .072$) when controlling for all other aspects of identification, and even more strongly by the affective subscale ($B = .266$, $p = .001$) when all other subcomponents of identification were controlled for. The most significant contributions to the experience of fear, when all other aspects of identification were controlled for, came from the membership importance subscale ($B = .148$, $p = .103$) and the oneness subscale ($B = .146$, $p = .110$), both marginal effects.

These analyses suggest that the importance of being an American to participants' sense of self was central to the intensity of both of the emotional reactions they had to imagining terrorist attacks on their country. This is certainly consistent with IET and its assumption of a social identification mechanism that includes group memberships in the self, thus making the experience of group-based emotions possible. In this case, the more central the group membership to the self, the more our UCSB student participants reported emotions on behalf of the group as a whole.

These results also offer some preliminary evidence that some aspects of identification might be more central to specific emotional reactions to such events than others. Specifically, affective identification was very important in predicting reactions of anger. The affect subscale includes items that seem to reflect a sense of pride that one belongs to their group. Perhaps pride in the group emboldens members with feelings of strength and injustice, appraisals that are more likely to result in anger reactions (and the concomitant desire to strike back). On the other hand, oneness appeared to be a more important aspect of identification in predicting fear. Perhaps the sense that they are interchangeable members of the group (the gist of many of the oneness scale items) makes participants more likely to imagine themselves as a possible target of attacks and thus more likely to feel greater fear.

The results of this study provided correlational support for IET's prediction that an important issue in experiencing intergroup emotions on behalf of your group is the extent to which individuals feel identified with their group. The results also provided preliminary evidence that different aspects of identification might be more important in predicting the experience of specific different emotional reactions to specific situations.

Given the highly emotionally charged nature of both the group membership and the target events investigated in this initial study, we wanted to provide a conceptual replication of these findings. Therefore, in our next study, we assessed the relationship between identification and emotions for a much less emotionally charged group membership. In this second study, we sought to replicate the finding of a relationship between overall identification and emotions that might be experienced in a threatening intergroup interaction, but focused this time on identification as a UCSB student. Cognizant of the additional role that the salience of American identity might have played in our post–September 11 findings, we also wished to assess the impact of category salience on the identification–emotion relationship. We reasoned that with a less chronically important or salient group membership, as UCSB affiliation is for most of our students, identification might be a significant predictor of intergroup emotions only when category membership was made salient.

Forty-three female participants, all UCSB undergraduates, completed the same identification measure described, but modified to assess identification as a UCSB student (e.g., "I am glad to belong to the UCSB community."). To manipulate category salience, half of our participants read a one-page neutral historical description of UCSB (salience condition), whereas the other half of our participants read a one-page equally neutral historical description of a well-known Santa Barbara landmark. Participants believed they were reading these descriptions for a reading comprehension task and took a simple, four-item true/false test about what they read to maintain this cover story before being thanked for their participation.

In an ostensibly unrelated study, all participants were then taken to private cubicles and were asked to imagine themselves in a threatening intergroup situation designed to elicit fear. Participants were asked to imagine themselves (either alone or with a group of UCSB students) walking down a local street at night and being wrongly accused of breaking a car mirror by either a single or a group of Santa Barbara City College students (a relevant local outgroup). Participants then reported, among other measures, how much fear they felt while imagining themselves in this scenario. (This was a one-item assessment of how fearful they felt, on the same scale as our previous study.)

All participants reported experiencing fear in this scenario, and there was no difference in level of fear experienced across the control and group membership salience conditions (nor between conditions where they were alone or with a group). Our primary interest was the relationship between identification and fear when group membership was made salient or not.

As expected, there was a strong relationship between overall identification with UCSB and expressed fear for participants whose group membership had previously been made salient ($B = .497$, $p < .03$). However, for participants in the control condition (in which group membership was not previously made salient), identification was unrelated to feelings of fear ($B = -.015$, $p > .1$). These findings, which have yet to be replicated, suggest the intriguing possibility that both categorization (as indicated by the effect of salience) and identification are necessary for the experience of intergroup emotions. That is, although increasing identification went hand in hand with increasing emotion, this relationship was true only for participants for whom the category was already activated. Thus, the effect of identification (the implications of the affective significance of group membership) might be moderated by categorization (or the knowledge of group membership).

As in the previous study, we had the opportunity to examine the particular components of identification that were related to fear in this situation. When membership identity was salient, all of the subscales except for similarity/typicality were significantly related to participants' feelings of fear. To determine which of the four subscales were central to participants' feelings of fear, a series of hierarchical regressions were performed. Analyses revealed that the importance subscale was the only significant independent predictor of fear ($B = .556$, $p < .04$), when controlling for all other aspects of identification. As expected, given the results of the overall analysis, none of the five subscales was significantly related to participants' expressed fear in the control condition.

Once again, we found that importance of group membership to our participants' sense of self played a central role in the relationship between identification and feelings of fear in a threatening intergroup interaction. These findings, in conjunction with the findings from the aforementioned study, increase our confidence that "importance identification" is a critical part of these types of intergroup situations for large groups like Americans and UCSB students, and for the emotions of fear (in both studies) and anger (in the first study). Further research needs to be directed at determining if different aspects of identification are more or less central to this relationship with different group memberships, different situations, and different emotions.

These results provide further support of the critical role that identification with group membership can play in determining whether intergroup emotions will or will not be experienced. Identification with a salient group membership appears to increase the intensity with which emotions are experienced on behalf of that membership. In both these cases, group membership was made situationally salient, although for very different reasons and in very different ways. Of course, some group memberships are no doubt chronically salient and may need no additional situational boost before the strong relations between identification and emotion observed here become visible.

Finally, although not designed to test this idea explicitly, results from one of our first studies (Mackie et al., 2000) provided some support for the role of identification in producing intergroup emotion. In these studies, participants self-identified as members of one of two conflicting groups. For example, participants identified themselves as part of the group of people who supported equal rights for homosexuals or part of the group opposed to such rights. After various manipulations designed to influence appraisals about antagonism between the groups, we measured anger, fear, and contempt toward the opposing group across a series of three studies. The relevant finding for our purposes here was that the relationship between appraisals and emotions was significantly, although not completely, mediated by identification. That is, the impact of appraisals on emotions was significantly determined by the extent to which individuals identified with the group.

All this work thus provides strong support for the role, not just of categorization, but of identification, in intergroup emotion. Our studies have focused on demonstrating that highly identified individuals experience group-linked emotions more intensely. Of course, these individuals might also be more likely to appraise the world in group-relevant terms, experience any resultant emotions more frequently, or be more likely to act on them, relations we have not yet explored. There is also reason to believe that the relation between identification and emotion is more subtle and complex than our demonstration of an association between increased identity and increased emotion suggests. For example, Doosje, Branscombe, Spears, and Manstead (1998, Study 2; see also Branscombe, Doosje, & McGarty, 2002) presented Dutch participants with an account of Dutch colonial history that was ambiguously negative. Participants who were high in chronic identification with their national group experienced *less* collective guilt than the low identifiers, just the opposite of the relation we have been describing. As those authors suggest, high identification in this case is no doubt predictive of an equally strong desire to defend the group and to maintain it in a positive light. Such motivations then dictate various reappraisals that lead to dampening of emotions, such as guilt, that suggest wrong-doing on the group's part.

Emotion Arising from Group Rather than Personal Concerns

Perhaps the best evidence for emotion as an intergroup phenomenon comes from situations such as those described in our opening examples. Consider what might happen when our national team loses the World Cup, for example. We are not at all involved in the action that produces the outcome – we did not play a bad game, we were not personally outmatched. Nor will the consequences of losing affect us directly – we will not lose our Nike endorsement, or be relegated to the second-string team. Yet, if our disappointment is bitter, we clearly feel an emotion by connection or extension. If we feel such an emotion even when the harms and benefits do not apply to us personally, we have experienced an emotion with intergroup roots. Can events that befall fellow group members, even if not directly to the self, trigger emotional reactions? If so, are such group-based emotions similar in appraisal antecedents and reported experience regardless of whether the emotion-triggering event has personal impact or not?

The clearest answers to these questions came from a study in which we asked our female participants to imagine that they were walking alone at night, as a single UCSB student, down a local street and that they were accosted by a single SBCC student who wrongly accused them of breaking his car's side mirror (D. Mackie, L. Silver, & E. Smith, unpublished data). The context – an unsubstantiated accusation made to a female on a deserted street at night – was designed to induce the appraisal of relative weakness and the emotion of fear. In these "categorization" conditions, participants are alone but categorized: Single-labeled members of the ingroup and outgroup interact. In a second set of conditions, we asked participants to imagine themselves as one of a group of UCSB students accosted in the same way by a group of SBCC students. We refer to these conditions as "intergroup" conditions. When asked to appraise the situation and to report their feelings, our participants reported the expected feelings of relative weakness and significant levels of fear. The level of fear experienced in the intergroup condition was slightly, but not significantly, reduced from that experienced in the categorization conditions: Both situations elicited reports of experienced fear that averaged between 7 and 8 on a 9-point scale.

Of course, in these categorization and intergroup situations, participants were imagining that the events were happening to them personally. In a parallel set of conditions, we described exactly the same scenarios – intergroup categorization and intergroup interactions – as if they occurred to other people. Thus, participants were asked to imagine a single UCSB student other than the self, or a group of UCSB students not including the self, in the situation. Thus, the events were imagined as impacting other ingroup members, but explicitly not the participant herself. Once again, we asked participants to report their own emotions (*not* the emotions felt by those involved in the action). Despite finding that less fear overall was reported when the self was not personally involved, the level of fear reported in the comparison conditions was considerable (averaging between 6 and 7 on the 9-point scale), indicating that fear was experienced even when the action did not directly involve the self. Once again, the weakness felt and fear experienced in the intergroup condition were slightly less than that experienced in the categorization condition.

The emotions reported in these conditions are thus good evidence for *intergroup* emotion – emotion experienced because of the impact of events on a group to which one belongs, even when events do not directly impact the self. The finding that emotions may be experienced on behalf of others because of shared group membership, even when events are not personally involving, demonstrates that experienced emotions are not purely individual-level phenomena.

These results are consistent with and confirm other studies that have demonstrated that emotions can be experienced as a group member, rather than only when due to personal experience. For example, individual group members do feel happy or sad depending on the success or failure of a group with which they identify, even if they do not personally contribute to that outcome (Cialdini et al., 1976). Similarly, Gordijn et al. (1999) provided evidence supportive of this position when they focused participants' attention on either their similarities or on their differences (manipulating social categorization and in all probability identity) with people who were harmed by a third party. They found that participants were angrier and less happy when similarities with the harmed group were salient, although they were not individually affected. In each of these cases, people reported experiencing emotions because of events that had occurred to other members of a membership group, although not to them individually. The demonstration that group membership does indeed have emotional implications independent of personal involvement thus suggests that currently individualistic theories of emotion might profitably be broadened to include intragroup- and intergroup-based emotions.

Regulation of Intergroup Behavior

One of our key motivations in developing IET was the promise of better ability to predict and explain intergroup behavior. For practical reasons, our studies of intergroup emotions to date have not yet measured actual intergroup behavior (although such studies are planned for the future). Still, we can advance several less direct arguments for the proposition that intergroup emotions should be causally tied to specific, particular intergroup behaviors.

First, several of our studies have shown that the ways in which one group wants to interact with another depend on what emotions the target group arouses. In Mackie et al. (2000), for example, we asked participants to indicate desires to take a number of different kinds of actions, ranging from leaving the outgroup alone (items like "I want to avoid/have nothing to do with/keep at a distance from/get away from them.") to trying to hurt them (items such as "I want to confront/oppose/argue with/attack them."). Factor analysis indicated that the items representing moving away from the other group were closely associated and quite distinct from the multiple closely associated items that reflected movement against the other group. Moreover, manipulations of appraisals that made the ingroup appear strong, which had produced anger, increased the desire to take action against the outgroup, while having no impact on behavioral tendencies to avoid the outgroup.

These studies also provided evidence that emotion regulates intergroup behavior in the sense that the impact of intergroup appraisals on intergroup behavior is mediated by intergroup emotions. Our earliest studies (Mackie et al., 2000) showed that anger significantly mediated the relationship between appraisals of strength and the desire to take action against the outgroup. To clearly demonstrate that this mediational relationship was not unique to scenarios involving anger, we also showed that fear significantly mediated the relationship between appraisals of weakness and the desire to move away from the outgroup (Mackie et al., 2002). Importantly, this was true not only in the conditions in which the self was personally involved in the intergroup interactions, but also, although more weakly, in conditions in which the self was not involved. All these findings, then, suggest that intergroup emotions (like all emotions) are closely linked to action tendencies, specifically to desires or tendencies to behave in specific ways toward outgroups.

A second reason that we believe intergroup emotions will prove to be deeply involved in regulating intergroup behavior is that they are closely related to prejudice. Prejudice – an overall positive or negative orientation or attitude toward an outgroup – has been studied for more than half a century within social psychology and has been shown to be related to many forms of intergroup behavior. These include voting for candidates from ethnic outgroups (Vanneman & Pettigrew, 1972), avoiding contact with outgroup members (Dovidio, Kawakami, & Gaertner, 2002), and many other types of behavioral discrimination (see Dovidio, Brigham, Johnson, & Gaertner, 1996, for a review). Thus, to the extent that intergroup emotions are causally related to prejudice, we can be confident that these emotions will indirectly cause concrete behavioral outcomes such as those just listed. We regard the emotions that people have experienced in past encounters (real or imagined) with outgroups as causally prior to their general level of prejudice toward those groups. This is because (as most theorists would agree) overall prejudice is some kind of average or summary of the past positive and negative experiences, thoughts, and feelings that people have had with regard to the group. Past instances of negative emotions, therefore, as well as negative stereotypes and negative behavioral encounters, should be among the most important causes of prejudice.

Evidence of the key role played by intergroup emotions comes from a recent study on the impact of two of the major causes of prejudice: a person's history of intergroup contact and broad political predispositions. Recent research indicates that intergroup contact (particularly when it involves actual friendship) is effective in reducing prejudice (Pettigrew, 1997; Wright et al., 1997), and also that broad predispositions such as Social Dominance Orientation (SDO; the general tendency to favor and support group-based hierarchies; Pratto et al., 1994) are strongly linked to prejudice. To investigate what role intergroup emotions might play in these relationships, Smith, Miller, and Mackie (2002) asked college students how frequently they had experienced specific positive and negative emotions with regard to African Americans, as well as measuring students' past personal contact with members of that group and their SDO. Dependent measures were a feeling thermometer and the Modern Racism Scale, two standard measures of prejudice against African Americans.

Regression analyses confirmed earlier research by indicating that the history of intergroup contact and SDO both predicted both measures of prejudice. Most important for our current argument, the impact of past contact and SDO on prejudice against African Americans, were both significantly mediated by negative emotions. That is, contact and SDO caused decreases and increases, respectively, in negative emotion, which in turn was a major cause of prejudice. Thus, the results of this study demonstrate that emotions play a key role in the overall processes that produce prejudice.

Besides mediating the effects of SDO and of past intergroup contact, we also found that both positive and negative emotions have powerful direct effects on prejudice. This means that anything else that causes intergroup emotions will also affect prejudice. Additional analyses found that, when intergroup emotions are included in the model, stereotypes of African Americans play little or no role in the overall process. Once emotions are controlled, the effects of stereotypes on prejudice are minimal, and this holds for the Modern Racism Scale and the more affectively tinged feeling thermometer measure of prejudice. However, if emotions are mistakenly left out of the analysis, the results misleadingly suggest that stereotypes play a role – but our findings show that their relation is spurious and not causal. These results support the theoretical claims made by Gordon Allport a half-century ago (1954), and by other researchers as recently as Brewer and Alexander (2002), that stereotypes may often be after-the-fact rationalizations for preexisting feelings or emotions about a group. Of course, we would not claim that stereotypes never have an impact on prejudice that is independent of that of emotion; for example, stereotypes would likely be more influential than emotions when people have little direct personal contact with a group that they only know about by reputation or media reports. Further research must examine the relative power of these two classes of causes under differing circumstances.

Prejudice has been the central variable in virtually all conceptualizations and empirical investigations of the causes of negative and discriminatory intergroup behaviors, including job discrimination, physical attacks, and even genocide. For this reason, our demonstrations that intergroup emotions play an important role as causes of prejudice, and as mediators of other variables' effects on prejudice, give emotions an important role. Emotions are part of the story of how intergroup behaviors are regulated, just as they are an obvious and important part of the regulation of individual actions. Intergroup fear, anger, anxiety, gratitude, respect, and the like motivate specific and differentiated types of intergroup behavior, thereby contributing to the overall positive or negative relationship between groups in society.

THE INTERGROUP NATURE OF EMOTION

In this chapter, we have argued that emotions should be considered intergroup phenomena, as well as intrapersonal phenomena. We have reviewed some evidence from our own and other social psychology laboratories consistent with this claim. Our work indicates that the experience of emotion can depend on the nature of group membership, that emotions can be experienced on behalf of other group members even when events are not personally impactful, and that emotions can regulate group and intergroup behavior. These conclusions led to several implications for points of commonality and difference between IET and other models of emotion.

First, we believe that intergroup emotion has quite different bases than interpersonally shared emotion. There is, of course, a sizable literature on empathy, the experience of emotion on behalf of another individual. Empathy is typically defined as an other-oriented affective response, similar to what another is or could be expected to feel, that stems from the apprehension or comprehension of that other individual's emotional state (Batson, 1987; Eisenberg, 2000). Despite the power of empathy to increase some forms of prosocial behavior and decrease some forms of aggressive behavior under some conditions (Eisenberg, 2000; Eisenberg & Fabes, 1998; Miller & Eisenberg, 1988), the concept does not seem to help explain the kinds of intergroup-based emotions that we have studied. We are not thrilled when our national team wins because the members of the team are feeling good; we do not feel angry when protesters in another country burn our flag because of how they feel – to the very contrary. Rather, such emotional experiences seem rooted in the common group membership and not in emotions shared with other specific individuals.

In fact, important differences between individually oriented empathy and more group-based emotions have been demonstrated in experimental attempts to improve the solution of social dilemmas. Social dilemmas are problems in which individual self-interest (to take as much of a resource as one can, for example) is in conflict with the overall interest of the group (since if every individual acted this way, the resource would be depleted and the entire group would suffer). Inducing empathy for the plight of another individual group member can increase the amount of resource shared with that particular other, but does little to help successfully solve the social dilemma (Batson, Klein, Highberger, & Shaw, 1995; Batson et al., 1999). In contrast, the induction of group-wide shared feelings of identity or bondedness seems to be one of the few manipulations that reliably increase successful solution of social and public goods dilemmas (Brewer & Kramer, 1986). The further similarities and differences in antecedents and consequences of interpersonally shared and group-based emotional experiences awaits further research.

Second, from the IET perspective, intergroup emotions are rooted in evaluatively laden interactions between and among groups. In this sense, our theory makes connections with other proposals that even more explicitly relate emotion to the structural relations among and between groups. Image theory, for example (Alexander, Brewer, & Hermann, 1999; Hermann & Fischerkeller, 1995), argues that the nature of the relationship between groups – whether dominant or subordinate, competitive or exploitative, threatening or secure, for example – produce appraisals that dictate both "images" (stereotypes) of and emotional reactions to outgroups. Thus, reactions are differentiated in this approach by the competitive and status relations between groups, but those interactions are also explicitly translated into appraisals that then serve as proximal determinants of emotion. Status relations among groups is also an important component of recent investigations of *schadenfreude* and gloating at the misfortunes of other groups, whose stumbles may or may not have relevance to the ingroup's standing (see Spears & Leach, this volume). Image theory, in turn, has much in common with Kemper's (1990) structural approach to social relations and emotions. According to Kemper, much human behavior is oriented toward attaining either power and control or support and status. Relations between groups are dictated by the combinations of those two kinds of behaviors, and specific emotions result from interpretations or appraisals of intergroup interactions that have consequences for power and status. Smith and Kessler's work (see this volume) on the anger that might result from an appraisal of relative deprivation is relevant here also, as it is the relative standing of groups in comparison, rather than absolutely, that generates the emotion. In addition, the affect control model (Smith-Lovin, 1990) views emotion as the result of confirmation and disconfirmation of identity, defined as an expected impression of standing on three key dimensions of goodness, potency, and activity. According to this perspective, emotions arise as a result of interactions that cause (especially unexpected) perceived change in people's or groups' goodness, potency, or activity. Emotions are indicators of how well a particular interaction is maintaining or changing one's identity along the three key dimensions.

IET is alone among these models in explicating the relationship between the individual and the group, and thus how individual emotions become group phenomena. All of the approaches have in common with IET an intepretational or appraisal mechanism that assesses situations or events in terms of the relative well-being of a group, the output of which triggers certain emotions. These models differ from IET (and from one another) in the dimensions on which situations or interactions are deemed to be important, and the extent to which certain forms of relationships appear to dominate interactions and thus dictate emotions between groups. Whereas IET has built from explicitly individual models of emotion, image theory and Kemper's social relations model in particular start with typical relations between groups. Perhaps unsurprisingly, it is the two dimensions of power/dominance/competitiveness/mastery and support/nurturance/cooperation/connectedness that best define these typical patterns. Perhaps intergroup emotion can be adequately accounted for merely by concentration on these two dimensions. Or, perhaps introducing more of the nuanced dimensions of individual or interpersonal models of emotion will explain significant additional variance in the occurrence of intergroup emotion. These issues, as well as the other differences among the various theories, remain open and empirical questions.

Our claim that emotion has intergroup roots is consistent with other recent theoretical developments that together argue for the truly social psychological nature of behavior. Our argument is that emotion, initially assumed to be an intraindividual mechanism, in fact has collective components, particularly components that reflect intergroup relationships. Similar developments have occurred in theorizing about, for example, motivation and self-esteem, which have also been assumed to be individual processes, but which are now known to have collective components (Sedikides & Brewer, 2001). It is perhaps surprising that it has taken so long to make these connections about emotion, given its central regulatory role in almost every aspect of social life. We intend our work to add to a growing recognition of the multiple ways in which emotions are founded in, and in turn provide a foundation for, the complexity of social relationships.

References

Alexander, M. G., Brewer, M. B., & Hermann, R. K. (1999). Images and affect: A functional analysis of out-group stereotypes. *Journal of Personality and Social Psychology, 77*, 78–93.

Allport, G. W. (1954). *The nature of prejudice*. Cambridge, MA: Addison Wesley.

Batson, C. D. (1987). Self-report ratings of empathic emotion. In N. Eisenberg & J. Strayer (Eds.), *Empathy and its development. Cambridge studies in social and emotional development* (pp. 356–360). New York: Cambridge University Press.

Batson, C. D., Ahmed, N., Yin, J., Bedell, S. J., Johnson, J. W., Templin, C. M., & Whiteside, A. (1999). Two threats to the common good: Self-interested egoism and empathy and empathy-induced altruism. *Personality and Social Psychology Bulletin, 25*, 3–16.

Batson, C. D., Klein, T. R., Highberger, L., & Shaw, L. L. (1995). Immorality from empathy-induced altruism: When compassion and justice conflict. *Journal of Personality and Social Psychology, 68*, 1042–1054.

Branscombe, N., Doosje, B., & McGarty, C. (2002). Antecedents and consequences of collective guilt. In Mackie, D. M. & Smith, E. R. (Eds.), *From prejudice to intergroup emotions: Differentiated reactions to social groups* (pp. 49–66). New York: Psychology Press.

Brewer, M. B., & Alexander, M. G. (2002). Intergroup emotions and images. In D. M. Mackie & E. R. Smith (Eds.), *From prejudice to intergroup emotions: Differentiated reactions to social groups* (pp. 209–226). New York: Psychology Press.

Brewer, M. B., & Brown, R. J. (1998). Intergroup relations. In D. T. Gilbert, S. T. Fiske, & G. Lindzey (Eds.), *The handbook of social psychology* (4th Edition, Vol. 2; pp. 554–594). New York: McGraw-Hill.

Brewer, M. B., & Kramer, R. M. (1986). Choice behavior in social dilemmas: Effects of social identity, group size, and decision framing. *Journal of Personality and Social Psychology, 50*(3), 543–549.

Brown, R. J., & Gaertner, S. L. (2001). *The Blackwell handbook of social psychology: Intergroup processes*. Malden, MA: Blackwell Press.

Cialdini, R. B., Borden, R. J., Thorne, A., Walker, M. R., Freeman, S., & Sloan, L. R. (1976). Basking in reflected glory: Three football field studies. *Journal of Personality and Social Psychology, 34*, 366–375.

Doosje, B., Branscombe, N. R., Spears, R., & Manstead, A. S. R. (1998). Guilty by association: When one's group has a negative history. *Journal of Personality and Social Psychology, 75*, 872–886.

Dovidio, J. F., Brigham, J. C., Johnson, B. T., & Gaertner, S. L. (1996). Stereotyping, prejudice, and discrimination: Another look. In N. Macrae, C. Stangor, & M. Hewstone (Eds.), *Stereotypes and stereotyping* (pp. 276–319). New York: Guilford.

Dovidio, J. F., Kawakami, K., & Gaertner, S. L. (2002). Implicit and explicit prejudice and interracial interaction. *Journal of Personality and Social Psychology, 82*, 62–68.

Eisenberg, N. (2000). Emotion, regulation, and moral development. *Annual Review of Psychology, 51*, 665–697.

Eisenberg, N., & Fabes, R. A. (1998). Prosocial development. In W. Damon (Series Ed.) & N. Eisenberg (Volume Ed.), *Handbook of child psychology: Vol. 3. Social, emotional, and personality development* (5th Edition; pp. 701–778). New York: Wiley.

Fiske, S. T. (1998). Stereotyping, prejudice, and discrimination. In D. T. Gilbert, S. T. Fiske, & G. Lindzey (Eds.), *Handbook of social psychology* (4th Edition, Vol. 2; pp. 357–411). New York: McGraw-Hill.

Gordijn, E. H., Wigboldus, D., & Yzerbyt, V. (2001). Emotional consequences of categorizing victims of negative outgroup behavior as ingroup or outgroup. *Group Processes and Intergroup Relations, 4*(4), 317–326.

Hermann, R. K., & Fischerkeller, M. (1995). Beyond the enemy image and spiral model: Cognitive-strategic research after the cold war. *International Organization, 49*, 415–450.

Hogg, M. A., & Abrams, D. (1988). *Social identifications: A social psychology of intergroup relations and group processes*. London: Routledge.
Kemper, T. D. (1990). Social relations and emotions: A structural approach. In T. D. Kemper (Ed.), *Research agendas in the sociology of emotions* (pp. 207–237). Albany, NY: State University of New York Press.
Lazarus, R. S. (1991). *Emotion and adaptation*. London: Oxford University Press.
Lazarus, R. S., & Folkman, S. (1984). *Stress, appraisal, and coping*. New York: Springer-Verlag.
Mackie, D. M., Devos, T., & Smith, E. R. (2000). Intergroup emotions: Explaining offensive action tendencies in an intergroup context. *Journal of Personality and Social Psychology, 79*, 602–616.
Mackie, D. M., & Smith, E. R. (1998). Intergroup relations: Insights from a theoretically integrative approach. *Psychological Review, 105*, 499–529.
Miller, P. A., & Eisenberg, N. (1988). The relation of empathy to aggression and externalizing/antisocial behavior. *Psychological Bulletin, 103*, 324–344.
Pettigrew, T. F. (1997). Generalized intergroup contact effects on prejudice. *Personality and Social Psychology Bulletin, 23*, 173–185.
Pratto, F., Sidanius, J., Stallworth, L. M., & Malle, B. F. (1994). Social dominance orientation: A personality variable predicting social and political attitudes. *Journal of Personality and Social Psychology, 67*, 741–763.
Sedikides, C., & Brewer, M. B. (Eds.). (2001). *Individual self, relational self, collective self*. Philadelphia: Psychology Press/Taylor & Francis.
Sedikides, C., Schopler, J., & Insko, C. A. (Eds.). (1998). *Intergroup cognition and intergroup behavior*. Mahwah, NJ: Lawrence Erlbaum.
Silver, M. D. (2001). *The multidimensional nature of ingroup identification: Correlational and experimental evidence*. Doctoral dissertation, Ohio State University.
Silver, M. D. (2002). *On the multidimensional nature of ingroup identification*. Unpublished data.
Smith, E. R. (1993). Social identity and social emotions: Toward new conceptualizations of prejudice. In D. M. Mackie & D. L. Hamilton (Eds.), *Affect, cognition, and stereotyping: Interactive processes in group perception* (pp. 297–315). San Diego: Academic Press.
Smith, E. R. (1999). Affective and cognitive implications of group membership becoming part of the self: New models of prejudice and of the self-concept. In D. Abrams & M. Hogg (Eds.), *Social identity and social cognition* (pp. 183–196). Oxford: Blackwell Publishers.
Smith, E. R., & Henry, S. (1996). An in-group becomes part of the self: Response time evidence. *Personality and Social Psychology Bulletin, 22*, 635–642.
Smith, E. R., & Ho, C. (2002). Prejudice as intergroup emotion: Integrating relative deprivation and social comparison explanations of prejudice. In I. Walker & H. Smith (Eds.), *Relative deprivation: Specification, development, and integration*. Boulder: Westview Press.
Smith, E. R., Miller, D. A., & Mackie, D. M. (2002). Effects of intergroup contact and political predispositions on prejudice: Role of intergroup emotions. Unpublished manuscript, Purdue University.
Smith, H. J., & Kessler, T. (this volume). Group-based emotions and intergroup behavior: The case of relative deprivation.

Smith-Lovin, L. (1990). Emotion as the confirmation and disconfirmation of identity: An affect control model. In T. D. Kemper (Ed.), *Research agendas in the sociology of emotions* (pp. 238–270). Albany, NY: State University of New York Press.

Spears, R. & Leach, C. W. (this volume). Intergroup Schadenfreude: Conditions and Consequences.

Tajfel, H. (1982). *Social identity and intergroup relations*. Cambridge: Cambridge University Press.

Vanneman, R. D., & Pettigrew, T. F. (1972). Race and relative deprivation in the urban United States. *Race, 13*(4), 461–486.

Wright, S. C., Aron, A., McLaughlin-Volpe, T., & Ropp, S. A. (1997). The extended contact effect: Knowledge of cross-group friendships and prejudice. *Journal of Personality and Social Psychology, 73*, 73–90.

12

Intergroup Contact and the Central Role of Affect in Intergroup Prejudice

Linda R. Tropp and Thomas F. Pettigrew

Decades of research have studied the role of intergroup contact in reducing intergroup prejudice (see Allport, 1954; Hewstone & Brown, 1986; Pettigrew & Tropp, 2000, 2003), yet little consensus has emerged regarding its effects. Past reviews of this extensive literature have reached sharply conflicting conclusions. Some indicate that intergroup contact leads to positive changes in intergroup prejudice, especially when the contact occurs under optimal conditions (e.g., Jackson, 1993; Pettigrew, 1971, 1998; Riordan, 1978). Others take a more critical stance. They hold that intergroup contact has relatively little or no effect on broad-scale changes in intergroup prejudice (e.g., Amir, 1976; Ford, 1986; Rothbart & John, 1985).

At first blush, these perspectives appear to be fundamentally inconsistent, reflecting the long-standing debates that have engulfed this research literature during the last half century. We believe this divergence in perspectives has grown out of an overemphasis on the general question of *whether* intergroup contact will reduce prejudice, with the phenomenon of intergroup prejudice construed as a single dimension. Close examination of the research contributing to these perspectives suggests that many different components of intergroup prejudice – including both affective and cognitive components – must be considered as potential outcomes of intergroup contact. Thus, it may be that different branches of the research literature have emphasized different aspects of the intergroup relationship. We pursue this possibility in this chapter, and we propose that affective dimensions of intergroup relationships are especially important for understanding the effects of contact on intergroup attitudes.

HISTORICAL APPROACHES TO THE STUDY OF INTERGROUP PREJUDICE

Following World War II, American social psychology sought to combine affective, motivational, and cognitive processes in the study of psychological phenomena. This multidimensional emphasis shaped the study of prejudice when the landmark study on the authoritarian personality appeared (Adorno et al., 1950). In the mid-1950s, however, two major events sharply changed the scene – Allport's (1954) *The Nature of Prejudice* and "the cognitive revolution."

Stressing cognitive factors, Allport (1954) countered the then fashionable assumption that group stereotypes were simply the aberrant distortions of "prejudiced personalities." Advancing the view now universally accepted, Allport insisted that cognitive components of prejudice were natural extensions of normal cognitive processes. Stereotypes, he concluded, were not aberrant at all, but unfortunately all too human. Reflecting a general emphasis on cognition throughout psychology, social cognition research took hold in social psychology in the 1970s. This work greatly enhanced our understanding of the nature and function of stereotyping, but its focus on cognitive concerns largely ignored the affective dimensions of prejudice.

By the 1980s, social psychologists began to broaden the scope of theory and research on prejudice, coinciding with a general move away from purely cognitive concerns to increased attention to affect and motivation. Two seminal volumes on stereotypes, both edited by David Hamilton, highlight the shift in emphasis. In *Cognitive Processes in Stereotyping and Intergroup Behavior* (Hamilton, 1981a), affect received only brief mention, and mood and emotion are not included in the index. By contrast, a dozen years later, *Affect, Cognition and Stereotyping* (Mackie & Hamilton, 1993a) centers on the role of affect.

AFFECTIVE TIES TO OUTGROUP MEMBERS AND REDUCTIONS IN INTERGROUP PREJUDICE

Corresponding to this shift, researchers have demonstrated a renewed interest in affect, both in terms of the bonds we create through our relationships with outgroup members, and the outcomes that can result from intergroup contact (e.g., Herek & Capitanio, 1996; Pettigrew, 1997a, 1998; Wright, Aron, & Tropp, 2002).

Pettigrew (1997a) proposes that the close ties generated by cross-group friendships can lead to greater feelings of liking for and identification with outgroup members; in turn, these affective ties feed into more positive feelings toward the entire outgroup. To test these possibilities, Pettigrew (1997a) analyzed survey responses from seven European samples. The survey asked participants to state whether they had any friends of a different culture, nationality, race, ethnicity, or social class, as well as to complete several measures of intergroup prejudice. These analyses revealed that cross-group friendships were consistently, highly, and negatively associated with intergroup prejudice. Moreover, the effects were especially strong for those prejudice measures based on affective responses, such as feelings of sympathy and admiration for the outgroup. By contrast, contact with outgroup members as co-workers or neighbors yielded far smaller effects (see also Hamberger & Hewstone, 1997).

Similarly, Wright, Aron, and their colleagues (McLaughlin-Volpe et al., 2000; Wright et al., 2002; Wright & Van der Zande, 1999) propose that greater feelings of intimacy and closeness to a single outgroup member can promote reductions in intergroup prejudice toward the outgroup as a whole. To examine these issues, McLaughlin-Volpe et al. (2000) assessed both the quantity (number) and quality (closeness) of respondents' cross-group interactions, along with asking respondents to report their feelings toward outgroup members using six word pairs (e.g., warm/cold, friendly/hostile). Across questionnaire and diary studies, these authors found that greater contact quality was significantly associated with less intergroup prejudice. Furthermore, contact quality moderated the relationship between quantity of contact and prejudice, such that greater numbers of cross-group interactions were associated with lower levels of prejudice only among those who had close cross-group relationships.

Focusing on empathy, Batson et al. (1997) also describe how personal connections to individual outgroup members may provide a route to improving attitudes toward stigmatized groups in general (see also Stephan & Finlay, 1999). These authors propose that, by attempting to relate to the experiences of the stigmatized, and imagining how they are affected by their stigmatized status, people will become more inclined to feel concern for a stigmatized person. This enhanced concern for the stigmatized person should in turn generalize to more positive attitudes toward the entire stigmatized group. With multiple studies involving a range of stigmatized groups, Batson et al. (1997) found support for this view, showing that greater empathy toward a stigmatized individual can promote positive changes in attitudes toward the stigmatized group as a whole.

In sum, recent studies, both within and beyond the contact literature, suggest that establishing affective ties with a single outgroup member can promote positive feelings toward the outgroup as a whole. But investigations that focus on basic cognitive processes are less optimistic regarding the potential for generalization of positive contact outcomes.

COGNITIVE PROCESSES AND THE POTENTIAL FOR REDUCING INTERGROUP PREJUDICE

The examination of cognitive processes underlying intergroup phenomena grew out of a broader interest in understanding people as processors of information who seek to classify and organize the stimuli they encounter in the social world. In a seminal paper, Tajfel (1969) described the simplifying function of categorization, elaborating on how the mere categorization of people into different groups can have profound effects on social perception and behavior (see also Tajfel, 1981). Cognitively oriented research on intergroup processes then flourished throughout the 1970s. This work placed particular emphasis on the role of categorization in the perpetuation of stereotypes (see Hamilton, Stroessner, & Driscoll, 1994). Thus, the research marked a notable shift from the earlier focus on motivation and affect to an emphasis on cognitive functions that underlie social perception and intergroup bias (Pettigrew, 1981, 1997b; Rothbart & Lewis, 1994).

This generation of research highlighted how stereotypes can be highly resistant to change (Hamilton, 1981b). When a person is categorized as a group member, stereotypes of that group are activated, and we tend to select, interpret, and recall information that is consistent with the outgroup stereotype (Hamilton et al., 1994; Wilder, 1986). The consensus view also held that information inconsistent with the stereotype is stored separately as either subtypes or "exceptions to the rule," thereby maintaining intact the original group stereotype (Taylor, 1981; Weber & Crocker, 1983; Wilder, 1984).

Growing out of these contentions, social psychologists began to question whether positive contact experiences with an individual outgroup member would in fact contribute to more positive views toward the outgroup as a whole (Hewstone & Brown, 1986; Rothbart & John, 1985; Wilder, 1986). Rothbart and John (1985) proposed that we view generalization largely in terms of the cognitive processes that negotiate relationships between stereotypical characteristics of a group and characteristics of those individuals who belong to the group (see also Rothbart, 1996; Rothbart & John, 1993). A basic premise of their argument is that, when viewing individuals as potential group representatives, people grant more weight to outgroup individuals who confirm the group stereotype and less weight to those who disconfirm the group stereotype (but see Rojahn & Pettigrew, 1992). Thus, when people are asked to make judgments about that group, individuals who possess those characteristics that are consistent with the group stereotype are more likely to come to mind as group "representatives" than those who do not possess those characteristics (see Rothbart, Sriram, & Davis-Stitt, 1996).

These perceptual processes directly influence the likely outcomes of intergroup contact (Rothbart & John, 1985, 1993). Interacting members of different groups can learn individuating information about each other that could potentially reduce their reliance on negative stereotypes. As we receive individuating information that disconfirms the group stereotype, we may become *more* likely to see outgroup members in a positive light, but we may also become *less* likely to see them as good representatives of their group. This process would severely limit the potential for any positive changes at the individual level to generalize to positive changes in views of the whole outgroup.

This reasoning led many researchers to focus on the role of typicality as a crucial determinant for the generalization of contact outcomes (Hewstone & Brown, 1986; Weber & Crocker, 1983; Wilder, 1984). In particular, Wilder's (1984) research indicates that positive contact experiences with an outgroup member may only generalize to the entire outgroup when the outgroup member is perceived to be typical of the outgroup. Wilder (1984) and others recognize that positive changes in intergroup perceptions from intergroup contact are possible, but they hold that such generalization is difficult to achieve given the rigid nature of stereotyping and other cognitive processes associated with categorization.

DEVELOPING A DIFFERENTIATED VIEW OF CONTACT OUTCOMES: AFFECTIVE AND COGNITIVE APPROACHES

These brief reviews suggest that two research traditions have emerged in examining the potential generalization of contact effects. One tradition focuses on *affective* dimensions of the intergroup relationship, and indicates that affective ties to individual outgroup members can propel positive feelings toward the outgroup as a whole. The other tradition concentrates on *cognitive* dimensions of the intergroup relationship, and suggests that the inertial nature of stereotyping and categorization makes the generalization of positive contact outcomes extremely difficult. Viewing these traditions together (Mackie & Hamilton, 1993b; Mackie & Smith, 1998), we believe a reconciliation and integration of these traditions seems possible, depending on the types of generalization we wish to consider. Rather than simply asking whether positive outcomes of contact will or will not generalize, it is useful to ask about the *kinds* of contact outcomes that are likely to generalize. Indeed, based on the research reviewed, we predict that *affective outcomes of intergroup contact are more likely to generalize than cognitive outcomes.*

This differentiated view of contact outcomes fits nicely with other research and theory on attitudes and the components of intergroup prejudice. Attitudes are generally defined as evaluative responses to objects or classes of objects (Eagly & Chaiken, 1993; Ostrom, 1969; Zanna & Rempel, 1988). Yet, rather than being conceptualized as a single construct, cognition and affect represent conceptually distinct components of both attitudes in general (Breckler & Wiggins, 1989; Eagly & Chaiken, 1993; Ostrom, 1969; Zanna & Rempel, 1988) and prejudiced attitudes in particular (Brewer, Campbell, & Levine, 1971; Esses, Haddock, & Zanna, 1993; Mann, 1959; Stangor, Sullivan, & Ford, 1991). Cognitive components of prejudice are commonly expressed in terms of one's perceptions, judgments, and beliefs about a group (Ashmore & Del Boca, 1981; Katz & Hass, 1988; Ostrom, Skowronski, & Nowak, 1994), whereas affective components of prejudice are based on one's feelings and emotional responses to a group (Esses et al., 1993; Smith, 1993; Stangor et al., 1991).

Here, by emphasizing a distinction between cognitive and affective dimensions of intergroup prejudice, we do not intend to imply that cognition and affect are entirely independent processes (see Eagly & Chaiken, 1993). We recognize that cognitive and affective processes often interact with each other, as has been noted in recent research (see Mackie & Smith, 2002; Stephan & Stephan, 1993, for reviews). Rather, we raise the distinction because we believe it highlights different ways in which we think about intergroup relationships and respond to outgroup members as the targets of our attitudes. Focusing on cognitive dimensions, such as making judgments and stating beliefs, may guide us toward evaluating outgroup targets as relatively detached observers, where we maintain a degree of psychological distance between ourselves and those outgroup targets. By contrast, affective dimensions may shift the focus of our attitudes such that they are more relational in nature, reflecting our feelings and emotional responses to outgroup members in the context of our relationships with them (see Zajonc, 1980; Zanna & Rempel, 1988, for related arguments). Thus, given that affective ties to outgroup members grow from intergroup contact – and particularly that involving close cross-group relationships – it is likely that such contact would generally produce greater attitudinal shifts on affective dimensions of prejudice relative to the effects observed for cognitive dimensions.

Furthermore, we suspect that these shifts should be especially likely to occur for those affective dimensions that relate directly to group members' contact experiences and denote *affective ties* to the outgroup, such as feelings of closeness to outgroup members, and feelings of comfort in cross-group interactions. Over several decades, researchers have noted that intergroup contact can promote greater feelings of warmth and closeness toward outgroup members (e.g., Cook, 1984; Deutsch & Collins, 1951; Pettigrew, 1997a; Wright et al., 2002). Much of the recent literature has concentrated on the role that anxiety plays in intergroup contact (e.g., Britt, Boniecki, Vescio, & Biernat, 1996; Islam & Hewstone, 1993; Stephan et al., 2002), as well as group members' concerns about feeling comfortable and accepted in cross-group interactions (e.g., Devine & Vasquez, 1998; Vorauer, Main, & O'Connell, 1998). Thus, though a wider range of emotions may be implicated depending on relations between the specific groups involved (Mackie & Smith, 2002), our discussion of affect focuses primarily on those dimensions that represent *affective ties* with the outgroup.

For the remainder of this chapter, we will examine variability in the generalization of different kinds of contact outcomes. We will consider whether the effects of contact on intergroup prejudice differ, depending on how prejudice is defined and assessed. In line with the two traditions of contact research, we compare relationships across affective and cognitive indicators of intergroup prejudice with two distinct types of data. First, we analyze data from our extensive meta-analytic review of research on the relationships between intergroup contact and prejudice (Pettigrew & Tropp, 2000, 2003). Here, we will contrast the magnitudes of contact-prejudice effects in relation to the many measures of prejudice used in prior research studies. We then examine these relationships further in a questionnaire study (see Tropp & Pettigrew, 2004), in which participants completed a wide range of prejudice measures paralleling those most commonly used in the broader contact literature.

RELATIONSHIPS BETWEEN INTERGROUP CONTACT AND PREJUDICE: META-ANALYTIC FINDINGS

Our recent meta-analysis examining relationships between contact and prejudice reveals the great variability with which prejudice has been defined and assessed in past research (Pettigrew & Tropp, 2000, 2003). For this analysis, we gathered studies through intensive searches of many research literatures, and we utilized a wide range of procedures to locate appropriate studies. First, we conducted computer searches of the psychological (*PsychLIT* and *PsycINFO*), sociological (*SocAbs* and *SocioFile*), political science (*GOV*), education (*ERIC*), dissertation (*UMI Dissertation Abstracts*), and general research periodical (*Current Contents*) abstracts through December 2000. These searches used 54 different search terms that range from single words (e.g., "intergroup," "contact") to combined terms (e.g., "age + intergroup contact," "disabled + contact"). Across the databases, we conducted three types of searches with these terms – by "title words," "key words," and "subject" – to maximize our chances of finding all relevant studies. Using the *Social Sciences Citation Index*, we checked on later citations of especially seminal contact studies, following the "descendancy approach" described by Johnson and Eagly (2000). We also requested published and unpublished papers through psychology e-mail networks, and we wrote personal letters to researchers who have published relevant work. Finally, we searched through reference lists from the studies we found and previous reviews of the contact literature.

As we gathered these papers, we evaluated whether they should be included in the analysis on the basis of four primary criteria (see Pettigrew & Tropp, 2003).

1. Because our focus is on the relationship between intergroup contact and prejudice, we considered *only those empirical studies in which intergroup contact can act as an independent variable for predicting intergroup prejudice*. This requirement excluded research that treats contact as a dependent variable in explaining how and why contact occurs.

2. We included *only studies that involve contact between members of discrete groups*. This rule allows for inclusion of studies involving cross-cutting categories, but only if the categories are clearly defined.
3. For inclusion, *the research must involve some degree of actual face-to-face interaction between members of the different groups*. Thus, the interaction must be observed or reported, or occur in such focused, long-term situations in which direct contact is unavoidable. This rule excludes research that utilizes rough proximity or group proportions to *infer* intergroup interaction. Our only exceptions involve research that carefully demonstrated that the intergroup proximity correlated highly with actual contact. This rule also omits investigations that attempt to assess contact using such indirect measures as information about an outgroup. We also excluded studies that asked about attitudes toward contact unless the researchers directly linked such indicators to prior intergroup experience. Finally, this inclusion rule eliminates research that categorizes participants into groups that do not directly interact – as in many minimal group studies.
4. *The prejudice dependent variables must be collected on individuals rather than simply as a total aggregate outcome, and data must be available to evaluate variability in prejudice in relation to intergroup contact*. These points allow for the inclusion of studies that examine relationships between contact and prejudice in within-group designs, or experimental tests of the effects of contact on prejudice in between-group designs.

Our full analysis includes 515 individual studies, with 714 independent samples and 1,365 nonindependent tests. Combined, 250,513 participants from 38 nations participated in the studies reported in this analysis. These studies span from the early 1940s through the year 2000, and they involve a wide variety of target groups, contact settings, study designs, and research procedures (Pettigrew & Tropp, 2000, 2003).

Our meta-analysis reveals that greater intergroup contact is significantly associated with lower levels of prejudice. Although the magnitude of this general relationship varied widely across studies, 93% of the studies showed an inverse relationship between contact and prejudice. Table 12.1 shows the mean estimates for the contact-prejudice effect size are quite consistent across the three units of analysis. For both the 515 studies and the 714 samples, the mean Cohen's d is $-.47$ (or a mean r of $-.23$). For the 1,365 tests, the mean d is $-.45$ (mean $r = -.22$). These estimates are only slightly reduced when two data corrections are imposed (assigning ceilings on sample sizes for five extremely large studies, and omitting fifteen studies that reported "nonsignificant" effects). It is these files – with "non-significant" studies removed and the largest studies, samples and tests capped – that we utilize in subsequent analyses.

TABLE 12.1. *Summary of Effect Sizes for Contact-Prejudice Relationship Across Studies, Samples, and Tests*

	d	95% CL	*Z*	*p*	*k*	*r*	*g*	*N*
All studies	−.467	−.47/−.46	−145.2	<.000	515	−.227	−.450	250,513
With data corrections[a]	−.425	−.43/−.42	−115.2	<.000	500	−.208	−.463	203,174
All samples	−.466	−.47/−.46	−145.0	<.000	714	−.227	−.454	250,513
With data corrections[a]	−.427	−.43/−.42	−115.2	<.000	697	−.209	−.465	199,967
All tests	−.452	−.46/−.45	−198.4	<.000	1,365	−.221	−.475	507,867
With data corrections[a]	−.416	−.42/−.41	−151.4	<.000	1,349	−.203	−.481	382,412

[a] For data reported with corrections, 15 cases reporting "nonsignificant" results have been removed (Johnson & Eagly, 2000; Rosenthal, 1995), and cases with extremely large sample sizes have been capped at 5,000 for studies, 3,000 for samples, and 2,000 for tests to avoid overweighting their results in the analysis. These corrected data files have been used in all subsequent analyses reported in this chapter.

Note: d = mean effect size weighted by the reciprocal of the variance; 95% CL = the 95% confidence limits of d; Z = standard score or deviate; p = probability of d; k = number of studies, samples, or tests involved in the analysis; r = correlation; g = unweighted mean effect; N = total number of subjects.

The studies included in this final sample are highly diverse as to participants, target groups, study designs, and contextual factors – all of which are potential moderators of the relationship between intergroup contact and prejudice. The clear majority of tests included in the analysis (85%) shows generalization of contact outcomes to the outgroup as a whole, with a mean contact-prejudice effect size only slightly lower ($d = -.41, r = -.20$) than that obtained for contact outcomes for individuals in the original contact situation ($d = -.42, r = -.21$). In addition, the more rigorous research studies reveal stronger associations between contact and prejudice (see Pettigrew & Tropp, 2000, 2003).

Relevant to the present discussion, our analysis includes studies that use a wide range of prejudice indicators. This inclusive net allows us to investigate the many ways in which researchers have measured prejudice, and to test whether relationships between contact and prejudice vary, depending on how prejudice is measured.

To preface this investigation, we first examine whether there were particular trends in the assessment of prejudice in contact research over past decades. For each test of the contact-prejudice relationship ($k = 1,349$), we coded whether the prejudice measure represented one of four broad types of indicators (beliefs, social distance, stereotypes, and affect). Those coded as *beliefs* ($k = 515$; 38%) ask participants to report the degree to which they endorse particular beliefs about the nature and experiences of a specified group, and how that group fits within the broader society. *Social distance* measures ($k = 263$; 19%) consist mostly of Bogardus-like instruments, in which participants indicate their willingness to interact with outgroup members across a variety of social contexts (Bogardus, 1928). Assessments of *stereotypes* (15%) involve two kinds of measures: items that directly assess the degree to which participants see certain characteristics as being associated with a group ($k = 145$), and those that use a semantic-differential format to ask participants about outgroup traits ($k = 58$; Osgood, Suci, & Tannenbaum, 1957). *Affect* measures (18%) include favorability ratings ($k = 113$) and semantic-differential scales assessing liking and intergroup evaluations ($k = 57$), along with measures concerning felt or anticipated emotions in cross-group interactions ($k = 68$). Although there is substantial variability in how emotions have been assessed in contact research, most of the emotion-based measures touched on feelings of comfort and anxiety (either as its primary focus, or as part of a more general measure of affective responses), with a few additional cases focusing on other, more specific emotions (e.g., fear, sympathy). Prejudice measures that do not fit in any of these categories ($k = 127$; 10%) are classified as *other*.

By decade, we tallied the number of tests corresponding to each type of prejudice indicator. We then divided these values by the total number of tests reported in each decade to compute the proportion of tests representing each kind of prejudice indicator in each decade. Figure 12.1 reveals that

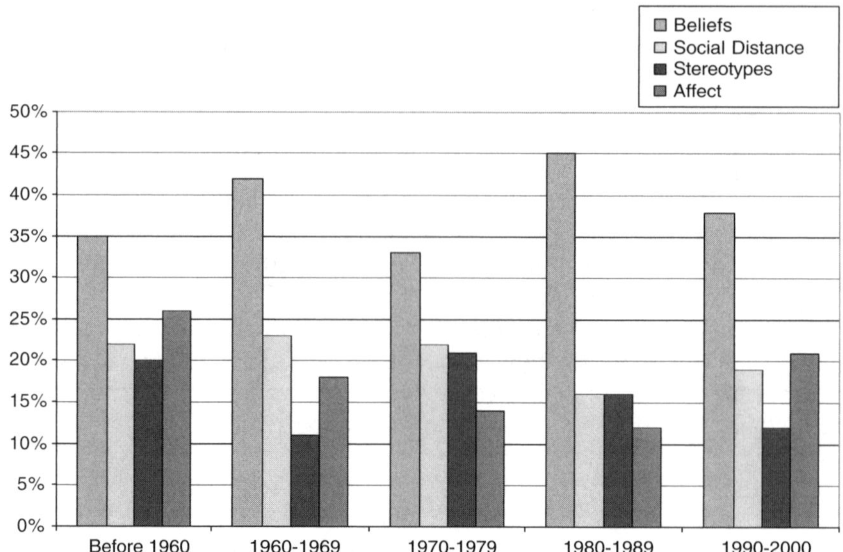

FIGURE 12.1. Proportion of tests reported for different prejudice indicators in contact studies from the 1940s to 2000.

intergroup belief measures have traditionally been, and continue to be, the most commonly used prejudice indicators in intergroup contact studies. The use of social distance measures has been reasonably constant, decreasing only slightly in recent decades. The use of stereotype measures peaked during the 1970s as the focus on affect waned. But a renewed interest in affect surfaced in studies from the 1990s.

Using the test level of analysis, Table 12.2 examines effect sizes across the contrasting types of prejudice measures. These results reveal that various measures of affect yield particularly strong effects, whether they were emotion-based measures (mean $d = -.53, r = -.26$), favorability ratings (mean $d = -.41, r = -.20$), or semantic-differential scales assessing liking and intergroup evaluations (mean $d = -.56, r = -.27$). Belief (mean $d = -.43, r = -.21$) and social distance (mean $d = -.44, r = -.21$) measures of prejudice also secure strong effects. Stereotype indicators produce weaker effects (mean $d = -.26, r = -.13$), but their results vary, depending on their form of measurement. The 147 tests that directly measure stereotypes yield meaningful, though significantly reduced effects (mean $d = -.32, r = -.16$). But the fifty-eight tests that use a semantic-differential format to tap stereotypes provide much smaller effects (mean $d = -.10, r = -.05$).

These patterns of findings shift only slightly when just the 1,148 tests concerning generalization to the outgroup are included in the analysis. Here, both affect and social distance measures show the strongest overall

TABLE 12.2. *Estimates of Contact-Prejudice Relationship Across Different Types of Prejudice Indicators*

Prejudice Indicator	*d*	95% CL	*Z*	*p*	*k*	*r*	*g*	*N*
Beliefs	−.426	−.43/−.42	−105.604	<.000	518	−.208	−.495	161,684
Social Distance	−.436	−.45/−.42	−69.889	<.000	263	−.213	−.436	85,252
Stereotypes	−.261	−.28/−.24	−30.364	<.000	203	−.130	−.410	47,170
Affect	−.463	−.48/−.45	−71.911	<.000	238	−.226	−.563	65,576
Other	−.370	−.39/−.35	−34.763	<.000	127	−.182	−.472	22,730

Note: The tests used in this table have had ceilings placed on their sample sizes and reports of "nonsignificance" omitted, as indicated in Table 12.1. As in Table 12.1, d = mean effect size weighted by the reciprocal of the variance; 95% CL = the 95% confidence limits of d; Z = standard score or deviate; p = probability of d; k = number of studies, samples, or tests involved in the analysis; r = correlation; g = unweighted mean effect; N = total number of subjects.

effects (mean $d = -.45, r = -.22$), with the emotion and affect-based semantic-differential measures yielding particularly strong effects (mean $d = -.52$ and $-.55$, respectively; $r = -.25$ and $-.26$). Belief measures show moderate effects (mean $d = -.41, r = -.20$). Stereotype measures show the weakest effects (mean $d = -.24, r = -.12$), though they again vary, depending on how stereotypes are assessed. Tests involving direct measures of stereotypes render modest effects (mean $d = -.29, r = -.15$), whereas tests involving semantic-differential measures of stereotypes reveal especially weak effects (mean $d = -.09, r = -.05$). Thus, although the results generally show that greater levels of contact are associated with lower levels of prejudice, additional analyses reveal that the strongest contact-prejudice relationships occur with affect-based measures. Measures of beliefs and social distance also provide strong contact-prejudice effects, yet the effects are markedly weaker for stereotype measures.

In sum, results from this analysis indicate a significant, inverse relationship between contact and prejudice, with greater levels of contact associated with lower levels of prejudice. Furthermore, the analysis reveals that the positive effects of contact tend to generalize from the immediate contact situation to the outgroup as a whole. However, the findings also point to systematic differences in the magnitudes of the contact-prejudice relationship depending on the prejudice measures used. The strongest contact-prejudice effects occur for affect measures, and the weakest effects emerge for stereotype measures. Together, these results lead us to question whether we should expect all potential outcomes to be affected equally by intergroup contact, given that there may be differences in orientation associated with affective and cognitive dimensions of intergroup prejudice. To reconcile divergent perspectives regarding the generalization of contact outcomes, we suggest that generalization may be achieved more readily for affective indicators of prejudice, relative to effects achieved for cognitive indicators.

RELATIONSHIPS BETWEEN INTERGROUP CONTACT AND MULTIPLE INDICATORS OF INTERGROUP PREJUDICE

Although these meta-analytic results are robust, there are limitations on the comparisons we can conduct with these data. Indeed, skeptics often criticize meta-analysis for conducting comparisons across studies in which variables, samples, and testing procedures are not uniform (see Rosenthal, 1991). In the meta-analysis, we had to group different prejudice measures together across studies to create broad categories of prejudice indicators for which contact-prejudice effect sizes could be compared.

Although the results of these procedures are informative, the classification of prejudice measures into broad categories reduces our ability to conduct a fine-grained analysis of what the various measures represent. For example, although semantic-differentials and favorability ratings are often used to assess affect in a broad sense, we find that these kinds of measures vary across different studies in the response scales offered to participants. In some cases, the measures are primarily designed to assess people's feelings toward and liking for other groups (e.g., Riordan, 1987; Stangor et al., 1996); whereas, in others, the measures focus on people's impressions or evaluations of other groups (e.g., Luiz & Krige, 1981; Patchen et al., 1977). In still other cases, such measurement details are not included in the research reports, thus making it difficult to determine distinctions in contact effects across different kinds of contact outcomes.

Thus, we conducted a separate study in which we asked participants to complete a wide range of measures pertaining to intergroup contact and prejudice (see Tropp & Pettigrew, 2004). Their responses allow for the simultaneous examination of relationships between multiple indicators of contact and prejudice, along with providing an opportunity to explore how different types of prejudice measures cluster together.

For this study, we recruited 126 white undergraduate participants (forty-six males and eighty females), with ages ranging from eighteen to twenty-two (mean age = 19.39 years). We informed participants that the study concerned people's experiences with and impressions of black Americans, after which they completed a questionnaire. The participants completed a wide variety of prejudice measures in reference to black Americans, using 7-point Likert-type scales. We gathered the following measures from an examination of studies in the meta-analysis (Pettigrew & Tropp, 2000, 2003), selecting them to represent the broad range of outcomes most commonly assessed in intergroup contact research.

POSITIVE AND NEGATIVE AFFECT. Participants reported the extent to which they would feel five positive emotional states (e.g., relaxed, secure) and five negative emotional states (e.g., awkward, threatened) in response to an imagined interaction with a black person ($\alpha = .91$ and .85, respectively; Stephan & Stephan, 1985).

INTERGROUP ANXIETY. Participants indicated the degree to which they feel anxious about discussing cultural differences and interacting with black people ($\alpha = 85$; Britt et al., 1996).

IDENTIFICATION. Participants indicated the extent to which they "identify" and "feel strong ties" with black people ($\alpha = .87$; Brown et al., 1986).

EXPECTATIONS. Participants indicated the degree to which they hold positive expectations (e.g., would get along, could trust) for interactions with black people ($\alpha = .88$; Tropp, 2003).

WARMTH. A single item assessed how "cold" or "warm" participants generally feel toward black people, using a procedure similar to a feeling thermometer (*NES Guide to Public Opinion and Electoral Behavior*, 1995–2000).

SEMANTIC DIFFERENTIAL. Participants indicated how they view black people in response to five word pairs (e.g., beautiful-ugly, strong-weak; $\alpha = .91$; see Osgood et al., 1957).

SOCIAL DISTANCE. Participants indicated their willingness to interact with black people in eight different social contexts (e.g., classroom, neighborhood; $\alpha = .94$; see Bogardus, 1928).

PRO-BLACK AND ANTI-BLACK RACIAL ATTITUDES. Participants indicated responses of sympathy and/or disapproval regarding the experiences of black Americans ($\alpha = .84$ and .76, respectively; see Katz & Hass, 1988).

BELIEFS. Items from the Attitudes toward Blacks Scale (Brigham, 1993), the Modern Racism Scale (McConahay, Hardee, & Batts, 1981), and the Racial Resentment Scale (Kinder & Sanders, 1996) assessed participants' symbolic beliefs about black people ($\alpha = 87$).

We first calculated correlations among these measures to examine their interrelationships (see Table 12.3). Nearly all the measures significantly correlate with each other at the .05 level of significance. Yet even among those relationships that are significant, there is considerable variability in the magnitudes of the correlations, with absolute values of r ranging from .17 to .72. Only four relationships between the measures were not statistically significant: Positive Affect did not correlate significantly with either Beliefs or Anti-Black Racial Attitudes, and neither Positive Affect nor Intergroup Anxiety correlated significantly with Pro-Black Racial Attitudes.

We then entered these measures into a principal-axis factor analysis with oblique rotation to explore how the measures cluster together. Two factors emerged, accounting for 55% of the variance in participants' scores (Table 12.4). A first factor included primarily *affective* indicators of prejudice, with strong loadings on Positive Affect, Negative Affect, Intergroup Anxiety, Identification, Expectations, and Warmth (rotated factor loadings from .40 to .85). A second factor included mostly *cognitive* indicators of prejudice, with strong loadings on the Semantic Differential, Social Distance, Intergroup Beliefs, and Pro-Black and Anti-Black Racial Attitudes (rotated factor loadings from .51 to .91). The two factors were only moderately correlated, $r = .40$, and a principal components analysis using orthogonal factors obtained virtually identical results.

One may wonder why Social Distance loaded highly in the cognitive factor rather than on the affective factor. After all, social distance measures are commonly used to assess people's responses to cross-group interactions across social contexts. However, these measures typically ask participants to report their *willingness to interact* with other groups (Bogardus, 1928), rather than asking them how they would expect *to feel* during those interactions. As such, social distance measures may reflect people's detached views of outgroup targets more than their emotional responses to them.

TABLE 12.3. *Correlations Among the Prejudice Measures*

	1	2	3	4	5	6	7	8	9	10	11
1. Positive Affect		$-.69^{***}$	$-.59^{***}$	$.40^{***}$	$.48^{***}$	$.39^{***}$	$-.36^{**}$	$-.23^{**}$	$-.11$	$.06$	$-.15$
2. Negative Affect			$.72^{***}$	$-.47^{***}$	$-.46^{***}$	$-.42^{***}$	$.30^{***}$	$.38^{***}$	$.21^{*}$	$-.18^{*}$	$.19^{*}$
3. Intergroup Anxiety				$-.47^{***}$	$-.46^{***}$	$-.36^{***}$	$.27^{**}$	$.29^{***}$	$.24^{**}$	$.02$	$.17^{*}$
4. Identification					$.62^{***}$	$.30^{***}$	$-.38^{***}$	$-.33^{***}$	$-.30^{***}$	$.22^{*}$	$-.29^{**}$
5. Expectations						$.41^{***}$	$-.51^{***}$	$-.52^{***}$	$-.41^{***}$	$.27^{**}$	$-.38^{***}$
6. Warmth							$-.55^{***}$	$-.40^{***}$	$-.33^{***}$	$.28^{**}$	$-.30^{***}$
7. Semantic Differential								$.50^{***}$	$.46^{***}$	$-.31^{***}$	$.55^{***}$
8. Social Distance									$.59^{***}$	$-.38^{***}$	$.54^{***}$
9. Intergroup Beliefs										$-.67^{***}$	$.65^{***}$
10. Pro-Black Attitudes											$-.41^{***}$
11. Anti-Black Attitudes											

Note: $^{*}p < .05$; $^{**}p < .01$; $^{***}p < .001$.

TABLE 12.4. *Rotated Factor Loadings from Factor Analysis of Prejudice Measures*

Measure	Factor 1	Factor 2
Positive Affect	**−.82**	.12
Negative Affect	**.85**	−.05
Intergroup Anxiety	**.82**	−.09
Identification	**−.54**	−.18
Expectations	**−.52**	−.35
Warmth	**−.40**	−.31
Semantic Differential	.35	**.51**
Social Distance	.19	**.64**
Intergroup Beliefs	−.07	**.91**
Pro-Black Racial Attitudes	.11	**−.67**
Anti-Black Racial Attitudes	−.01	**.74**

Note: Loadings of .40 or higher have been highlighted in **bold**.

We then examined participants' responses to these measures in relation to three indicators of intergroup contact. Participants were asked to report: (1) the number of black people they know, at least as acquaintances; (2) the number of black people they would consider to be friends; and (3) how close they feel to the black people they know on a scale ranging from 1 (not at all) to 7 (very close). Additionally, participants completed two 6-item measures concerning internal and external motivation to control prejudice ($\alpha = .83$ and .88, respectively; Dunton & Fazio, 1997; Plant & Devine, 1998). We used these measures as controls in the following analyses, because participants may resist admitting to prejudices toward other groups.

Table 12.5 provides the correlations between the contact and prejudice measures, both with and without controlling for motivation to control prejudice. Consistent with the meta-analytic results, many significant relationships emerge between the contact and prejudice measures, revealing that greater intergroup contact is associated with more positive intergroup outcomes. At the same time, notable differences in the relationships emerge across the prejudice indicators. Those measures loading highly on the affective factor significantly and more consistently relate to the contact indicators than those loading highly on the cognitive factor; furthermore, these patterns are particularly pronounced for those contact indicators that indicate close cross-group ties, such as outgroup friends and intergroup closeness. Note, too, that the more evaluative measures from the cognitive factor (semantic-differential, social distance) reveal some significant relationships with the contact indicators, particularly when motivations to control prejudice are partialed out, whereas the belief measures did not.

These findings underscore how affective and cognitive dimensions of intergroup prejudice may have different implications for intergroup relations. Exploratory factor analysis distinguished between prejudice

TABLE 12.5. *Correlations Between Prejudice Measures and Three Indicators of Intergroup Contact*

	Outgroup Acquaintances		Outgroup Friends		Outgroup Closeness	
Measure	r	Partial r	r	Partial r	r	Partial r
Affective Factor						
Positive Affect	.22*	.24**	.31***	.36***	.23***	.23***
Negative Affect	−.21*	−.24**	−.32***	−.39***	−.27**	−.27**
Intergroup Anxiety	−.21*	−.19*	−.34***	−.40***	−.31***	−.32***
Identification	.26**	.27**	.38***	.42***	.32***	.33***
Expectations	.13	.18*	.26**	.34***	.27***	.28***
Warmth	.11	.15	.30***	.34***	.22*	.21*
Cognitive Factor						
Semantic Differential	−.05	−.10	−.14	−.22*	−.15	−.15
Social Distance	.04	−.06	−.15	−.27**	−.17*	−.21*
Intergroup Beliefs	.03	−.02	−.01	−.06	−.13	−.15
Pro-Black Attitudes	.02	.10	.04	.09	.04	.05
Anti-Black Attitudes	.01	−.04	−.03	−.07	−.15	−.16

Note: Partial r's control for internal and external motivation to control prejudice. $^{*}p < .05$; $^{**}p < .01$; $^{***}p < .001$.

measures representing affective ties with the outgroup (Positive Affect, Negative Affect, Anxiety, Identification, Expectations, and Warmth) and those representing cognitive and evaluative responses to the outgroup (Semantic Differential, Social Distance, Intergroup Beliefs, Pro-Black and Anti-Black Racial Attitudes). Measures loading highly on the affective factor also showed more consistent and significant relationships with contact indicators than measures loading on the cognitive factor, particularly for those contact indicators concerning close ties to outgroup members. Thus, together, our results suggest that affective dimensions of intergroup relationships are especially important considerations for achieving positive outcomes from intergroup contact.

CONCLUSIONS

In this chapter, we have reviewed two branches of contact research that often reach different conclusions regarding the potential for intergroup contact to reduce prejudice. We propose that the nature of their disagreement lies in their tendency to focus on different aspects of the intergroup relationship. On the one hand, cognitively oriented theorists are correct in highlighting the importance of the many cognitive barriers to stereotype change that can limit contact effects. But, in neglecting affective factors, they overlook the many positive, generalizable outcomes that can grow from intergroup contact. On the other hand, affectively oriented theorists are correct in showing how contact – especially that involving close relationships – can render meaningful changes in how people feel toward outgroups. But they are, perhaps, too enthusiastic about the potential for contact to reduce prejudice in all its forms.

In line with these proposals, the combined results of the meta-analysis and questionnaire study confirm that prejudice indicators cannot be treated interchangeably. Different patterns of relationships emerge, depending on the measures used. Results from these studies also mesh nicely with a host of other recent findings that point to the pivotal role of affect in intergroup prejudice (Smith, 1993). For example, a meta-analysis reveals that relative deprivation strongly predicts prejudice only when it taps anger and resentment, as well as a perceived group difference (Walker & Smith, 2001). Stephan and colleagues (2002) demonstrate the critical role of anxiety in the contact-prejudice relationship, with intergroup anxiety mediating the effects of contact on racial attitudes for both black and white American participants. Similarly, Esses and Dovidio (2002) show that emotions mediate most of the effect of a video depicting racial discrimination on their white college participants' willingness to engage in interracial contact.

The marked contrast between relatively large contact effects on affective dimensions of prejudice and much smaller effects on stereotypes presents an interesting problem. We agree with Mackie and Smith (1998) that future research needs to combine cognitive and affective considerations toward a more integrated understanding of intergroup prejudice. We suspect that, whereas stereotypes may still be activated, and the content of stereotypes may be slow to change, the affective tone of stereotypes may shift as a result of intergroup contact. Thus, after optimal contact, the "lazy" outgroup may still be seen as "lazy" – but "lazy" might take on such new affective qualities as "laid back" and cultivating a relaxed enjoyment of life. To explore these possibilities, future contact research must be careful to measure intergroup prejudice both in terms of affective connections to and cognitive representations of outgroup members.

References

Adorno, T. W., Frenkel-Brunswik, E., Levinson, D. J., & Sanford, R. N. (1950). *The authoritarian personality*. New York: Harper.

Allport, G. W. (1954). *The nature of prejudice*. Reading, MA: Addison-Wesley.

Amir, Y. (1976). The role of intergroup contact in change of prejudice and ethnic relations. In P. A. Katz (Ed.), *Toward the elimination of racism* (pp. 245–308). Elmsford, NY: Pergamon Press.

Ashmore, R. D., & Del Boca, F. K. (1981). Conceptual approaches to stereotypes and stereotyping. In D. L. Hamilton (Ed.), *Cognitive processes in stereotyping and intergroup behavior* (pp. 1–35). Hillsdale, NJ: Erlbaum.

Batson, C. D., Polycarpou, M. P., Harmon-Jones, E., Imhoff, H. J., Mitchener, E. C., Bednar, L. L., Klein, T. R., & Highberger, L. (1997). Empathy and attitudes: Can feelings for a member of a stigmatized group improve feelings toward the group? *Journal of Personality and Social Psychology, 72*, 105–118.

Bogardus, E. S. (1928). *Immigration and race attitudes*. Boston: Heath.

Breckler, S. J., & Wiggins, E. C. (1989). Affect versus evaluation in the structure of attitudes. *Journal of Experimental Social Psychology, 25*, 253–271.

Brewer, M. B., Campbell, D. T., & Levine, R. A. (1971). Cross-cultural test of the relationship between affect and evaluation. *Proceedings of the Annual Convention of the American Psychological Association, 6*, 213–214.

Brigham, J. C. (1993). College students' racial attitudes. *Journal of Applied Social Psychology, 23*, 1933–1967.

Britt, T. W., Boniecki, K. A., Vescio, T. K., & Biernat, M. (1996). Intergroup anxiety: A person × situation approach. *Personality and Social Psychology Bulletin, 22*, 1177–1188.

Brown, R., Condor, S., Mathews, A., Wade, G., & Williams, J. (1986). Explaining intergroup differentiation in an industrial organization. *Journal of Occupational Psychology, 59*, 273–286.

Cook, S. W. (1984). Cooperative interaction in multiethnic contexts. In N. Miller & M. B. Brewer (Eds.), *Groups in contact: The psychology of desegregation* (pp. 155–185). Orlando: Academic Press.

Deutsch, M., & Collins, M. E. (1951). *Interracial housing: A psychological evaluation of a social experiment*. Minneapolis: University of Minnesota Press.

Devine, P. G., & Vasquez, K. A. (1998). The rocky road to positive intergroup relations. In J. L. Eberhardt & S. T. Fiske (Eds.), *Confronting racism: The problem and the response* (pp. 234–262). Thousand Oaks, CA: Sage.

Dunton, B. C., & Fazio, R. H. (1997). Categorization by race: The impact of automatic and controlled components of racial prejudice. *Journal of Experimental Social Psychology, 33*, 451–470.

Eagly, A. H., & Chaiken, S. (1993). *The psychology of attitudes*. Fort Worth: Harcourt Brace Jovanovich.

Esses, V. M., & Dovidio, J. F. (2002). The role of emotions in determining willingness to engage in intergroup contact. *Personality and Social Psychology Bulletin, 28*, 1202–1214.

Esses, V. M., Haddock, G., & Zanna, M. P. (1993). Values, stereotypes, and emotions as determinants of intergroup attitudes. In D. Mackie & D. Hamilton (Eds.), *Affect, cognition, and stereotyping: Interactive processes in group perception* (pp. 137–166). San Diego: Academic Press.

Ford, W. S. (1986). Favorable intergroup contact may not reduce prejudice: Inconclusive journal evidence, 1960–1984. *Sociology and Social Research, 70*, 256–258.

Hamberger, J., & Hewstone, M. (1997). Inter-ethnic contact as a predictor of blatant and subtle prejudice: Tests of a model in four West European nations. *British Journal of Social Psychology, 36*, 173–190.

Hamilton, D. L. (Ed.). (1981a). *Cognitive processes in stereotyping and intergroup behavior*. Hillsdale, NJ: Erlbaum.

Hamilton, D. L. (1981b). Stereotyping and intergroup behavior: Some thoughts on the cognitive approach. In D. L. Hamilton (Ed.), *Cognitive processes in stereotyping and intergroup behavior* (pp. 333–353). Hillsdale, NJ: Lawrence Erlbaum Associates.

Hamilton, D. L., Stroessner, S. J., & Driscoll, D. M. (1994). Social cognition and the study of stereotyping. In P. G. Devine, D. L. Hamilton, & Ostrom, T. M. (Eds.), *Social cognition: Impact on social psychology* (pp. 291–321). New York: Academic Press.

Herek, G. M., & Capitanio, J. P. (1996). "Some of my best friends": Intergroup contact, concealable stigma, and heterosexuals' attitudes toward gay men and lesbians. *Personality and Social Psychology Bulletin, 22*, 412–424.

Hewstone, M., & Brown, R. (1986). Contact is not enough: An intergroup perspective on the 'contact hypothesis.' In M. Hewstone & R. Brown (Eds.), *Contact and conflict in intergroup encounters* (pp. 1–44). Oxford, UK: Basil Blackwell.

Islam, M. R., & Hewstone, M. (1993). Dimensions of contact as predictors of intergroup anxiety, perceived outgroup variability, and outgroup attitude: An integrative model. *Personality and Social Psychology Bulletin, 19*, 700–710.

Jackson, J. W. (1993). Contact theory of intergroup hostility: A review and evaluation of the theoretical and empirical literature. *International Journal of Group Tensions, 23*, 43–65.

Johnson, B. T., & Eagly, A. H. (2000). Quantitative synthesis of social psychological research. In H. T. Reis & C. M. Judd (Eds.), *Handbook of research methods in social psychology*. London: Cambridge University Press.

Katz, I., & Hass, R. G. (1988). Racial ambivalence and American value conflict. *Journal of Personality and Social Psychology, 55*, 893–905.

Kinder, D. R., & Sanders, L. M. (1996). *Divided by color: Racial politics and democratic ideals*. Chicago: University of Chicago Press.

Luiz, D., & Krige, P. (1981). The effect of social contact between South African white and colored adolescent girls. *Journal of Social Psychology, 113*, 153–158.

Mackie, D. M., & Hamilton, D. L. (1993a). *Affect, cognition, and stereotyping*. San Diego: Academic Press.

Mackie, D. M., & Hamilton, D. L. (1993b). Affect, cognition, and stereotyping: Concluding comments. In D. M. Mackie & D. L. Hamilton (Eds.), *Affect, cognition, and stereotyping: Interactive processes in group perception* (pp. 371–383). San Diego: Academic Press.

Mackie, D. M., & Smith, E. R. (1998). Intergroup relations: Insights from a theoretically integrative approach. *Psychological Review, 105*, 499–529.

Mackie, D. M., & Smith, E. R. (2002). Intergroup emotions and the social self: Prejudice reconceptualized as differentiated reactions to outgroups. In J. P. Forgas & K. D. Williams (Eds.), *The social self: Cognitive, interpersonal, and intergroup perspectives* (pp. 309–326). New York: Psychology Press.

Mann, J. H. (1959). The relationship between cognitive, affective, and behavioral aspects of racial prejudice. *Journal of Social Psychology, 49*, 223–228.

McConahay, J. B., Hardee, B. B., & Batts, V. (1981). Has racism declined in America? It depends on who is asking and what is asked. *Journal of Conflict Resolution, 25*, 563–579.

McLaughlin-Volpe, T., Aron, A., Wright, S. C., & Reis, H. T. (2000). *Intergroup social interaction and intergroup prejudice: Quantity versus quality*. Manuscript submitted for publication.

NES Guide to Public Opinion and Electoral Behavior, 1995–2000. Ann Arbor: National Election Studies, Center for Political Studies, University of Michigan. Retrieved from: http://www.umich.edu/~nes/nesguide/nesguide.htm

Osgood, C. E., Suci, G. J., & Tannenbaum, P. H. (1957). *The measurement of meaning*. Urbana, IL: University of Illinois Press.

Ostrom, T. M. (1969). The relationship between the affective, behavioral, and cognitive components of attitude. *Journal of Experimental Social Psychology, 5*, 12–30.

Ostrom, T. M., Skowronski, J. J., & Nowak, A. (1994). The cognitive foundation of attitudes: It's a wonderful construct. In P. G. Devine, D. L. Hamilton, & Ostrom, T. M. (Eds.), *Social cognition: Impact on social psychology* (pp. 195–258). New York: Academic Press.

Patchen, M., Davidson, J. D., Hofmann, G., & Brown, W. R. (1977). Determinants of students' interracial behavior and opinion change. *Sociology of Education, 50*, 55–75.

Pettigrew, T. F. (1971). *Racially separate or together?* New York: McGraw-Hill.

Pettigrew, T. F. (1981). Extending the stereotype concept. In D. L. Hamilton (Ed.), *Cognitive processes in stereotyping and intergroup behavior* (pp. 303–331). Hillsdale, NJ: Erlbaum.

Pettigrew, T. F. (1997a). Generalized intergroup contact effects on prejudice. *Personality and Social Psychology Bulletin, 23*, 173–185.

Pettigrew, T. F. (1997b). The affective component of prejudice: Empirical support of the new view. In S. A. Tuch & J. K. Martin (Eds.), *Racial attitudes in the 1990s: Continuity and change* (pp. 76–90). Westport, CT: Praeger.

Pettigrew, T. F. (1998). Intergroup contact theory. *Annual Review of Psychology, 49*, 65–85.

Pettigrew, T. F., & Tropp, L. R. (2000). Does intergroup contact reduce prejudice? Recent meta-analytic findings. In S. Oskamp (Ed.), *Reducing prejudice and discrimination: The Claremont Symposium on Applied Social Psychology* (pp. 93–114). Mahwah, NJ: Erlbaum.

Pettigrew, T. F., & Tropp, L. R. (2003). *A meta-analytic test of intergroup contact theory.* Manuscript submitted for publication.

Plant, E. A., & Devine, P. G. (1998). Internal and external motivation to respond without prejudice. *Journal of Personality and Social Psychology, 75*, 811–832.

Riordan, C. (1978). Equal-status interracial contact: A review and revision of the concept. *International Journal of Intercultural Relations, 2*, 161–185.

Riordan, C. (1987). Intergroup contact in small cities. *International Journal of Intercultural Relations, 11*, 143–154.

Rojahn, K., & Pettigrew, T. F. (1992). Memory for schema-relevant information: A meta-analysis resolution. *British Journal of Social Psychology, 31*, 81–109.

Rosenthal, R. (1991). *Meta-analytic procedures for social research.* Newbury Park: Sage.

Rosenthal, R. (1995). Writing meta-analytic reviews. *Psychological Bulletin, 118*, 183–192.

Rothbart, M. (1996). Category-exemplar dynamics and stereotype change. *International Journal of Intercultural Relations, 20*, 305–321.

Rothbart, M., & John, O. P. (1985). Social categorization and behavioral episodes: A cognitive analysis of the effects of intergroup contact. *Journal of Social Issues, 41*, 81–104.

Rothbart, M., & John, O. P. (1993). Intergroup relations and stereotype change: A social-cognitive analysis and some longitudinal findings. In P. M. Sniderman, P. E. Tetlock, & E. G. Carmines (Eds.), *Prejudice, politics, and the American dilemma* (pp. 32–59). Stanford, CA: Stanford University Press.

Rothbart, M., & Lewis, S. (1994). Cognitive processes and intergroup relations: A historical perspective. In P. G. Devine, D. L. Hamilton, & Ostrom, T. M. (Eds.), *Social cognition: Impact on social psychology* (pp. 347–382). New York: Academic Press.

Rothbart, M., Sriram, N., & Davis-Stitt, C. (1996). The retrieval of typical and atypical category members. *Journal of Experimental Social Psychology, 32*, 309–336.

Smith, E. R. (1993). Social identity and social emotions: Toward new conceptualizations of prejudice. In D. Mackie & D. Hamilton (Eds.), *Affect, cognition, and stereotyping: Interactive processes in group perception* (pp. 137–166). San Diego: Academic Press.

Stangor, C., Jonas, K., Stroebe, W., & Hewstone, M. (1996). Influence of student exchange on national stereotypes, attitudes, and perceived group variability. *European Journal of Social Psychology, 26*, 663–675.

Stangor, C., Sullivan, L. A., & Ford, T. E. (1991). Affective and cognitive determinants of prejudice. *Social Cognition, 9*, 359–380.

Stephan, W. G., Boniecki, K. A., Ybarra, O., Bettencourt, A., Ervin, K. S., Jackson, L. A., McNatt, P. S., & Renfro, C. S. (2002). The role of threats in the racial attitudes of blacks and whites. *Personality and Social Psychology Bulletin, 28*, 1242–1254.

Stephan, W. G., & Finlay, K. (1999). The role of empathy in improving intergroup relations. *Journal of Social Issues, 55*, 729–743.

Stephan, W. G., & Stephan, C. W. (1985). Intergroup anxiety. *Journal of Social Issues, 41*, 157–175.

Stephan, W. G., & Stephan, C. W. (1993). Cognition and affect in stereotyping: Parallel interactive networks. In D. M. Mackie & D. L. Hamilton (Eds.), *Affect, cognition, and stereotyping: Interactive processes in group perception* (pp. 111–136). San Diego: Academic Press.

Tajfel, H. (1969). Cognitive aspects of prejudice. *Journal of Social Issues, 25*, 79–97.

Tajfel, H. (1981). *Human groups and social categories*. Cambridge: Cambridge University Press.

Taylor, S. (1981). A categorization approach to stereotyping. In D. Hamilton (Ed.), *Cognitive processes in stereotyping and intergroup behavior* (pp. 83–114). Hillsdale, NJ: Erlbaum.

Tropp, L. R. (2003). The psychological impact of prejudice: Implications for intergroup contact. *Group Processes and Intergroup Relations, 6*, 131–149.

Tropp, L. R., & Pettigrew, T. F. (2004). *Examining relationships between intergroup contact and multiple indicators of prejudice*. Manuscript submitted for publication.

Vorauer, J. D., Main, K. J., & O'Connell, G. B. (1998). How do individuals expect to be viewed by members of lower status groups? Content and implications of meta-stereotypes. *Journal of Personality and Social Psychology, 75*, 917–937.

Walker, I., & Smith, H. (Eds.). (2001). *Relative deprivation: Specification, development and integration*. New York: Cambridge University Press.

Weber, R., & Crocker, J. (1983). Cognitive processes in the revision of stereotypic beliefs. *Journal of Personality and Social Psychology, 45*, 961–977.

Wilder, D. A. (1984). Intergroup contact: The typical member and the exception to the rule. *Journal of Experimental Social Psychology, 20*, 177–194.

Wilder, D. A. (1986). Cognitive factors affecting the success of intergroup contact. In S. W. Worchel & W. G. Austin (Eds.), *Psychology of intergroup relations* (pp. 49–66). Chicago: Nelson-Hall.

Wright, S. C., Aron, A., & Tropp, L. R. (2002). Including others (and groups) in the self: Self-expansion and intergroup relations. In J. P. Forgas & K. D. Williams (Eds.), *The social self: Cognitive, interpersonal, and intergroup perspectives* (pp. 343–363). New York: Psychology Press.

Wright, S. C.,, & Van der Zande, C. C. (October, 1999). *Bicultural friends: When cross-group friendships cause improved intergroup attitudes*. Paper presented at the annual meeting of the Society for Experimental Psychology, St. Louis.

Zajonc, R. B. (1980). Feeling and thinking: Preferences need no inferences. *American Psychologist, 35*, 151–175.

Zanna, M. P., & Rempel, J. K. (1988). Attitudes: A new look at an old concept. In D. Bar Tal & A. Kruglanski (Eds.), *The social psychology of knowledge* (pp. 315–334). Cambridge: Cambridge University Press.

13

Judgments of Deserving and the Emotional Consequences of Stigmatization

Cheryl R. Kaiser and Brenda Major

Prejudice and discrimination are a part of all human cultures (Sidanius & Pratto, 1999). In all societies, some social groups are valued, treated respectfully, and can easily access important material and social resources, whereas other groups are stigmatized – they are devalued, treated disrespectfully, and often have difficulty obtaining even basic resources. Members of stigmatized groups face prejudice in economic, interpersonal, and political domains. For instance, relative to European Americans, African Americans on average possess less formal education and have less access to resources, such as health insurance, housing, and employment opportunities (Braddock & McPartland, 1987; Massey, Gross, & Shibuya, 1994; Snowden & Thomas, 2000). Gay men and lesbians and the obese frequently experience social rejection, even from their own families (Baker, 2002; Crandall, 1995). These threats call into question one's basic worth as a human being and can thus pose threats to psychological well-being.

In this chapter, we examine the emotional consequences of being a target of prejudice and discrimination. Individuals are targets of prejudice and discrimination when they or members of their social group are viewed and treated in an unjust negative manner because of their social identity (Major, Quinton, & McCoy, 2002). It is important to note that individuals may *objectively* be targets of prejudice but not *perceive* themselves as such. Furthermore, individuals may blame their own (or their groups') outcomes on their *social identity*, but not perceive those outcomes as unjust. Additionally, to the extent that social identities function as self-aspects, appraisals of events with respect to those social identities will trigger emotions similar to those experienced at the individual level (Smith, 1993). Thus, individuals need not personally experience prejudice to experience it as a threat against the self and to experience strong emotion in response (Smith, 1993).

Allport (1954/1979) observed that responses to being a victim of prejudice can be either intropunitive (i.e., directed toward the self) or extropunitive (i.e., directed toward others). We believe a similar distinction can be applied to emotional responses to prejudice. Examples of self-directed emotions include feelings of shame, guilt, and humiliation. Examples of other-directed emotions include feelings of anger, hostility, and resentment toward others.[1] Emotions are directed inward when individuals appraise themselves as responsible for an outcome (Abramson, Seligman, & Teasdale, 1978; Lazarus, 1999). In contrast, emotions are directed outward when others are appraised as responsible for an outcome (Weiner, 1995).

Although prejudice researchers have sometimes combined self-directed and other-directed emotions into composite measures of general negative affect, we believe this is a mistake. Self- and other-directed emotional responses to prejudice may sometimes co-exist, but theoretically these types of emotional responses are quite distinct and result from different types of responsibility appraisals (Abramson et al., 1978; Weiner, 1995). Additionally, several studies on prejudice illustrate the importance of differentiating between self-directed and other-directed emotions (e.g., Major, Kaiser, & McCoy, 2003; Vorauer & Kumhyr, 2001).

In addition to this distinction between self-directed and other-directed emotions, emotional responses can also be experienced at the individual or group level (Doosje et al., 1998; Mackie, Devos, & Smith, 2000; Smith, 1993). According to self-categorization theory (Turner, 1985), when social identities are salient, individuals define themselves as interchangeable group members rather than distinct individuals. In other words, the ingroup becomes incorporated into the self (Smith & Henry, 1996). Recent theory and research illustrate how emotions can be experienced on behalf of social groups (Doosje et al., 1998; Mackie et al., 2000; Smith, 1993). For example, drawing on self-categorization theory, Smith and colleagues propose that, when social identity is salient, individuals consider group outcomes rather than personal outcomes when appraising social identity-relevant threats. Furthermore, appraisals of whether the ingroup will be hurt or benefited by events influence emotional consequences. According to Mackie et al. (2000, p. 603), "When appraisals occur on a group basis, emotions are experienced on behalf of the ingroup, and the ingroup and outgroup become the targets of emotion." For members of stigmatized groups, encountering evidence that one's group is a target of prejudice can influence ingroup-directed feelings, such as collective self-esteem. Likewise, the stigmatized might respond to a single outgroup member's prejudicial behavior by experiencing other-directed emotions, such as anger, toward the entire outgroup.

Although certainly not the only dimensions along which emotions can be distinguished, these inner-directed versus outer-directed and

[1] Although emotional responses to prejudice could conceivably be positive, we are aware of no theory or research leading to this prediction. Accordingly, we focus exclusively here on negative emotional responses to prejudice.

Direction of Emotion

Target of Emotion	Inner-Directed	Outer-Directed
Individual	Individual Self-Directed Emotions	Individual Outer-Directed Emotions
Collective	Collective Self-Directed Emotions	Collective Outer-Directed Emotions

FIGURE 13.1. Emotional responses to prejudice.

individually experienced versus collectively experienced dimensions suggest four broad categories of emotional response to prejudice (see Figure 13.1): (1) self-directed emotions experienced on behalf of the individual self; (2) self-directed emotions experienced on behalf of the collective self (groups with which one identifies), (3) other-directed emotions experienced toward a particular individual (e.g., a single prejudiced person), or (4) other-directed emotions experienced toward a collective (e.g., prejudiced outgroups).

In this chapter, we first review research and theory on the relationship between prejudice and emotion. Our review highlights the complexity of this relationship. Sometimes prejudice results in negative individual or collective self-directed or other-directed emotions, but sometimes it does not. In some cases, groups who chronically face prejudice have more positive feelings toward themselves and their group than groups who infrequently face prejudice. Sometimes victims of prejudice display anger against individuals or entire outgroups; sometimes they do not. We argue that judgments of deserving are the proximal determinant of individual and collective emotional responses to prejudice. We discuss two antecedents to deserving judgments: situational cues to justice and chronic ideologies about fairness.

PREJUDICE AND EMOTION

Individual Self-Directed Emotions

The majority of research addressing emotional responses to being the target of prejudice has focused on the implications of prejudice for personal self-esteem. Although scholars disagree about whether self-esteem is best characterized as an affective state tied to specific self-relevant emotions or a self-attitude with a large valence component (see Baumeister, 1998, for a review), in this chapter, we will treat self-esteem as a self-directed affective state characterized primarily by the emotions pride and shame. We use this approach because research investigating specific self-directed emotions experienced by targets of prejudice is rare, and because historical and recent analyses suggest that self-esteem is closely tied to shame and pride (Brown & Marshall, 2001; James, 1890). For example, William James (1890) described self-esteem as a self-directed evaluation marked by specific emotions such as pride and shame that arise from our successes and failures in life. More recently, Brown and Marshall (2001) examined the relationship between self-esteem and a large number of positive and negative affective states. Across three studies, self-esteem was most closely characterized by feelings of pride and shame.

Classic theoretical perspectives on responses to prejudice assumed that prejudice lowers the self-esteem of its targets because they come to internalize society's negative attitudes toward them. For example, in commenting on their observation that a large percentage of African American children in their study seemed to prefer white skin coloring to black skin coloring, Clark and Clark (1950) wrote,

> They [their data] would seem to point strongly to the need for a definite mental hygiene and educational program that would relieve children of the tremendous burden of feelings of inadequacy and inferiority which seem to become integrated into the very structure of the personality as it is developing. (p. 350)

These predictions stem from reflected appraisal self-theories (e.g., Cooley, 1956), which predict that self-views are a function of how one is perceived by others.

Although scholars have searched for evidence that prejudice lowers self-esteem, the empirical evidence is mixed. There is not a direct relationship between membership in an objectively stigmatized group and lower personal self-esteem (Crocker & Major, 1989). Members of some groups that are chronic targets of prejudice and discrimination (e.g., African Americans) have higher self-esteem on average, compared with nonstigmatized groups (e.g., European Americans) (Twenge & Crocker, 2002), whereas members of other devalued groups (e.g., overweight white women) report lower self-esteem on average compared with groups more valued and privileged in society (e.g., nonoverweight individuals) (Miller & Downey, 1999). Within the same stigmatized group, some individuals report high self-esteem and others report low self-esteem (Friedman & Brownell, 1995). The link between *perceived* prejudice and self-esteem is more consistent. A number of questionnaire studies have found that the more members of stigmatized groups, such as women and ethnic and racial minorities perceive themselves (or their group) as targets of discrimination, the lower their self-esteem (Branscombe, Schmitt, & Harvey, 1999; Schmitt et al., 2002) (but see Major et al., 2002, for a critique of this research).

Collective Self-Directed Emotions

Research examining collective self-directed (ingroup directed) emotions in response to prejudice is rare. One type of ingroup-directed emotion that has received attention, is collective self-esteem. Collective self-esteem, the group-level equivalent of personal self-esteem, is an overall feeling of self-perceived worthiness of one's social groups (Luhtanen & Crocker, 1992). It reflects global feelings toward the group and is marked by feelings such as group pride and group shame. One frequently used measure of collective self-esteem is Luhtanen and Crocker's (1992) Collective Self-Esteem Scale. Though this scale has four subscales, research indicates that the private regard subscale, on which participants indicate their agreement with statements such as, "I feel good about the social groups I belong to" and "I often regret that I belong to some of the social groups I do" (reverse scored) best characterizes the construct collective self-esteem (Crocker et al., 1994; Ethier & Deaux, 1994).

Internalization perspectives suggest that members of devalued groups will experience negative ingroup-directed feelings. For example, Allport (1954/1979) argued, "A Jew may hate his historical religion (for if it did not exist he would not be marked out for persecution).... Since he cannot escape his own group, he thus in a real sense hates himself – or at least the part of himself that is Jewish" (p. 151). Likewise, Allport discusses how for African Americans "... some degree of in-group hate seems almost inevitable" (p. 152). Branscombe and colleagues argue that because prejudice threatens social identity, an important part of the self, it will have negative implications for collective self-esteem (Branscombe et al., 1999).

As with the findings for personal self-esteem, empirical findings regarding the impact of prejudice on collective self-esteem are mixed. Contrary to the aforementioned predictions, being a member of a group that is regularly a target of prejudice does not presume low collective self-esteem. Members of devalued ethnic groups (African Americans and Asians), for example, do not report lower collective self-esteem relative to members of more valued ethnic groups (European Americans) (Crocker et al., 1994). In fact, African Americans report higher collective self-esteem relative to both Asians and European Americans (Crocker et al., 1994). The finding that African Americans (who frequently face racial discrimination) report higher collective self-esteem than European Americans (who rarely face racial discrimination) is clearly inconsistent with theories arguing that being a target of prejudice directly lowers collective self-esteem.

Research examining the correlation between *perceptions* of prejudice and collective self-esteem is also mixed. Several questionnaire studies found that perceiving oneself or one's group as a target of prejudice is negatively correlated with collective self-esteem among African Americans and women (Branscombe et al., 1999; Schmitt et al., 2002). Likewise, perceiving that others do not have positive beliefs about one's ethnic group is related to lower collective self-esteem among Asians (Crocker et al., 1994). Among African Americans, however, perceiving that others do not like their group is unrelated to collective self-esteem (Crocker et al., 1994; Rowley et al., 1998).

Individual and Collective Other-Directed Emotions

It is frequently assumed that the experience of prejudice will result in negative emotions directed toward those felt to be responsible, emotions such as anger, resentment, and hostility (Adams, 1965; Crosby, 1976; Tajfel & Turner, 1986; Walster, Walster, & Berscheid, 1978). The assumption that prejudice leads directly to outgroup derogation is captured in the following quote from a Jewish student described in Allport (1954/1979):

> I am intolerant because I have been a victim of intolerance during my early formative years. The hatreds and prejudices I have developed are reactions used as defense mechanisms. If Joe Doakes hates me I naturally will return the compliment.

Studies exploring the prevalence and nature of other-directed emotions among targets of prejudice are rare. Furthermore, little attempt has been made to differentiate emotions felt toward a prejudiced individual from those felt toward a prejudiced outgroup. Empirical evidence addressing whether being the target of prejudice leads to negative other-directed emotions is mixed. Correlational data show that African Americans who more readily perceive themselves or their group as targets of prejudice are also more likely to experience hostility toward European Americans (Branscombe et al., 1999). Likewise, women who perceive themselves as targets of sexism frequently report experiencing anger (Swim et al., 2001). However, relative deprivation research demonstrates that people who are objectively disadvantaged often do not report feeling angry about their situations (Crosby, 1982).

Summary

Although theories about the impact of prejudice on the emotions of its targets abound, empirical studies exploring this issue are surprisingly rare. Furthermore, research findings are mixed. Some research suggests that membership in a group that is a target of prejudice is associated with negative self-directed emotions, such as low personal and collective self-esteem. Likewise, other research suggests that perceiving oneself or one's group as a victim of prejudice is associated with low personal and collective self-esteem. In contrast, other research has failed to find these links, suggesting that the association between prejudice and individual and collective self-directed emotions is more complex. Similar inconsistencies are characteristic of the limited research investigating the link between being a target of prejudice and other-directed emotions. How can we resolve these inconsistencies?

THE MODERATING ROLE OF DESERVING

We believe that an important moderator of how individuals respond emotionally to negative outcomes that they perceive are linked to their group membership is whether they cognitively appraise those outcomes as deserved. The concept of deserving is central to many social justice theories (e.g., Adams, 1965; Crosby, 1976; Deutsch, 1985; Walster et al., 1978).[2] Judgments of deserving are cognitive judgments with affective consequences, and refer to the relationship between individuals and their outcomes (Lerner, 1987). The cognitive aspect of deserving is "the judgment, often tacit, that someone or some category of people, is entitled to a particular set of outcomes by virtue of who they are and what they have done" (Lerner, 1987, p. 108). Individuals feel they deserve outcomes to the extent that they have engaged in appropriate behaviors to achieve those outcomes or have certain ascribed characteristics that are deemed worthy for possessing those outcomes. The affective component of deserving stems from "... an imperative, a sense of requiredness between the actor's perceived outcomes and the person's attributes of acts" (pp. 107–108). That is, the affective consequences of deserving stem from moral judgments about the relationship between one's inputs or attributes and resulting outcomes. Although most theory and research have focused on judgments of the deserving of individuals, Lerner's definition makes clear that judgments also are made about the deserving of groups. Categories of people (convicted felons, women) may not be seen as deserving of certain

[2] Historically, the term deserving often has been used interchangeably with that of entitlement. Because of their substantial overlap, we too will use these terms interchangeably. The main distinction between entitlement and deserving is that judgments of deserving are made about outcomes that are contingent on an individual's actions, whereas judgments of entitlement are made about outcomes that are based on adherence to norms or rules without any particular reference to an individual's actions (Feather, 1999). Individuals feel entitled to outcomes because of ascribed characteristics (e.g., sex and race), whereas they feel deserving of outcomes because of achieved characteristics (e.g., a strong work ethic). The distinction between entitlement and deserving is particularly subtle within the context of prejudice, because ascribed characteristics are often used to draw judgments about a group or individual's achieved characteristics (Jost & Banaji, 1994).

outcomes (e.g., the right to vote) because of assumptions about their inferior characteristics.

Several theorists (e.g., Crosby, 1982; Feather, 1999; Major, 1994) assert that judgments of deserving are the proximal determinant of emotional responses to socially distributed outcomes, such as emotions of anger and sadness. According to Shaver and colleagues (1987), the critical factor determining whether one experiences anger or sadness in response to negative events is the judgment that the negative event was "illegitimate, unfair, wrong, contrary to what ought to be" (Shaver et al., 1987) or, in other words, undeserved. When negative outcomes are judged to be deserved, the result is sadness; when they are judged to be undeserved, the result is anger. With respect to emotional responses to stigmatization, we suggest that the more members of stigmatized groups judge their own negative outcomes, devalued status, or poor treatment as deserved, the more likely they are to experience negative personal self-directed emotions such as sadness and shame (Crocker & Major, 1994; Major, 1994). Likewise, to the extent that the ingroup is part of the self, negative personal self-directed emotions may be experienced when the *ingroup*'s poor treatment, negative outcomes, or devalued status are judged as deserved. Furthermore, the judgment that the ingroup deserves their poor outcomes may also lead to negative *collective* self-directed emotions (e.g., being ashamed of one's group). This prediction is grounded in theory, and data showing that self-blame is damaging to self-esteem if the aspect of self that is blamed cannot be changed (e.g., one's character) (Janoff-Bulman & Lang-Gunn, 1988). A similar process may operate at the group level, whereby blaming the poor outcomes of one's group on stable, internal attributes of the group (e.g., a lack of intelligence) is apt to lead to lower collective self-esteem.

In contrast, seeing oneself or one's group as undeserving of negative treatment or devalued status should mitigate these negative personal and collective self-directed emotions. Members of stigmatized groups who perceive either their own personal treatment, or the treatment of their group, as undeserved are likely to experience anger and negative other-directed emotions in response (Shaver et al., 1987). Note that it is possible for outcomes to be judged as deserved when those outcomes are in fact due to prejudice. Likewise, outcomes may be judged as undeserved even when they are indeed an accurate reflection of inputs. Furthermore, it is possible that outcomes may be judged as deserved even when individuals recognize that discrimination may have been a factor. This may occur if individuals have an *independent* basis for assessing personal or group deserving (such as knowledge of their own or their group's performance, or beliefs about their own or their group's qualifications). Under these conditions, the effects of procedural fairness cues on assessments of deserving, and subsequent emotions, are likely to be minimized.

Our deserving analysis applies best to situations in which principles of equity theory (Adams, 1965) or social exchange theory (Thibaut & Kelley, 1959) are relevant – that is, in situations in which it is generally believed that a person's or group's outcomes (broadly defined) should, to some degree, reflect that person's or group's inputs or contributions. Although research has demonstrated the usefulness of exchange and equity theories for understanding individual's reactions to outcomes in a wide variety of domains (Walster et al., 1978), there are some domains in which principles of equity are considered less appropriate than other distributive justice principles (e.g., family relationships). Our analysis is not intended to apply to those domains. We also confine our analysis to understanding emotional reactions to outcomes perceived as linked to one's membership in a social group.

Antecedents to Judgments of Deserving

What leads individuals to feel that their own poor outcomes, treatment, or status, or those of their ingroup, are deserved or undeserved? Many factors shape deserving judgments, including laws, social comparisons, and goals (Major, 1994). A full discussion of this complex issue is beyond the scope of this chapter (see Adams, 1965; Deutsch, 1985; Feather, 1999; Major, 1994). Social exchange theory and equity theory suggest that outcomes are judged as deserved when they are believed to accurately reflect the relevant contributions or qualities of the individual(s) or group(s) receiving those outcomes. Accordingly, judgments of deserving with respect to outcomes linked to stigma are likely to be influenced by beliefs about how accurately personal or group outcomes reflect personal or group inputs, and by beliefs about the fairness of the procedures by which outcomes are distributed generally in society. In the following section, we briefly discuss perceptions of procedural justice and ideologies about fairness as antecedents to judgments of deserving.

Procedural Justice

Perceptions of the fairness of the procedures used to allocate outcomes to individuals or groups affect whether outcomes are judged to accurately reflect contributions (Lind & Tyler, 1988). Thus, within an equity-relevant context, information pertinent to violations of procedural fairness should affect judgments of deserving (and through these judgments, emotions). Unfair procedures include those characterized by disrespect, inconsistent application, bias, or insufficient information (Lind & Tyler, 1988). Individuals who learn that they received poor outcomes in the context of unfair procedures are likely to feel undeserving of those outcomes, because the outcomes are not assumed to accurately reflect their inputs. In contrast, the perception that rules of procedural fairness were followed can lead to perceptions of deserving, even when individuals and groups actually had no influence over the actual distribution of outcomes (Lind & Tyler, 1988).

Justice-Related Ideologies

Judgments of deserving with respect to specific outcomes also are influenced by individuals' ideologies about the fairness of societal distributions of rewards and punishments. Ideologies are attitudes, beliefs, and values that are collectively held within society. Some ideologies are *legitimizing ideologies* (Sidanius & Pratto, 1999), in that they serve to justify and legitimize unequal status and outcome distributions among groups or individuals. Legitimizing ideologies justify social inequality by attributing good or poor outcomes to dispositions and behaviors of that person or group and holding them responsible for their outcomes. In North America, examples of legitimizing ideologies include the beliefs in a Just World (Lerner, 1977), in the Protestant Work Ethic (Mirels & Garrett, 1971), and in individual mobility (Tajfel & Turner, 1986). The Belief in a Just World, for example, leads to the inference that individuals and groups get what they deserve, and deserve what they get. Consequently, those who are devalued and disadvantaged must somehow deserve their poor fate. The Protestant Work Ethic ideology includes the belief that individual hard work leads to success and that lack of success is caused by moral failings. Thus, those who fare well deserve positive outcomes because they work hard and are morally superior, whereas those who fare poorly deserve negative outcomes because they are lazy and morally flawed. Stereotypes about disadvantaged groups, such as those portraying African Americans as lazy or women as indecisive, also function as legitimizing ideologies (Jost & Banaji, 1994). Stereotypes may be used to justify denying valuable outcomes to entire categories of people.

In sum, we argue that judgments of individual and collective deserving are proximal determinants of individual and collective emotional responses to prejudicial treatment. Judgments of personal and group deserving are shaped, among other things, by perceptions of procedural justice and by ideologies about the ways in which outcomes are distributed to individuals and groups in society. In the remainder of this chapter, we discuss our research examining the impact of perceived prejudice on personal and collective emotional responses, and discuss how perceptions of deserving moderate this link.

DESERVING AND PERSONAL SELF-DIRECTED EMOTIONS

In an attempt to account for the high personal self-esteem observed among many stigmatized groups, Crocker and Major (1989) hypothesized that the perception of prejudice can, under some circumstances, provide members of devalued groups with a means of personal self-esteem protection.

Specifically, they proposed that when individuals can attribute negative outcomes to prejudice based on their group membership, rather than to internal, stable, aspects of the self, this will protect their personal self-esteem. They based their hypothesis on theoretical models of emotion positing that blaming negative events on causes for which one is not responsible (such as the prejudice against one's group) protects personal affect and self-esteem, compared with blaming negative outcomes on causes for which one is responsible (such as one's lack of ability) (e.g., Abramson et al., 1978; Weiner, 1995). From a deserving perspective, the perception of prejudice signals that outcome allocations are procedurally unfair and hence are not an accurate reflection of inputs. Accordingly, the perception of prejudice should reduce the extent to which negative outcomes are judged as personally deserved. By so doing, they should buffer personal self-esteem.

Prejudice as a Cue to Procedural Injustice

Several studies demonstrate that cues to prejudice-related injustice can protect the stigmatized from experiencing negative personal self-directed emotions following receipt of negative outcomes (Crocker et al., 1991; Major, Kaiser, & McCoy, 2003; Major, Quinton, & Schmader, 2003; Major et al., 1998). For example, in one study (Crocker et al., 1991), women received negative performance feedback on an essay from a man who expressed either very traditional (sexist) or liberal views toward women. Women who were negatively evaluated by a sexist man reported fewer depressed emotions (e.g., blue, sad) relative to women evaluated by a liberal man. In another study (Major, Kaiser, et al., 2003), men and women imagined that a professor rejected their request to enroll in a course. One group learned that the professor did not admit any members of their own gender group into the course, but let in ten members of the other gender group. Another group learned that they were the only students not permitted to add the course (because the professor thought they were unintelligent). Participants who assumed sexism was responsible for their rejection blamed themselves less and reported fewer depressed emotions compared with those who assumed the rejection was due to their lack of intelligence. Furthermore, blaming the rejection on prejudice rather than on a lack of intelligence mediated emotional responses to the rejection. Thus, these studies suggest that perceived prejudice can buffer personal self-directed emotions via its effects on judgments of personal deserving.

Caveats

Both of the aforementioned studies used paradigms in which procedural cues indicating the presence of prejudice were blatant. Crocker and Major (1989, p. 621) hypothesized that

> ... overt prejudice or discrimination should be less damaging to the self-esteem of its targets than is prejudice or discrimination that is disguised or hidden behind a cloak of fairness. When one is faced with blatant prejudice ... it is clear that the proper attribution for negative outcomes is prejudice ... the ambiguity surrounding both positive and negative treatment that may result from covert prejudice is problematical for the stigmatized individual.

From a deserving perspective, when prejudice is subtle rather than overt, recipients of negative feedback may not be certain that their negative feedback was not deserved and hence their personal self-esteem may suffer.

Major et al. (2003) found evidence consistent with this hypothesis. Women in this experiment completed a test of creative thinking in small mixed-gender groups. They were told that a male judge would grade the test and select one member of the group to serve in a desirable leadership position during a following task. While participants waited for their grades, a female confederate in the group commented that the male evaluator was either blatantly prejudiced, possibly prejudiced, or made a neutral comment unrelated to the evaluator or prejudice. All participants then received negative feedback on their test, were informed that they were not selected to be leader, and completed a measure of self-esteem. Women in the blatant prejudice condition blamed their feedback more on prejudice and reported higher personal self-esteem than women in the ambiguous or no prejudice conditions. These latter two groups did not differ from each other in self-esteem. Thus, self-esteem was buffered among women who perceived their negative treatment as clearly and unambiguously undeserved (because they faced blatant sexism). It is important to recognize, however, that devalued groups have unique histories, and these histories can lead to different thresholds for deciding when cues to prejudice are strong. For example, African Americans have a strong sense of their group's devalued status and of the injustice (lack of deservedness) of this status (Kluegel & Smith, 1986). This history may make them more sensitive to cues to injustice relative to groups with a more poorly developed sense of themselves as disadvantaged (e.g., women; Kluegel & Smith, 1986). In fact, among African Americans, even subtle cues to procedural injustice can protect them from experiencing negative self-directed emotions. For example, in one study (Major et al., 1998), African Americans received negative feedback on an intelligence test and then completed a self-esteem measure. One half of the participants learned that the researchers were interested in examining whether the test was racially biased, and the other half received no information about potential test bias. As predicted, African Americans reported higher self-esteem when potential test bias was primed, compared with when it was not primed. Thus, just raising the specter of potential bias may protect African Americans from the negative self-directed emotional consequences that might occur if they saw their failure as deserved.

It is also important to point out that attributing negative outcomes to one's social identity, or even to prejudice based on that identity, does not necessarily protect self-esteem. Individuals can attribute negative outcomes to their social identities and can even recognize that others are prejudiced against them, but still perceive this treatment as deserved (Crocker & Major, 1994). Depending on their beliefs about their own (or their group's) attributes, and their assumptions about their own or their groups' responsibility for those attributes, targets can interpret negative outcomes as a form of deserved negative treatment. A study by Crocker, Cornwell, and Major (1993) demonstrates how this can occur. In this study, overweight women were rejected as a dating partner by a man who could either see them (and hence knew they were overweight) or could not see them (and hence did not know they were overweight). Overweight women who were seen attributed the rejection to their weight, but they did not hold the man responsible for his decision. This type of attributional pattern was associated with increased depressed emotions. Thus, if individuals view themselves as deserving of their disadvantaged status (e.g., because it is assumed to be controllable), they will likely experience increased self-directed negative emotional outcomes when faced with negative treatment stemming from their social identity.

In sum, a number of studies demonstrate that procedural justice cues (in particular, the presence or absence of prejudice against one's group) influence how negative outcomes affect personal self-esteem and self-directed emotions. According to our deserving analysis, procedural justice cues affect self-directed emotional responses by either increasing (in the case of fair procedures) or decreasing (in the case of unfair procedures) judgments of personal deserving.

Ideology as a Cue to Deserving

Ideologies about the relationship between people and their outcomes also influence emotions in response to perceived prejudice against the group. In one of the first studies to investigate this issue, Quinn and Crocker (1999) asked overweight and standard weight women to read a paragraph that primed either the Protestant Work Ethic ideology or a more inclusive ideology and then to read an article describing prejudice against the overweight. All women subsequently completed a composite measure of well-being assessing depression, anxiety, and self-esteem. Overweight women in the Protestant Work Ethic prime condition reported lower levels of well-being relative to overweight women in the inclusive prime condition. Standard weight women were unaffected by the prime. According to our deserving analysis, this pattern of emotional responses occurred because overweight women who endorsed the Protestant Work Ethic were more likely than those who did not endorse this legitimizing ideology to feel that their group (and themselves personally, as a group member) deserved the prejudicial treatment that they experienced.

We (Major & Kaiser, 2002) recently obtained similar findings among women exposed to sexism. In our first study, women (all of whom had previously completed measures of the Protestant Work Ethic, the Belief in a Just World, and personal self-esteem) were randomly assigned to read an article describing pervasive sexism against women or one of two control articles (a neutral article or an article describing how prejudice against women is rare). Personal self-esteem was then reassessed. As predicted, women who read that prejudice against women was pervasive and who strongly endorsed the Belief in a Just World or the Protestant Work Ethic ideology reported decreased self-esteem (controlling for initial self-esteem) relative to women who less strongly endorsed these status-legitimizing ideologies. This was not the case in the control conditions. Indeed, when women read neutral information, these same legitimizing ideologies were positively associated with self-esteem.

We replicated and extended these findings in a second study in which women, all of whom had previously completed a measure of the Protestant Work Ethic and self-esteem, were randomly assigned to read an article describing prejudice against female students and alumni from their own university or an article describing prejudice against an unknown group. Among women who read about prejudice against their own group, the more strongly they endorsed the Protestant Work Ethic ideology, the lower their self-esteem. In contrast, among women who read about prejudice against an unknown group, endorsing the Protestant Work Ethic was positively associated with self-esteem. Collectively, the Quinn and Crocker (1999) and Major and Kaiser (2002) studies demonstrate that endorsing (or being primed with) status-legitimizing ideologies, such as the Protestant Work Ethic and the Belief in a Just World, makes individuals vulnerable to experiencing low personal self-esteem when they read about prejudice against their own group, but not when they read about prejudice against other groups or when they are not exposed to prejudice against their group. According to our deserving analysis, this pattern occurs because endorsing legitimizing ideologies leads individuals to believe that groups (and by extension the self as a member of those groups) deserve their treatment in society. Furthermore, this applies to group memberships that are presumably under one's control (weight), as well as those not under one's control (gender).

DESERVING AND COLLECTIVE SELF-DIRECTED EMOTIONS

The aforementioned studies illustrate that cues relevant to deserving (procedural justice cues or ideologies) influence personal self-directed emotions in response to observing prejudice directed against oneself or against one's social group. Do these same cues influence emotions directed toward the group as a whole? Do individuals who believe that outcomes are fairly distributed feel differently about their social groups than individuals who believe they are unfairly distributed? From a deserving perspective, to the extent that the group as a whole is viewed as deserving of their lower status (e.g., women would be paid as much as men if they only had different work priorities or worked as hard as men), prejudice against the group may lead to emotions such as ingroup-directed shame.

Correlational evidence supports the proposition that legitimizing ideologies are associated with negative collective-self-directed emotions among groups that face pervasive prejudice. For example, Levin, Sidanius, Rabinowitz, and Federico (1998) examined the relationship between endorsement of status-legitimizing ideologies and feelings toward group membership among members of socially valued ethnic groups (i.e., whites and Asian Americans) and less-valued groups (i.e., Latinos and blacks). Results generally revealed that the relationship between legitimizing ideologies and ingroup-directed feelings (this was a composite measure of ingroup-directed feelings and cognitions, so interpretation is limited to some extent) was different for members of valued and devalued social groups. For Latino and African Americans, the more they endorsed legitimizing ideologies, the less they reported feeling close to their ingroup. In contrast, the relationship between legitimizing ideologies and ingroup closeness was positive for whites and Asian Americans. This study suggests that, for disadvantaged groups that frequently face discrimination, endorsing legitimizing ideologies can come at the cost of positive emotions toward the part of the self that is defined by group memberships.

The Major and Kaiser (2002) studies described also demonstrated that endorsing legitimizing ideologies can lead to negative collective self-directed emotions among groups exposed to prejudice. In those studies, we assessed women's collective self-esteem prior to and after reading an article about prejudice against women or a control article. Across both experiments, endorsing legitimizing ideologies was related negatively to collective self-esteem among women assigned to the prejudice conditions. In contrast, endorsing these same ideologies was unrelated or even positively related to collective self-esteem among women assigned to the control conditions. These findings suggest that legitimizing ideologies lead to negative feelings toward the group when members of the group are faced with evidence that the group is a target of prejudice. According to our deserving analysis, this occurs because legitimizing ideologies lead to the inference that groups are responsible for their devalued social position.

DESERVING AND OTHER-DIRECTED EMOTIONS

Theories of emotion predict that, when negative outcomes are seen as illegitimate, feelings of anger are likely to result (Shaver et al., 1987). According to relative deprivation theory (Crosby, 1976; Runciman, 1966), people will experience relative deprivation when they compare their own outcomes with others and come to the conclusion that they are receiving less than they deserve. Feelings of relative deprivation can be felt on behalf of oneself (egoistical relative deprivation) or on behalf of one's group (fraternal deprivation). The emotions that most closely accompany feelings of relative deprivation are resentment and anger (Crosby, 1982). Accordingly, the more members of disadvantaged groups perceive negative treatment directed against themselves or their group as undeserved, the more they should experience anger, resentment, or other outer-directed emotions, either on behalf of themselves or their group.

Relative deprivation theory emerged, however, to explain the paradoxical finding that people who are objectively disadvantaged often do *not* report anger or discontent with their situations (Crosby, 1976). For example, even though women are typically paid less than men for comparable work and contribute a greater share of family work than do their husbands, they typically report no less satisfaction with their lives, jobs, or marriages than do men (see Crosby, 1982; Major, 1994). One reason is that members of disadvantaged groups often come to feel they deserve their lower status and less positive treatment (Major, 1994).

Olson and Hafer (2001) proposed that endorsing legitimizing ideologies, such as the Belief in a Just World, prevents the expression of anger and hostile other-directed emotions among stigmatized groups. They argue that individuals who endorse the Belief in a Just World are likely to blame negative events on themselves rather than on prejudice. This attributional pattern is proposed to result in increased perceived deserving, which then leads to negative self-directed emotions rather than emotions of discontent and anger. Although studies that measure legitimizing ideologies and other-directed emotions, such as anger, among disadvantaged groups are rare, legitimizing ideologies are related to behaviors that can be considered "consequences" of anger emotions. In particular, Olson and Hafer (2001) argue that discontentment and anger lead to assertive actions to remedy prejudiced situations. They found that the more underpaid working women endorsed the Belief in a Just World, the less they reported engaging in group-based advocacy in their employment settings, such as arguing for better opportunities for women (Hafer & Olson, 1993).

Based on this, one might expect that the more individuals blame negative outcomes on prejudice, rather than on their own lack of personal deserving, the angrier they will feel against those who they view as prejudiced. Correlational evidence is consistent with this expectation. Branscombe and colleagues (1999) found that the more African Americans perceive their racial group as targets of prejudice, the more hostile they feel toward European Americans.

Research using experimental paradigms, however, has not found that individuals are angrier when prejudice is the likely cause of their own negative outcomes than when their own lack of deserving is the likely cause. For instance, Major et al. (2003) found that participants who blamed rejection from a course on a sexist professor experienced fewer negative self-directed emotions, but not more hostile emotions than those who blamed the rejection on their own lack of intelligence. Both groups were equally angry, and both were angrier than women who imagined that their request was denied because the professor was a jerk. Other studies (Crocker et al., 1991) have also found that individuals rejected because of prejudice and because of a lack of deserving are equally angry. At first glance, it seems surprising that participants whose rejection is due to prejudice are not angrier than those whose rejection is due to their own inadequacies. We suspect this pattern occurs because it is difficult to tease apart within a single experiment the hostile emotional effects of rejection due to prejudice from rejection due to other personal attributes (Twenge et al., 2001).

In sum, there are compelling theoretical reasons to anticipate that the more stigmatized individuals reject legitimizing ideologies that lead to the inference that they personally, or their group, deserves their ill treatment, the more likely they will be to report anger, hostility, and other extropunitive emotions, especially toward those individuals and groups responsible for prejudice. However, data do not yet provide strong support for this relationship. This may be an artifact of the methodologies typically used in stigma experiments. Additionally, members of devalued groups may be reluctant to report hostile emotions because their welfare is often dependent on the benevolence of higher status groups and because it is also oftentimes socially unacceptable to express anger (Olson & Hafer, 2001). We believe that anger is potentially an important emotion for members of devalued social groups. Although anger is rarely seen as a healthy emotion, anger may be necessary for people to engage in collective action. Clearly, more research needs to examine the relationships among perceived prejudice, perceived deserving, and anger among members of stigmatized groups.

SUMMARY AND CONCLUSIONS

Prejudice has a number of emotional consequences for its targets. Prejudice can influence emotions directed at the individual and collective self, as well as emotions directed toward other individuals and groups. In this chapter, we argued that judgments of personal and group deserving moderate the emotional impact of prejudice on its targets. Although judgments of deserving are influenced by a number of factors, we focused our attention on legitimizing ideologies and cues to procedural justice as processes that influence the extent to which members of stigmatized groups come to feel that they personally, or their group, is deserving or undeserving of poor outcomes.

We reviewed research showing that when members of stigmatized groups face negative outcomes, strong cues that prejudice may have influenced outcomes can result in decreased levels of negative personal self-directed emotions. Evidence of prejudice decreases the extent to which outcomes are seen as accurately reflecting inputs and hence the extent to which negative outcomes are judged as deserved. We also reviewed evidence showing that endorsing legitimizing ideologies can be a double-edged sword for members of groups frequently exposed to prejudice. On the one hand, these ideologies are psychological resources. For instance, in contexts unrelated to prejudice, individuals who endorse legitimizing ideologies view their world as more controllable, display more task persistence, and report higher levels of well-being (Taylor & Brown, 1988). On the other hand, when members of stigmatized groups face blatant prejudice, legitimizing beliefs are a source of emotional vulnerability. Because legitimizing ideologies hold individuals and groups responsible for negative outcomes, they lead to the inference that groups that are targets of prejudice must deserve their devalued status.

Finally, despite compelling theoretical reasons for predicting that exposure to blatant prejudice and rejection of legitimizing ideologies will be associated with higher levels of hostile emotions directed toward individuals or outgroups thought to be responsible for one's disadvantage, evidence is scarce. Because anger is a motivator of action, this research avenue holds a great deal of promise.

ACKNOWLEDGMENTS

This chapter was supported by a grant from the National Institute of Mental Health (1F32MH64308) to the first author and by a grant from the National Science Foundation (BCS-9983888) to the second author.

References

Abramson, L. Y., Seligman, M. E., & Teasdale, J. D. (1978). Learned helplessness in humans: Critique and reformulation. *Journal of Abnormal Psychology, 87*, 49–74.

Adams, J. S. (1965). Inequality in social exchange. *Advances in Experimental Social Psychology, 2*, 267–299.

Allport, G. (1954/1979). *The nature of prejudice* (pp. 151–152). New York: Doubleday Anchor.

Baker, J. M. (2002). *How homophobia hurts children: Nurturing diversity at home, at school, and in the community*. New York: Hawthorn Press.

Baumeister, R. F. (1998). The self. In D. T. Gilbert, S. F. Fiske, & G. Lindzey (Eds.), *The handbook of social psychology* (Vol. 1; pp. 680–740). New York: Oxford University Press.

Braddock, J. H., & McPartland, J. M. (1987). How minorities continue to be excluded from equal employment opportunities: Research on labor market and institutional barriers. *Journal of Social Issues, 43*, 5–39.

Branscombe, N. R., Schmitt, M. T., & Harvey, R. D. (1999). Perceiving pervasive discrimination among African Americans: Implications for group identification and well-being. *Journal of Personality and Social Psychology, 77*, 135–149.

Brown, J. D., & Marshall, M. A. (2001). Self-esteem and emotion: Some thoughts about feelings. *Personality and Social Psychology Bulletin, 27*, 575–584.

Clark, K. B., & Clark, M. P. (1950). Emotional factors in racial identification and preference in Negro children. *Journal of Negro Education, 19*, 341–350.

Cooley, C. H. (1956). *Human nature and the social order*. Glencoe, IL: Free Press.

Crandall, C. S. (1995). Do parents discriminate against their heavyweight daughters? *Personality and Social Psychology Bulletin, 21*, 724–735.

Crocker, J., Cornwell, B., & Major, B. (1993). The stigma of overweight: Affective consequences of attributional ambiguity. *Journal of Personality and Social Psychology, 64*, 60–70.

Crocker, J., Luhtanen, R., Blaine, B., & Broadnax, S. (1994). Collective self-esteem and psychological well being among White, Black, and Asian college students. *Personality and Social Psychology Bulletin, 20*, 503–513.

Crocker, J., & Major, B. (1989). Social stigma and self-esteem: The self-protective properties of stigma. *Psychological Review, 96*, 608–630.

Crocker, J., & Major, B. (1994). Reactions to stigma: The moderating role of justifications. In M. P. Zanna and J. M. Olson (Eds.), *The psychology of prejudice: The Ontario symposium* (Vol. 7; pp. 289–314). Hillsdale, NJ: Erlbaum.

Crocker, J., Voelkl, K., Testa, M., & Major, B. (1991). Social stigma: The affective consequences of attributional ambiguity. *Journal of Personality and Social Psychology, 60*, 218–228.

Crosby, F. J. (1976). Model of egoistical relative deprivation. *Psychological Review, 83*, 85–113.

Crosby, F. J. (1982). *Relative deprivation and working women*. New York: Oxford University Press.

Deutsch, M. (1985). *Distributive justice: A social-psychological approach*. New Haven, CT: Yale University Press.

Doosje, B., Branscombe, N. R., Spears, R., & Manstead, A. S. R. (1998). Guilty by association: When one's group has a negative history. *Journal of Personality and Social Psychology, 75*, 872–886.

Ethier, K. A., & Deaux, K. (1994). Negotiating social identity in a changing context: Maintaining identification and responding to threat. *Journal of Personality and Social Psychology, 67*, 243–251.

Feather, N. (1999). Judgments of deservingness: Studies in the psychology of justice and achievement. *Personality and Social Psychology Review, 3*, 86–107.

Friedman, M. A., & Brownell, K. D. (1995). Psychological correlates of obesity: Moving to the next research generation. *Psychological Bulletin, 117*, 3–20.

Hafer, C. L., & Olson, J. M. (1993). Beliefs in a just world, discontent, and assertive actions by working women. *Personality and Social Psychology Bulletin, 19*, 30–38.

James, W. (1890). *The principles of psychology* (Vol. 1). New York: Dover.

Janoff-Bulman, R., & Lang-Gunn, L. (1988). Coping with disease, crime, and accidents: The role of self-blame attributions. In L. Y. Abramson (Ed.), *Social cognition and clinical psychology: A synthesis* (pp. 116–147). New York: The Guilford Press.

Jost, J. T., & Banaji, M. R. (1994). The role of stereotyping in system-justification and the production of false consciousness. *British Journal of Social Psychology, 33*, 1–27.

Kluegel, J. R., & Smith, E. R. (1986). *Beliefs about inequality: Americans' views of what is and what ought to be*. Hawthorne, NJ: Aldine de Gruyer.

Lazarus, R. S. (1999). *Stress and emotion: A new synthesis*. New York: Springer.

Lerner, M. J. (1977). The justice motive: Some hypotheses as to its origins and forms. *Journal of Personality, 45*, 1–52.

Lerner, M. J. (1987). Integrating societal and psychological rules of entitlement: The basic task of each actor and fundamental problem for the social sciences. *Social Justice Research, 1*, 107–125.

Levin, S., Sidanius, J., Rabinowitz, J. L., & Federico, C. (1998). Ethnic identity, legitimizing ideologies, and social status: A matter of ideological asymmetry. *Political Psychology, 19*, 373–404.

Lind, E. A., & Tyler, T. R. (1988). *The social psychology of procedural justice*. New York: Plenum Press.

Luhtanen, R., & Crocker, J. (1992). A collective self-esteem scale: Self-evaluation of one's social identity. *Personality and Social Psychology Bulletin, 18*, 302–318.

Mackie, D. M., Devos, T., & Smith, E. R. (2000). Intergroup emotions: Explaining offensive action tendencies in an intergroup context. *Journal of Personality and Social Psychology, 79*, 602–616.

Major, B. (1994). From social inequality to personal entitlement: The role of social comparisons, legitimacy appraisals, and group membership. In M. P. Zanna (Ed.), *Advances in experimental social psychology* (Vol. 26; pp. 293–348). San Diego: Academic Press.

Major, B., & Kaiser, C. R. (2002). Fairing well in an unfair world: Ideology endorsement and the impact of prejudice on self-esteem. Unpublished manuscript. University of California, Santa Barbara.

Major, B., Kaiser, C. R., & McCoy, S. K. (2003). It's not my fault: When and why attributions to prejudice protect well-being. *Personality and Social Psychology Bulletin, 29*, 772–781.

Major, B., Quinton, W. J., & McCoy, S. K. (2002). Antecedents and consequences of attributions to discrimination: Theoretical and empirical advances. In M. P. Zanna (Ed.), *Advances in experimental social psychology* (Vol. 34; pp. 251–330). New York: Academic Press.

Major, B., Quinton, W. J., & Schmader, T. (2003). Attributions to discrimination and self-esteem: Impact of group identification and situational ambiguity. *Journal of Experimental Social Psychology, 39*, 220–231.

Major, B., Spencer, S., Schmader, T., Wolfe, C., & Crocker, J. (1998). Coping with negative stereotypes about intellectual performance: The role of psychological disengagement. *Personality and Social Psychology Bulletin, 24*, 34–50.

Massey, D. S., Gross, B., & Shibuya, K. (1994). Migration, segregation, and the geographic concentration of poverty. *American Sociological Review, 59*, 425–445.

Miller, C. T., & Downey, K. T. (1999). A meta-analysis of heavyweight and self-esteem. *Personality and Social Psychology Review, 3*, 68–84.

Mirels, H., & Garrett, J. (1971). The Protestant ethic as a personality variable. *Journal of Consulting and Clinical Psychology, 36*, 40–44.

Olson, J., & Hafer, C. L. (2001). Tolerance of personal deprivation. In J. T. Jost & B. Major (Eds.), *The psychology of legitimacy: Emerging perspectives on ideology, justice, and intergroup relations* (pp. 157–175). New York: Cambridge University Press.

Quinn, D. M., & Crocker, J. (1999). When ideology hurts: Effects of belief in the Protestant ethic and feeling overweight on the psychological well-being of women. *Journal of Personality and Social Psychology, 77*, 402–414.

Rowley, S. J., Sellers, R. M., Chavous, T. M., & Smith, M. A. (1998). The relationship between racial identity and self-esteem in African American college and high school students. *Journal of Personality and Social Psychology, 74*, 715–724.

Runciman, W. G. (1966). *Relative deprivation and social justice: A study of the attitudes to social inequality in 20th century England*. Berkeley: University of California Press.

Schmitt, M. T., Branscombe, N. R., Kobrynowicz, D., & Owen, S. (2002). Perceiving discrimination against one's gender group has different implications for well-being in women and men. *Personality and Social Psychology Bulletin, 28*, 197–210.

Shaver, P., Schwartz, J., Kirson, D., & O'Connor, C. (1987). Emotion knowledge: Further explorations of a prototype approach. *Journal of Personality and Social Psychology, 52*, 1061–1086.

Sidanius, J., & Pratto, F. (1999). *Social dominance: An intergroup theory of social hierarchy and oppression*. New York: Cambridge University Press.

Smith, E. R. (1993). Social identity and social emotions: Toward new conceptualizations of prejudice. In D. M. Mackie & D. L. Hamilton (Eds.), *Affect, cognition, and stereotyping: Interactive processes in group perception* (pp. 297–315). San Diego: Academic Press.

Smith, E. R., & Henry, S. (1996). An in-group becomes part of the self: Response time evidence. *Personality and Social Psychology Bulletin, 22*, 635–642.

Snowden, L. R., Thomas, K. (2000). Medicaid and African American outpatient mental health treatment. *Mental Health Services Research, 2*, 115–120.

Swim, J. K., Hyers, L. L., Cohen, L. L., & Ferguson, M. J. (2001). Everyday sexism: Evidence for its incidence, nature, and psychological impact from three daily diary studies. *Journal of Social Issues, 57*, 31–53.

Tajfel, H., & Turner, J. C. (1986). The social identity theory of intergroup behavior. In S. Worchel & W. G. Austin (Eds.), *The psychology of intergroup relations* (pp. 7–24). Chicago: Nelson-Hall.

Taylor, S. E., & Brown, J. D. (1988). Illusion and well-being: A social psychological perspective on mental health. *Psychological Bulletin, 103*, 193–210.

Thibaut, J. W., & Kelley, H. H. (1959). *The social psychology of groups*. New York: Wiley.

Turner, J. C. (1985). Social categorization and the self-concept: A social cognitive theory of group behavior. In E. J. Lawler (Ed.), *Advances in group processes: Theory and research* (Vol. 2; pp. 77–121). Greenwich, CT: JAI Press.

Twenge, J. M., Baumeister, R. F., Tice, D. M., & Stucke, T. S. (2001). If you can't join them, beat them: The effects of social exclusion on antisocial vs. prosocial behavior. *Journal of Personality and Social Psychology, 81*, 1058–1069.

Twenge, J., & Crocker, J. (2002). Race, ethnicity, and self-esteem: Meta-analyses comparing Whites, Blacks, Hispanics, Asians, and Native Americans, including a commentary on Gray-Little and Hafdahl (2000). *Psychological Bulletin, 128*, 371–408.

Vorauer, J., & Kumhyr, S. M. (2001). Is this about you or me? Self- versus other-directed judgments and feelings in response to intergroup interaction. *Personality and Social Psychology Bulletin, 27*, 706–719.

Walster, E., Walster, G. W., & Berscheid, E. (1978). *Equity theory and research*. Boston: Allyn & Bacon.

Weiner, B. (1995). *Judgments of responsibility: A foundation for a theory of social conduct*. New York: The Guilford Press.

14

Group-based Emotions and Intergroup Behavior

The Case of Relative Deprivation

Heather J. Smith and Thomas Kessler

When researchers discuss relative deprivation (RD), they refer to the perception of an undeserved disadvantage, the accompanying emotions, and associated action tendencies. People who notice an unfair relative disadvantage might feel a variety of emotions, including disappointment, depression, surprise, envy, anger, resentment and outrage (Corning, 2000; Folger, 1986, 1987; Mikula, Petri, & Tanzer, 1990). This list of possible emotions raises two questions. First, are some of these emotions more typical than others as a reaction to a perceived unfair disadvantage? Second, what conditions determine which of these emotions are felt? According to cognitive appraisal theories of emotion (Frijda, 1993; Ellsworth, 1994; Roseman, Spindel, & Jose, 1990), people's perceptions or cognitive appraisals of the situation shape how they will feel. The purpose of this chapter is to explore a variety of appraisal dimensions that may distinguish among the various RD emotions. We believe that a closer examination of the specific emotions elicited by perceptions of unfair disadvantages will clarify the relationship between perceptions of RD and subsequent behavioral reactions. We describe the important complexities that emerge as we consider five appraisal dimensions proposed by RD theorists as antecedents of RD: (1) the legitimacy of the intergroup context, (2) who is responsible for the disadvantage, (3) feasibility of any change, (4) social support, and (5) social comparisons. Finally, we discuss whether the cognitive appraisals we describe: (1) cause feelings of deprivation, (2) are the cognitive components of the deprivation experience, or (3) are the consequence of feeling deprived.

EARLY DEVELOPMENTS OF RD

Stouffer and his colleagues (1949) first articulated the concept of RD to explain a series of unexpected relationships between feelings of satisfaction and one's position in the army. By unhooking subjective evaluations from objective circumstances, the RD concept suggested solutions to two puzzling findings. First, RD suggested why objective inequities do not always incite protest. RD researchers argue that people do not always make the subjective comparisons that reveal the status quo to be illegitimate (Major, 1994). Second, RD suggested why sometimes even "objectively advantaged" people feel deprived and resentful. RD researchers propose that if people feel that they are entitled to have more than they have, they will feel deprived, regardless of how many resources or other advantages they may possess. One of the most important conceptual distinctions within RD theory is the distinction between individual and group RD (see Walker & Smith, 2002, for a review). Individual RD (IRD) develops from interpersonal comparisons, whereas group RD (GRD) arises through intergroup comparisons. It is GRD, rather than IRD, that is more strongly associated with political protest and active attempts to change the social system (Smith & Pettigrew, 2002). Moreover, IRD is presumably associated with individual emotions, whereas GRD is an excellent example of an intergroup emotion (Smith, 1993). GRD emotions are experienced with respect to one's social identity as a group member, based on appraisals of the intergroup context and associated with specific action tendencies. Similar to other intergroup emotions (e.g., Mackie, Devos, & Smith, 2000; Smith, 1993), we expect the emotional experience associated with GRD to mediate the relationship between perceived collective disadvantage and collective behavior.

However, most RD researchers assume rather than measure the emotions that mediate the relationship between perceptions of disadvantage and action (for exceptions, see Leach, Iyer, & Pederson, 2003; Mummendey et al., 1999; Pettigrew, 2002). Even when researchers measure emotions, they use terms that vary widely in intensity (compare dissatisfaction to outrage). More importantly, these terms often represent different basic emotions or different clusters of emotion terms within a basic emotion category (see Shaver et al., 1987). For example, disappointment and hopelessness represent sadness, whereas resentment and frustration represent anger. Rage, frustration, envy, and resentment all represent different natural word clusters within the basic emotion of anger (Shaver et al., 1987). Yet researchers often combine several of these individual terms into a single scale intended to measure RD. Although we believe that measuring emotions is an improvement over assuming their existence, by paying attention to the basic emotions to which our measures refer, we can improve the predictive power of RD. We propose that a simple perception of a negative intergroup comparison outcome may be the triggering event of a complex appraisal process that can lead to frustration, distress, disappointment, envy, or – if a particular interpretation of the situation emerges – resentment or outrage. These emotions do not have not to be felt constantly to motivate collective action. Recurrent similar appraisals of a particular intergroup context may be maintained as a set of beliefs about the intergroup relationship that predispose people to feel and react in particular ways. Following Klandermans's (1997) notion of a collective action frame, if group members share an interpretation of an intergroup relation (including legitimacy concerns and resources such as social support), they also will share feelings of group-based resentment, and, therefore, will be motivated to organize group members in collective action. However, there is no reason to expect that perceptions of a disadvantaged intergroup comparison always lead to collective action. Therefore, we have to consider in more detail the variety of ways people might react to feeling deprived.

BROADENING THE PERSPECTIVE ON THE OUTCOMES ASSOCIATED WITH GRD

Traditionally, RD researchers have been most interested in the explanation (and post-hoc prediction) of political unrest and collective action. These behaviors are seen as consequences of subjectively experienced "upward" contrasting (intergroup) comparisons (Leach, Snider, & Iyer, 2002; Tyler, Boeckmann, Smith, & Huo, 1997). Although introduced as an explanation of collective behavior, researchers also applied the RD concept to explain a wide variety of attitudes and behaviors ranging from participation in U.S. inner-city riots during the 1960s to committing date rape to feelings of powerlessness (see Smith & Pettigrew, 2002). This inclusion of a wide variety of reactions is both a strength and a problem within RD research (Ellemers, 2002; Smith & Pettigrew, 2002). On the one hand, it illustrates that RD can be applied to a broader range of reactions (attitudes as well as behavior) than some social scientists assume (e.g., Finkel & Rule, 1987). On the other hand, it suggests that the assumption that perceptions of unfair group disadvantages always lead to anger – and, in turn, collective challenge of the injustice – may be too simple (Mackie et al., 2000, p. 603).

In particular, we should distinguish between action and inaction (Crosby, 1976; Mark & Folger, 1984; Wright, Taylor, & Moghaddam, 1990). Regardless of how people might feel, the most common response to a grievance against another person or organization is to do nothing (see Tyler et al., 1997, for a review). To challenge injustice is costly. In fact, both field and experimental studies show that the majority of women who report experiencing sexual harassment and discrimination do not challenge it (Koss et al., 1994; Swim & Hyers, 1999). However, research on sexual harassment also consistently shows that discrimination and harassment are associated with significant psychological and physical stress (e.g., Koss et al., 1994). For example, a daily experience study shows that African American women who felt personally mistreated in comparison with others have increased cardiovascular activity, compared with other African American and European American women (Guyll, Matthews, & Bromberger, 2001).

Thus, inaction does not mean the absence of an emotional experience. In fact, we think that this is an area in which direct measures of people's emotional state will prove most useful to RD researchers. Does increased physical stress occur because people cannot express their anger? Or is the emotional experience in this case closer to sadness? In a meta-analysis of RD research (Smith & Pettigrew, 2002), GRD was not associated with measures of stress (average $r = .05$), whereas IRD was slightly related to stress measures (average $r = .15$). However, the relationship between stress and feeling deprived may depend on other variables. In one intriguing study, members of a disadvantaged group who reported GRD showed more signs of mental health problems over time (Schmitt & Maes, 2002). However, this relationship was qualified by the degree of ingroup bias; disadvantaged group members who reported more bias toward their ingroup did not show decreased mental health, despite feeling group deprived. Although these findings are provocative, we believe a clearer understanding of these relationships requires explicit measures of the experienced emotions and related appraisal dimensions.

APPRAISALS ASSOCIATED WITH RD

All RD theorists assume that the RD experience begins with wanting something one does not have, and all RD theorists also include a comparison with some standard, be it an ideal, person, or group, (Walker & Pettigrew, 1984). However, as shown in Table 14.1, RD theorists have proposed a variety of antecedents that might lead to feeling deprived. Crosby (1976, 1982) and Folger (1986, 1987) present two of the most influential models of RD. Crosby (1976) proposed that, to feel deprived, people who lack some object or opportunity must (1) perceive that someone else has it, (2) want it, (3) feel entitled to it, (4) think that it is feasible to obtain it, and (5) lack a sense of responsibility for not having it. Subsequent research by Crosby (1982) and others pared the number of preconditions to just two: (1) wanting what one does not have, and (2) feeling that one deserves whatever it is one wants but does not have.

Drawing on Crosby's (1976) model and refined versions of the simulation heuristic (Kahneman & Tversky, 1982), Folger (1986, 1987) proposed that the current state of affairs forms a narrative or a story to which different alternative stories can be compared. People will evaluate their current outcome negatively and feel resentful and angry if they can imagine (1) much better alternative outcomes (high referent outcomes), (2) more legitimate contingencies and procedures that might have led to better outcomes (high referent instrumentalities), and (3) the current situation will not improve in the near future (low likelihood of amelioration). More recent research on the influence of mental simulations on people's outcome evaluations is found within counterfactual thinking research (Olson & Roese, 2002).

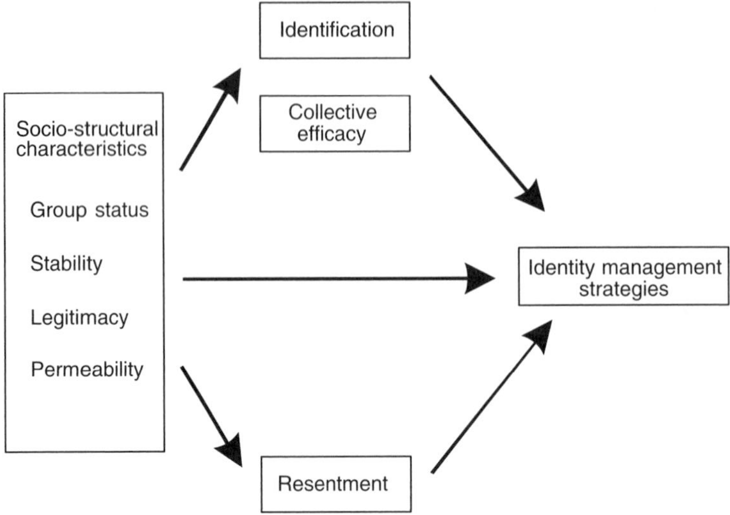

FIGURE 14.1. Integrated model for the combination of social identity theory and relative deprivation theory with socio-structural characteristics and ingroup situation as predictors; identification, fraternal resentment, and group efficacy as mediators; and six identity management strategies as criteria (adapted from Mummendey et al., Journal of Personality and Social Psychology 1999, 76. Copyright © 1999 by the American Psychological Association. Reprinted with Permission).

Other researchers propose that feeling deprived represents the outcome of particular sets of causal attributions (Crosby, 1982; Walker, Wong, & Kretzschmar, 2002). For example, Walker and his colleagues argue that perceived disadvantages that are linked to external and stable causes prompt the strongest feelings of deprivation (Walker et al., 2002).

The focus of these models is the experience of IRD, but recent integrations of GRD with social identity principles (Ellemers, 2002; Kawakami & Dion, 1992; Mummendey et al., 1999; Walker & Pettigrew, 1984) suggest three appraisals of the intergroup situation that shape feeling group deprived. First, if people perceive the intergroup situation as stable (or the likelihood of amelioration as low), they will feel more group deprived. Second, if people perceive the intergroup situation as illegitimate, they will feel more group deprived. And finally, if people perceive the group boundaries are impermeable, they will feel more group deprived (see Figure 14.1). As Mummendey and her colleagues (1999) discuss, if group boundaries are impermeable, people cannot easily avoid the group's disadvantaged fate, and feelings of group-based resentment should be greater. Moreover, impermeable group boundaries tend to increase identification with the ingroup and thereby enhance the likelihood that people will feel GRD when a relative intergroup disadvantage is perceived. In a test of their integration of both models with former East German participants, Mummendey and colleagues (1999) showed that impermeable group boundaries and stable and illegitimate intergroup relationships enhanced feelings of group-based resentment. This group-based resentment, in turn, was more closely associated with collectively oriented strategies of social and realistic competition than with individual responses (such as individual mobility).

Although previous RD researchers describe sets of attributions or cognitive heuristics, we think several of the terms presented in Table 14.1 can be interpreted as dimensions of appraisal – evaluations of events and situations that elicit particular emotional experiences (Roseman & Smith, 2001). We consider five appraisals in more detail: (1) legitimacy, (2) responsibility, (3) agency, (4) social support, and (5) social comparisons. Different sets of appraisals should be associated with different specific emotional experiences (resentment or disappointment) and different specific action tendencies (acceptance, normative or nonnormative, individual or collective action; see Wright et al., 1990).

Legitimacy

As shown in Table 14.1, explicit in almost all RD models is the concept of deserving – people compare their situation to another possibility using principles about what "ought to be" (Tyler et al., 1997). If people believe negative discrepancies to be justified or legitimate, they are unlikely to feel resentful or frustrated, even though they recognize their disadvantage (Ellemers, 2002; Folger, 1987). In fact, it may be perceived illegitimacy that changes people's comparison motives from self-improvement (one reason for comparing upward; Buunk et al., 1990; Wood, 1989) or self-enhancement (one reason for comparing downward instead; Wood, 1989) to an evaluation of the larger intergroup context (Taylor, Moghaddam, & Bellerose, 1989).

Appraisals of legitimacy may also distinguish among different emotional reactions to perceived disadvantage. First, if another group's advantage is viewed as undeserved, but sanctioned by the larger society, people may experience envy rather than resentment (Feather & Sherman, 2002). As Williams (1975) writes, to receive less than one wants results in a sense of deprivation, to receive less than one expects results in feelings of disappointment, but to receive less than is "mandated by accepted social rules and values (that to which one is entitled)" results in resentment (p. 356). Williams' reference to accepted social rules and values reflects how legitimacy is defined within the procedural justice literature (Tyler, 1997).

Finally, legitimacy appraisals may determine whether the reaction to GRD is normative or nonnormative. Researchers define normative reactions as reactions that conform to the standards of the larger social system and nonnormative reactions as reactions that are seen as outside of existing social rules or norms (Kawakami & Dion, 1992; Wright et al., 1990). If we

TABLE 14.1. *Suggested Antecedents for Feeling Deprived*

Runciman, 1966	**Davis, 1959**	**Gurr, 1970**	**Crosby (1976, 1982)**	**Referent Cognitions Theory (Folger, 1986, 1987)**	**Causal Attribution Theory (Walker, 2002)**	**Corning, 2000**	**Social Identity Theory (Ellemers, 2002; Kawakami & Dion, 1992; Mummendey & Kessler, 2002; Walker & Pettigrew, 1984)**
Want something do not have	Want something do not have	Want something do not have	Want something do not have*	–	Want something do not have	Want something do not have	–
Feel entitled to it	Feel entitled to it	Feel entitled to it	Feel entitled to it*	Current outcomes not justified	–	Feel entitled to it	Legitimacy
Some person or group has it	Ingroup member has it	–	Someone else has it	Can imagine alternative situation	–	Compare with group that has it	–
Feasible to get it	–	– –	Feasible to get it	–	–	–	–
–	–	Less and less likely over time to get it	–	Don't think current situation will improve	Stable vs. unstable attribution	–	Stability
–	–	–	–	–	Controllable vs. Uncontrollable	–	Collective efficacy
–	–	–	No personal responsibility for not having it	–	Internal vs. external attribution	–	–
–	–	–	–	–	–	–	Permeability

Note: Crosby (1982) revised the preconditions.

believe that it is feelings of anger and frustration (an attack emotion; e.g., Averill, 1983) that RD engenders, it suggests that RD should be more closely related to nonnormative than to normative behaviors. If people view their disadvantage as the product of illegitimate procedures, they may prefer to challenge the procedures or act outside the realm of those procedures. In a recent experiment involving classes of students, feeling that one's class was deprived in comparison with another class mediated the relationship between legitimacy (manipulated as the way in which a test was completed) and collective nonnormative action (Boen & Vanbeselaere, 2002). Students assigned to the illegitimate experimental condition were also significantly less likely to simply accept the current disadvantaged state of affairs.

Of course, the perception of actions as nonnormative or normative may depend on one's perspective (see Mummendey & Wenzel, 1999). Although members of a disadvantaged group may view their action as normative, the challenged advantaged group may view actions against established procedures as nonnormative. This divergence in perspectives (Mummendey & Wenzel, 1999) is arguably an additional factor that promotes intergroup conflict.

Responsibility

Judgments of responsibility for negative events are central appraisal dimensions to most conceptualizations of anger (Averill, 1983; Weiner, 1995), but are only included in Crosby and Walker's models of RD (see Table 14.1). Appraisals of responsibility may shape the emotional experience in two ways. First, it may move the focus from the self to another person, group, or system. Self-blame for a negative outcome is associated with depression, whereas attributing the same negative event to discrimination by another leads to anger (Major, Quinton, & McCoy, 2002). Second, it might increase people's certainty about their understanding of an event, moving them from sadness-related emotions to anger-related emotions.

Furthermore, we believe that it may be the combination of responsibility appraisals that is most important. For example, in new analyses of the German unification survey studies (see Mummendey et al., 1999), high outgroup responsibility – together with low ingroup responsibility for the current outcome – leads to the most resentment about the intergroup situation. Moreover, combinations of responsibility appraisals also might distinguish envy from resentment – with envy the product of feeling one is not responsible for one's current deprived situation, but resentment as the product of feeling one is not responsible and another is responsible for the situation.

Understanding reactions to GRD also requires understanding who is considered responsible (see Mark & Folger, 1984; Walker et al., 2002). The implications of responsibility attributions for action might be clearest if we consider members of an advantaged group who experience GRD. Will the focus of attention be the disadvantaged group who ostensibly are getting more than they deserve? Or will the focus be the system that enables this inequity to occur? Interestingly, this distinction may be blurred for members of the disadvantaged group, because they may view the larger system and the advantaged group as the same (see Wenzel et al., 2003). However, regardless of the group's status, distinguishing between the system and another group is not an idle theoretical exercise. As Potter and Reicher's (1987) careful analysis of the St. Paul's riots in Britain shows, even in the midst of an intense situation, participants carefully attacked the property (such as stores) that belonged to the people who were seen as most responsible for the participants' grievances.

A last question is how responsibility and legitimacy appraisals might be related. For example, in the study of East Germans, ratings of responsibility to the ingroup and outgroup completely explained ratings of legitimacy. This redundancy is supported by other studies of responsibility attributions. By itself, a negative outcome or a severe disaster (such as an earthquake) does not lead to perceptions of illegitimacy. However, if one or several agents could be blamed for being responsible either by omission or commission (e.g., governmental organizations that do not promote help for the victims of the earthquake or an architect who has constructed the building that collapsed during the earthquake), then the disaster is viewed as illegitimate (Shklar, 1992). How can we reconcile these findings with the earlier argument that legitimacy is about procedures? Perhaps the piece that is missing is that procedures are typically the responsibility of the advantaged group, so from the disadvantaged group's perspective, they may represent the same thing. Certainly, the evaluation of authority intentions is a key part of relational definitions of procedural justice (Tyler, 1997). One interesting question for future research is whether the redundancy documented in previous research continues to occur when the sources of legitimacy and responsibility are more clearly distinguished.

Feasibility

Within RD research, appraisals of the feasibility of alternative outcomes are an important feature in the evaluation of current outcomes (Crosby, 1982; Folger, 1986, 1987). Folger (1987) distinguishes between past feasibility (the belief that the current outcome could have been avoidable) and the likelihood of amelioration (the likelihood that the situation might improve). We think past feasibility is more closely related to our discussion of responsibility attributions for the outcome. In contrast, we believe that the likelihood of amelioration is a complex construct that should be decomposed into appraisals of (1) the stability of the intergroup relations, (2) the permeability of the group boundaries, and (3) efficacy or agency.

When intergroup relations are perceived as highly stable, there is little possibility for change, and the related emotions may be closer to distress or depression. But when the likelihood of amelioration is high or the intergroup situation is unstable, people may feel hope or anger. On the one hand, an expected improvement of the current situation by fortunate or cooperative conditions or the support of another party might trigger hope. On the other hand, if improvement requires active challenge, it may trigger anger, resentment, and effort to communicate with others to develop a consensus for collective action. In this case, when intergroup relations are perceived as unstable, efficacy or agency concerns become important appraisals. Differences in the sense of efficacy or power may be involved in the differential development of either hopelessness or depression (associated with low perceived efficacy) or resentment and anger (associated with high perceived efficacy).

We define agency or efficacy as people's assessments of their individual or group abilities to change the situation (cf. Roseman et al., 1990). This definition links RD models directly to resource mobilization research (Klandermans, 1997). Research suggests that, when mobilization resources (including material resources and social support) are present, people are more likely to engage in "nonnormative" forms of collective behavior (Martin, 1986; see also Mackie et al., 2000).

Beyond mobilization resources, psychological assessments of efficacy may be particularly important predictors of reactions to GRD. Individual self-efficacy is defined as a belief in one's ability to reach one's goals and accomplish tasks (Bandura, 1995). Assessments of individual efficacy may be closely associated with people's reactions to permeable and nonpermeable group boundaries. We know from field and experimental research that members of low status groups who believe group boundaries are permeable will be more likely to pursue individual mobility strategies than members who believe group boundaries are impermeable (Wright et al., 1990).

However, individual efficacy should only be related to people's assessment about their own abilities to change the situation and should not be related to collective action (Azzi, 1995). More recently, Bandura and others have proposed that collective efficacy represents the same beliefs as individual efficacy, but about a particular group (Abrams, 1990; Bandura, 1995; Mummendey et al., 1999). In experimental studies (Ouwerkerk & Ellemers, 2002), participants who reported greater collective efficacy worked harder to improve their group's performance. Azzi (1995) proposes an even more nuanced clarification of efficacy. He defines collective efficacy as including assessments that (1) collective action will yield at least some of the outcomes desired by the group, (2) other group members are willing to participate, and (3) the group possesses needed resources to defend counterattacks. He also proposes a second type of efficacy: participatory self-efficacy. Azzi defines participatory self-efficacy as the belief that "the individual's participation is seen as having a potential incremental effect on collective action" (Azzi, 1995, p. 104). It is people who are high in both participatory self-efficacy and collective efficacy who should be most willing to participate in collective action.

To our knowledge, participative efficacy has not been systematically explored (but see research on common dilemmas, e.g., Yamagishi & Sato, 1986.) However, Azzi's distinction between participative and collective efficacy is an important reminder of the distinction between group-based emotion (I feel this because I see myself as a member of this group) and collective emotions – given these circumstances, all members of my group should share this feeling (see Manstead & Fischer, 2001). Both types of emotional experience might be necessary for prompting commitment to collective action.

Social Support

If the antecedents proposed by RD theorists are compared with various lists of emotional appraisals, one key dimension missing from earlier lists of RD antecedents is social support. In fact, Bies and Tripp (1996) argue that the most frequent reaction to any type of fairness is to verify the event with others – was it really unfair? This kind of social validation is particularly important because in the evaluation of single events, one often faces attributional ambiguity (Major et al., 2002). Klandermans (1997) captures this idea with the normative motive for participating in collective action – derived from people's ratings of the reactions they expect from significant others and how important they feel those reactions are. Similarly, Mackie and her colleagues (2000) argue that anger toward an outgroup is more likely when people feel there is broad collective support for their group's position.

Although not discussed explicitly as a dimension of appraisal, we might argue that one type of social support, identification with the group, is included in many analyses of GRD (e.g., Mummendey et al., 1999; Walker & Pettigrew, 1984). Groups can act as a source of emotional or instrumental support and provide social validation for one's perceptions (see Major et al., 2002). If a particular group is more relevant or important for people, they will show and expect greater commitment to the group, thereby perceiving greater social support by the group. As outlined in social identity and self-categorization theories (Ellemers, Spears, & Doosje, 1999; Turner, 1999), when people define themselves in terms of a shared group membership, they accentuate intragroup similarities and intergroup differences. They see themselves less as unique and different individuals and more as similar prototypical representatives of the ingroup (Turner, 1999). For example, when a woman defines a negative personal experience as gender discrimination, she identifies the experience as something that can happen to other women and not just to herself (Foster, 2000). This perceptual shift suggests that simply interpreting the situation in intergroup terms may give people a greater sense of certainty about their appraisals, social support, and collective efficacy (e.g., Hogg & Grieve, 1999). In field and experimental studies with natural groups, degree of identification with the group is a more important influence than the permeability of group boundaries on group members' decision to stay or try to leave the group (Ellemers et al., 1999).

However, just because members identify with a disadvantaged group does not mean that they view the intergroup situation as illegitimate. In some cases, identification could be associated with the view that the intergroup situation is appropriate (see Crocker, 1999; Crocker et al., 1999). Imagine a female employee who feels mistreated by her male boss. If she associates gender with a feminist ideology, she might feel empowered (and angry), but if she associates gender with a traditional ideology, she might feel the mistreatment is acceptable or deserved. If we pay attention to the content of the collective representations associated with particular group memberships, we might be able to predict when a salient group membership might protect against the negative self-implications of disadvantage and when it will not. In other words, we can talk about politicized and nonpoliticized group identities (Kelly & Breinlinger, 1996; Simon & Klandermans, 2001). In fact, as Major and her colleagues (2002) propose, politicized collective identification or group consciousness combine group identification with elements of injustice and collective efficacy. In other words, politicized collective identities include the feelings of GRD as part of the social identity.

APPRAISAL FUNCTION OF SOCIAL COMPARISONS

Within RD theory, negative outcomes of group-based social comparisons initiate the emotional experience of GRD. In general, the stronger the discrepancy between the group's outcome and the comparison referent, the stronger the feeling of GRD will be. However, RD research reminds us that the size of status differences is important. Sometimes, minor differences between groups may be more easily tolerated than perceptions of blatant inferiority; at other times, minor differences may be more problematic (see Brown, 1984).

RD research also reminds us that people are likely to consider multiple comparison sources (Messe & Watts, 1983). In fact, Pettigrew and his colleagues initially defined GRD as the product of two comparisons – disadvantaged comparisons between one's ingroup and an outgroup, and favorable comparisons between oneself and the ingroup. This formulation allowed for a distinction between GRD and "double" deprivation, in which one feels deprived in comparison with one's ingroup and as a group representative in comparison with an outgroup (Vanneman & Pettigrew, 1972; Walker & Pettigrew, 1984). For example, the African American men most likely to participate in the urban riots reported feelings of "double deprivation" – they felt African Americans were deprived in comparison with European Americans, and that they personally were deprived in comparison with other people (Dibble, 1981; see also Vanneman & Pettigrew, 1972). Moreover, recent research on the relationship between IRD and GRD suggests that within-group comparisons may be important complements to between-group comparisons (e.g., Pettigrew, 2002; Tougas & Beaton, 2002). When ingroup boundaries are perceived as permeable, personally advantaged but group disadvantaged participants may be quite willing to acknowledge the problem but not address it (Smith, Spears, & Oyen, 1994). If the ingroup boundaries are perceived to be impermeable, personally advantaged but group disadvantaged folks may have the most resources and motivation to challenge the system (Pettigrew, 1978; Wright et al., 1990).

This treatment of IRD and GRD is different from reformulations of RD within self-categorization and social identity frameworks. Within a Social Identity Theory/Self Categorization Theory (SIT/SCT) theoretical framework, IRD and GRD are assumed to be independent from each other because IRD develops from a salient personal identity, whereas GRD develops from a salient social identity (Kessler, Mummendey, & Leisse, 2000; Postmes et al., 1999). The assumption and related research suggest that, when a person thinks of him/herself as a group representative, within-group comparisons or interpersonal comparisons and motives will not influence perceptions of group disadvantage. In contrast, when a person conceives him/herself as an unique individual, intergroup comparisons and motives will not influence feelings of personal disadvantages (Kessler et al., 2000; Postmes et al., 1999). Although *interpersonal* comparisons and motives may be independent of intergroup comparisons and processes, we think that a full understanding of GRD, its antecedents, and its consequences requires a consideration of *intragroup* processes, as well as intergroup processes. In future research, evaluations of ingroup respect (Smith & Tyler, 1997) or participative efficacy (Azzi, 1995) may provide the bridge between perceptions of personal and group disadvantages. However, this possibility requires researchers to measure comparisons carefully (e.g., are people thinking of themselves as group members or as unique individuals?) and to not assume or construct comparison combinations post hoc (see Smith & Pettigrew, 2002). An important future question will be to examine under what conditions personal and group disadvantages are independent and under what conditions they work in concert in the development of collective action.

Not only might people combine personal and group-level comparisons, they also might use temporal comparisons (at the personal and group level) to frame intergroup comparisons. If comparisons with an imagined future suggest improvement, people may be more likely to tolerate current intergroup inequalities (Klandermans, 1997; Mummendey & Kessler, 2000; Ouwerkerk & Ellemers, 2002). Alternatively, dramatic changes across time might make current intergroup inequities less tolerable. For example, during the German unification process, East Germans were expected to assimilate to West German economic and political conditions (Mummendey & Kessler, 2000). As the lower status group, they were faced with enormous change over time. For East Germans, comparisons across time were rated as more informative, important, and frequent than comparisons with West Germans. Both types of comparisons influenced their feelings of resentment. However, for West Germans who did not face massive changes in their lifestyle, neither comparisons with East Germans nor temporal comparisons influenced their feeling of resentment. However, social comparisons with the United States were seen as relevant and therefore affected West Germans' feelings of resentment.

APPRAISALS AS ANTECEDENT CONDITIONS OR AS COGNITIVE CONTENT

According to cognitive theories of emotions, a current state of affairs elicits emotions depending on the way the current state of affairs is appraised (Frijda, 1993; Roseman & Smith, 2001). Therefore, it is tempting to interpret the proposed antecedents of RD as appraisal dimensions for feeling deprived. However, we must recognize the ambiguity in the concept of appraisal (e.g., Parkinson & Manstead, 1992; Russell, 1987). According to Frijda (1993), one should distinguish between appraisals as the antecedents of emotions and appraisals as the cognitive content of the emotional experience. Many emotions researchers have measured the appraisal of events, the phenomenological experience, tendencies toward various actions, and different emotion-related goals as aspects of the cognitive experience (Frijda, 1993; Roseman et al., 1990). These components of emotions are introspectively observable and form stable patterns in self-report studies. However, what really causes these emotions remains unclear. Moreover, the implicit assumption of a "linear model" of emotion processes (Frijda, 1993; Lewis, 1996) does not recognize that emotions also inform us about the current states of affairs (see Schwartz & Clore, 1996) and does not allow for some recursive relationships between different components of emotions. A simplified linear model does not offer a good explanation for how complex emotions develop out of scarce information or simpler emotions, or why some emotions require more cognitive elaboration than others.

Initial evidence that the appraisal dimensions that we discussed do not relate in a simple "linear fashion," but form a belief system comes from longitudinal surveys of former East Germans' experiences with the German unification process (Kessler & Mummendey, 2002). Mummendey and colleagues (1999) showed that resentment about the relationship between East and West Germans mediates the impact of socio-structural (perceived status, stability, legitimacy, and permeability) characteristics on collective behavior, such as social and realistic competition. Moreover, because perceived status depends crucially on social comparisons (Kessler, Mummendey, & Leisse, 2000), resentment also mediates the relationship between comparisons and intergroup behavior.

Similarly, there is also evidence for a recursive relationship between the strength of ingroup identification and feeling deprived. On the one hand, experiments, field studies, and longitudinal field surveys show that greater identification with the group creates greater sensitivity to disadvantageous intergroup comparisons and more GRD (e.g., Abrams, 1990; Kessler & Mummendey, 2002; Mummendey et al., 1999). On the other hand, experimental evidence shows that GRD can increase identification with the disadvantaged group (Walker, 1999) and that people who view the intergroup relationship as illegitimate and group boundaries as impermeable identify more strongly with the disadvantaged group (Ellemers, 1993). Direct manipulations of emotional states also change the degree of ingroup identification (Hollbach & Kessler, 2002). In their study, participants had to report either positive or negative emotions that were either directed to the ingroup or the outgroup. In addition, they measured ingroup identification before and after the emotion manipulation to assess the change in identification. The results indicate that positive emotions toward the ingroup and negative emotions toward the outgroup enhanced ingroup identification, whereas negative emotions toward the ingroup and positive emotions toward the outgroup reduced ingroup identification.

We believe that including recursive relationships among ingroup identification, emotional experiences, and appraisals of the intergroup context is especially important for understanding the tendency toward collective action. Moreover, these recursive relationships may also occur in conjunction with interactions within the social context. As Manstead & Fischer (2001) argue, other group members' reactions to an emotional event may shape the intensity, duration, and expression of an emotion. Thus, the development of a complex emotion (like group-based resentment) may not only depend on an individual's belief system, but also on communication and validation of those beliefs by other group members (e.g., Haidt, 2001).

CONCLUSIONS

RD gained its notoriety as an explanation of collective action. However, to understand what motivates collective action, we need to specify the particular emotional experiences associated with perceptions of relative intergroup disadvantage. Unfortunately, RD emotions are rarely discussed in detail; they have often been inferred and seldom measured (and if measured, then without differentiating different emotions from each other). In this chapter, we propose that depending on the appraisals of responsibility, stability, social support, and different types of efficacy, emotional reactions to perceptions of relative disadvantage may vary from disappointment and distress to resentment and indignation. The specific action tendencies associated with different emotions can help to specify which behavioral course is taken from the wide variety of potential reactions and strengthen the predictive value of RD theory. We believe that it is the cognitive appraisals that elicit group-based resentment that will be most closely associated with collective challenges of the injustice, but further appraisals of the situation may encourage or hinder that reaction.

Reviewing the antecedents suggested by RD researchers to be associated with feeling deprived also suggests that certain dimensions should be redefined. For example, feasibility may include assessments of situational stability, concerns about personal and collective efficacy, and also shared predictions, expectancies, and hopes. By clarifying the concept of feasibility, we can consider a broader range of outcomes more systematically; in particular, we can consider when perceptions of relative disadvantage will lead to increased physical stress. Our discussion also reveals the importance of considering multiple comparisons (e.g., how social comparisons may be shaped by people's temporal comparisons, how intergroup comparisons may be related to people's assessments of their position within the group) and multiple attributions (people's assessments of the ingroup's lack of responsibility in combination with the outgroup's responsibility, people's assessment of the ingroup's collective efficacy in combination with the outgroup's reactions).

Finally, a model in which appraisal dimensions are considered to be part of a constellation of beliefs about the intergroup situation, rather than part of a linear sequence of antecedents and consequences may prove to be the most descriptive. A detailed exploration of the temporal evolution of emotional reactions to a perceived disadvantage could be beneficial because it might explain how group-based emotions can become a collective phenomenon that ultimately leads to collective action. Moreover, this extended perspective on emotions provides researchers with the opportunity to analyze the influence of the social context and, particularly, the presence of other ingroup members on people's emotional experiences.

ACKNOWLEDGMENTS

Preparation of this chapter was supported in part by NIMH Grant 1 R15 MH62096 01A1. We thank the editors for their very helpful comments on an earlier draft.

References

Abrams, D. (1990). *Political identity: Relative deprivation, social identity and the case of Scottish nationalism.* WSRC 16-19 Initiative – Occasional Papers.

Averill, J. R. (1983). Studies on anger and aggression: Implications for theories of emotion. *American Psychologist, 38*, 1145–1160.

Azzi, A. (1995). From competitive interests, perceived injustice, and identity needs to collective action: Psychology mechanisms in ethnic nationalism. In C. Dandeleer (Ed.), *Nationalism and violence* (p. 104). New Brunswick, NJ: Transaction.

Bandura, A. (1995). Exercise of personal and collective efficacy in changing societies. In A. Bandura (Ed.), *Self-efficacy in changing societies* (pp. 1–45). Cambridge: Cambridge University Press.

Bies, R. J., & Tripp, T. M. (1996). Beyond distrust: "getting even" and the need for revenge. In R. Kramer and T. R. Tyler (Eds.), *Trust in organizations*. Beverly Hills, CA: Sage.

Boen, F., & Vanbeselaere, N. (2002). The relative impact of socio-structural characteristics on behavioral reactions against membership in a low status group. *Group Processes / Intergroup Relations, 5*, 299–318.

Brown, R. J. (1984). The effects of intergroup similarity and cooperative vs. competitive orientation on intergroup discrimination. *British Journal of Social Psychology, 23*, 21–33.

Buunk, B., Collins, R., Taylor, S., VanYperon, N., & Dakof, G. (1990). The affective consequences of social comparisons: Either direction has its ups and downs. *Journal of Personality and Social Psychology, 59*, 1238–1249.

Corning, A. F. (2000). Assessing perceived social inequity: A relative deprivation framework. *Journal of Personality and Social Psychology, 78*, 463–477.

Crocker, J. (1999). Social stigma and self-esteem: Situational construction of self-worth. *Journal of Experimental Social Psychology, 35*, 89–107.

Crosby, F. (1976). A model of egotistical deprivation. *Psychological Review, 83*, 85–113.

Crosby, F. (1982). *Relative deprivation and working women*. New York: Oxford University Press.

Davis, J. A. (1959). A formal interpretation of the theory of relative deprivation. *Sociometry, 22*, 280–296.

Dibble, U. (1981). Socially shared deprivation and the approval of violence: Another look at the experience of American Blacks during the 1960s. *Ethnicity, 8*, 149–169.

Ellemers, N. (1993). The influence of socio-structural variables on identity management strategies. *European Review of Social Psychology, 4*, 27–57.

Ellemers, N. (2002). Social identity and relative deprivation. In I. Walker, & H. J. Smith (Eds.), *Relative deprivation: Specification, development and integration*. Cambridge: Cambridge University Press.

Ellemers, N., Spears, R., & Doosje, B. (1999). *Social identity: Context, commitment, content*. Oxford, UK: Blackwell Publishers.

Ellsworth, P. C. (1994). Sense, culture, and sensibility. In S. Kitayama & H. R. Markus (Eds.), *Emotion and culture: Empirical studies of mutual influence* (pp. 23–50). Washington, DC: American Psychological Association.

Feather, N. T., & Sherman, R. (2002). Envy, resentment, Schadenfreude, and sympathy: Reactions to deserved and undeserved achievement and subsequent failure. *Personality and Social Psychology Bulletin, 28*, 953–961.

Finkel, S., & Rule, J. (1987). Relative deprivation and related psychological theories of civil violence: A critical review. *Research in Social Movements: Conflicts and Change, 9*, 47–69.

Folger, R. (1986). A referent cognitions theory of relative deprivation. In J. Olson, C. P. Herman, and M. Zanna (Eds.), *Relative deprivation and social comparison: The Ontario Symposium*. Hillsdale, NJ: Lawrence Erlbaum.

Folger, R. (1987). Reformulating the preconditions of resentments: A referent cognitions model. In J. Masters & W. Smith (Eds.), *Social comparison, social justice and relative deprivation*. Hillsdale, NJ: Lawrence Erlbaum Associates.

Foster, M. D. (2000). Positive and negative responses to personal discrimination: Does coping make a difference? *Journal of Social Psychology, 140*, 93–106.

Frijda, N. H. (1993). The place of appraisal in emotion. *Cognition and Emotion, 7*, 357–387.

Gurr, T. (1970). *Why men rebel*. Princeton, NJ: Princeton University Press.

Guyll, M., Matthews, K. A., & Bromberger, J. T. (2001). Discrimination and unfair treatment: Relationship to cardiovascular reactivity among African American and European American women. *Health Psychology, 20*, 315–325.

Haidt, J. (2001). The emotional dog and its rational tail: A social intuitionist approach to moral judgment. *Psychological Review, 108*, 814–834.

Hogg, M. A., & Grieve, P. (1999). Social identity theory and the crisis of confidence in social psychology. *Asian Journal of Social Psychology, 2*, 79–93.

Hollbach, S., & Kessler, T. (2002). *Emotions in intergroup context: Group-based emotions as determinants of ingroup identification*. Poster presented at the 13th General Meeting of the European Association of Experimental Social Society, San Sebastian, Spain, June 26–29.

Kahneman, D., & Tversky, A. (1982). Availability and the simulation heuristic. In D. Kahneman, P. Slovic, & A. Tversky (Eds.), *Judgment under uncertainty: Heuristics and biases*. New York: Oxford University Press.

Kawakami, K., & Dion, K. (1992). The impact of salient self-identities on relative deprivation and action intentions. *European Journal of Social Psychology, 23*, 525–540.

Kelly, C., & Breinlinger, S. (1996). *The social psychology of collective action*. London, UK: Taylor and Francis.

Kessler, T., & Mummendey, A. (2002). Sequential or parallel processing? A longitudinal field study concerning determinants of identity-management strategies. *Journal of Personality and Social Psychology, 82*, 75–88.

Kessler, T., Mummendey, A., & Leisse, U.-K. (2000). The personal-group discrepancy: Is there a common information basis of personal and group judgment? *Journal of Personality and Social Psychology, 79*, 95–109.

Klandermans, B. (1997). *Principles of movement participation*. Basil Blackwell: Oxford.

Koss, M. P., Goodman, L. A., Browne, A., Fitzgerald, L. F., Keita, G. P., & Russon, N. F. (1994). *No safe haven: Male violence against women at home, at work and in the community*. Washington, DC: American Psychological Association.

Lalonde, R. N., & Silverman, R. A. (1994). Behavioral preferences in response to social injustice: The effects of group permeability and social identity salience. *Journal of Personality and Social Psychology, 66*, 78–85.

Leach, C. W., Iyer, A., & Pederson, A. (2003). *The politics of emotion: The role of intergroup guilt and anger in apology to Aboriginal Australians*. Unpublished manuscript, University of California, Santa Cruz.

Leach, C. W., Snider, N., & Iyer, A. (2002). "Poisoning the consciences of the fortunate": The experience of relative advantage and support for social equality. In I. Walker & H. J. Smith (Eds.), *Relative deprivation: Specification, development and integration*. Cambridge, UK: Cambridge University Press.

Lewis, M. D. (1996). Self-organising cognitive appraisals. *Cognition and Emotion, 10*, 1–25.

Mackie, D. M., Devos, T., & Smith, E. R. (2000). Intergroup emotions: Explaining offensive action tendencies in an intergroup context. *Journal of Personality and Social Psychology, 79*, 602–616.

Major, B. (1994). From social inequality to personal entitlement. *Advances in Experimental Social Psychology, 26*, 293–355.

Major, B., Quinton, W. J., & McCoy, S. K. (2002). Antecedents and consequences of attributions to discrimination: Theoretical and empirical advances. *Advances in Experimental Social Psychology, 34*, 251–330.

Manstead, A. S. R., & Fischer, A. H. (2001). Social appraisal: The social world as object and influence on appraisal processes. In K. Scherer, A. Schorr, & T. Johnstone (Eds.), *Appraisal processes in emotion: Theory, methods, research*. Oxford, UK: Oxford University Press.

Mark, M., & Folger, R. (1984). Response to relative deprivation: A conceptual framework. *Review of Personality and Social Psychology: Emotion, Relationship and Health, 5*, 192–218.

Martin, J. (1986). The psychology of injustice. In J. Olson, C. P. Herman, and M. Zanna (Eds.), *Relative deprivation and social comparison: The Ontario Symposium*. Hillsdale, NJ: Lawrence Erlbaum.

Messe, L. A., & Watts, B. L. (1983). The complex nature of the sense of fairness: Internal standards and social comparisons as bases for reward evaluation. *Journal of Personality and Social Psychology, 21*, 480–500.

Mikula, G., Petri, B., & Tanzer, N. (1990). What people regard as unjust: Types and structures of everyday experiences of injustice. *European Journal of Social Psychology, 20*, 133–149.

Mummendey, A., & Kessler, T. (2000). Deutsch–deutsche Fusion und sozial Identität: Sozialpsychologische Perspektiven auf das Verhältnis von Ost-zu Westdeutschen. [German–German fusion and social identity: Social psychological perspectives on the relations between East and West Germans.] In H. Esser (Hrsg.), *Der Wandel nach der Wende. Gesellschaft, Wirtschaft, Politik in Ostdeutschland* (pp. 277–307). Wiesbaden: Westdeutscher Verlag.

Mummendey, A., Kessler, T., Klink, A., & Mielke, R. (1999). Strategies to cope with negative social identity: Predictions by social identity theory and relative deprivation theory. *Journal of Personality and Social Psychology, 76*, 229–245.

Mummendey, A., & Wenzel, M. (1999). Social discrimination and tolerance in intergroup relations: Reactions to intergroup differences. *Personality and Social Psychology Review, 3*(2), 158–174.

Olson, J. M., & Roese, N. J. (2002). Relative deprivation and counterfactual thinking. In I. Walker & H. J. Smith (Eds.), *Relative deprivation: Specification, development and integration*. Cambridge, UK: Cambridge University Press.

Ouwerkerk, J. W., & Ellemers, N. (2002). The benefits of being disadvantaged: Performance-related circumstances and consequences of intergroup comparisons. *European Journal of Social Psychology, 32*(1), 73–92.

Parkinson, B., & Manstead, A. S. R. (1992). Appraisal as a cause of emotion. In M. S. Clark (Ed.), *Emotion. Review of the personality and social psychology* (Vol. 13; pp. 122–149). Newbury Park, CA: Sage.

Pettigrew, T. F. (1978). Three issues in ethnicity: Boundaries, deprivations and perceptions. In J. M. Yinger & S. J. Cutler (Eds.), *Major social issues* (pp. 25–49). New York: Free Press.

Pettigrew, T. F. (2002). Summing up: Relative deprivation as a key social psychology concept. In I. Walker & H. J. Smith (Eds.), *Relative deprivation: Specification, development and integration*. Cambridge, UK: Cambridge University Press.

Postmes, T., Young, H., Branscombe, N. R., & Spears, R. (1999). Personal and group motivational determinants of perceived discrimination and privilege discrepancies. *Journal of Personality and Social Psychology, 76*, 320–338.

Potter, J., & Reicher, S. (1987). Discourses of community and conflict: The organization of social categories in accounts of a "riot." *British Journal of Social Psychology, 26*, 25–40.

Roseman, I. J., & Smith, C. R. (2001). Appraisal theory: Overview, assumptions, varieties, controversies. In K. Scherer, A. Schorr, & T. Johnstone (Eds.), *Appraisal processes in emotion: Theory, methods, research*. Oxford, UK: Oxford University Press.

Roseman, I. J., Spindel, M. S., & Jose, P. E. (1990). Appraisals of emotion-eliciting events: Testing a theory of discrete emotions. *Journal of Personality and Social Psychology, 59*, 899–915.

Runciman, W. G. (1966). *Relative deprivation and social justice: A study of attitudes to social inequality in twentieth-century England*. Berkeley: University of California Press.

Russell, J. A. (1987). Comment in articles by Frijda and by Conway and Bekerian. *Cognition and Emotion, 1*, 193–197.

Schmitt, M., & Maes, J. (2002). Stereotypic ingroup bias as self-defense against relative deprivation: Evidence from a longitudinal study of the German unification process. *European Journal of Social Psychology, 32*, 293–434.

Schwartz, N., & Clore, G. L. (1996). Feelings and phenomenal experiences. In E. T. Higgins & A. W. Kruglanski (Eds.), *Social psychology: Handbook of basic principles* (pp. 433–465). New York: Guilford Press.

Shaver, P., Schwartz, J., Kirson, D., & O'Connor, C. (1987). Emotion knowledge: Further exploration of a prototype approach. *Journal of Personality and Social Psychology, 52*, 1061–1086.

Shklar, J. (1992). *The faces of injustice*. New Haven: Yale University Press.

Simon, B., & Klandermans, B. (2001). Politicized collective identity: A social psychological analysis. *American-Psychologist, 56*(4), 319–331.

Smith, E. (1993). Social identity and social emotions: Towards new conceptualizations of prejudice. In D. Mackie & D. Hamilton (Eds.), *Affect, cognition and stereotyping* (pp. 297–315). San Diego, CA: Academic Press.

Smith, H. J., & Pettigrew, T. F. (2002). *Relative deprivation. A conceptual critique and meta-analysis*. Unpublished manuscript, University of California, Berkeley.

Smith, H. J., Spears, R., & Oyen, M. (1994). People like us: The influence of personal deprivation and salience of group membership on justice evaluations. *Journal of Experimental Social Psychology, 30*, 277–299.

Smith, H. J., & Tyler, T. R. (1997). Choosing the right pond: How group membership shapes self-esteem and group-oriented behavior. *Journal of Experimental Social Psychology, 33*, 146–170.

Stouffer, S. A., Suchman, E. A., DeVinney, L. C., Starr, S. A., & Williams, R. M. (1949). *The American soldier: Adjustment to army life* (Vol. 1). Princeton, NJ: Princeton University Press.

Swim, J., & Hyers, L. L. (1999). Excuse me – What did you just say?!: Women's public and private responses to sexist remarks. *Journal of Experimental Social Psychology, 35*, 68–88.

Taylor, D. M., Moghaddam, F. M., & Bellerose, J. (1989). Social comparison in an intergroup context. *Journal of Social Psychology, 125*, 89–109.

Tougas, F., & Beaton, A. M. (2002). Personal and group relative deprivation: Connecting the I to the we. In I. Walker & H. J. Smith (Eds.), *Relative deprivation: Specification, development, and integration* (pp. 119–135). New York: Cambridge University Press.

Turner, J. C. (1999). Some current issues in research on social identity and self-categorization theories. In N. Ellemers, R. Spears, & B. Doosje (Eds.), *Social identity: Context, commitment, content*. Oxford, UK: Blackwell Publishers.

Tyler, T. R. (1997). The psychology of legitimacy. *Personality and Social Psychology Review, 1*, 323–344.

Tyler, T. R., Boeckmann, R. J., Smith, H. J., & Huo, Y. J. (1997). *Social justice in a diverse society*. Denver, CO: Westview Press.

Vanneman, R. D., & Pettigrew, T. F. (1972). Race and relative deprivation in the urban United States. *Race, 13*, 461–485.

Walker, I. (1999). Effects of personal and group relative deprivation on personal and collective self-esteem. *Group Processes and Intergroup Relations, 2*, 365–380.

Walker, I., & Pettigrew, T. F. (1984). Relative deprivation theory: An overview and conceptual critique. *British Journal of Social Psychology, 23*, 301–310.

Walker, I., & Smith, H. J. (2002). *Relative deprivation: Specification, development and integration*. Cambridge, UK: Cambridge University Press.

Walker, I., Wong, N. K., & Kretzschmar, K. (2002). Relative deprivation and attribution: From grievance to action. In I. Walker, & H. J. Smith (Eds.), *Relative deprivation: specification, development and integration* (pp. 288–312). Cambridge, UK: Cambridge University Press.

Weiner, B. (1995). Inferences of responsibility and social motivation. In M. P. Zanna (Ed.), *Advances in experimental social psychology* (Vol. 27; pp. 1–47). San Diego: Academic Press.

Wenzel, M., Mummendey, A., Weber, U., & Waldzus, S. (2003). The ingroup as pars pro toto: Projection from the ingroup onto the inclusive category as a precursor to social discrimination. *Personality and Social Psychology Bulletin, 29*, 461–473.

Williams, R. M. (1975). Relative deprivation. In L. A. Coser (Ed.), *The idea of social structure: papers in honor of Robert K. Merton* (p. 356). New York: Harcourt Brace Jovanovich.

Wood, J. (1989). Theory and research concerning social comparisons of personal attributes. *Psychological Bulletin, 106*, 231–248.

Wright, S. C., Taylor, D. M., & Moghaddam, F. M. (1990). Responding to membership in a disadvantaged group: From acceptance to collective protest. *Journal of Personality and Social Psychology, 58*, 994–1003.

Yamagishi, T., & Sato, K. (1986). Motivational basis of the public goods problem. *Journal of Personality and Social Psychology, 50*, 67–73.

15

Interpreting the Ingroup's Negative Actions Toward Another Group

Emotional Reactions to Appraised Harm

Nyla R. Branscombe and Anca M. Miron

Social identity theory (Tajfel & Turner, 1986) claims that how people interpret group-relevant events depends on their own group membership and the structural relations that exist between the ingroup and a salient comparison outgroup. When people think of themselves as a member of a social group, they are motivated to protect the identity of their group, and this can lead them to appraise the ingroup's actions in ways that benefit their ingroup (Baumeister & Hastings, 1997; Iyer, Leach, & Pedersen, in press). We argue that such ingroup-serving motivations affect the appraisal of ingroup actions and the emotions that group members experience when they self-categorize as members of their group (Branscombe, Doosje, & McGarty, 2002; Montada & Schneider, 1989).

Even when the self has clearly played no causal role in an event, depending on the meaning that event has for a valued social identity, differential emotional reactions can occur (Branscombe et al., 1993; Cialdini et al., 1976; Doosje et al., 1998; Yzerbyt et al., 2002). As Smith (1999) notes, group-based emotional responses rest on appraisals that consider the event's implications for one's *social identity*, whereas personal emotional responses are based on appraisals that consider the event in terms of its implications for *personal identity*. In this chapter, we explore the processes that are instigated when people are reminded of their ingroup's past or present harmful actions toward another group. We focus on how appraisals that reduce the severity and injustice of the ingroup's actions can undermine the experience of collective guilt. Specifically, we consider how social identity concerns encourage appraisals that justify and protect the ingroup when group members are confronted with the harm done to another group. We examine two distinct emotional response mediators of the effects of perceiving the harm-doing as illegitimate for the degree to which collective guilt is experienced. Specifically, empathy for the harmed group and distress at exposure to their suffering are both assessed

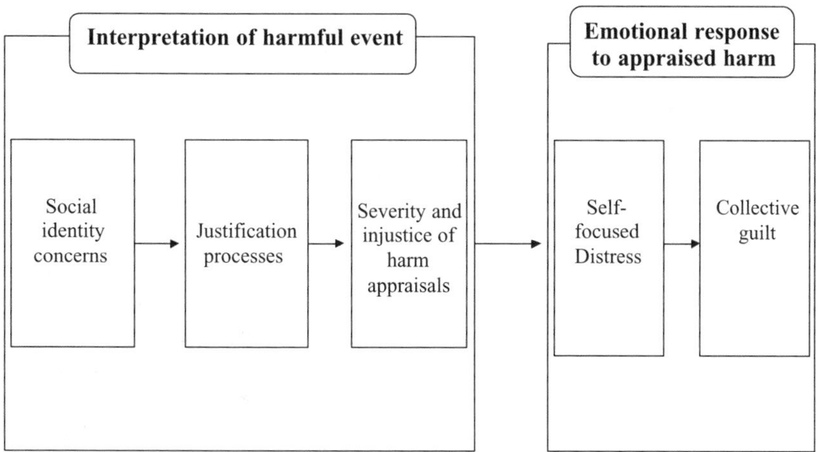

FIGURE 15.1. Self-focused distress and collective guilt responses as a function of severity and injustice appraisals when the ingroup's harmful actions toward another group are confronted.

to determine which is the primary mediator of how much collective guilt is experienced.

We argue that the motivation to see the ingroup's actions as moral can color ingroup members' appraisals of group-relevant events. Indeed, there are several types of group-protection strategies that will allow the ingroup's actions to be appraised as just and moral. We suggest that, when ingroup members are confronted with the harm done by their ingroup, the perceived illegitimacy of that event is most likely to evoke self-focused distress and collective guilt. As illustrated in Figure 15.1, we propose that social identity concerns affect whether ingroup actions are appraised as harmful and unjust or not. To the extent that the harm done is appraised as an injustice for which the ingroup is responsible, more distress and collective guilt will be experienced. When the event the ingroup is responsible for is appraised as legitimate and just, these aversive emotional reactions are unlikely to be experienced.

COLLECTIVE GUILT AS A GROUP-LEVEL AVERSIVE EMOTION

Guilt has been defined as regret for wrongdoing (Eisenberg, 2000). More specifically, it has been conceptualized as "an agitation-based emotion that is aroused when the actor actually causes, anticipates causing, or is associated with an aversive event" (Ferguson & Stegge, 1998, p. 20). The experience of personal guilt involves acceptance of responsibility for actions that cause harm to another or otherwise represent a violation of moral standards, and it is often accompanied by a desire to make amends for the wrongdoing (Ferguson & Stegge, 1998; Hoffman, 2000; Tangney, 1995).

Collective guilt has been defined as a group-based emotion that is experienced when people categorize themselves as members of a group that has committed unjustified harm to another group (Branscombe et al., 2002). In contrast to personal guilt, the individual need not feel responsible for the harmful event to experience collective guilt. When people categorize themselves as group members, reminders of their ingroup's harmful actions can result in feelings of *guilt by association* (Heider, 1958; Hoffman, 1987, 1991). According to Hoffman (1987, p. 50), guilt by association can be experienced when one's relatively advantaged group is seen as the cause of the distress evoked in the victims. For collective guilt to be aroused, the ingroup's responsibility for the harm experienced by the other group must be acknowledged (Branscombe et al., 2002; Iyer, Leach, & Crosby, 2003).

Collective guilt has been conceptualized as an aversive emotion. For this reason, the circumstances needed to induce it may occur relatively infrequently (Branscombe et al., 2002; Iyer et al., in press). When people encounter *social identity threats* that imply their group has illegitimately harmed another group (Branscombe et al., 1999), they can use multiple strategies as means of justifying that particular harmful action. To the extent that such justification strategies are effective, the event caused by the ingroup will be appraised as just and, as a result, little guilt will be experienced.

Perceptions of illegitimacy have been shown to be an important predictor of personal guilt (Roseman, 1984; Frijda, Kuipers, & Ter Schure, 1989). Likewise, perceiving the ingroup's actions as illegitimate predict collective guilt. For example, Montada and Schneider (1989) found that guilt for intergroup inequality is best predicted by dominant group members' appraisals of discrimination against minorities as unjust. Collective guilt is highest when the relative status advantage of a privileged ingroup is perceived to be illegitimate (Branscombe et al., 2002; Iyer et al., 2003; Schmitt et al., 2000).

HOW EVENT APPRAISALS CAN PREVENT COLLECTIVE GUILT

Appraising the ingroup's actions or higher status as legitimate should be an important means of preventing collective guilt. We argue that when an intergroup situation is appraised as unfair, members of advantaged groups experience distress when they are confronted with the suffering of the victimized outgroup. To the extent that the ingroup is accepted as responsible for illegitimately causing the harm done to the other group, then collective guilt may be induced. However, when the perceiver's own *identity concerns* are activated by the social context, then the ingroup's actions should be more likely to be appraised as legitimate, which will result in little collective guilt.

As the negativity of the event that people are confronted with increases, the potential threat to the ingroup's positive social identity is greater. As a result, ingroup members may be motivated to appraise their ingroup's actions as less harmful or unjust. Dominant group members do legitimize the victimized group's outcomes, especially when their own advantage was illegitimately obtained (Hornsey et al., 2003) or they believe they cannot correct the harm done (Bandura, 1990; Berscheid & Walster, 1967; Lerner & Simmons, 1966; Schmitt, Branscombe, & Brehm, in press). When the harm done involves economically disadvantaging the other group, exaggerating the input and worth of the overbenefited group or minimizing the deservingness of the disadvantaged group can lead to appraisals of inequality as just (Branscombe et al., 2003; Mallett & Swim, in press; Walster, Berscheid, & Walster, 1973). Therefore, to the extent that inequality is appraised as legitimate or fair, the basis for inequity distress will be undermined.

EFFECT OF IDENTITY CONCERNS ON EVENT APPRAISALS

Social identity theory (Tajfel & Turner, 1986) assumes that intergroup event appraisals are shaped by people's membership in social groups. When people value or identify with their group, they will be especially prone to interpreting the ingroup's actions in ways that provide justification for its harmful consequences. By doing so, the value of the group's identity can be protected even in the face of threats to its value, which considerable research has demonstrated is particularly likely among high identifiers (Branscombe et al., 1999).

Branscombe et al. (2003) found that group identification moderated responses to a disadvantaged group, depending on the perceived fairness of the ingroup's status advantage. When highly identified white participants were asked to think about their illegitimate racial privileges, they attempted to minimize the harmful consequences of their advantages and derogated the victims (i.e., showed increased modern racism). In contrast, those who were lower in white identification showed reductions in modern racism when exposed to the same social identity threat of illegitimate privilege, suggesting that they experienced guilt when the inequality that favors their ingroup was made salient. Likewise, when men are confronted with gender-based inequality, they exhibit signs of defensive legitimization the more they identify with their gender group. Specifically, Miron, Branscombe, and Schmitt (2003) found in two studies that gender group identification in men significantly predicted acceptance of gender inequality legitimizations. We argue that dominant group members who highly identify with their group are indeed more motivated to defend the justice of their group's actions, and do so by minimizing the harm done, derogating the victims, or by appraising the intergroup inequality as legitimate.

JUSTIFICATION PROCESSES

A variety of theorists (Baumeister & Hastings, 1997; Branscombe et al., 2002; Iyer et al., in press) have argued that, when members of a group are confronted with information about their negative past, they will be motivated to defend their group. We illustrate with three strategies how the experience of collective guilt can be prevented.

Minimization of the Harm Done

Because justification processes permit ingroup members to appraise their group's actions as fair, people will attempt to do so as a means of protecting their ingroup's identity when intergroup inequality is made salient. Even when the ingroup's harmful actions cannot be denied, people can still appraise the gravity of the harm done as less severe. A. M. Miron and N. R. Branscombe (unpublished data) reasoned that social identity concerns could be activated when an intergroup event description indirectly reminds the perceiver of the ingroup's history of having harmed another group. Indeed, implicit national history comparisons may be rather likely to be provoked at this historical juncture, given the global nature of communication and the widespread publicity of actions taken by some nations to address the wrongs of their nation's past (Barkan, 2000; Brooks, 1999). Therefore, information about another national group's *similar* negative history might have the potential to engage perceivers' defensive assessments of the harm done – even when the historical information that is directly presented is not about the ingroup per se. We consider whether such comparative assessments at the group level can lead ingroup members to engage in a process of minimization of the harm done *by another group* as a means of protecting their own group's identity. If another group's actions in an event description remind ingroup members of the harm that was *also* committed by the ingroup, then group members may be motivated to appraise the harm done as minimal.

A. M. Miron and N. R. Branscombe (unpublished data) assessed whether implicit comparisons with another nation in terms of harmful past actions could lead to different appraisals of the harm done, depending on the similarity of the national histories. To test this hypothesis, we first made white Americans' ($N = 66$) social identities salient. Participants were required to indicate their racial group membership and to self-categorize as an American citizen. We then gave them an account of the historical harm committed by one national group against another. The information provided to all of our participants concerned Britain's historical use of another group as unpaid labor. Britain's exploitation of the victimized group was described as a crucial factor in their acquisition of great wealth.

To manipulate the ingroup-identity relevance of the comparison, we varied what group the British were said to have harmed. In one condition, participants read that the British exploited Africans as unpaid labor, the same group White Americans also historically harmed. In the other condition, participants read that the British used East Indians as unpaid labor, a group our participants' ingroup had no history of having harmed. To assess the possibility that ingroup identity concerns can lead ingroup members to appraise the harm done as less severe, participants rated how serious and how unjust the harm was that the British caused to the other group. We expected that when the harmed group was Africans, a group that Americans also used as unpaid labor, the motivation to protect the ingroup's identity would be present. In contrast, when the harmed group was East Indians, this motivation should be absent. As a result of the different degrees of group-protective motivation activated – depending on the target group harmed – minimization of the harm done should differentially occur. We predicted and obtained a significant difference in the perceived severity of the injustice of Britain's actions, depending on which group the British were said to have victimized. When the harm was done to Africans, participants considered it to be reliably less serious and less unjust than when the harm was done to East Indians. We argue that when the group that was harmed by the British was the same as that also harmed by the participants' own ingroup, reductions in the perceived severity and injustice of those actions reflect participants' attempts to protect their social identity.

Halbwachs (1992) has suggested that the collective memory of a nation's past is shaped by the concerns of the present. Our research indicates that perceived injustice and the "worthiness" of victims are indeed dependent on salient social identity concerns. The perception of the "value" of victims depends on what group is harmed and who committed the harm against them. Our study suggests that the worthiness of Britain's victims – expressed in terms of minimization of the harm done to them – depends on whether the perceiver's own national group has or has not also harmed those same people. We argue that it is not simply the amount of harm done per se that determines the perceived severity or injustice of the harm done, for that was identical in both of the victim group conditions of our study. Nor was it that our participants perceived the harm done to Africans as less serious because they are more familiar with, and consequently less surprised to learn about, exploitation of that group compared to Indians. When we asked participants to rate the extent to which they were surprised by Britain's actions and the events in the historical account they read, we found no differences by victim group condition in perceived surprise concerning the events described. The crucial determinant in this study for perceived injustice was whether the perceiver's own social identity was implicated by the historical event description or not. When the perceiver's social identity was implicated, event severity was minimized compared with when the ingroup's moral standing was not at stake.

Perhaps the most extreme method of minimizing the harm caused by the ingroup would be to deny that the event even occurred. Although such outright denial may be relatively rare, a number of groups do show evidence of minimization of the harm committed against another group. Churchill's (1997) summary of recent international survey data is illuminating in this regard. For example, he notes that in 1991 nearly 40% of adult Austrians reported having "doubts" about whether a European Holocaust of the magnitude depicted in history texts actually occurred. Similar data from Italy reveals that approximately 25% of the adult population believes that the severity of the Holocaust has been "overstated." Likewise, white Australians frequently minimize the numbers of Aboriginal children who were harmed by their government's policy of forcibly removing them from their families (Augoustinos & LeCouteur, in press).

The perceived severity of the harm done can also be minimized by selectively using different standards for judging injustice depending on whether it is an ingroup's actions being considered or not. A higher standard might need to be met to conclude that the ingroup is guilty of moral violations, whereas a relatively lower standard might be used when another group's harmful actions are being judged. Groups favor employment of judgment standards that allow their ingroup's actions to be perceived as moral. For example, by shifting to a standard that is assumed to have been normative during "some less moral time," the present-day ingroup can be judged more favorably by comparison with the low standards that were in effect during those "dark" times, when everyone did it, and when many countries acted on colonial agendas. Marques, Paez, and Sera (1997) describe this strategy among Portuguese participants who claim that their ingroup was no worse than others because all of the colonial countries did wrong then. By diffusing of responsibility for the harm-doing across nations and selective use of standards, the ingroup's actions can be judged as more moral and less worthy of present compensation.

Nagata (1990) discusses shifts in the standards used by Caucasian Americans in their attempts to justify the internment of Japanese Americans during World War II. Caucasian Americans frequently contrast the internment of Japanese Americans to the Nazi death camps, which in effect reduces by comparison the severity of the suffering of the group victimized by the ingroup. Similarly, white New Zealanders frequently suggest that their ingroup's past actions reflect pervasive human tendencies that have "gone on for thousands of years" (Wetherell & Potter, 1992), and this results in less distress concerning the harm done to the Indigenous Maori population. Indeed, such selective use of pervasiveness of wrongdoing standards can exert a powerful impact on the victimized groups' own perceptions of perpetrator responsibility for the harm committed. Victimized group members (see Wohl & Branscombe, in press) who perceive the harmful actions committed against them as historically pervasive and not unique to one particular perpetrator group (e.g., "everyone did it") assign contemporary perpetrator group members less guilt for the harm done than those who perceive the wrongdoing as specific to one perpetrator group.

Derogating the Victims

Derogating the victims harmed by the ingroup is another effective justification strategy. Indeed, there is considerable evidence that derogation of victims helps perpetrators to be "less burdened by distress" when faced with their harm-doing (Bandura, 1990, p. 39). We argue that derogation at the group level is an important means by which people protect themselves against collective guilt. Hornsey et al. (2003) showed that high-power groups display more derogation of low-power groups when their high-power position is perceived as illegitimate. By imagining that the disadvantaged outgroup is inferior or unworthy, members of high-power groups can justify the conditions that provided them with greater power in the first place. Thus, when confronted with the ingroup's advantaged position, less distress and guilt will be experienced to the extent that derogation of the disadvantaged group allows the ingroup's privileged position to be justified (Branscombe et al., 2003).

Many groups have used some variation on the "victims deserved their treatment" method of justification. By suggesting provocation on the part of the victims, perpetrator groups can justify their own harmful actions (Staub, 1989). At its most extreme, victims can be excluded from the category "human" entirely so they can be seen as not deserving humane treatment at all, permitting any harm done to them to be seen as completely justified (Bar-Tal, 1990).

Legitimization of Harm

Harm-doing can be justified when the actions are perceived as either necessary for the victim's own good or as serving larger moral purposes (Bar-Tal, 1990; Brock & Buss, 1964; Opotow, 1990). One example of legitimization of harm-doing is offered by the German Nazi officer, Rudolph Hoess, the commandant of Auschwitz, who said that "killing millions of Jews was done as a service to his country" (Staub, 1989, p. 132). Ideologies that suggest harm-doing serves noble ingroup purposes allow perpetrator groups to potentially rationalize any harmful treatment. Even when perpetrator groups accept that their actions did result in harmful outcomes, they can still argue that their intentions were positive. For example, Australians often report that their government's policy of removing Aboriginal children from their families was actually due to a desire to improve the victims' lives because Aboriginal parenting and culture were deemed to be inferior (Augoustinos & LeCouteur, in press).

Group inequality can be legitimized in advantaged group members either in terms of their greater input or the disadvantaged group's lesser input. To the extent that either method results in inequality being seen as just, then the perceived suffering of the other group will not arouse collective guilt in advantaged group members. The question of how such justice appraisals lessen the experience of collective guilt is an important one that we will now consider in detail. Theoretically, appraising the victims' suffering as minimal or just could undermine the experience of collective guilt either by reducing self-focused distress or by decreasing other-oriented empathy. We sought to determine by which mechanism appraising the harm done as just undermines collective guilt – via self-focused distress or other-oriented empathy.

HOW LEGITIMACY APPRAISALS UNDERMINE COLLECTIVE GUILT

One means by which appraisals of legitimacy could undermine the experience of collective guilt might be via their impact on feelings of *empathy and concern for the victimized group*. Batson, Fultz, and Schoenrade (1987; see also Davis, 1983) defined *empathy* as an other-focused emotional response that is congruent with the other's welfare. Feelings of sympathy, compassion, softheartedness, and tenderness in response to exposure to another's suffering are thought to reflect empathic concern.

Considerable evidence has accumulated in support of the idea that feeling empathy for another in need leads to increased helping with the ultimate goal of benefiting that person (Coke, Batson, & McDavis, 1978; Dovidio, Allen, & Schroeder, 1990; see Batson, 1991, for a review). Furthermore, some forms of helping at both the personal and group levels can be predicted by feelings of guilt (Doosje et al., 1998; Tangney et al., 1996). Indeed, empathy has been considered a precursor of guilt in children, and there is some evidence that empathy is correlated with guilt (Tangney, 1995). Moreover, both guilt and empathy can motivate people to want to make up for their misdeeds and to desire forgiveness (Baumeister, Stillwell, & Heatherton, 1994; Roseman, Wiest, & Swartz, 1994). Thus, to the extent that empathy and guilt actually have similar functions – to motivate helping – factors that undermine empathy might also undermine collective guilt.

As with collective guilt, empathy could be affected by whether the victim's suffering is appraised as legitimate. To the extent that harmful outcomes or status inequality are seen as justified, perceivers show less empathy for the victims (Montada & Schneider, 1989; Stephan & Finlay, 1999;

Tangney, 1995; Weber, Mummendey, & Waldzus, 2002). Empathic emotion and helping are not aroused when victims are perceived as responsible for their suffering (Weiner, 1980). In the context of intergroup relations, empathy could be undermined when the disadvantaged group is perceived as deserving its lesser outcomes. Such legitimization among advantaged group members would allow for perceived equity restoration without the advantaged needing to actually give up their benefits. Thus, appraising the other group's disadvantage as legitimate could undermine the victim group's perceived need, which both empathy and collective guilt might serve to address. In fact, it is not uncommon for historical perpetrator groups to exaggerate the benefits that victimized groups have already or are expected to receive in the future, which could effectively reduce perceived victim need. For example, Iyer et al. (in press) have noted that a substantial proportion of white Australians falsely believe that Aboriginal people receive more social security benefits than do Non-Indigenous people. Such beliefs could undermine the victim group's perceived need, which might lower both empathy and collective guilt in perpetrator group members.

Legitimacy appraisals might, however, primarily affect collective guilt by a rather different route – via *the self-focused distress* that is aroused when the ingroup's action is perceived as causing suffering in another group (Leach, Snider, & Iyer, 2002; Mallett & Swim, in press; Walster et al., 1973). In short, collective guilt stemming from distress might be expected when a moral imperative or standard is perceived as having been transgressed by the ingroup, and this should be greater as the severity of the violation and harm increases (Branscombe et al., 2002; Lazarus, 1991).

Appraising the harm done as illegitimate could result in increased distress for several reasons. Distress has been defined as one's own anxiety when witnessing another's suffering (Batson, 1991; Davis, 1983). Such distress when exposed to another's suffering can be induced even when the ingroup is not perceived as responsible for that suffering. Considerable research has demonstrated that feeling distress by exposure to the suffering of another evokes an egoistic motivation to reduce one's own vicarious emotional arousal (Batson, 1991). In addition, the degree of suffering experienced by victims may inform perpetrator group members about the injustice of their ingroup's actions, which would reflect negatively on the social identity of ingroup members. Increased distress responses to harm do seem to depend on the degree to which a discrepancy exists between how the ingroup is perceived to be in actuality and how people believe their ingroup ought to be (Bizman, Yinon, & Krotman, 2001). At the group identity level, perceiving the ingroup as responsible for the illegitimate suffering of another group could taint the social identity of members of privileged groups. For these reasons, we expect that collective guilt will be a function of the degree to which self-focused distress occurs when the harm experienced by the outgroup is made salient (see also Estrada-Hollenbach & Heatherton, 1998; Roseman et al., 1994).

Exposure to unjustified group-based inequality also has the potential of threatening principles of justice. Equity theory (Walster et al., 1973) proposed that people prefer outcomes to be fair and proportional to inputs (or other causes of deservingness). Deviations from equity can produce emotional distress. Baumeister et al. (1994) define guilt for inequity as the distress suffered by people who know they are overrewarded at others' expense. However, if the unequal outcomes are perceived as legitimate or as carrying few consequences for the disadvantaged, then the basis for experiencing inequity distress is undermined.

We argue that distress at another group's disadvantage and collective guilt are similar precisely because both are *self-focused* aversive emotional responses to perceiving others' distress. Indeed, Eisenberg et al. (1989) are explicit that personal distress should be considered a form of self-centered anxiety and that it is not a component of empathy. Distress at another's suffering is positively correlated with self-rumination, whereas empathy is not (Joireman, Parrott, & Hammersla, 2002).

Batson, Early, and Salvarani (1997) provided experimental evidence supporting the self-focused nature of distress. The distress reported in response to a person in need was higher in the condition in which participants were asked to imagine how *they* would have felt if they were in the victim's situation, compared with when they were asked to imagine how *the victim* would feel. Empathy, however, did not differ in the imagine-self and imagine-other conditions. As Hoffman (2000) has pointed out, when observers are confronted with information about others' distress, an "egoistic drift" is likely to occur. That is, when people mentally put themselves in the victim's place, it turns attention away from the victim's experience and toward the self. Thus, imagine-self instructions are likely to produce a self-focused distress response, whereas imagine-other will produce an empathetic reaction. Consistent with this reasoning, Iyer et al. (2003) found that collective guilt in European Americans emerged when the ingroup's role as perpetrators of racial discrimination was the focus, but not when the discrimination victims' suffering was the focus.

Thus, we believe the existing evidence implies that both distress and collective guilt are self-focused emotional responses that primarily motivate people to try to reduce their own distress rather than that of the victim. This reasoning suggests that collective guilt reflects a concern for one's own identity-based pain rather than stemming from an empathy-based concern for the harmed others (Batson, 1991; Iyer et al., in press; Steele, 1990). Experiencing self-focused distress and collective guilt should therefore only motivate ingroup members to restore justice in a salient intergroup relationship if doing so represents a means of restoring the ingroup's moral identity. Empathy, in contrast, is an other-focused emotional response to the victimized group's distress, and it should motivate observers to help with the ultimate goal of benefiting that group. Based on these theoretical assumptions, we conducted two studies to test whether distress or empathy drives collective guilt. We predicted that distress, but not empathy, would mediate the effect of appraising the disadvantaged group's situation as illegitimate on the experience of collective guilt. When ingroup members are given information about the harm done to an outgroup, legitimizing the victimized group situation should undermine guilt by undercutting self-focused feelings of distress rather than by reducing feelings of empathic concern for outgroup members.

LEGITIMACY APPRAISALS UNDERMINE COLLECTIVE GUILT VIA SELF-FOCUSED DISTRESS

We sought to examine the role of these two potential mechanisms of collective guilt avoidance: lowered empathy for the victimized group versus decreased distress at exposure to the suffering of the victimized group. Batson et al. (1987) have shown that, when people are exposed to a victim in need, each of these emotional responses can occur. They argue that responses on distress adjectives (e.g., upset and troubled) reflect an egoistic motivation to reduce the perceiver's own distress, whereas empathic concern adjectives (e.g., compassionate and softhearted) reflect an altruistic motivation to improve the welfare of the victim.

In two studies, Miron et al. (2003) examined how appraising inequality as legitimate serves to inhibit collective guilt. In the first study, we measured legitimacy appraisals, whereas in the second study we manipulated these appraisals. In Study 1, male participants ($N = 52$) were first informed about the various ways that the considerable inequality between men and women continues in present-day American society. Because previous research has documented that dominant groups subscribe to ideologies that justify status differences that favor them (Montada & Schneider, 1989; Schmitt, Branscombe, & Kappen, 2003), we assessed the extent to which participants concur with common legitimizations for gender inequality. We measured agreement with justifications of gender inequality with nine items, $\alpha = .84$ (e.g., "Men are better suited for leadership roles than women are; women are better suited for nurturing roles than men are."). To the extent that men appraise the existing gender inequality as legitimate and just, then the bases for empathy, distress, and collective guilt should be undermined.

The extent to which participants reported feeling collective guilt concerning the inequality that exists between them was measured with four items, $\alpha = .80$ (e.g., "I feel guilty about the inequality that exists between men and women."). Empathic concern for women and their plight, as well as self-focused distress, were assessed as two different emotional reactions that can occur when the harmful inequality that exists between the gender groups is made salient. Two items assessed empathic concern when the victimized group is the focus, $\alpha = .92$ (e.g., "I feel compassionate toward women who experience gender discrimination." "I feel softhearted when I hear about women who are discriminated against."). Three distress items captured the extent to which participants felt distressed, upset, and alarmed by the discrimination that their ingroup perpetrates against women, $\alpha = .82$ (e.g., "I feel upset when I think about what men do to women." "I feel troubled when men benefit at the expense of women."). In our gender group context, consistent with Batson et al. (1987), the empathy and distress items loaded on two different factors that together accounted for 82% of variance in these items, and the two indexes were moderately correlated, $r = .51, p < .001$.

As predicted, appraising gender inequality as legitimate significantly predicted collective guilt, $\beta = -.28, p = .05$. As the perceived legitimacy of inequality increased, the experience of collective guilt decreased. To test whether the effect of legitimacy of inequality on collective guilt was mediated by empathy for the victims or by self-focused distress, we conducted a mediational analysis. Baron and Kenny (1986) have pointed out several criteria that must be met to show that a variable is a reliable mediator. First, the dependent variable must be affected by the independent variable. As noted, legitimacy of inequality significantly predicted collective guilt. Second, the mediator must be affected by the independent variable. Legitimacy of inequality significantly predicted distress, $\beta = -.42, p = .002$, and empathy for the victims, $\beta = -.31, p = .028$. Third, the mediator must reliably affect the dependent variable when the effect of the independent variable is controlled. To test for mediation, we simultaneously regressed collective guilt on the independent variable, with both empathy and distress included as potential mediators. As shown in Figure 15.2, we found that distress was a significant predictor of collective guilt, $\beta = .38, p = .019$. Furthermore, controlling for distress resulted in legitimacy appraisals no longer significantly affecting collective guilt, $\beta = -.09, p = .51$. Empathy did not, however, reliably predict collective guilt, $\beta = .08, p = .59$. We also conducted a Sobel test to assess the extent to which each mediator (empathy and distress) attenuated the relationship between appraisal of inequality as legitimate and collective guilt. Based on this test, we concluded that the effect of legitimacy appraisals on collective guilt is not mediated by empathy, $z = -1.37, p = .17$, whereas distress is a reliable mediator of this relationship, $z = -2.20, p < .03$.

In Study 2, we manipulated the perception of the legitimacy of gender inequality that benefits men and harms women. We created a manipulation that either supported or refuted the beliefs assessed in the legitimacy appraisal measure used in Study 1. Because previous research has shown that people do blame the victims of harm-doing (Bandura, 1990; Bar-Tal,

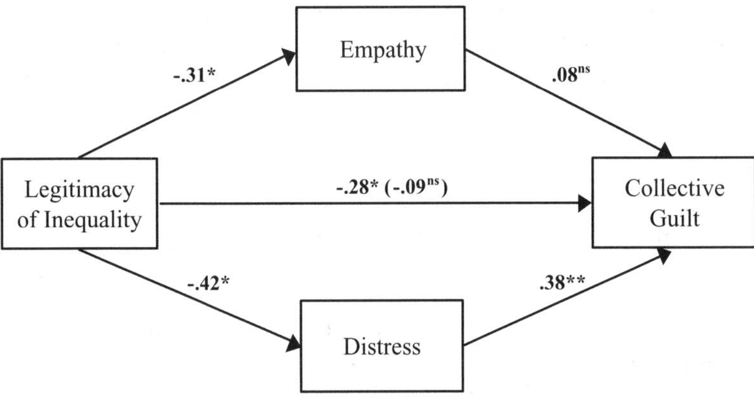

FIGURE 15.2. Mediational analyses: Self-focused distress mediates the effect of legitimacy appraisals on collective guilt, whereas empathy does not. The direct effect coefficient shown in parentheses reflects the inclusion of both potential mediators in the equation. All coefficients with an asterisk are significant at $p < .05$.

1990; Lerner & Simmons, 1966), in Study 2 we also included items that tap the perceived deservingness of the victims as a legitimization of gender inequality (e.g., women do not have the capabilities needed for the particular jobs they are excluded from). Importantly, we manipulated only the appraisal of inequality as legitimate or illegitimate and held constant the severity of inequality across the two conditions.

Study 2 began with male participants ($N = 73$) reading a bogus 2002 newspaper article entitled, "Why does gender inequality persist in American society?" In both conditions, the male author of the article first provided accurate statistics about the extent of gender inequality in the United States today. Facts were presented showing that women earn less money than men, and that the wage gap between women and men cuts across a wide spectrum of occupations. Perception of the inequality as legitimate was induced with the argument that differential ability is the cause of the differences in the status positions of men and women. Specifically, for half of the participants (*legitimacy-supported condition*), legitimacy of inequality appraisals for why women are not in high-paid, high-status jobs (i.e., engineering and business) were supported with "evidence" that "even though on objective psychological tests such as intelligence women score as high as men do, women score far lower than men do on other abilities required by these types of high-status professions (e.g., assertiveness, achievement-oriented personality, leadership, and competitiveness)." In this condition, it was argued that gender inequality is not due to subtle, systematic, and intentional discrimination strategies, but to the fact that men and women possess different abilities that make them better suited for different jobs. For the other half of our participants (*legitimacy-undermined condition*), the legitimacy of existing inequality was undermined by arguing that women score as high as men do on intelligence tests *and* on the abilities required by these professions. Furthermore, it was argued that the inequality that exists is not due to natural gender differences, but to subtle, systematic, and intentional discrimination.

In this study, we measured collective guilt with ten items, empathy with seven items, and distress with seven items. A factor analysis confirmed that we captured three separate constructs as intended with these items. The indices formed included all of the items used in Study 1, plus additional items assessing each construct. The distress index ($\alpha = .90$) included all of the distress items used by Batson et al. (1987): distressed, upset, alarmed, troubled, disturbed, perturbed, and saddened. The reference for all of the items was the suffering of the women (e.g., "I am disturbed when I learn about how much women suffer from discrimination." "I feel upset when I think about the discrimination that men do to women."). The empathy index ($\alpha = .85$) included the following adjectives: compassionate, soft-hearted, sympathetic, moved, compassionate, and empathize with (e.g., "I feel sympathetic toward women who do not have as much opportunity as men do." "I feel compassionate toward those women who encounter inequality in their workplace."). The distress and empathy indices were again positively correlated, $r = .69$, $p < .001$. Collective guilt ($\alpha = .89$) was assessed with items referencing the guilt felt for the benefits men gain from gender inequality, for the harm women suffer because of discriminatory practices, and the responsibility men deserve for the existing inequality (e.g., "I feel guilty because men receive benefits at the expense of women." I feel guilty because my gender group's actions have harmed the other gender." "I feel men are responsible for gender inequality.").

The results of this experiment replicated those obtained in the previous correlational study. Legitimacy of inequality significantly predicted collective guilt, $\beta = -.31$, $p < .05$. When we simultaneously regressed collective guilt on empathy, distress, and the manipulation of legitimacy, distress reliably predicted collective guilt, $\beta = .46$, $p < .001$, whereas empathy did not, $\beta = .22$, $p = .07$. With both mediators included in the regression equation, the manipulation of legitimacy no longer predicted collective guilt, $\beta = -.17$, $p = .06$. Finally, we conducted a Sobel test to examine the extent to which empathy and distress attenuated the effect of the manipulation of legitimacy on collective guilt. Empathy failed to mediate this relationship, $z = -0.08$, $p = .43$, whereas distress was a marginally significant mediator of this relationship, $z = -1.87$, $p = .06$.

The results of both studies offer clear support for the hypothesis that appraising inequality as legitimate undermines the experience of collective guilt by reducing the distress that is experienced when confronted with information about the ingroup's privileged status. These results provide little support for the idea that empathic concern for the victims is a determinant of collective guilt, or that it is a reliable mediator of the effect of legitimacy of inequality on collective guilt. Therefore, if status inequality is perceived as legitimate (i.e., due to natural differences between men and women, or the lack of leadership ability in women), distress and collective guilt will be undermined when the disadvantaged group's suffering is made salient.

Previous research (Bandura, 1990; Montada & Schneider, 1989; Schmitt et al., 2000) has shown that appraisals of legitimacy are correlated with both empathy and guilt. Nonetheless, the results of our studies indicate that appraising gender inequality as legitimate undermines the potential for collective guilt by undermining the distress felt rather than by undermining empathy following exposure to information about the economic disadvantage of the outgroup. These results are consistent with Iyer et al.'s (2003) finding that collective guilt requires participants to focus on their own group's role as perpetrators of injustice. Collective guilt therefore reflects a selfish concern for one's own pain rather than a sympathetic concern for the disadvantaged others. Our studies indicate that collective guilt results from increased distress rather than increased empathy, and this supports the idea that collective guilt reflects self-focused identity concerns. For this reason, dominant groups might be expected to deal with information about the injustice of their group's actions, when possible, by escaping or avoiding exposure to the distress experienced by the outgroup.

IMPLICATIONS FOR GROUP-BASED HELPING

When collective guilt cannot be avoided, the distress that group members experience when they are confronted with the illegitimate actions of their group may motivate group-based apologies and reparations on behalf of the ingroup. Previous research on the link between group-based emotions and helping disadvantaged groups indicates that both collective guilt and empathy can predict helping. Iyer et al. (2003) found that white guilt was predictive of support for affirmative action programs that are aimed at compensating African Americans, but not of support for noncompensatory efforts such as increased opportunities. Moreover, they found that other-focused empathy predicted support for social equality aimed at benefiting the disadvantaged group. Their work suggests that the self-focused nature of collective guilt might prevent sustained forms of helping, and this may be precisely because advantaged group members are focused on their own distress when they are confronted with the disadvantaged group's need (see Hoffman, 2000).

Given the self-focused nature of collective guilt, an interesting question is whether the anticipated difficulty of helping primarily affects the magnitude of the distress and collective guilt experienced, or the degree to which empathy is induced. Batson et al. (1987) showed that, when participants feel personal distress in response to another's need, they do not help if they can escape the situation. The ability to escape the situation did not affect participants who felt empathy for the person in need. When empathy was experienced, help occurred regardless of whether escape was possible or not.

Given that collective guilt stems from the self-focused distress that occurs when the victimized group's suffering is deemed to be illegitimate, providing an escape from distress should undermine dominant group members' motivation to help repair the harm done. The perceived costs of helping the victimized group does influence appraisal of the situation and collective guilt (Schmitt, Branscombe, & Brehm, in press; Shaw, Batson, & Todd, 1994). If the costs of helping the victimized group are perceived to be too high, people may appraise the situation as legitimate, which will undermine both guilt and helping. Miron et al. (2003) found some evidence that the perceived difficulty of helping the victims influences the emotional responses that are aroused by exposure to the harm done to the victimized group. Men who agreed that the existing inequality cannot be changed reported significantly less empathy, $\beta = -.55$, $p = .001$, less distress, $\beta = -.65$, $p = .001$, and less collective guilt, $\beta = -.44$, $p = .001$.

Schmitt et al. (in press) provided additional evidence that collective guilt for the harm done by the ingroup can be undermined when high costs for correcting the harm are anticipated. They found that the intensity of collective guilt varied as a function of the magnitude of reparations that would be required. When the compensation needed to correct the past wrong was framed as moderately difficult to achieve, collective guilt was greater than when the compensation was framed as extremely difficult. In addition, when the compensation available is perceived as too little to cover the harm done or is seen as requiring little effort to achieve, collective guilt is also less likely to be experienced. In this case, intervention may be perceived as not needed, with matters being expected to right themselves of their own accord. These results suggest that, for perpetrator groups to maintain their motivation to make reparations stemming from collective guilt, they must perceive that there is a difficult but manageable form of compensation available to them. If either the harm done seems impossible to correct, or it is believed that the wrong done will simply right itself with time, the motivation to make reparations may be rather low.

CONCLUSIONS

Collective guilt is a distress-based emotional response that occurs when the harm done to another group is appraised as illegitimate. Because it is threatening to perceive the actions of one's ingroup as unjust, people are likely to appraise the harm done as either having minimal consequences or as justified. We showed that, when social identity concerns are aroused, the perceived severity and injustice of the harm-doing are reduced. Collective guilt stems from the self-focused distress that is aroused when injustice is confronted, rather than empathy for those suffering from the injustice. To the extent that justification processes are effective, the harm-doing will be appraised as just and little collective guilt will be experienced. To arrive at such identity-protective appraisals, a number of justification strategies can be used. The gravity of the harm done can be minimized, the victims can be derogated, and the intergroup situation can be legitimized. Each of these has the potential of preventing the experience of collective guilt when group-based inequality is made salient.

When justification processes succeed, the harm done is appraised as legitimate, and the basis for collective guilt is undermined. In light of our findings, collective guilt appears to be a fragile emotional response that can be rather easily disrupted. Because ideological beliefs that support gender inequality specifically are widely subscribed to (Schmitt, Ellemers, & Branscombe, 2003), collective guilt for gender inequality may be routinely avoided. However, as our findings indicate, to the extent that such legitimacy beliefs are effectively undermined and people appraise the existing inequality as unjust, then collective guilt can be induced. When this occurs, dominant group members may become motivated to restore justice. In contrast to guilt, empathy appears to be primarily affected by the perceived severity of the victim's need (Batson et al., 1997). Therefore, the motivation evoked by distress-based guilt may be to restore perceived justice rather than to address the need of the victimized group. For collective guilt to lead to helping and motivate sustained social change among dominant group members, the costs of restoring justice may need to be perceived as lower than the identity costs involved in not restoring justice.

References

Augoustinos, M., & LeCouteur, A. (in press). On whether to apologize to Indigenous Australians: The denial of white guilt. In N. R. Branscombe & B. Doosje (Eds.), *Collective guilt: International perspectives*. New York: Cambridge University Press.

Bandura, A. (1990). Selective activation and disengagement of moral control. *Journal of Social Issues, 46*, 27–46.

Barkan, E. (2000). *The guilt of nations*. New York: W. W. Norton.

Baron, R. M., & Kenny, D. A. (1986). The moderator-mediator variable distinction in social psychological research: Conceptual, strategic, and statistical considerations. *Journal of Personality and Social Psychology, 51*, 1173–1182.

Bar-Tal, D. (1990). Causes and consequences of delegitimization: Models of conflict and ethnocentrism. *Journal of Social Issues, 46*, 65–81.

Batson, C. D. (1991). *The altruism question: Toward a social-psychological answer*. Hillsdale, NJ: Erlbaum.

Batson, C. D., Early, S., & Salvarani, G. (1997). Distress and empathy: Two qualitatively distinct vicarious emotions with different motivational consequences. *Personality and Social Psychology Bulletin, 23*, 751–758.

Batson, C. D., Fultz, J., & Schoenrade, P. A. (1987). Distress and empathy: Two qualitatively distinct vicarious emotions with different motivational consequences. *Journal of Personality, 55*, 19–39.

Baumeister, R. F., & Hastings, S. (1997). Distortions of collective memory: How groups flatter and deceive themselves. In J. W. Pennebaker, D. Paez, & B. Rime (Eds.), *Collective memory and political events: Social psychological perspectives* (pp. 277–293). Mahwah, NJ: Erlbaum.

Baumeister, R. F., Stillwell, A. M., & Heatherton, T. F. (1994). Guilt: An interpersonal approach. *Psychological Bulletin, 115*, 243–267.

Berscheid, E., & Walster, E. (1967). When does a harm-doer compensate a victim? *Journal of Personality and Social Psychology, 6*, 435–441.

Bizman, A., Yinon, Y., & Krotman, S. (2001). Group-based emotional distress: An extension of self-discrepancy theory. *Personality and Social Psychology Bulletin, 27*, 1291–1300.

Branscombe, N. R., Doosje, B., & McGarty, C. (2002). Antecedents and consequences of collective guilt. In D. M. Mackie & E. R. Smith (Eds.), *From prejudice to intergroup emotions: Differentiated reactions to social groups* (pp. 49–66). Philadelphia: Psychology Press.

Branscombe, N. R., Ellemers, N., Spears, R., & Doosje, B. (1999). The context and content of social identity threat. In N. Ellemers, R. Spears, & B. Doosje (Eds.), *Social identity: Context, commitment, content* (pp. 35–58). Oxford, UK: Blackwell.

Branscombe, N. R., Schmitt, M. T., Schiffhauer, K., & Valencia, L. (2003). *Racial attitudes in response to thinking about White privilege*. Manuscript submitted for publication.

Branscombe, N. R., Wann, D. L., Noel, J. G., & Coleman, J. (1993). Ingroup or outgroup extremity: Importance of the threatened identity. *Personality and Social Psychology Bulletin, 19*, 381–388.

Brock, T., & Buss, A. H. (1964). Effects of justification for aggression and communication with the victim on postaggression dissonance. *Journal of Abnormal and Social Psychology, 68*, 403–412.

Brooks, R. L. (1999). The age of apology. In R. L. Brooks (Ed.), *When sorry isn't enough: The controversy over apologies and reparations for human injustice* (pp. 3–12). New York: New York University Press.

Churchill, W. (1997). *A little matter of genocide*. San Francisco: City Lights Books.

Cialdini, R. B., Borden, R. J., Thorne, A., Walker, M. R., Freeman, S., & Sloan, R. L. (1976). 'Basking in reflected glory': Three (football) field studies. *Journal of Personality and Social Psychology, 34*, 366–375.

Coke, J. S., Batson, C. D., & McDavis, K. (1978). Empathic mediation of helping: A two-stage model. *Journal of Personality and Social Psychology, 36*, 752–766.

Davis, M. H. (1983). Measuring individual differences in empathy: Evidence for a multidimensional approach. *Journal of Personality and Social Psychology, 44*, 113–126.

Doosje, B., Branscombe, N. R., Spears, R., & Manstead, A. S. R. (1998). Guilty by association: When one's group has a negative history. *Journal of Personality and Social Psychology, 75*, 872–886.

Dovidio, J. F., Allen, J. L., & Schroeder, D. A. (1990). The specificity of empathy-induced helping: Evidence for altruistic motivation. *Journal of Personality and Social Psychology, 59*, 249–260.

Eisenberg, N. (2000). Emotion, regulation, and moral development. *Annual Review of Psychology, 51*, 665–697.

Eisenberg, N., Fabes, R. A., Miller, P. A., Fultz, J., Mathy, R. M., Shell, R., Shea, C., & Reno, R. R. (1989). The relations of sympathy and personal distress to prosocial behavior: A multimethod study. *Journal of Personality and Social Psychology, 57*, 55–66.

Estrada-Hollenbach, M., & Heatherton, T. F. (1998). Avoiding and alleviating guilt through prosocial behavior. In J. Bybee (Ed.), *Guilt and children* (pp. 215–231). San Diego: Academic Press.

Ferguson, T. J., & Stegge, H. (1998). Measuring guilt in children: A rose by any other name still has thorns. In J. Bybee (Ed.), *Guilt and children* (pp. 19–74). San Diego: Academic Press.

Frijda, N. H., Kuipers, P., & Ter Schure, E. (1989). Relations among emotion, appraisal, and emotional action readiness. *Journal of Personality and Social Psychology, 57*, 212–228.

Halbwachs, M. (1992). *On collective memory*. Chicago: University of Chicago Press.

Heider, F. (1958). *The psychology of interpersonal relationships*. New York: Wiley.

Hoffman, M. (2000). *Empathy and moral development: Implications for caring and justice*. Cambridge, UK: Cambridge University Press.

Hoffman, M. L. (1987). The contribution of empathy to justice and moral judgment. In N. Eisenberg (Ed.), *Empathy and its development* (pp. 47–80). Cambridge, UK: Cambridge University Press.

Hoffman, M. L. (1991). Development of prosocial motivation: Empathy and guilt. In N. Eisenberg (Ed.), *The development of prosocial behavior* (pp. 281–313). New York: Academic Press.

Hornsey, M. J., Spears, R., Cremers, I., & Hogg, M. A. (2003). Relations between high and low power groups: The importance of legitimacy. *Personality and Social Psychology Bulletin, 29*, 216–227.

Iyer, A., Leach, C. W., & Crosby, F. J. (2003). White guilt and racial compensation: The benefits and limits of self-focus. *Personality and Social Psychology Bulletin, 29*, 117–129.

Iyer, A., Leach, C. W., & Pedersen, A. (in press). Racial wrongs and restitutions: The role of guilt and other group-based emotions. In N. R. Branscombe & B. Doosje (Eds.), *Collective guilt: International perspectives*. New York: Cambridge University Press.

Joireman, J. A., Parrott, G. L. III, & Hammersla, J. (2002). Empathy and the self-absorption paradox: Support for the distinction between self-rumination and self-reflection. *Self and Identity, 1*, 53–65.

Lazarus, R. C. (1991). *Emotion and adaptation*. New York: Oxford University Press.

Leach, C. W., Snider, N., & Iyer, A. (2002). "Poisoning the consciences of the fortunate": The experience of relative advantage and support for social equality. In I. Walker & H. J. Smith (Eds.), *Relative deprivation: Specification, development and integration* (pp. 136–163). New York: Cambridge University Press.

Lerner, M. J., & Simmons, C. H. (1966). Observer reactions to the "innocent victim": Compassion or rejection? *Journal of Personality and Social Psychology, 4*, 203–210.

Mallett, R. K., & Swim, J. K. (in press). Collective guilt in the United States: Predicting support for social policies to alleviate social injustice. In N. R. Branscombe &

B. Doosje (Eds.), *Collective guilt: International perspectives*. New York: Cambridge University Press.

Marques, J., Paez, D., & Sera, A. F. (1997). Social sharing, emotional climate, and the transgenerational transmission of memories: The Portuguese Colonial war. In J. W. Pennebaker, D. Paez, & B. Rime (Eds.), *Collective memory and political events: Social psychological perspectives* (pp. 253–275). Mahwah, NJ: Erlbaum.

Miron, A. M., Branscombe, N. R., & Schmitt, M. T. (2003). *Collective guilt as distress over illegitimate ingroup advantage*. Manuscript submitted for publication.

Montada, L., & Schneider, A. (1989). Justice and emotional reactions to the disadvantaged. *Social Justice Research, 3*, 313–344.

Nagata, D. K. (1990). The Japanese-American internment: Perceptions of moral community, fairness, and redress. *Journal of Social Issues, 46*, 133–146.

Opotow, S. (1990). Moral exclusion and injustice: An introduction. *Journal of Social Issues, 40*, 1–20.

Roseman I. J. (1984). Cognitive determinants of emotions. A structural theory. In P. Shaver (Ed.), *Review of Personality and Social Personality, 5*, 11–35.

Roseman, I. J., Wiest, C., & Swartz, T. S. (1994). Phenomenology, behaviors, and goals differentiate discrete emotions. *Journal of Personality and Social Psychology, 67*, 206–221.

Schmitt, M., Behner, R., Montada, L., Muller, L., & Muller-Fohrbrodt, G. (2000). Gender, ethnicity, and education as privileges: exploring the generalizability of the existential guilt reaction. *Social Justice Research, 13*, 313–337.

Schmitt, M. T., Branscombe, N. R., & Brehm, J. W. (in press). Determinants of the intensity of gender-based guilt in men. In N. R. Branscombe & B. Doosje (Eds.), *Collective guilt: International perspectives*. New York: Cambridge University Press.

Schmitt, M. T., Branscombe, N. R., & Kappen, D. M. (2003). Attitudes toward group-based inequality: Social dominance or social identity? *British Journal of Social Psychology, 42*, 161–186.

Schmitt, M. T., Ellemers, N., & Branscombe, N. R. (2003). Perceiving and responding to gender discrimination in organizations. In S. A. Haslam, D. van Knippenberg, M. J. Platow, & N. Ellemers (Eds.), *Social identity at work: Developing theory for organizational practice* (pp. 277–292). Philadelphia: Psychology Press.

Shaw, L. L., Batson, C. D., & Todd, R. M. (1994). Empathy avoidance: Forestalling feeling for another in order to escape the motivational consequences. *Journal of Personality and Social Psychology, 67*, 879–887.

Smith, E. R. (1999). Affective and cognitive implications of a group becoming part of the self: New models of prejudice and of the self-concept. In D. Abrams & M. A. Hogg (Eds.), *Social identity and social cognition* (pp. 183–196). Oxford, UK: Blackwell.

Staub, E. (1989). *The roots of evil: The origins of genocide and other group violence* (p. 132). New York: Cambridge University Press.

Steele, S. (1990). *The content of our character*. New York: Harper Perennial.

Stephan, W. G., & Finlay, K. (1999). The role of empathy in improving intergroup relations. *Journal of Social Issues, 55*, 729–743.

Tajfel, H., & Turner, J. C. (1986). The social identity theory of intergroup conflict. In S. Worchel & W. G. Austin (Eds.), *Psychology of intergroup relations* (pp. 7–24). Chicago: Nelson-Hall.

Tangney, J. P. (1995). Shame and guilt in interpersonal relationships. In J. P. Tangney & K. W. Fischer (Eds.), *Self-conscious emotions: The psychology of shame, guilt, embarrassment, and pride* (pp. 115–139). New York: Guilford Press.

Tangney, J. P., Miller, R. S., Flicker, L., & Barlow, D. H. (1996). Are shame, guilt, and embarrassment distinct emotions? *Journal of Personality and Social Psychology, 70*, 1256–1269.

Walster, E., Berscheid, E., & Walster, G. M. (1973). New directions in equity research. *Journal of Personality and Social Psychology, 25*, 151–176.

Weber, U., Mummendey, A., & Waldzus, S. (2002). Perceived legitimacy of intergroup status differences: Its prediction by relative ingroup prototypicality. *European Journal of Social Psychology, 32*, 449–470.

Weiner, B. (1980). A cognitive (attribution) – emotion action model of motivated behavior: An analysis of judgments of help giving. *Journal of Personality and Social Psychology, 39*, 186–200.

Wetherell, M., & Potter, J. (1992). *Mapping the language of racism: Discourse and the legitimation of exploitation*. New York: Columbia University Press.

Wohl, M. J. A., & Branscombe, N. R. (in press). Importance of social categorization for forgiveness and assignment of collective guilt for the Holocaust. In N. R. Branscombe & B. Doosje (Eds.), *Collective guilt: International perspectives*. New York: Cambridge University Press.

Yzerbyt, V., Dumont, M., Gordijn, E., & Wigboldus, D. (2002). Intergroup emotions and self-categorization: The impact of perspective-taking on reactions to victims of harmful behavior. In D. M. Mackie & E. R. Smith (Eds.), *From prejudice to intergroup emotions: Differentiated reactions to social groups*. Philadelphia: Psychology Press.

16

Intergroup Schadenfreude

Conditions and Consequences

Russell Spears and Colin Wayne Leach

People can feel just as strongly about their membership in groups as they do about any other feature of their lives. Recent theory and research marrying social identity theory with appraisal and other approaches to emotion is beginning to show how important emotions are to the group and intergroup aspects of social life. In this chapter, we develop the intergroup emotion perspective by focusing on *schadenfreude* – a malicious pleasure that group members can take in the suffering of another group. We believe schadenfreude is an important, if somewhat obscure, emotion because it is an insidious expression of a malevolent feeling that can do serious harm to intergroup relations.

THE SOCIAL IDENTITY THEORY OF INTERGROUP RELATIONS

The social identity theory tradition has been particularly useful in defining the group level of self and specifying the relations between groups that can structure psychological experience (Tajfel & Turner, 1986). Although Tajfel (1978, p. 63) referred to the "emotional significance" attached to group membership as a defining feature of social identity, classic social identity theory offers a rather generic account of the affective side of group life. Thus, the evaluation of ingroups and outgroups is typically characterized along a single dimension of valence that ranges from the self-directed positivity of ingroup favoritism to the other-directed negativity of outgroup derogation. This fairly simple characterization of group evaluation is belied by other aspects of a theoretical framework that emphasizes the complexities of intergroup relations. Although social identity theory conceptualizes the experience of an ingroup's relation to other groups as the complex product of status, stability, legitimacy, and the permeability of group boundaries (Tajfel & Turner, 1986; see Spears, Jetten, & Doosje, 2002), the quality of the experience produced by these factors is not typically conceptualized with such richness.

Related to this point, social identity theory has been viewed as better placed to explain ingroups' attempts to differentiate themselves from, or favor themselves over, other groups to secure positive identity and psychological well-being. For example, the minimal group paradigm typically reveals evidence of enhancement of the ingroup rather than direct derogation of outgroups (for reviews, see Diehl, 1990; Mummendey & Otten, 1998). Although the "pride" and "satisfaction" ingroup members can take in their group's superiority over others is an important form of group bias, it does not appear to damage social relations in the same way as the antipathy associated with the derogation of outgroups (Leach, Snider, & Iyer, 2002; Mummendey & Otten, 1998). As a result, some argue that social identity theory fails to capture the more pernicious forms of prejudice and discrimination that involve explicit derogation or malice (Brewer, 1999; Struch & Schwarz, 1989). Whether this apparent limitation is intrinsic to social identity theory or not, greater attention to the emotional bases of malice toward outgroups may be important to the development of social identity theory.

Intergroup Emotion

The intergroup emotion perspective represents an important extension of social identity theory's conceptualization of intergroup experience (see Mackie, Silver, & Smith, this volume; Smith, 1993). An emotion-based approach to intergroup experience promises to capture better the specific meaning and motives produced by the specific group relations conceptualized by social identity theory (Leach et al., 2002). At present, there is a burgeoning of research in this area (for reviews, see Mackie & Smith, 2002, as well as this volume). For example, Mackie, Devos, and Smith (2000) recently examined how intergroup anger and fear color different behavioral reactions against outgroups (see also Alexander, Brewer, & Herrmann, 1999; Fiske et al., 1999). Emotion-based approaches have also been developed to understand group-based guilt as a basis of restitution to harmed outgroups (Doosje et al., 1998; Iyer, Leach, & Crosby, 2003).

These studies show the advantages of studying the specific emotions at work in intergroup relations. Importantly, because emotions are highly suggestive of the behavioral tendencies groups have toward one another (Arnold, 1960; Frijda, 1986), they also give insights into how forms of prejudice grounded in distinct emotions will be manifested in specific forms of discrimination. Our examination of intergroup schadenfreude extends this work on emotion in social identity and intergroup relations. Although the limited research on schadenfreude has conceived it as an interpersonal emotion (e.g., R. H. Smith et al., 1996), our interest is in schadenfreude occurring at the intergroup level. Thus, we examine group members' enjoyment of the suffering of another group.

We now proceed by defining schadenfreude and considering its social consequences in the intergroup domain. Addressing the conditions that facilitate and constrain this emotion in the intergroup context is a central task of this chapter and provides insights into the psychological factors that illustrate schadenfreude's distinctive qualities.

Intergroup Schadenfreude

"What a fearful thing is it that any language should have a word expressive of the pleasure which men [and women] feel at the calamities of others; for the existence of the word bears testimony to the existence of the thing" (R. C. Trench, 1852, p. 29, as cited in the *Oxford English Dictionary*, 1989).

The German word schadenfreude describes the pleasure felt in response to another person's misfortune (Ortony, Clore, & Collins, 1988; *Oxford English Dictionary*, 1986). Although schadenfreude may be experienced as a feeling of joy, or satisfaction, or happiness, the term is specific to the pleasure that comes from observing another's misfortune. As the aforementioned quote suggests, languages may have a word to describe this particular form of pleasure precisely because it is untoward. Given that moral precepts dictate that we should feel sympathy toward those who suffer a misfortune (Heider, 1958), feelings of pleasure require special acknowledgment and attention.

The philosopher Nietzsche (1887/1967) was one of the first in the modern period to discuss the particularities of schadenfreude. He emphasized the fact that the feeling of schadenfreude is dependent on the passive observation of another's suffering, rather than an active attempt to make another suffer by defeating them directly. Although Nietzsche thought the pleasure of taking "pride" in or "gloating" over making another suffer was preferable (see Leach & Spears, 2002), he saw schadenfreude as a passive, indirect, and opportunistic way to gain pleasure from others' suffering.

What makes schadenfreude particularly disturbing and destructive (and interesting) is that pleasure is a divergent response to another's suffering (Heider, 1958); we feel pleasure while the other feels pain. Whereas sympathy toward the suffering of others implies psychological closeness and emotional convergence, schadenfreude implies psychological distance and emotional divergence (see section II of this volume for discussions of emotional convergence and divergence). Although schadenfreude does not necessarily involve ill-will toward others, pleasure at others' pain is, by definition, malicious because it is a divergent response to others' suffering (Heider, 1958).

A character in a (true life) short story by Truman Capote (1975) remarks that humans are unique in the animal kingdom in their capacity for malice (see also Nietzsche, 1887/1967). Implicit here is the notion that the malice inherent in schadenfreude is restricted to the higher social beings, making schadenfreude a complex, secondary emotion. The desk Nazi may show fewer outward signs of aggression than the mountain lion, but it is the former that appears more malevolent. The conscious awareness and volition necessary to malice explain why the concept of evil is reserved for distinctly human acts (Staub, 1989). This reminds us that some forms of savagery may ironically require a degree of sophistication (e.g., a social memory with which to build up resentments and bear grudges).

Malice, however, is rarely directed indiscriminately. Because sympathy is a more morally legitimate and socially acceptable response to another's suffering, the malicious pleasure of schadenfreude appears to be particularly sensitive to the social circumstances that surround it. Schadenfreude should be most clearly felt under circumstances that make it appear more morally legitimate to enjoy another's suffering. In the case of intergroup schadenfreude, it seems that outgroups who are seen as rivals or who are otherwise the targets of malice may invite the most schadenfreude in response to their misfortunes.

Social Consequences, Historical Examples

Intergroup schadenfreude may well have played a pivotal role in some of the worst atrocities of the twentieth century. Perhaps the most obvious concerns the fate of the Jews in Nazi Germany. To be sure, the Nazis were hardly passive bystanders in their persecution and extermination of the Jews, or other groups. However, historians have noted that the holocaust cannot be understood unless the passive tolerance and even encouragement of members of the civilian population are taken into account (Goldhagen, 1996).

Although other emotions endorsed by the Nazi ideology (e.g., contempt, disgust) may have been important to the promulgation of persecution of other groups (e.g., gypsies and homosexuals), the Jews were in many ways the classic targets of intergroup schadenfreude because their success was widely envied. Indeed, the antisemitism endemic in Weimar Germany and Poland had already been alive for centuries, fed by Christian conspiracy theories to be sure, but also by the culture of envy toward a group that had become prosperous, forced by previous waves of antisemitism into money-lending professions (see Bettelheim & Janowitz, 1964; Fiske et al., 2002). Given that Jews were an envied group seen as undeserving of their success, many Germans may have felt schadenfreude, rather than sympathy or outrage, in response to their persecution.

The fate of the Jews in Nazi Germany is not the only example of intergroup schadenfreude with ghastly consequences. In many other cases, victims of atrocity and even genocide appear to have garnered little sympathy when they were in a position to attract envy and rivalry from those who could do something to stop the violence. Recent examples include the intellectuals in Cambodia (with a similar but less extreme precedent set during the cultural revolution in China), the Muslims in Bosnia, and the Tutsis in Rwanda. Closer to home, but on a less deadly scale, tolerance of attacks on Asian communities in the United States and in the United Kingdom in periods of unrest in socially deprived neighborhoods may stem from similar intergroup dynamics. In all these cases, schadenfreude may have enabled onlookers idly to accept aggression, atrocity, and even genocide against envied or rival outgroups.

As we have noted, schadenfreude is a passive emotion, and therefore cannot explain the active persecution of rival groups, only the celebration of their suffering once it has been begun. However, if this emotion is recognized by agents of persecution, it can provide a context in which aggression is tolerated or even becomes normative. The famous dictum of Edmund Burke that all it takes for evil to triumph is for good men to do nothing speaks to the passive power of intergroup schadenfreude.

Intergroup schadenfreude may therefore be particularly dangerous in unstable social systems and in times of social upheaval, when high status groups start to lose ground and the protection of the previously powerful authorities. This analysis can be applied to many of the historical examples we have cited above. Under these conditions, it may become more legitimate to celebrate the loss of the rival group openly. It also seems possible that times of great upheaval can transform passive schadenfreude into the more active derogation of gloating. The dehumanization of the Jews in Nazi ideology and practice can be seen as the rhetorical means by which passive tolerance of suffering becomes justified as active persecution. Intergroup schadenfreude may therefore provide important seeds for direct aggression toward outgroups, by creating a climate in which the suffering becomes publicly accepted and enjoyed. Tracking the social transitions that facilitate these shifts from schadenfreude to gloating is an important question for future consideration, but is beyond the scope of the present research program (but see Leach & Spears, 2002).

THE PSYCHOLOGICAL CONDITIONS OF INTERGROUP SCHADENFREUDE

Atrocity and genocide are highly consequential but hardly everyday occurrences. So far, our case for intergroup schadenfreude has been made writ large. But what is the actual evidence for intergroup schadenfreude? Before our recent program of research, what little research there was on schadenfreude focused on the interpersonal variety. For example, a pioneering study by R. H. Smith et al. (1996) examined the pleasure students took in seeing a peer suffer a setback in their academic careers (see also Van Dijk et al., 2002).

In Smith et al. (1996), students were exposed to a highly successful (or unsuccessful) peer whose superiority (or inferiority) to them was made clear. As expected, the successful peer highlighted the participants' relative inferiority. The peer then suffered (or did not suffer) the misfortune of being denied admission to medical school. Those exposed to the superior peer felt more pleasure when he suffered a setback. Importantly, Smith et al. (1996) showed that feeling inferior to the successful peer is what led to schadenfreude in response to his setback. They also showed that schadenfreude in this case was not simply a product of disliking the peer, but reflected the fact of the peer's failure. Recent research has also shown interpersonal schadenfreude to result from feelings of personal inferiority (e.g., Feather & Sherman, 2002).

The few studies of interpersonal schadenfreude show that people can feel pleasure in response to another's suffering, but they offer no support for the notion that this emotion can exist at the intergroup level. Although intergroup schadenfreude should be conceptually similar to the interpersonal variety, it should be the product of concerns for the group self and intergroup, rather than interpersonal, inferiority. Thus, the rest of this chapter provides a conceptual frame and adds empirical flesh to our conceptualization of intergroup schadenfreude. We are especially concerned with conditions that might facilitate and constrain intergroup schadenfreude, and that might help to explain when it is most likely to occur. Showing how this intergroup emotion varies according to certain social conditions may provide evidence that it occurs, as well as when and how it operates. Thus, we outline the conditions that facilitate or constrain intergroup schadenfreude and offer empirical support, mainly from our own program of research, for this particular intergroup emotion.

Facilitating Conditions

Interest in the Domain of the Outgroup's Failure

As we have already argued, schadenfreude is specific to particular intergroup relations, being directed toward outgroups who have suffered a setback. The state of rivalry implies that the outgroup has suffered a misfortune in a domain that is valued by the ingroup. Obviously, if the domain of the outgroup's misfortune is not important to the ingroup, the misfortune of the outgroup is unlikely to have psychological impact. As Nietzsche (1887/1967) suggested, schadenfreude is likely increased when rivals suffer in a domain of interest to ingroup identity. The notion that ingroup bias will occur in domains of interest to the group has already received support among social identity researchers (e.g., Mummendey & Simon, 1989), and we address this issue with particular reference to schadenfreude.

The Threat of Ingroup Inferiority

Nietzsche (1887/1967, p. 127) also proposed that schadenfreude should be exacerbated when the ingroup's status is threatened in some way, proposing that schadenfreude might serve as a "defensive retaliation" for such threats (see also Heider, 1958; Wills, 1981, 1991). According to Nietzsche, it is the threat of one's inferiority that leads to "a desire to deaden pain by means of affect" (p. 127). That interpersonal schadenfreude is increased after the threat of personal inferiority was shown by Smith et al. (1996). There is also research within the social identity literature suggesting that threats to group status will evoke derogation of outgroups more generally (see Branscombe et al., 1999; Mummendey & Otten, 1998). For example, members of real world low-status groups, whose group identity is "chronically" threatened by the presence of higher status groups, show the highest levels of bias against outgroups (Mullen, Brown, & Smith, 1992). More "acute" threats to group identity, in the form of poor performance on a specific task, have also been shown to increase the derogation of outgroups (see Mummendey & Otten, 1998). Research shows that such derogation of outgroups can enhance feelings of group worth (e.g. Branscombe & Wann, 1994), suggesting the motivation for such imaginary revenge. The question here then is whether threat actually exacerbates feelings of schadenfreude. In our research, we assess the effects of both chronic and acute forms of threat.

Constraining Conditions

Social conditions may also work to constrain intergroup schadenfreude. We believe that the conditions surrounding a schadenfreude opportunity may work to constrain either the experience of schadenfreude itself or the degree to which schadenfreude, once experienced, is expressed openly.

Emotional Experience

Although schadenfreude can be pleasing it is not always morally legitimate to experience it (see R. H. Smith, 1991). For this reason, Nietzsche described schadenfreude as extremely opportunistic – relying on circumstances that make it morally legitimate for one to enjoy another's misfortune. As he put it (1885/1961, p. 123), our "most secret tyrant-appetite disguises itself in words of virtue." In line with Nietzsche, we believe that people's experience of intergroup schadenfreude should be sensitive to circumstances that make it appear more or less legitimate. For example, schadenfreude should be less legitimate in response to the misfortune of an outgroup that is deservedly superior to the ingroup (cf. Feather & Sherman, 2002). Although the ingroup should want to be pleased at the misfortune of a superior outgroup, the outgroup's superiority should make schadenfreude at a single misfortune seem morally wrong. Indeed, schadenfreude toward legitimately superior outgroups who suffer a single misfortune should be difficult to legitimate even privately, to oneself. In cases where an outgroup appears deservedly superior, respect – however grudging – is a more morally legitimate feeling than schadenfreude (lest we be accused of sour grapes). Under circumstances that make schadenfreude morally illegitimate, the feeling itself should be constrained.

Emotional Expression

It is important to start by stating the obvious: The expression of schadenfreude may often be considered socially undesirable. It seems likely that most cultures have some prohibition against openly expressing pleasure at other people's misfortunes, although there may be great variation in the circumstances under which expressions of schadenfreude are seen as untoward. Given the likelihood of such prohibitions, it may not always be possible to express schadenfreude openly when it is experienced. This suggests that the expression of schadenfreude may be moderated by a more general concern for social desirability. Thus, a general concern for seeing oneself as a good person or having others see one as a good person (Paulhus' two dimensions of social desirability) may lead to the suppressed expression of schadenfreude. It is also possible that the expression of the schadenfreude that ingroups experience may be moderated by more strategic concerns about the intergroup relation.

Strategic Concerns

Given that schadenfreude is a malicious feeling directed toward an outgroup, ingroups may be very strategic about when and where it is expressed. This is consistent with the social identity theory-based argument that the "reality constraints" of intergroup status inequalities can constrain the expression of negative evaluations of outgroups (Doosje, Spears, & Koomen, 1995; Ellemers et al., 1997; Jetten et al., 2000; see Spears, Jetten, & Doosje, 2002). For example, R. Spears, C. W. Leach, and H. Mitchell (unpublished data) have argued that it is less socially acceptable for lower status groups to publicly claim that they are superior to higher status groups given the social reality of their relative status. Although lower status groups may contest the degree to which their inferior status is fair, the reality of their position makes malice toward superior outgroups less credible and less defensible. For this reason, lower status or less powerful groups may (strategically) avoid open expression of schadenfreude in circumstances that make them vulnerable to challenge from the outgroup that has suffered a misfortune.

Lower status or less powerful groups may have to be especially strategic about their expression of schadenfreude, given a realistic fear of reprisal from higher status outgroups. For example, expressing schadenfreude in the face of a wounded rival is dangerous, lest the group regain its original position and exact revenge. Consistent with this notion, there is some evidence in the social identity literature that group members moderate behavior that might unduly antagonize the outgroup, especially when the intergroup hierarchy is unstable (e.g., Scheepers et al., 2002; for a discussion, see Leach et al., 2002).

Expressing schadenfreude in front of powerful authorities who have the ability to sanction such expression is equally dangerous. This is shown in the social identity model of deindividuation effects (Reicher, Spears, & Postmes, 1995; Spears & Lea, 1994). It has been shown that group members are strategic in their expression of behavior that authorities may see as unacceptable, expressing such behavior more often when they are not identifiable and thus not accountable. Thus, there are numerous ways in which the expression of intergroup schadenfreude may be constrained. We now follow these ideas into the laboratory to assess the evidence for intergroup schadenfreude and to examine the conditions that facilitate and constrain it.

EMPIRICAL SUPPORT

In the following sections, we examine experimental evidence for intergroup schadenfreude, with special attention to the factors that facilitate and constrain it. This evidence comes from research we have conducted in the Netherlands. We begin by considering facilitating conditions (the specificity of the intergroup rivalry, interest in the domain of the outgroup's misfortune, and the threat of ingroup inferiority) and then consider the conditions that might constrain schadenfreude (the legitimate superiority of the outgroup, general concern for social desirability). Although our empirical work has often addressed more than one of these factors at once, for clarity here we separate these themes and address them in turn. These factors not only produce main effects, but do interact with each other (because schadenfreude is especially sensitive to the social circumstances that surround it, the more that optimal conditions are in place, the more likely it will be found). We address these interactions in the later sections.

Measurement of Schadenfreude

In general, we measure schadenfreude by asking people to report the degree to which they feel specific emotion terms (translated from the Dutch, these terms are equivalent to schadenfreude, happiness, and various synonyms for satisfaction) regarding the misfortune of an outgroup protagonist. These positive feelings about an outgroup's misfortune tend to be quite distinct from the negative feelings that signal a more convergent reaction to another's misfortune (e.g., sympathy, compassion, sadness; see Leach et al., 2003).

Providing evidence for intergroup schadenfreude involves demonstrating that it is a function of group-level concerns, rather than more personal or interpersonal issues. For this reason, we always measure, and control for, people's dispositional tendency to experience schadenfreude at the interpersonal level. As indicated previously, we also control for liking toward the outgroup, as well as identification with the ingroup, to ensure that reactions to the fall cannot be accounted for by more general (dis)affiliations with either group.

Facilitating Conditions

In this section, we consider two factors that can facilitate the experience of schadenfreude in line with Nietzsche's insights, namely interest in the domain of the outgroup's fall and the threat to identity caused by a sense of inferiority.

Interest in the Domain of the Outgroup's Misfortune

One important aspect of the setback suffered by the rival is that it should be important to the potential beneficiary. If perceivers consider the others' misfortune trivial or irrelevant, then it is unlikely that they will be able to derive pleasure when the misfortune befalls the outgroup. We refer to this as domain interest.

To test this idea, we have measured interest in the domain of the loss in all of our research on schadenfreude. The majority of these studies show a clear main effect of domain interest such that schadenfreude is higher for those higher in domain interest. We now describe the first two studies testing this and then briefly summarize the subsequent demonstrations of this effect.

In the first study, we presented participants with a questionnaire concerned with reactions to certain matches played during the Soccer World Cup played in France in the summer of 1998 (see Leach et al., 2003, for further details). The fact that Germany was knocked out in an early stage of the championship (by Croatia) provided us with the schadenfreude opportunity. It is important to explain that Germany forms a key rival for our Dutch respondents, both for historical and political reasons, and especially in the domain of soccer. Although Germany has historically been more successful in major tournaments, the Dutch have always had a talented national team, especially in recent years. That the German team is not clearly superior to the Dutch one suggests that the German loss was likely to be seen as deserved. The sporting context may also make it more acceptable to express schadenfreude. We reasoned that it might be more socially acceptable to express schadenfreude in a sporting context of such close rivalry, in which emotional reactions to victory and defeat are more acceptable and normative – football is after all only a game.

We measured the degree of interest in football, predicting that those more interested in this domain would show more pleasure in response to the German defeat. This is what we found. Football interest was a reliable predictor of intergroup schadenfreude, controlling for our standard covariates. Moreover, we replicated this effect in a somewhat similar study conducted in the aftermath of the European Championship for soccer in 2000. In this case, we examined reactions to the losses of both Germany and Italy. The predicted main effect of football interest was highly reliable: Those with greater interest experienced more schadenfreude at the loss of the rival.

A further study used a different domain and different group membership. In this study, we capitalized on the rivalry between students at the University of Amsterdam (our participants) and the other local university (the Free University). The cover story was that we were conducting research assessing the viability of an interuniversity quiz tournament that a national TV channel was interested in televising. In line with the cover story, we also measured people's interest in TV quiz shows. Because final-year students made up the teams, we could convince our first-year participants that this national quiz had been going for a number of years and used this to provide feedback about previous duels with the outgroups. Moreover, this year, the University of Amsterdam had been knocked out by its local rival (an acute threat), raising the stakes. Participants then received the opportunity to show schadenfreude in response to their rival's loss to another Dutch university (Maastricht) in the final of the competition. As predicted, we found that schadenfreude toward the loss of the rival was reliably higher for those who had interest in TV quiz shows. In other studies in which we have measured interest in the domain in which the outgroups' misfortune occurs, we have also found evidence of increased intergroup schadenfreude as a function of such interest.

The Threat of Ingroup Inferiority

A further factor that might facilitate schadenfreude is threat to ingroup status. Recall that Nietzsche saw intergroup schadenfreude as the revenge of the impotent, so that one of the functions of schadenfreude is to deaden the pain evoked by the ingroup's own inferiority. On this basis, we expect that people who feel threatened by the superiority of the outgroup, or more precisely their own inferiority (which might be less constrained by the legitimate superiority of the outgroup), may find the forbidden fruit of schadenfreude more tasty.

We examined the effects of status threat in the soccer studies already described. In the World Cup study, we manipulated the threat of ingroup inferiority on the same dimension as the schadenfreude opportunity (i.e., the perceived inferiority of the national football team) in two ways: chronic threat and acute threat (in a 2 × 2 design). In the chronic threat condition, we preceded the schadenfreude opportunity with a page of questions concerned with the previous national success in World Cup competitions. Participants were forced to acknowledge that the Dutch team had never previously won this prestigious tournament, whereas the other countries mentioned had (Brazil and even England). In the acute threat condition, we simply preceded the schadenfreude opportunity, with a similar set of questions regarding the Dutch loss to Brazil in the same tournament, reminding participants of the painful exit of their side to a superior rival. Note that, in both of these threat manipulations, we did not make a direct reference to the superiority of Germany in this domain. In the chronic threat manipulation, we highlighted the previous success of other nations, such as Brazil, and in the acute threat manipulation the ingroup was eliminated by Brazil also. This allows us to emphasize the inferiority of the ingroup without making explicit the superiority of the rival Germany that might introduce the legitimacy constraints we consider shortly.

Both forms of inferiority threat resulted in increased levels of schadenfreude at the German loss, supporting our prediction. Interestingly, the chronic threat manipulation also interacted with the football interest measure discussed in the previous section: Soccer interest was a more positive predictor of schadenfreude for those who were not chronically threatened (i.e., threat had more impact on those low in interest). It seems likely that those high in football interest are already primed to experience intergroup schadenfreude without help from this threat manipulation, perhaps because they themselves are chronically threatened by the soccer rivalry with Germany and the schadenfreude opportunity their loss provides.

We also investigated the effect of acute threat in increasing schadenfreude in the European Championship study. Directly before the schadenfreude opportunity, we reminded participants of the match in which the Dutch team was eliminated (by Italy). Once again, this produced greater schadenfreude toward the German rival, and again primarily under conditions of low interest.

To summarize, the soccer studies provide clear evidence that threatening the ingroup by making clear their inferior status, at least on the same dimension of the schadenfreude opportunity, can increase the tendency to seize the opportunity for schadenfreude. We are currently engaged in research to assess whether threats to group status in general (and perhaps even threats to personal status) might also increase intergroup schadenfreude as a form of compensation for these threats.

Constraining Conditions

In this section, we review our research addressing conditions that can constrain intergroup schadenfreude. We first consider the possibility that there may be a general opprobrium on expressing this emotion because of its malicious character, addressed under the rubric of "social desirability." We then proceed to assess whether expressions of schadenfreude are more contingent on contextual factors that constrain schadenfreude by affecting the legitimacy of the emotional experience itself or its public expression.

Social Desirability

As we saw from the first study, generating evidence for direct intergroup schadenfreude is not straightforward. Moreover, although the soccer studies do show predicted variations in intergroup schadenfreude, it is possible that it may be limited to sporting contexts in which a degree of malicious pleasure is de rigeur. This raises a methodological question, namely the possibility that schadenfreude is constrained or underreported because it is generally seen as socially undesirable. We tried to address this issue to some extent in the European Championship study in which we attempted to encourage honest responding by manipulating a norm valorizing this part of Dutch identity. This proved only partially successful, however, in so far as this norm only increased schadenfreude under specific conditions, and a satisfactory "no norm" control condition was missing (effects were compared with another Dutch norm of tolerance). This finding already raises doubts about the possibility of a blanket social desirability main effect. We also doubt that the expression of intergroup schadenfreude is suppressed due to a general fear that is socially undesirable, because we have found no association between expressed schadenfreude and Paulhus' (1991) measures of social desirability (see Leach et al., 2003).

In a series of studies, we adopted another technique for trying to assess whether schadenfreude is generally constrained by socially desirable responding. In these studies, we used the bogus pipeline procedure (Jones & Sigall, 1971) to give respondents the impression that we could measure their emotions directly. This involves attaching a sensor linked up to the computer on which the respondents rate their emotional reactions. The cover story indicates that the computer is able to measure the "Galvanic Skin Response" that allows us to assess emotional states, and thus (by inference) this operates as a sort of lie detector if they report emotions different to those actually felt.

In this first study, we also deviated from the sporting domain and presented people with a scenario involving the European Parliament and elections for an important European Union commissioner. In two different conditions the protagonist running for this position came either from the ingroup (The Netherlands) or the rival outgroup (Germany), and in both cases they lost out to a candidate from another nationality. This provided the schadenfreude opportunity. We applied the bogus pipeline manipulation in half of the conditions to assess the effect of desirable responding. We expected intergroup schadenfreude only where it involved the rival outgroup (Germany) and especially when the bogus pipeline was on, resulting in a two-way interaction in the 2 × 2 design.

Although the predicted interaction was reliable, and schadenfreude toward the outgroup was higher when the bogus pipeline was applied, schadenfreude toward the Dutch ingroup was actually higher to the ingroup under no pipeline conditions. Indeed this cross-over interaction reflected the fact that schadenfreude toward the Dutch target fell when the pipeline was introduced – schadenfreude to the German rival did not increase reliably in the pipeline condition ($p < .13$).

These results suggest that that the bogus pipeline did have an effect on the reporting of schadenfreude, but they do not give strong support for a blanket effect of social desirability constraining schadenfreude. Moreover, it is not clear why schadenfreude toward the ingroup should drop, or indeed be higher than toward the outgroup under no pipeline conditions. Although the ingroup ratings are not directly relevant to our analyses of intergroup schadenfreude (this was intended as a comparison control group or baseline), it is interesting to speculate why this occurred. It possible that a certain level of schadenfreude, within the ingroup at least, may be socially desirable, or at least culturally sanctioned. This fits with the Dutch "tall poppy" norm (see Feather,1994, for a similar phenomenon in Australia and Japan) that encourages schadenfreude toward high achievers who subsequently fall from grace. This is captured in the Dutch phrase: "just be average, that's more than plenty" ("doe maar gewoon dat is gek genoeg"). Although our measure of depositional schadenfreude did not mediate this effect, dispositional schadenfreude might not capture this cultural norm.

Whatever the basis of this effect, the general conclusion on the basis of this study, and the honesty norm manipulation, is that there does not appear to be strong evidence for a general social desirability norm constraining intergroup schadenfreude. Indeed, the results for the ingroup in the bogus pipeline study suggest that there may be social conditions under which schadenfreude becomes more socially acceptable, and this may also be true of the intergroup variant of schadenfreude under certain social conditions (see the section on social consequences in which we considered historical examples where this may have been the case). For example, one might expect that intergroup schadenfreude is more acceptable to an ingroup audience, and we have found some evidence for this in another study (R. Spears et al., unpublished data). With these caveats and complexities in mind, we now move on from the idea that social desirability forms a general constraint on expression to consider how more specific and contingent legitimacy concerns might affect intergroup schadenfreude.

Legitimacy Concerns and Strategic Considerations

As we have argued, the actual experience of intergroup schadenfreude may be compromised by social reality constraints concerning the legitimacy of the rival's superiority. Although a rival's failure provides the opportunity for schadenfreude, the circumstances of the fall must legitimate taking advantage of the opportunity. If a highly successful rival fails when his/her superiority suggests that s/he should have succeeded, schadenfreude is likely to be constrained by the social reality of that superiority. This is one reason why schadenfreude can be seen as an opportunistic emotion. Although ingroup inferiority, which gives schadenfreude its raison d'être, often goes hand in hand with outgroup superiority, it is also constrained by it for reasons of legitimacy.

We investigated this issue in the European Championship study. Recall that in this study we varied the nature of the rival providing the schadenfreude opportunity (Germany vs. Italy). Recall also that we manipulated acute threat by reminding participants of the Dutch elimination from the tournament by Italy directly before the schadenfreude opportunity. Whereas we expected this manipulation to operate as an acute threat in the case of the German rival (similar to the reminder of the loss to Brazil in the World Cup study), in the case of the Italian rival the Dutch loss to Italy should limit legitimate schadenfreude toward Italy by forming a social reality constraint. To revel in the loss of the Italians after being forced to acknowledge their superiority could appear hypocritical and unseemly (sour grapes). Moreover, we expected this reality constraint to be particularly apparent when the honesty norm was salient, forcing respondents to admit the legitimate superiority of the Italian rival. Results confirmed this prediction, but only for the low-interest respondents, in line with the greater sensitivity these respondents showed to threat in the World Cup study.

Further evidence for the constraining role of legitimacy was obtained in the university quiz study. Some further design details of this study are pertinent here. We manipulated the history of previous duels between the University of Amsterdam and the Free University in this study, such that the outgroup was clearly superior (having won all six previous meetings in the quiz) or such that the score was equal (three wins apiece). In this case, we would expect the history of equal spoils to present the weakest social reality constraint to experiencing schadenfreude. Moreover, equal status can intensify rivalry, competition, and ingroup bias, as social identity theorists have noted (Tajfel & Turner, 1986).

However, expressing schadenfreude openly in the equal success condition may still present problems for strategic reasons. Precisely because the situation is equal it may also seem unstable, and to openly celebrate their failure may provoke the opposition (Scheepers et al., 2002) or attract the opprobrium of other audiences, such as the experimenter (Spears & Smith, 2001). With this in mind, we once again introduced a bogus pipeline procedure to prevent the emotion from being strategically suppressed. Specifically, we predicted that there would be greater schadenfreude in the equal condition, but that this would primarily be expressed when the bogus pipeline was applied. The pain of the competitive rivalry should increase the schadenfreude untempered by legitimacy concerns, and the bogus pipeline should allow the ingroup (even encourage them) to admit to this pain. When the outgroup is superior, however, schadenfreude may be moderated by the legitimacy of the outgroup superiority, and the effect of the pipeline should be reduced or absent as a result (less or no pain to be expressed).

This is what we found. Intergroup schadenfreude increased in the equal condition, but was only expressed when the bogus pipeline was applied. Moreover, in this study, we measured the threat and pain experienced at the loss of the ingroup to the rival and showed that this mediated intergroup schadenfreude in the equal condition. In short, the competitive intergroup situation created by equality provided optimal conditions for the legitimate experience of intergroup schadenfreude, and the bogus pipeline removed any obstacles to its socially undesirable expression for strategic reasons (e.g., because it might antagonize the outgroup). Clearly, we need to investigate the precise reasons for suppressing schadenfreude under conditions of equality more fully in further research. However, the reduced schadenfreude in the superior outgroup condition, and the lack of a bogus pipeline effect, illustrate clearly the social reality constraints that can limit schadenfreude because of legitimacy concerns.

SUMMARY AND CONCLUSIONS

In this chapter, we have addressed a number of issues concerning intergroup schadenfreude, including questions of definition, evidence of its occurrence, its distinctness from more interpersonal and dispositional forms of schadenfreude, and the factors that can facilitate and constrain it. We have provided evidence that intergroup schadenfreude occurs, both by showing its variation as a function of the key predictors, and constraints by legitimacy and possible strategic concerns. The notion that intergroup schadenfreude, although malicious, is generally constrained by its socially undesirable nature appears at this stage to be oversimplistic. Although intergroup schadenfreude can be constrained, this appears to be contingent on contextual and relational factors that affect legitimacy and social desirability considerations, hence its opportunistic nature.

The contingent impact of techniques originally designed to transcend effects of social desirability on schadenfreude is consistent with our more general argument that given the "right" (i.e., morally wrong) social and historical conditions, intergroup schadenfreude may even become socially acceptable. In this sense, intergroup schadenfreude can perhaps prefigure as well as reflect the conditions that lead to more active forms of persecution, along with their emotional correlates, such as gloating. Such social changes may then reflect deeper changes to the social hierarchy, and thus undermine the very status differentials that can constrain schadenfreude in a more material sense. Intergroup schadenfreude may therefore not just implicate emotional opportunism, but also the social opportunism relating to social and historical conjunctures.

An emotion-based approach allows us to understand the specificity, extremity, and the variety of distinct forms of discrimination and the distinct emotional experiences underlying them. In theoretical terms, this also takes us beyond the ingroup favoritism often associated with the social identity approach and addresses one emotional basis of clear outgroup derogation. This emotion-based approach to intergroup relations provides a sensitive tool for analyzing the emotional character of specific social relations in context. This approach also allows us to appreciate the social and psychological conditions that thwart schadenfreude and prevent it from progressing into more active forms of persecution. As social psychologists, we can analyze the factors that cause such emotions, but clearly this approach needs to be supplemented by other forms of social, economic, and historical analyses to explain fully the social conditions that can give rise to intergroup schadenfreude.

References

Alexander, M. G., Brewer, M. B., & Herrmann, R. K. (1999). Images and affect: A functional analysis of out-group stereotypes. *Journal of Personality and Social Psychology, 77*, 78–93.

Arnold, M. B. (1960). *Emotions and personality, Volume 1. Psychological aspects*. New York: Columbia University Press.

Bettelheim, B., & Janowitz, M. (1964). *Social change and prejudice*. New York: Free Press.

Branscombe, N. R., Ellemers, N., Spears, R., & Doosje, B. (1999). The context and content of social identity threat. In N. Ellemers, R. Spears, & B. Doosje (Eds.), *Social identity: context, commitment, content* (pp. 35–58). Oxford, UK: Blackwell.

Branscombe, N. R., & Wann, D. L. (1994). Collective self-esteem consequences of outgroup derogation when a valued social identity is on trial. *European Journal of Social Psychology, 24*, 641–658.

Brewer, M. B. (1999). The psychology of prejudice: Ingroup love or outgroup hate? *Journal of Social Issues, 55*, 429–444.

Capote, T. (1975). *Music for chameleons*. Vintage: New York.

Diehl, M. (1990). The minimal group paradigm: Theoretical explanations and empirical findings. *European Review of Social Psychology, 1*, 263–292.

Doosje, B., Branscombe, N. R., Spears, R., & Manstead, A. S. R. (1998). Guilty by association: When one's group has a negative history. *Journal of Personality and Social Psychology, 75*, 872–886.

Doosje, B., Spears, R., & Koomen, W. (1995). When bad isn't all bad: The strategic use of sample information in generalization and stereotyping. *Journal of Personality and Social Psychology, 69*, 642–655.

Ellemers, N., Van Rijswijk, W., Roefs, M., & Simons, C. (1997). Bias in intergroup perceptions: Balancing group identity with social reality. *Personality and Social Psychology Bulletin, 23*, 186–198.

Feather, N. T. (1994). Attitudes toward high achievers and reactions to their fall: Theory and research concerning tall poppies. *Advances in Experimental Social Psychology, 26*, 1–73.

Feather, N. T., & Sherman, R. (2002). Envy, resentment, schadenfreude, and sympathy: Reactions to deserved and undeserved achievement and subsequent failure. *Personality and Social Psychology Bulletin, 28*, 953–961.

Fiske, S. T., Cuddy, A. J. C., Glick, P., & Xu, J. (2002). A model of (often mixed) stereotype content: Competence and warmth respectively follow from perceived status and competition. *Journal of Personality and Social Psychology, 82*, 878–902.

Fiske, S.T., Xu, J., Cuddy, A. C., & Glick, P. (1999). (Dis)respecting vs. (dis)liking: Status and interdependence predict ambivalent stereotypes of competence and warmth. *Journal of Social Issues, 55*, 473–489.

Frijda, N. (1986). *The emotions*. Cambridge: Cambridge University Press.

Goldhagen, D. J. (1996). *Hitler's willing executioners: Ordinary Germans and the Holocaust*. New York: Knopf.

Heider, F. (1958). *The psychology of interpersonal relations*. New York: J. Wiley & Sons.

Iyer, A., Leach, C. W., & Crosby, F. (2003). White guilt and racial compensation: The benefits and limits of self-focus. *Personality and Social Psychology Bulletin, 29*, 117–129.

Jetten, J., Spears, R., Hogg, M. A., & Manstead, A. S. R. (2000). Discrimination constrained and justified: Variable effects of group variability and in-group identification. *Journal of Experimental Social Psychology, 36*, 329–356.

Jones, E. E., & Sigall, H. (1971). The bogus pipeline: A new paradigm for measuring affect and attitude. *Psychological Bulletin, 76*, 349–364.

Leach, C. W., Snider, S., & Iyer, A. (2002). "Poisoning the consciences of the fortunate": The experience of relative advantage and support for social equality. In I. Walker & H. J. Smith (Eds.), *Relative deprivation: Specification, development, and integration* (pp. 136–163). New York: Cambridge University Press.

Leach, C. W., & Spears, R. (2002). "Without cruelty there is no festival": Gloating over the suffering of a lower status group. Manuscript under review, University of California, Santa Cruz.

Leach, C. W., Spears, R., Branscombe, N. R., & Doosje, B. (2003). Malicious pleasure: Schadenfreude at the suffering of another group. *Journal of Personality and Social Psychology, 84*, 932–943.

Mackie, D. M., Devos, T., & Smith, E. R. (2000). Intergroup emotions: Explaining offensive action tendencies in an intergroup context. *Journal of Personality and Social Psychology, 79*, 602–616.

Mackie, D. M., Silver, L. A., & Smith, E. R. (this volume). Intergroup emotions: Emotion as an intergroup phenomenon.

Mackie, D. M., & Smith, E. R. (Eds.). (2002). *From prejudice to intergroup relations: Differentiated reactions to social groups*. Philadelphia: Psychology Press.

Mullen, B., Brown, R., & Smith, C. (1992). Ingroup bias as a function of salience, relevance, and status: An integration. *European Journal of Social Psychology, 22*, 103–122.

Mummendey, A., & Otten, S. (1998). Positive-negative asymmetry in social discrimination. *European Review of Social Psychology, 9*, 107–143.

Mummendey, A., & Simon, B. (1989). Better or different? III: The impact of importance of comparison dimension and relative ingroup size upon inter-group discrimination. *British Journal of Social Psychology, 28*, 1–16.

Nietzsche, F. (1961). *Thus spoke zarathustra* (trans. R. J. Hollingdale) (p. 123). New York: Penguin. (Original work published 1883–1885.)

Nietzsche, F. (1967). *On the genealogy of morals* (trans. W. Kaufmann & R. J. Hollingdale) (p. 127). New York: Random House. (Original work published 1887.)

Ortony, A., Clore, G. L., & Collins, A. (1988). *The cognitive structure of emotions*. New York: Cambridge University.

Oxford English Dictionary. (1989). Oxford, UK: Oxford University Press.

Paulhus, D. L. (1991). Measurement and control of response bias. In J. P. Robinson, P. R. Shaver, & L. S. Wrightsman (Eds.), *Measures of personality and social psychological measures* (Vol. 1; pp. 17–59). San Diego, CA: Academic Press, Inc.

Reicher, S. D., Spears, R., & Postmes, T. (1995). A social identity model of deindividuation phenomena. *European Review of Social Psychology, 6*, 161–198.

Scheepers, D., Spears, R., Doosje, B., & Manstead, A. S. R. (2002). *Diversity in discrimination: Structural factors, situational features, and social functions*. Manuscript submitted for publication.

Smith, E. R. (1993). Social identity and social emotions: Toward a new conceptualization of prejudice. In D. M. Mackie & D. L. Hamilton (Eds.), *Affect, cognition, and stereotyping* (pp. 297–315). San Diego, CA: Academic Press, Inc.

Smith, R. H. (1991). Envy and the sense of injustice. In P. Salovey (Ed.), *The psychology of jealousy and envy* (pp. 79–99). New York: Guilford Press.

Smith, R. H., Turner, T. J., Garonzik, R., Leach, C. W., Urch, V., & Weston, C. (1996). Envy and schadenfreude. *Personality and Social Psychology Bulletin, 22*, 158–168.

Spears, R., Jetten, J., & Doosje, B. (2002). The (il)legitimacy of ingroup bias: From social reality to social resistance. In J. Jost & B. Major (Eds.), *The psychology of legitimacy: emerging perspectives on ideology, justice, and intergroup relations* (pp. 332–362). New York: Cambridge University Press.

Spears, R., & Lea, M. (1994). Panacea or panopticon? The hidden power in computer-mediated communication. *Communication Research, 21*, 427–459.

Spears, R., & Smith, H. J. (2001). Experiments as politics. *Political Psychology, 22*, 309–330.

Staub, E. (1989). *The roots of evil: The origins of genocide and other group violence*. New York: University Press.

Struch, N., & Schwartz, S. H. (1989). Intergroup aggression: Its predictors and distinctness from ingroup bias. *Journal of Personality and Social Psychology, 56*, 364–373.

Tajfel, H. (1978). Social categorization, social identity and social comparison. In Tajfel, H. (Ed.), *Differentiation between social groups: Studies in the social psychology of intergroup relations* (pp. 61–76). London: Academic Press.
Tajfel, H., & Turner, J. C. (1986). The social identity theory of intergroup behavior. In S. Worchel & W. G Austin (Eds.), *Psychology of intergroup relations* (pp. 7–24). Chicago: Nelson Hall.
Van Dijk, W. Yedema, M., Goslinga, S., & Ouwerkerk, J. (2002). Jammer joh! [What a shame!] In D. A. Stapel, M. Hagendoom & E. Van Dijk (Eds.), *Jaarboek Sociale Psychologie 2001* (pp. 271–310). Delft: Eburon.
Wills, T. A. (1981). Downward comparison principles in social psychology. *Psychological Bulletin, 90*, 245–271.
Wills, T. A. (1991). Similarity and self-esteem in downward comparison. In J. Suls & T. A. Wills (Eds.), *Social comparison: contemporary theory and research* (pp. 51–78). Hillsdale, NJ: Erlbaum.

Index